THE MARIJUANA CONVICTION

A History of Marijuana Prohibition in
the United States

The Marijuana Conviction

A History of Marijuana Prohibition in the United States

Richard J. Bonnie
and
Charles H. Whitebread II

The Lindesmith Center
New York

Library of Congress Cataloging Data:

Bonnie, Richard J.
        [Marihuana conviction]
        The marijuana conviction: A history of marijuana prohibition
in the United States / Richard J. Bonnie and Charles H. Whitebread II.
        p. cm.-- (A drug policy classic reprint from the Lindesmith
Center, New York)
        Originally published: The marihuana conviction. Charlottesville:
University of Virginia Press, [1974].
        Includes bibliographical references and index.
        ISBN 1-891385-06-2
        1. Marijuana—Government policy—United States—History.
2. Narcotics, Control of-- United States—History. 3. Drug Abuse—
United States—History. I. Whitebread, Charles H. II. Title.
III Series

HV5822.M3B65 1999
362.29'5'0973—dc21   99-15034
                                                CIP

Printed in the United States by North Wales Press

In loving memory of my mother
RJB

In memory of William Farhood
CHW II

Contents

A Note from the Publisher

SCHOLARLY histories of drugs and drug policies rarely reflect well upon current policies and their defenders. This book is no exception. There is simply too much in the historical record that reflects poorly upon the motivations and judgments of those who promoted and supported the criminal prohibition of marijuana in the United States, and too little about the roles of science, medicine and dispassionate analysis. Fearmongering and sloppy journalism, sham science and shameless propaganda, racism and xenophobia – all contributed to the emergence and institutionalization of marijuana prohibition in this country.

Richard J. Bonnie and Charles H. Whitebread II wrote this book in 1973. Bonnie had just completed a stint as Associate Director of the Shafer Commission appointed by President Nixon to evaluate the nation's drug policies. The Commission's reports gave legitimacy and momentum to the growing sentiment in favor of reforming federal, state and local drug laws, especially those concerning marijuana. During the following years, eleven states decriminalized marijuana possession, and top officials in President Carter's White House spoke openly in favor of federal decriminalization of marijuana.

The 1980s represented a partial return to the sentiments and harsh policies of earlier decades. Now the public opinion pendulum appears to be swinging once again (even as marijuana arrests and other sanctions increase each year). Perhaps the best indicator of the trend is the annual survey of college freshmen, which since 1968 has asked whether students believe that marijuana should be legalized. The proportion agreeing "strongly" or "somewhat" peaked at 52.9% in 1977, dropped to 16.7% in 1989, and has now increased to 33% (as of 1996). The debate over marijuana policy now also includes two somewhat distinct issues – whether and how to make marijuana legally available for medical uses; and whether the United States should join other nations in allowing hemp to be legally produced for industrial purposes. Recent polls now show more than sixty percent of adult

Americans supporting the legalization of marijuana for medical purposes, and 50-55% supportive of legalizing hemp production for industrial purposes.

This book – the second to be republished as part of The Lindesmith Center's drug policy classics reprint series – goes to press just months after a clean sweep of victories for drug policy reform on Election Day. Citizens in five states – Alaska, Washington, Oregon, Nevada, Colorado and Washington, D.C. endorsed ballot initiatives legalizing marijuana for medical purposes (although only three will effect immediate changes in state laws). In Oregon, two-thirds of voters also rejected an attempt by the state legislature to recriminalize marijuana. And in Arizona, voters similarly rejected efforts by the state legislature to undo a drug policy reform initiative that had passed in 1996.

Prospects for drug policy reform now appear better than anytime in the previous two decades. Many people suspect there is something not quite right about the nation's marijuana policies, but shy away from supporting reform in part because they assume there must have been good reasons for criminalizing marijuana in the first place. This book is scholarly and objective. It is also, in the final analysis, powerful evidence for reform.

ETHAN NADELMANN
Director
The Lindesmith Center
January, 1999

Foreword to the 1999 Edition

IN EARLY 1971, when I became Chairman of the National Commission on Marihuana and Drug Abuse, American society was deeply divided by the war in Vietnam, and college campuses were hotbeds of dissent. Marijuana use had become a potent symbol in the culture wars, and, as a result, the scientific facts about the drug were obscured by its social meaning. In this polemical context, the Commission set out to elicit the facts and to report them to the American people. In our first report, *Marihuana: A Signal of Misunderstanding* (1972), we recommended that marijuana use be depoliticized, deglamorized and decriminalized. In our second report, a year later, we said that drug use in America should be treated as a public health problem, and that it should be addressed through a balanced use of what are now called supply-side and demand-side policies. The Commission's work benefited enormously from the contributions made by University of Virginia law professor Richard Bonnie who served as our Associate Director and was a key architect of our two reports. One of Professor Bonnie's many contributions was research on the history of the marijuana laws in this country (conducted jointly with his colleague Charles Whitebread). Their work was published initially in an Appendix to the Commission's 1972 report and was subsequently expanded and published by the University Press of Virginia as a book entitled *The Marihuana Conviction* (1974).

It seems that our country has still been unable to sort out the scientific and medical information about marijuana. More than 25 years after the Commission issued its report, the facts about the medical usefulness of marijuana and the dangers associated with non-medical use are still obscured by emotion and political posturing. I hope republication of *The Marijuana Conviction* will help to dissipate some of the continuing misunderstanding.

GOVERNOR RAYMOND P. SHAFER
Chairman, National Commission on
Marihuana and Drug Abuse (1971-1973)

Authors' Preface to the 1999 Edition

WHEN *The Marihuana Conviction* was first published in 1974, the political winds were blowing in the direction of reform. Spurred by the 1972 report of the National Commission on Marihuana and Drug Abuse, a growing body of informed opinion supported decriminalization of possession of marijuana for personal use. Over the next several years, eleven states enacted decriminalization legislation, the Ford Administration tilted in the direction of reform, and the Carter Administration explicitly endorsed decriminalization.

The pace of reform suddenly slowed and came to a halt in the late 1970's. This reversal in marijuana politics was linked to the conservative swing in public opinion that eventually brought Ronald Reagan to the White House and to epidemiological evidence that marijuana use was rising among teenagers, a trend that reached its high point in 1979. Although it is doubtful that the increase in youthful marijuana use was attributable to decriminalization, it was troubling in public health terms and it posed a new challenge for reformers. We had often called attention to the symbolic or declarative functions of legislation *enacting* marijuana prohibition or raising penalties for drug offenses; now we had to contend with the declarative effects of legislative action *repealing* marijuana prohibition or ameliorating penalties for drug offenses. Drug law reform is a complicated business.

The nation's brief experiment in drug law reform during the 1970's was succeeded, almost overnight, by a repressive "war on drugs." "Zero tolerance" became the motto of national drug policy for nearly 15 years. Arrests for drug offenses have skyrocketed, filling the nation's jails and prisons with drug offenders. Some marijuana offenders are serving sentences even more excessive than those that had shaken public support for the marijuana laws in the 1960's and that had led us to begin the research that culminated in *The Marihuana Conviction.*

As these words are written, the political winds seem to be shifting once again in the direction of reform. A recent surge in adolescent drug use shows, once again, that repression doesn't "solve" drug problems. A more balanced approach toward drug use has been supported in recent months by the College on the Problems of Drug Dependence (CPDD), the leading scientific organization in the field, and by Physician Leadership on National Drug Policy, a new organization of distinguished physicians favoring a public health approach to drug control. In this context, we are pleased that the Lindesmith Center has decided to republish *The Marihuana Conviction* (now *The Marijuana Conviction*, to make it more accessible in computer databases) as part of its series of classic books on drug policy. We will be even more gratified if this effort helps to revive the cause of reform.

We should also enter two mild caveats. This is a republication of a book originally published in 1974. We have not attempted to update the story or to review what other authors have said about the history of the marijuana laws over the past 25 years. Although we have no reason to reconsider the basic outlines of our historical account, other authors have undoubtedly identified factual errors, uncovered additional sources, and offered different interpretations of the evidence we assembled. In short, while the book may be a "classic," it is no longer definitive.

Individually and jointly, we have made no secret of our support for marijuana law reform, then (in 1974) or now. However, our ideas about specific aspects of drug control policy have not remained unchanged over the past two decades, and republication of this book should not be taken as a reaffirmation of every opinion expressed in it.

RICHARD J. BONNIE
Charlottesville, Virginia
September, 1998

Foreword

MARIHUANA has been called the deceptive weed. Indeed, it has a nature so diverse as to make almost any statement about it a target for contradiction. Estimates of its physiological and psychological effects are notoriously unreliable. Its ambiguous nature appears to invite strong opinions that attempt to evoke certainty where none exists. Thus policy makers tend to become victims of their own propaganda. When marihuana first started to become a social problem in this country, members of Congress were led to make definitive judgments quite unsupported by reliable evidence. Laws were passed, based on definitions known to be unscientific. Criticisms that now appear valid and scientific were rejected out of hand. This book documents these and many other developments over the decades during which *Cannabis sativa* has been known in the United States.

This monograph is deceptive; it is far more exciting and informative than its title would suggest. Reading about efforts to control the use of marihuana through legal measures could be (and usually is) insufferably dull, but this volume is different. It is so illuminated by the authors' wide and complete knowledge of the problem's technical aspects, coupled with a sensitive awareness of its many psychological and sociological aspects, that the reading is both highly enjoyable and also throws much light on the capacity of a nation to fool itself as well as make a fool of itself.

Although the authors began to research and write on this subject in 1969, they have recently had the advantage of an enormous amount of work done by and under the auspices of the National Commission on Marihuana and Drug Abuse (1971-73). The senior author was one of the principal architects of this group's two reports. With the publication of this definitive history, a natural companion to the eight official volumes of the commission, anyone wishing to familiarize himself with all the intricate, delicate, and tricky aspects of the drug problem in this country has a comprehensive library at his disposal.

Who should read this book? Anyone who wishes to become aware of one of the most volatile issues of our time, which is, in turn, related to the great majority of all the other issues that plague a society attempting to achieve the best in living conditions for all its citizens. More specifically, it should be read by those who wish to become better informed about how social issues develop in ways not intended or even predictable. Law and medical students, sociologists, legislators at all levels, and policy makers come immediately to mind. Teachers, clergymen, and all those who counsel others (especially the young) will gain much to increase their own self-confidence.

In many ways the marihuana problem resembles many of our other social dilemmas: those who become involved do so gradually, compromise following compromise, until they are trapped in situations from which there is no easy way out.

Reading this book was enjoyable, enlightening, and stimulating. To produce such a volume, tracing a society's response to a single plant species, is a significant accomplishment. To read it carefully will add appreciably to one's knowledge of the way a free society can go astray in its methods and yet ultimately find ways of solving the complex problems that confront it.

DANA L. FARNSWORTH, M.D.
Vice Chairman, National
Commission on Marihuana
and Drug Abuse

Boston, Massachusetts
July 1973

Preface

THIS BOOK is about a controversial subject. Indeed, the debate about marihuana probably arouses considerably stronger psychological reactions than does the ingestion of marihuana. For this reason no "expert"—whatever his discipline—can credibly contend that he has no opinion on the pivotal questions of social and legal policy. We make no such pretense. In fact, we intend to clear the air at the outset by clarifying the general perspective from which we view the marihuana discussion.

Our intellectual interest in marihuana and its legal history began in the fall of 1969. The precipitating event was the assessment of a mandatory twenty-year sentence under Virginia law to a young college student for the possession of a small amount of marihuana. His case received national publicity and highlighted the individual injustices so often compelled by the nation's marihuana laws.

We resolved at that time to submit a brief to the Supreme Court of Appeals of Virginia as a "friend of the court" in the case. Distinctly legal issues were to be the focus of the brief: that the Virginia legislature did not intend that judges assess such sentences; that if it did, a twenty-year sentence for such a trivial offense was unconstitutionally excessive; that the legislative classification of marihuana as a narcotic was unreasonable; and that a criminal prohibition of possession for personal use infringed individual rights and was therefore beyond the legislature's power. At the same time, we planned to devote substantial attention to the political and judicial history of marihuana legislation and to the current state of scientific knowledge about the drug.

Not long after we had undertaken this effort, the General Assembly of Virginia revised the state's marihuana law, reducing the potency of our constitutional arguments. We suspected that the court would avoid all the constitutional questions in the cases pending under the old law and would permit all sentences not yet final to be altered to accord with the new law. Ultimately the court declared the mandatory twenty-year minimum sentence provided by the statute for opiate possession to be inapplicable to marihuana possession.

Nonetheless, our forays into the historical materials and into the contemporary literature had disturbed us for reasons much broader than the individual injustices perpetrated by the present law in Virginia and other states. Most important was the injury being suffered by the law as an institution, as growing numbers of people questioned the wisdom of marihuana prohibition, defied it, and began to doubt the capacity of our legal system to order society rationally. Further, we were alarmed by the extent to which the marihuana issue had become ensnared in broader social polemics. Change and stability, defiance and repression, hippieism and middle-Americanism, protest politics and "law and order" all helped define the cultural milieu which the marihuana issue came to symbolize. We were concerned that the assimilation of the marihuana issue into larger social conflicts had consigned the debate to the public viscera instead of the public mind.

We therefore continued to try to unearth the roots of the marihuana laws, hoping that an understanding of the origins of the prohibitory policy might moderate the challengers' hostile accusations and at the same time promote in policy makers an awareness of their own responsibility. Our first effort was an article which appeared in the October 1970 issue of the *Virginia Law Review* (vol. 56, pp. 971-1203), entitled "The Forbidden Fruit and the Tree of Knowledge: An Inquiry into the Legal History of American Marijuana Prohibition." Given the original focus of our research, this study was devoted for the most part to judicial and constitutional history. Yet our limited survey of the political and social history was perhaps the most fascinating aspect of the article and merely whetted our appetites for further research.

With the cooperation of the National Commission on Marihuana and Drug Abuse and the Bureau of Narcotics and Dangerous Drugs in the U.S. Department of Justice, we delved deeply into the historical documents. This book is the result of our efforts. In the course of writing it, we were constantly plagued by a conflict between readability and comprehensiveness. We have erred in the direction of thorough documentation due to our heavy reliance on primary source materials, many of which are not easily accessible.

Another matter of concern was the appropriate appellation for our subject. Throughout its tumultuous social history, the various mixtures of leaves, stems, tops, and resin of *Cannabis sativa* L. have been known by many names. In this country, Indian hemp and marihuana have been most common, although the latter has been spelled in a multitude of ways, including *marijuana, marywana, maraguana,* and *marajuana.* In recent years, we have even noted that the spelling of the word has a symbolic social significance, and a writer's social policy preference may frequently be predicted according to whether he begins the third syllable with an *h* or a *j.* We suspect that advocates of change insist on using the *j* because "marihuana" has always been the official spelling.

Although the *j* probably conforms more closely to the practice of Spanish translation, we have employed in this book the spelling most commonly found in the historical documents. Similarly, although "marihuana" now refers primarily to a loose mixture of leaves, stems, and tops generally rolled into cigarettes, and not to the more potent resinous mixtures ("hashish"), the potency of the mixture does not appear to have been of historical significance. Indeed, cannabis was known during the formative stages of its American prohibition as either "hasheesh," the term drawn from the Eastern literature, or "marihuana," the local term. Thus, no distinction is intended in the following pages between the resinous and loose mixtures unless the context requires otherwise.

In an endeavor requiring deep excursions into the bowels of so many libraries and file rooms, we were naturally assisted by a multitude of individuals too numerous to recount here. However, to the 1969-70 staff of the *Virginia Law Review*, three generations of student assistants at the University of Virginia Law School, the staff of the National Commission on Marihuana and Drug Abuse, and the personnel of the Bureau of Narcotics and Dangerous Drugs, we owe sincere thanks. Deserving of special mention are the research assistance of Ms. Evelyn Miller, Ms. Nathalie Gilfoyle, and Messrs. John Golden and Ronald Stevens, the helpful suggestions of Dr. David Musto, and the stenographic fortitude of Ms. Deloris

West and the secretarial pool at the University of Virginia Law School. We also gratefully acknowledge the support and encouragement of Medicine in the Public Interest, a Washington-based nonprofit foundation, and the University of Virginia Law School. Finally, for his kind and expert cooperation, we thank Mr. Michael R. Sonnenreich, formerly Executive Director of the National Commission on Marihuana and Drug Abuse.

R. J. B.

Charlottesville, Virginia   C. H. W. II
August 1973

THE MARIHUANA CONVICTION

A History of Marihuana Prohibition in
the United States

Prologue

THIS BOOK is an historical study of the American public policy response to marihuana, or Indian hemp. Labeled *Cannabis sativa* by Linneaus in 1753, this plant has been used for centuries in Asia and Africa as a medicine and an intoxicant. The same plant has been cultivated as a source of fiber, in North America since the early seventeenth century. Yet the story that will unfold in the succeeding pages spans only seventy years because cannabis was not used as an intoxicant in North America until the late nineteenth century, and in the United States until the early twentieth century.

The hemp plant has been used throughout history for three major purposes. From the fiber men have made rope, twine, and cloth; the seeds yield a useful, rapidly drying oil and also provide sustenance for birds. And in the resin men have discovered a psychoactive agent which they have used for medicinal, religious, and intoxicant purposes. Among different peoples at different times, some of these uses have been more predominant than others.

It seems likely that hemp cultivation originated in western China several millennia before Christ. Because of its prolific pollination and rapid propagation in both its cultivated and wild states, the plant and its use for fiber spread gradually throughout central Asia and India and from there to Asia Minor and to Africa.

Evidence exists of its use for psychoactive purposes perhaps a thousand years before Christ in India, where it became an integral part of Hindu culture, and later in other parts of Asia and the mid-East (South Russia, Assyria, and Persia). Its use as an intoxicant was clearly established in the Arab and Mediterranean worlds by the tenth century A. D., generating many references in Arabian literature. It has been suggested that the intoxicant use of cannabis permeated Islamic culture so thoroughly because alcohol was forbidden to Mohammed's followers. In any event, the expansionist Moslems probably introduced their preferred drug into all of

North Africa from Egypt to Morocco during the ensuing centuries. Whatever its source, the practice slowly took deep root in Egypt and neighboring lands.

How familiar was the hemp plant to Europeans? Evidence on this point is very sketchy. Some have suggested that the Scythians introduced the hemp plant to Europe in their westward migration about 1500 B.C. Others have concluded that it came later, after the fall of Rome. In any event, it is clear that the plant was widely cultivated for fiber purposes during the Renaissance. Henry VIII reportedly required its cultivation by English farmers.

On the other hand, there is no evidence of the use of cannabis as an intoxicant in Europe until the early nineteenth century despite the many previous cultural and commercial contacts between Europeans and the East. In France, medical writers had been aware for some time of the psychoactive use of the plant by Asians and Africans. Further interest was aroused by Napoleonic soldiers and scientists returning from Egypt, where the French colonial forces tried unsuccessfully to wipe out the practice of using hemp which was widespread among the lower classes. As so often happens, however, the curiosity of the occidental elite had thereby been whetted; and the previously passive awareness of cannabis' properties within the medical community was now augmented by the more acute interest of Europe's intellectuals and international traveling set.

Within the Parisian artistic community, interest was particularly intense. Moreau de Tours, the eminent French psychiatrist, wrote a book on cannabis in 1845. He described his own experiences and championed its use, both for therapeutic and euphoriant purposes. His interest was shared by other members of the avant-garde artistic classes, including Victor Hugo, Baudelaire, and Balzac. They recorded their experiences in writing and gathered at the *Club des Haschischins* to share them. It is important, however, to realize that Europeans had no general knowledge of or interest in the psychoactive properties of hemp well into the twentieth century.

Hemp cultivation was well established in the New World long before its intoxicant properties were known. Europeans eagerly transmitted the practice of growing the plant for fiber to the Americans with the early settlers. Probably the Spaniards first introduced it to the New World sometime around 1545 when

Almagro and Valdivia came to Chile. Importing the seeds from Europe, American colonists cultivated hemp for fiber as early as 1611 in Jamestown and 1632 in Massachusetts. As settlers fanned out across North America, so did the practice of cultivating hemp. From Virginia and Pennsylvania, the industry had spread to Kentucky by 1775 and from there to Missouri by 1835. On a smaller scale, hemp was also cultivated in the late nineteenth century in Illinois, Indiana, Nebraska, Iowa, and California. For the most part, seed production was centered primarily in the Kentucky and Illinois River valleys, and fiber production in the Great Lake states.

The American hemp industry reached its zenith in the mid-1800s. First, Kentucky farmers began to import Chinese rather than European seed, improving the quality of domestic hemp. Second, the substantial competition provided by importation of Indian hemp was lessened when the British government, desiring to reduce the plant's widespread intoxicant use in the colony, limited its cultivation there. However, by 1890 American domestic hemp production had declined substantially; the cotton industry was boosted by the development of labor-saving machinery, while hemp harvesting remained a laborious task. Aside from cotton, the demand for fiber was now being satisfied by increased importation of Indian jute. Nevertheless, this domestic flirtation with hemp production left an important legacy. The hemp plant now grew wild along the roadsides and in the fields of almost every state. By the end of the nineteenth century the hemp plant was well rooted and, for the time being, largely ignored in America.

As in Europe, the practice of eating or smoking hemp for its intoxicant qualities had not yet appeared on any significant scale in preindustrial America. But this country also had its travelers whose experiences with the alien drug "hasheesh" are reflected in a series of mid-nineteenth-century literary curios. Although they attracted little contemporary interest, these generally fictionalized and exaggerated accounts were to be resurrected three quarters of a century later in a new social context. The titles of these bizarre publications, analyzed in detail elsewhere, will convey their literary orientation. "The Vision of Hashish" and *The Hashish Eater* were both probably written by Bayard Taylor; published anonymously, they appeared in *Putnam's Monthly* in 1854 and 1856. *The Hashish*

Eater: Being Passages from the Life of a Pythagorean, a book, and "The Apocalypse of Hashish," a *Putnam's* article, were published in 1857 by Fitzhugh Ludlow.

Along with this short-lived literary interest in cannabis intoxication came a more important development: the sudden prominence of the drug as a therapeutic agent. Although there are recorded examples of early medicinal application of hemp in China, India, and Egypt, it was only after a series of enthusiastic reports by Aubert-Roche (1839), O'Shaughnessy (1843), and Moreau de Tours (1845) that the practice began in Europe and the United States. The drug quickly achieved popularity as a treatment for a wide variety of problems, particularly spastic conditions, headaches, and the labor of childbirth.

Over one hundred articles recommending cannabis use were published in medical journals between 1840 and 1900, and it was included in the U.S. pharmacopoeia in 1870. Pharmaceutical houses soon developed preparations of cannabis, and extracts, tinctures, and herb packages were readily available at any pharmacy. Ludlow, for example, secured his "hashish" not in the romantic East but in his local drug store in Poughkeepsie, New York. Ludlow's experience notwithstanding, there is no evidence that these pharmaceutical preparations of cannabis, most of them imported, were used for intoxicant purposes here during the nineteenth century.

By the middle of the nineteenth century the use of the hemp plant for fiber, seed, and medicine was well established both in Europe and in the United States. Indeed, its commercial use was on the increase, but, a few artistic experiments excepted, its use as an intoxicant had not yet begun on either continent.

Where did the American intoxicant use of marihuana come from? To answer this, we must go back to the late sixteenth century. The prevailing hypothesis is that intoxicant use of cannabis first came to the Americas with the African slave trade shuttling back and forth to Brazil. Persuasive evidence for this view is that Brazilians and West Africans use the same name for the plant and that ingestion by water pipe, a practice originating in Asia Minor and Northern Africa, was also prevalent in Brazil. It seems likely that the conjunction of expansive slave trade, Spanish mobility, intensive commercial activity, and tobacco-smoking gradually introduced the practice of smoking cannabis throughout the West Indies and Central America.

Whether or not it followed this route, the use of cannabis was reported in Mexico in 1880 and was prevalent by 1898. Widely cultivated and growing wild, the drug was readily available for eating, drinking, or smoking—the latter being by far the most common method of ingestion. Soldiers in Pancho Villa's army are reputed to have used the drug freely. A well-known Mexican folk song memorializes their practice by describing the inability of the cockroach to march without marihuana to smoke:

> La cucaracha, la cucaracha
> Ya no puede caminar
> Porque no tiene, porque no tiene
> Marihuana que fumar.

It seems clear that the introduction of marihuana-smoking into the United States came not from Europe, which transmitted the fiber, oil, and medicinal uses of hemp, but from Asia and Africa by way of South and Central America, particularly Mexico and the West Indies. This fact has had a substantial impact on the perspective with which the policy-making establishment—legislators, press, governmental agencies, and private opinion makers—have viewed the drug and its effects.

CHAPTER I

The Narcotics Consensus Is Born

IN THE DAYS before marihuana became a political issue in the United States, dissent was rarely voiced to the long-standing social policy vehemently opposed to its use and to the harsh legal policy of jailing its users. This consensus has been shattered, but an alternative one is not yet in view.

The pivotal issue in the current debate is which of the nation's contradictory policies toward intoxicant use will be applied to marihuana. Proponents of change never fail to raise in their behalf the relative dangers of alcohol use and inevitable repeal of its prohibition, predicting a similar fate for present marihuana policy. Opponents of change dismiss the comparison, asking whether this society should be satisfied with the consequences of repeal, and linking marihuana instead to a public consensus opposed to "narcotics" and "drug abuse."

In the following pages, we will trace the development of the original marihuana consensus during the first third of the twentieth century and will illustrate why, once challenged, it collapsed so easily. To do so, however, we must describe the policy-making environment in which the initial consensus was rooted. Paradoxically, that environment remains the same today as when the marihuana story began: American society was grappling inconsistently and inconclusively with the difficult moral, social, and legal issues surrounding the use and misuse of psychoactive drugs. Then, as now, policy makers were concerned about the widespread use of psychoactive drugs, and turned to the law for recourse, establishing two separate precedents in the course of the initial legal response. By the time marihuana appeared on the scene, a major social response had already been formulated, and marihuana policy was determined by the legal environment into which it was thrust. And so it is today.

Drug Use at the Turn of the Century

Alcohol, of course, had been around from the beginning. When the Puritans set sail for Massachusetts, they had brought with them 42 tons of beer and 10,000 gallons of wine.[1] Although alcohol was applied sporadically for therapeutic purposes, intoxication was its acknowledged role in colonial life, as had long been true of occidental civilization.

The first contribution of the New World to the drug habits of the Old was tobacco.[2] Previous successes in South and Central America encouraged John Rolfe to launch an experiment in tobacco cultivation in Virginia in 1613. As a result of his success, the leaf became the economic mainstay of the Southern colonies. Within seven years Virginia exported to England nothing else but tobacco and a little sassafras. The practices of sniffing and chewing tobacco spread quickly among the colonial population and made significant inroads in the mother country as well.

Charles Dickens, during his mid-nineteenth-century tour of the States, observed how deeply the habit permeated the American scene:

> Washington may be called the headquarters of tobacco-tinctured saliva. . . . In all the public places of America, this filthy custom is recognized. In the courts of law, the judge has his spittoon, the crier his, the witness his, and the prisoner his; while the jurymen and spectators are provided for. . . . The stranger will find [the custom] in its full bloom of glory, luxuriant in all its alarming recklessness, at Washington.[3]

Until the mid-nineteenth century, most domestically consumed tobacco was chewed. Then the pipe and the cigar attracted adherents, and after the Civil War the practice of cigarette-smoking was introduced, taking root despite widespread criticism. When the incidence of cigarette use increased substantially after World War I, this habit supplanted all other forms of tobacco consumption, and any pretense that the tobacco leaf had medicinal applications had all but vanished.

The Civil War period also marks another important development in the history of American drug use. Opium had long been available as a painkiller to practitioners of the healing arts, and was widely used in nineteenth-century America. The medical profession was aware that the oral use of opium could result in an "appetite" for the drug, a phenomenon regarded in the same category as the "alcohol habit." This awareness was apparently of insufficient moment to suggest the need for caution when morphine was discovered in 1803 and when the hypodermic syringe was introduced in the middle of the century.[4]

Human suffering was of untold dimensions during the Civil War, and the opiates, particularly morphine, were used indiscriminately for the wholesale relief of pain and, most significantly, for treatment of common gastrointestinal ailments; opiate withdrawal became known as the "army disease," and many veterans are thought to have returned addicted to these drugs.[5] Overmedication continued unabated after peace had been restored, for morphine, widely used in medical practice, was also readily available outside the medical system in proprietary medicines. Within a few years "morphinomania" became a recognizable medical entity, as persons given morphine for legitimate therapeutic purposes often found themselves addicted.[6] The problem was exacerbated by the absence of restrictions upon druggists in refilling prescriptions containing excessive amounts of morphine and other opiates.[7]

The scope of excessive medication increased in 1884 when Koller discovered the local anesthetic properties of cocaine, and again in 1898 when an advance in German chemistry produced heroin. Initially marketed as a cough suppressant, heroin was publicized as having many of the virtues and few of the dangers of morphine; some even suggested that it would be useful in the treatment of morphinism itself.[8] This drug was soon widely used for pain relief and other medicinal purposes.[9]

The drug habit reached still deeper into American society through the promotion and unrestricted use of proprietary medicines. Exotically labeled elixirs such as Dr. Brown's Snake Oil were advertised as general cures for ills ranging from snakebite to melancholia. Because the contents did not have to be printed on the label, many an unsuspecting person became addicted without ever knowing that the medicine that worked so well contained large quantities of opiates.[10]

In sum, careless prescriptions, repeated dispensation, and hidden distribution of harmful drugs whose dependence liability was unknown until too late, fostered a large addict population which continued to increase into the early twentieth century. Since accidental addiction and overmedication played such a large role, the addict population was middle class, included more females than males, more whites than blacks, and cut across geographic lines.[11] Although the medical profession became increasingly aware of this phenomenon of medically based opiate use in the last years of the century, it was invisible to the general public and was not a matter of major concern outside the profession until the first decade of the present century.

But not all opiate use was medicinal. The Chinese Opium Wars and the romantic appeal of the mysterious Orient whetted the interest of the Western intellectual elite in opium-smoking during the middle of the nineteenth century. Coleridge, De Quincey, and others memorialized their mystical experiences in their literature. Then, after the Civil War, the practice of opium-smoking gained a stronger foothold among the American population when Chinese immigrants began filtering into California, particularly San Francisco. Opium dens proliferated as the exotic oriental ritual attracted American curiosity. One observer noted in 1882 that sometime around 1875, "authorities became cognizant of the fact . . . that many women and young girls, and also young men of respectable family, were being induced to visit the dens . . . ."[12] Opium soon found its way into the underworld, and the practice spread among the deviant subcultures of the nation's cities. This population also began to sniff cocaine, the active ingredient of South American coca leaves.

This then was the nature and scope of American drug use at the turn of the twentieth century. Alcohol was well rooted across the entire population, particularly in the West; cigarette-smoking was seeping into the cultural mainstream; a significant percentage of the adult population (conservatively estimated at 125,000 persons) had innocently become addicted to the opiates; opium-smoking had developed a substantial following in the West and among the urban elite; and the intoxicant use of opium, morphine, and cocaine had now appeared in the streets of the nation's cities.

The Social Response to Twentieth-Century Drug Use

By the turn of the century, America was in the throes of a major social transformation. Rapid conversion from an agrarian to an industrial state wrought substantial changes in the style and composition of American life. Large businesses and corporations had developed vast economic power, slowly driving their smaller competitors out of business. The nation had become urbanized as the industrial cities siphoned off attention and manpower from the farms. As this process unfolded, the poverty and social disruption of the burgeoning cities drew horrified commentary from novelists, politicians, newspapers, and social observers. To satisfy the manpower needs of an expanding economy, the nation welcomed successive waves of immigrants in the nineteenth and early twentieth centuries. These immigrants brought with them different religions, strange languages, and distinctly "un-American" customs.

Leading the governmental response to this massive upheaval in the economic, political, and social life of America was an amorphous group of urban reformers who set out confidently to remedy the industrial and institutional ills plaguing their nation.[13] The nationalist spirit manifested in the Spanish-American War was now directed to fulfillment of America's highest domestic aspirations. Although their proposals had utilitarian dimensions, the reformers were engaged in a distinctly moral enterprise, seeking "good government" free of corruption, economic competition free of trusts and exploitation, and cities free of vice and degradation.

Moral reform had been a strong undercurrent of nineteenth-century American life, and—as in the case of alcohol—every social ill attracted its own group of organized adversaries. As the century progressed and the institutional evils of industrialization and urbanization became apparent, this reform sentiment gradually turned to the government and the law to protect the moral fiber of the nation. The moral strength of the individual was no longer believed sufficient to counter corporate selfishness, political corruption, and urban degradation.

By the end of the century, reform sentiment had entered the political arena in unusual strength. The resort to politics was not new; what was new was the serious manner with which the reformers went about the business of organizing and functioning within the practical confines of a political system. Perhaps the reformers had matured, no longer relying on moral exhortations alone. In any event, the most practical and, for this reason, perhaps, the most successful of the reforming groups, was that amorphous conglomerate called the Progressives. Slogans and social structure aside, Progressivism was propelled by a belief that legislation was an effective tool for achieving moral reform and by an organized political effort at every level of government to implement this creed.

The economic virtues of hard work, competition, and individualism, tempered by the social virtue of humanitarianism, formed the core of the reform ideology. Superimposed on the entire effort was a Calvinist urge to demonstrate superior moral status. Since they considered the morality of the nation to depend on the appearance of its institutions, the reformers engaged in a national campaign to purify the cities, the businesses, and the political process itself. Further, since national progress depended on the economic and political contribution of every individual, the reformers aimed to remove the urban vices impeding individual productivity and moral perfection.

The reform faith in the moral perfectibility of every citizen was concretely manifested in a continuing effort to cleanse the moral environment of the cities. Particularly important was reformers' protective attitude toward urban children who were exploited economically by day and tempted morally by night. Through the juvenile court movement, the reformers sought to extricate the errant child from his injurious environment and to redirect his path. Through child labor laws, the reformers aimed to curb the worst excesses of the giant industrial complexes hungry for the cheap labor offered by women, children, and immigrants.

Most reformers also opposed the political and economic exploitation of the immigrants, whose depressed wages facilitated economic concentration, and whose ignorance of American political institutions and unfamiliarity with the democratic system were the perfect cement in the urban political machines. These reformers were intolerant of the institutions rather than of the immigrants themselves. Taking a deterministic and democratic approach to the urban masses, the Progressives were generally not associated with the xenophobic pressure for immigration restriction that recurred throughout the late nineteenth and early twentieth centuries.

While the reform movement was not overtly nativistic, it is important to comprehend its ambivalence toward the immigrants gathering in the nation's urban areas. A number of reformers held the cosmopolitan view, according to which ethnic cross-pollination improved the quality of the American species. A more widely held opinion implicitly postulated the moral superiority of the white, Protestant, Anglo-Saxon breed and confidently affirmed its capacity to assimilate diverse cultural groups. To the nationalist image of America as a haven for the oppressed was added the heady optimism of belief in the melting pot. In Justice Holmes's words, the Americans were "the Romans of the modern world, the great assimilating people."[14]

Yet, as John Higham has demonstrated in his classic work *Strangers in the Land*,[15] the assimilationist attitude contained within it the seeds of nativism. Absorption, not cultural pluralism, was the preferred outcome. As one newspaper put it in 1888, "the strong stomach of American civilization will ultimately digest this unsavory and repellent throng."[16] Twenty years later one of the most race conscious of America's social scientists concluded that the "vortical suction of our civilization is stronger now than ever before."[17] But whenever this confidence in the native stock's ability to assimilate was shaken, a cry for immigration restriction was heard. And whenever fear—of economic adversity, internal subversion, or international militarism—gripped the population, national wrath was turned toward the foreign born.

During the Progressive era, however, confidence—not fear—was the controlling public policy, and its democratic, environmentalist ideology focused on integrating the immigrant into the American system rather than protecting that system from him. At the same time, the moral certainty of the reformers precluded toleration of any of the immigrants' "habits of life" which were inconsistent with the prevailing value system.

The unrestrained marketing practices of the pharmaceutical companies, which tended to foster the "drug habit evil" among the children, among the immigrants, and among the weak and unsuspecting, posed a ripe target for the reformers, as did the economic excesses of the liquor industry. Here, as in no other area of American life, governmental intervention was clearly needed to purify industries with so much power to harm the ordinary citizen. Further, drugs, like the cities themselves, were thought to be seductive, bidding pleasure and comfort as the first step on the inexorable path to addiction, immorality, criminality, and death. From this perspective, the reformers viewed all habit-forming drugs as interchangeable sources of misery, all of which had to be purged from the urban environment. Only then could the weak avoid temptation, the fallen be saved, and the immigrant be protected.

To summarize, the social response to drug use in the early twentieth century was framed by a policy-making ideology that combined faith in the moral superiority of the dominant social order, confidence in the inevitability of moral (and therefore social) progress, preference for cultural homogeneity, intolerance of institutional "evils," paternalism toward children and immigrants, and faith in governmental action. This response took two separate paths, one directed at "narcotics," meaning the opiates and cocaine, and another directed at alcohol and, to a lesser extent, tobacco. Narcotics policy, as it slowly emerged, was supported by a latent popular consensus; alcohol policy, however, was conceived and abandoned in conflict.

The Antinarcotics Consensus

Up until the last two decades of the nineteenth century, little concerted governmental action had been taken to control the manufacture, distribution, or consumption of psychoactive drugs. Legal restraints were confined for the most part to state laws regulating pharmacies and restricting the distribution of poisons (which generally included the opiates and other medicines). Despite a mushrooming opiate dependence problem arising from unrestrained distribution within the medical system, it was the "street" use of opiates and cocaine which accelerated professional and public interest in their habit-forming properties. Indeed, legislative attention (and medical understanding of drug properties as well) seems to have occurred only after each new drug achieved a significant degree of "street" use, especially when that use was identified with the poor, racial minorities and criminal classes. For example, the earliest state laws focused primarily on crime prevention and public education regarding the dangers of opiate use.[18] The first wave of prohibitory drug (nonalcohol) legislation pertained to opium-smoking, which first appeared on the West Coast after the Civil War, and gradually spread to the outcast populations of major cities. In 1875 a San Francisco ordinance prohibited the smoking or possession of opium, the possession of opium pipes, and the maintenance of opium dens. Then, beginning with the Nevada law which prohibited the retail sale of smoking opium in 1877, twenty states enacted statutes designed directly to eradicate the alien practice, either by prohibiting the operation of opium dens or by prohibiting the smoking and possession of opium altogether.[19]

These early opium prohibitions, the first drug legislation to criminalize the consumer for his indulgence, clearly had more to do with the drug's users than with the drug itself—most (eleven) were passed in western states where there was little pretense of assimilating the newly immigrated Chinese populations: Nevada (1877), South Dakota and North Dakota (1879), Utah (1880), California and Montana (1881), Wyoming (1882), Arizona (1883), Idaho and New Mexico (1887), and Washington (1890). The violence of the anti-Chinese agitation during the seventies and eighties was matched only by the viciousness of the rhetoric; in 1882 the federal government responded by forbidding further Chinese immigration. Called upon to test the constitutionality of opium prohibition, even the appellate judiciary recognized the law's ethnic origins: "Smoking opium is not our vice, and therefore, it may be that this legislation proceeds more from a desire to vex and annoy the "Heathen Chinee" in this respect, than to protect the people from the evil habit."[20]

While opium-smoking was attracting interest in the West, the use of cocaine was recorded in the South. By the turn of the century "cocainomania" among Southern blacks had become a matter of official concern, and violent criminal conduct was frequently attributed to the influence of cocaine.[21]

By the early years of the twentieth century, morphine had replaced smoking opium as the opiate of choice in the streets.[22] Now morphine and cocaine (heroin had not yet surfaced in the streets to any significant extent) were identified with the under-world of the "vicious" cities—the prostitutes, pimps, gamblers, and blacks—and the public was aroused against the "menace" of "morphinism." Law enforcement officials in the major cities led the attack;[23] as these drugs became identified with urban crime, opiate use was gradually shorn of its mystical appeal, and the image of the dope fiend took root in the public mind.

As the widespread use of opiates and cocaine inside and outside medical practice was brought forcefully to public attention, the medical profession, the law enforcement community, and the state legislatures intensified previously casual efforts to bring the medical distribution of "narcotics" under control, primarily by tightening the restrictions on prescription practices and pharmacies and by prohibiting nonmedical distribution.[24] Whereas only a handful of states restricted the availability of opiates and cocaine to prescriptions before 1900, most enacted laws "designed to minimize the drug-habit evil" by 1912. Prescriptions were required for distribution of cocaine in forty-four states, of opiates in thirty-three, and of chloral hydrate in fifteen.[25]

Meanwhile, pressure for comprehensive federal legislation was mushrooming as public alarm over the "narcotics evil" escalated year by year. In 1906 Congress passed the Pure Food and Drug Act, the first major federal drug legislation to require labeling of all preparations containing more than prescribed amounts of opiates, and the availability of proprietaries containing significant quantities of these drugs diminished dramatically.[26] The 1909 "Act to Prohibit Importation and Use of Opium," barred the importation of opium at other than specified ports and for other than medicinal use. The law further required the keeping of import records. The main force behind the passage of this statute was a desire to establish the United States' formal opposition to nonmedical use of opiates as the nation's delegation prepared for international proceedings.[27]

A few years later state antinarcotics legislation began to take on crusade proportions. New additional federal regulation of the inter-state trade in cocaine, morphine, and heroin was said to be necessary because effective control was beyond the competence of the states and was mandated by U.S. obligations under the recently formulated Hague Convention of 1912. Consequently, the Harrison

Act, for fifty-six years the foundation of federal law controlling narcotic drugs, was passed in 1914.[28]

The Harrison Act required registration and payment of an occupational tax by all persons who imported, produced, dealt in, sold, or gave away opium and coca leaves and their derivatives. All registered handlers were required to file returns setting forth in detail their use of the drugs and to use special order forms in making any transfer. Conversely, it was unlawful for anyone to purchase, sell, dispense, or distribute any of these "narcotic" drugs without having registered or paid the tax; and it was also unlawful to transfer these drugs without using an official written order form prepared by the recipient. Finally, mere possession of these drugs without a prescription was presumptive evidence of violation of the act.

An important objective of the Harrison Act was to regulate the legitimate commerce in the opiates and cocaine in order to bring this traffic into observable and controllable channels. Every transaction was subject to some official paperwork, and the regulatory devices went well beyond those necessary for the collection of the excise and registration taxes.

Why had Congress chosen this awkward revenue mechanism for what was clearly a regulatory enactment? In simple terms, Congress was attempting to do indirectly that which it believed it could not do directly: regulate the practice of medicine and the intrastate sale and possession of drugs. In 1914 when Congress enacted the Harrison Act, the prevailing interpretation of its powers to regulate interstate and foreign commerce and to raise revenue was that these powers were limited and that the power to regulate "local" affairs had been reserved to the states by the Tenth Amendment.[29] Thus, as the Supreme Court pointed out in 1925 in a case construing the act, "direct control of medical practice in the states is beyond the power of the Federal Government."[30] By using its taxing powers, however, Congress was regulating these local activities only "incidentally," in order to facilitate implementation of its primary intent—the raising of revenue. Ultimately, the Supreme Court allowed Congress to get away with this ruse, but only by a five-to-four margin.[31]

The Harrison Act crystallized a firm national policy of curtailing the availability of "habit-forming" substances. The previous failure of the medical profession to appreciate the dependence liability of new substances had now resulted in professional and legislative preoccupation with this issue. In addition, each of the so-called "narcotic" drugs had, in its turn, been associated with criminal behavior, an association which the popular imagination attributed to the drug rather than to the lifestyle of its street users.

In short, the drug habit led to crime and slothfulness, and any nonmedical use inevitably tended to excess. At its core, then, the Harrison Act embodied a strong ideological and moral antipathy to habitual drug use in general and to the nonmedical or "street" use of the "narcotic" drugs in particular.[32] "We are an opium-consuming nation today," thundered Congressman Harrison in 1913, lamenting that the "shameless traffic" in the opiates had created "criminal classes" and that their use "with such accompanying moral and economic degradation is widespread among the upper classes of society."[33]

As to the undesirability and immorality of the use of opiates or cocaine for pleasure, there was no debate. Such use was inconsistent with the entire ideology guiding public policy makers during this period. The "narcotic" drug severely impeded individual participation in the economic and political systems by enslaving its unsupervised users in the clutches of addiction. Increasingly associated with the slothful and immoral "criminal classes" who degraded the nation's cities, narcotics use threatened to retard national growth with pauperism, moral degeneracy, and crime. A consensus had emerged: the nonmedical use of "narcotics" was a cancer which had to be removed entirely from the social organism.

In the context of curtailing availability and use of habit-forming drugs, Congress undoubtedly intended to prohibit habitual drug use. Indeed, a wide spectrum of official and professional opinion considered the satisfaction of a preexisting drug habit to be an impermissible medical practice. Although Congress did not address the question of maintenance expressly, and congressional intent continues to be the subject of lively debate,[34] it is difficult to believe the legislators were oblivious to the fate of perhaps a quarter of a million opiate-dependent persons (about evenly divided between "medical" and "street" addiction).[35] Under the Harrison Act, persons possessing drugs secured pursuant to a prescription or received directly from a physician were naturally excepted from the general prohibitions of transportation and possession. In this connection, exceptions to the various order forms and transfer provisions were tied to "legitimate medical purposes" (or similar language). It was a common medical practice in many states[36] before the act for physicians to prescribe these drugs to maintain an addict on a "comfort" regimen or on a graduated withdrawal schedule, although the legislatures of at least ten states expressly forbade this practice.

One view is that Congress anticipated the early development of a drug-free "cure" for addiction and therefore intended to preclude maintenance, except perhaps on a temporary basis. The opposing view is that Congress did not intend to prohibit maintenance but that the Prohibition Unit of the Treasury Department, which became responsible for narcotics enforcement in 1920, cunningly converted the Harrison Act into a prohibitory statute by using the courts to discourage private physicians from having anything to do with narcotics addicts, and by closing the narcotics "clinics" or dispensaries which had developed to provide a controlled supply for addicts who were suddenly cut off from other drugs by the Harrison Act and by the Treasury's vigorous enforcement policy.[37]

The question of congressional intent is somewhat moot. A cure was not forthcoming, and the addict was ultimately closed off from medical assistance, and was forced underground to purchase his drug. By imposing the stamp of immorality and criminality on *all* habitual narcotics use outside limited medical channels, official-dom generated a self-fulfilling prophecy. Inflated underground prices often provoked criminal activity which in turn cemented the link between iniquity and drug addiction. Dr. Lawrence Kolb, who emerged during this period as one of the government's leading medical experts on addiction, has noted: "[A] result of the physician's resignation to pressure was that addicts to the opiates began to commit petty crimes in order to secure the drugs which could prevent their suffering. These inevitable law-induced crimes greatly accentuated the general public belief that opiates had some inherent sinister property which could change normal people into moral perverts and criminals."[38]

The net result of the nation's enforcement policy was to tighten the antinarcotics consensus. The nonmedical use of opiates and cocaine was washed completely of the mystical qualities formerly

ON THE HEELS OF "REFORM"

IN 1917 reports of the narcotic division of the Treasury Department showed 1,060 cases of violation of the laws against selling drugs; in 1925, they showed 10,297 cases of violation, about ten times as many as before the passage of the Volstead Act. Maybe there is no connection between this increase and Volsteadism, but the ugly follower seems close behind.

Chicago Herald and Examiner, 1926

associated with opium-smoking. By 1925 the medical problem had receded in the wake of the regulatory legislation and narcotics use was tied entirely to crime and slothfulness; and users—whether dependent or not—were sent to jail for their indulgence.

The Harrison Act, as it was enforced against maintenance and street use, was undoubtedly a prohibition statute. Total implementation of the prohibitory scheme, however, depended on residual state legislation since the federal government had neither the manpower nor the constitutional authority to fight street crime. The states responded without hesitation to the federal lead. Before 1914 only six states had prohibited mere possession of regulated (not including smoking opium) drugs by unauthorized persons (five of these laws pertained only to cocaine). However, by 1931 thirty-six had prohibited possession of cocaine, thirty-five had prohibited possession of opiates, and eight had prohibited possession of hypodermic syringes. A particularly significant feature of the state response to the Harrison Act was a sharp increase in criminal penalties which occurred between 1914 and 1931.[39]

Before leaving the antinarcotics developments, we should note that the Prohibition Unit was anxious to have a possession offense as well. Direct prohibition was of course beyond congressional power, and the Harrison Act had made possession of narcotics outside the stamped package presumptive evidence of violation of the revenue and registration provisions. In 1916 the Supreme Court noted that any congressional attempt to punish as a crime possession of any article produced in a state would probably be unconstitutional, and therefore held that the provision did not apply to mere possession of opium.[40] Six years later Congress found a way around this technicality as part of a new Narcotic Drugs Import and Export Act which tightened the Harrison Act's regulatory scheme.[41]

The 1922 act authorized the Federal Narcotics Control Board to determine how much opium, cocaine, and their derivatives were necessary for medical purposes and to set quotas accordingly as to amounts which could be imported to fill this need. Under Section 2f of this act, possession without a prescription was made presumptive evidence of concealment of drugs illegally imported in violation of the act. In other words, by tying possession for nonmedical purposes to importation, Congress got around the Supreme Court, and made possession a federal crime again.

Thus, within fifteen years after passage of the Harrison Act, American narcotics public policy had made a full turn. The likelihood of accidental addiction having been minimized, the image of the "dope fiend"—the immoral "street" user—now lay at the center of policy-making. What had been formerly viewed as an unfortunate sickness with organic causes was now viewed as yet another immoral behavior of the criminal class. The medical profession, never much interested in treating opiate dependence in the first place, had been intimidated and finally ousted from the addict's life; and now, deprived of any legitimate source of narcotic drugs, the user's entire lifestyle was criminalized—from possession of his needle and his drug to the thievery in which he had to engage to sustain his habit.

National Alcohol Prohibition: Conflict

There were many major differences between the temperance and antinarcotics movements. The temperance movement was a matter of vigorous public debate; the antinarcotics movement was not. Temperance legislation was the product of a highly organized nationwide lobby; narcotics legislation was largely ad hoc. The ultimate aim of the temperance movement was always clear—to eliminate consumption of alcohol; the aim of the antinarcotics movement, which was directed at two separate phenomena (pharmaceutical manufacturing and street use), was always ambiguous until a vociferous enforcement policy established a highly restrictive policy. Finally, alcohol prohibition never made criminals of consumers of the drug, while narcotics prohibition insinuated the criminal law into every aspect of the narcotic user's lifestyle.

On the other hand, there were striking similarities between the two movements. In both, legislative action was initially secured against the evils of unlimited availability, and only later against all use. Most of the rhetoric was the same: these drugs menaced the young and produced crime, pauperism, and insanity. Both movements began at the state level and later secured significant congressional action. Most important, both had dual dimensions: moralistic and nativistic. But therein lies their most important difference as well. Narcotics prohibition arose out of a consensus morality and

San Francisco Examiner, 1 April 1927

was directed toward the lifestyles of insulated minorities; the moral imperatives of alcohol prohibition, on the other hand, never achieved wholesale acceptance, and the lower class, immigrant populations at which it was aimed were not outside the political process.

Alcohol prohibition, achieved nationally five years after passage of the Harrison Act, had a puzzling ideological flavor. When the temperance movement surfaced in the early nineteenth century, it was dominated by moral considerations. Aggressive prohibition campaigns had been mounted in every state from 1851 to 1869, and again from 1880 to 1890. But in 1903 only Maine (1884), Kansas (1880), and North Dakota (1889) were completely dry states. Ernest Cherrington, chronicler par excellence of the prohibition movement, blamed the failure of the first thrust in part on the intervention of the slavery question, which diverted the moral fervor of the people from the temperance movement. The failure of the second campaign he attributed to the inability of the prohibition activists to compete politically with growing liquor interests that dominated state and local governments.

By 1906, however, the progress of the antisaloon arm of the temperance movement in local option contests and the prohibition of alcohol by the people of Oklahoma in a provision of their constitution (ratified upon admission to statehood) signaled a new crusade for state prohibitory legislation. The Oklahoma vote so "electrified the moral forces of other states" that by 1913 six additional states had enacted statewide prohibition, and half of the remaining states were contemplating action.

By November 1913, pressure was building. More than half the population and 71 percent of the area of the United States were under prohibitionary laws. Accordingly, the Fifteenth National Convention of the Anti-Saloon League of America unanimously endorsed immediate passage of national constitutional prohibition, whereupon the National Temperance Council was formed to combine forces of the various temperance organizations.[42]

This initial success reflected the continuing vitality in rural America of a fundamentalist opposition to the use of intoxicants which, nonetheless, engendered more guilt than observance. Members of Women's Christian Temperance Union, formed in 1874, and similar groups campaigned against the use of tobacco, alcohol, and coffee, and could count on the support of those members of the community who, although indulging occasionally themselves, were willing to concede the moral superiority of those who abstained.

Despite this substantial resurgence, however, the temperance movement would not have succeeded on the national level had it not drawn support from strains of the reform ideology and of the reformers themselves. In an article in *Appleton's Magazine* in 1908 the Reverend Charles F. Aked articulated the role of temperance in the reform movement: "We are spending our lives, many of us, in the effort to make the world a little better and brighter for those that shall come after us. . . . We want to open out life and liberty to all the sons of men. We want to make possible for all of life in the whole, the good and the beautiful . . . and the common sale of intoxicating liquor renders our work a thousand times more difficult. . . ."[43] Learning political tactics from their fellow reformers, and attracting many from among those who were horrified by the economic and social evils of excessive alcohol use, prohibition advocates finally succeeded in legislating the temperance morality.

Indeed, many elements of the reform value system did coincide with the aims of the temperance movement. Excessive use of alcohol, like use of narcotic drugs, prevented the individual from playing an active and productive role in society. For this reason, such use contravened the basic reform prescription for individuality and productivity in economic affairs. Excessive use increased with the commercialization of the production and distribution of alcohol and with the expansion of saloons. As the muckrakers and sensational journalists continued to point to the number of alcohol "addicts" in America and to portray their lives as ones of destruction and shame, more and more reformers were inclined to join the traditional fundamentalist temperance groups to press for a national alcohol prohibition. Public resentment against the corrupting influence of the large liquor dealers in local politics, especially in the bigger cities, tended to focus public attention on removing this cancer from the body politic.

Finally, the institution that most strongly aroused public sentiment against liquor traffic was the licensed saloon, the symbol of intemperance and corruption. Owned or controlled by the large brewers or wholesalers, centers of political activity, homes of commercialized vice, the saloons were the bête noires of native American public opinion. Here the linkage of excessive consumption of alcohol with the other city vices and with the Irish and Italian immigrant population increased the inclination of many reformers to oppose alcohol.

Beneath these more or less concrete considerations, however, was a cultural conflict for which prohibition was a potent symbol. No longer so certain of the assimilationist capacity of the dominant native Anglo-Saxon culture, reform leaders now felt threatened by the continuing aggregation of immigrant throngs. Riding the wave of the prewar drive for "100 percent Americanism," the Drys "identified their crusade to regulate behavior with preservation of the American way of life."[44] As Joseph Gusfield's *Symbolic Crusade* has so thoroughly demonstrated, native, Protestant, middle-class leaders, ideologically unopposed to moderate consumption of alcohol, joined the prohibitionist crusade to assert the continued superiority of their way of life.[45]

Adopted by the constitutionally required majority of both houses of Congress in December 1917, the Eighteenth Amendment was ratified by the thirty-sixth state on 16 January 1919 and became effective on 16 January 1920. The Eighteenth Amendment itself prohibited manufacture, sale, and transportation of "intoxicating liquors . . . for beverage purposes" within the United States. Congress and the states were given concurrent authority to enforce the amendment. The sponsors of the implementing federal legislation, the Volstead Act, were anxious to remedy the fact that the amendment did not prohibit possession, stating in the Senate report that "[u]nder a Constitutional Amendment which prohibits the manufacture of intoxicating liquor even for one's own use there can be no justification for permitting the possession of that which must be illegally manufactured or sold before it is possessed."[46]

Accordingly, Section 3, Title II of the Volstead Act prohibited possession "except as otherwise authorized." This exception was made for "authorized possession" because the Senate thought it had to protect the property rights of persons possessing liquor that had been legally secured prior to passage of the act. Section 33 authorized the possession of such liquor so long as it was within a private dwelling for the personal consumption of the owner, his family, or his bona fide guests. Although Section 33 excepted personal use of lawfully acquired liquor from the operation of the act, it also placed the burden of proof on the possessor in any action to prove that any liquor he consumed *was* lawfully acquired, possessed, and used.

Despite the express intent of Congress in formulating Sections 3 and 33 to forbid the possession of intoxicating beverages altogether, the courts ultimately vitiated the attempt to forbid personal use by liberally construing "authorized possession."[47]

The judicial attempts to immunize the individual alcohol consumer from prosecution should be compared to the judicial reticence to curtail the scope of criminal control over the narcotics consumer. In cases construing the Volstead Act, the federal courts bent over backwards to limit its coverage, the net result being that neither possession nor purchase of alcohol was a federal crime.

At the state level, only five states (Georgia, Idaho, Indiana, Kansas, and Tennessee) prohibited possession of alcohol for personal use. The remaining states utilized every conceivable statutory device to assure that the law would not reach into the consumer's home. For example, ten states prohibited possession only if it was for purposes of sale, and three others prohibited possession only if it was in public. Of the other twenty-eight states, some expressly excluded possession of small amounts from the general "possession" offense, others permitted home brew, and still others excluded private dwellings from any enforcement activity, thereby immunizing personal consumption.[48]

The prohibition experiment was doomed from the start. As the Wickersham Commission noted in 1931, the passage of the Eighteenth Amendment was attributable not to public opposition to the use of intoxicating beverages,[49] although this was indeed the view of many of the leaders of the movement, but rather to public hostility to three related evils: excessive consumption, political corruption, and licensed saloons.[50] Without a sincere moral commitment among a substantial majority of the population, enforcement of total abstinence under the Volstead Act was impossible.

It is apparent that antinarcotics legislation and alcohol prohibition followed different political paths and, further, that their concurrent passage was purely coincidental. Once opiate use became identified with otherwise immoral or unliked populations, prohibition was almost automatic; although consistent with the reform ideology of the period, such legislation required no ideological umbrella. Alcohol prohibition, on the other hand, was a misshapen child of social conflict never backed by a consensus; and the policy was never seriously implemented. Also consistent in part with reform objectives, alcohol prohibition nevertheless defied ideological characterization.

Public Policy Patterns

On the surface, it would appear that a cohesive social response to psychoactive drug use emerged during the first two decades of the twentieth century. Judging only from the prohibitory governmental response to narcotics and alcohol which had evolved by 1920, one might assume that American society had contracted a social allergy to the consumption of psychoactive substances for nonmedical purposes, and that no distinction was drawn between alcohol on the one hand and the opiates and cocaine on the other.

As we have suggested in the preceding pages, such an assumption would be erroneous. The alcohol and narcotics responses emerged independently of one another. The social situations were completely different as was the eventual impact of the formal response on individual beliefs and behavior. Prohibitory alcohol legislation was incapable of altering ingrained habits of alcohol consumption or public opinion regarding the drug (and the cycle of prohibition and repeal may actually have been counterproductive by erasing the dangers of alcohol from the public memory). The cultural conflict which precipitated the Eighteenth Amendment continued unabated during its tenure, finally tipping in favor of the urban immigrant masses and therefore in favor of repeal.

The initial narcotics legislation, on the other hand, responded to a commonly accepted regulatory need but to no preexisting public attitude toward use of these particular substances. Public attitude was predisposed by the identity and characteristics of persons who chose to use these substances, and the formal policy-making response tended to affirm and harden these predispositions.

The formative impact of legislative action on public attitude is illustrated by the meaning of the term "narcotics." This term referred medically to those substances which dulled a person's senses and put him to sleep when taken in small doses, and stupefied him ("narcosis") and caused complete insensibility and perhaps death when taken in large doses.[51] Frequently mentioned as examples were the opiates and the belladona group of drugs (datura, stramonium, hyosyamus). It appears that as the medical profession became aware of other psychoactive substances, they were immediately classified as narcotics if they could produce sleep like the opiates or hallucinations like the belladona group. The effect was that chloral hydrate, cannabis, and peyote were all defined as "narcotics." Conversely, there was some disagreement among the pharmacologists and medical lexicographers regarding whether alcohol was a "narcotic," even though it shared the depressant qualities of the opiates.[52]

The initial "narcotics" legislation clearly embodied the disapproval of the medical and law enforcement communities of the nonmedical use of these potent, stupor-producing substances—the opiates. As use of these substances became inseparably identified with a criminal, immoral lifestyle, public disapproval emerged as well, hardening into antipathy; and since this antipathy extended to "narcotics," it extended automatically to the unfamiliar substances to which the medical community (cannabis, chloral hydrate, peyote) or the law enforcement community (cocaine) referred as "narcotics." The narcotics image thus came to encompass addiction, lethargy, crime, insanity, and death. The term assumed a social meaning, one defined by the public policy bearing its name. If a drug appeared on the streets, it was presumed "habit-forming" and criminogenic and was therefore considered a "narcotic."

In this connection, then, we note that *neither* the antinarcotics nor alcohol responses manifested a societal opposition to the mere *use* of psychoactive substances for pleasure. The abstentionist strain in our culture, strongest in nineteenth-century rural America, never won majority acceptance, even during the prohibition triumph. The successful inclusion of alcohol prohibition in the United States Constitution is a testimonial to the depth of native concern about the sociopolitical consequences of urban distribution and consumption of alcohol rather than to the dominance of abstentionist sentiment. At the same time, the use of alcohol was deeply ingrained in the American culture, as Toqueville had noted almost a century earlier; and recent acceptance into that culture of multitudes of alcohol-drinking European immigrants had rooted the habit even deeper. Consequently, the new public policy required that a substantial number of people discard a habit which they considered innocuous.

Throughout the seventy-year history of prohibition agitation, its opponents argued—and its proponents admitted—that alcohol was used in moderation by the overwhelming number of its devotees. The predominance of moderate use, together with the lack of majority opposition to such use, forestalled nationwide prohibition for seven decades and sealed its fate even then. In regard to narcotics use, however, each of these elements was missing: the use of opiate drugs for pleasure was not an indigenous behavior; observers uniformly assumed that moderation was impossible and that use and abuse were synonymous; and there was no population with access to the public opinion process which could have challenged the validity of that assumption.

A second important policy pattern manifested in this amorphous legislative response is that private behavior is most likely to be criminalized if the population engaging in that behavior is already perceived as a criminal class. Until about 1915 the courts had insisted that there were constitutional restraints on the power of the government to coerce abstention (by prohibiting possession or consumption). In states which attempted to prohibit possession of alcohol, the courts generally held that such an enactment was beyond the state's "police power"—its power to regulate and protect the public health, safety, and morals.

At the same time, the courts were upholding prohibition of possession of opium, having accepted the narcotics imprint. For example, a California judge asserted in 1911: "But liquor is used daily in this and other countries as a beverage, moderately and without harm, by countless thousands . . .; whereas it appears there is no such thing as moderation in the use of opium. Once the habit is formed the desire for it is insatiable, and its use is invariably disastrous."[53]

When the temperance movement accelerated around 1913-15, however, the courts retreated and withdrew the constitutional restraints on the police power. Naturally, the movement's opponents were outraged and accused the courts of interpreting constitutional precepts to correspond with public opinion.[54] This indeed is what the courts did. As Brooks Adams noted in 1913, the scope of the "police power"

> could not be determined in advance by abstract reasoning.Hence, as each litigation arose, the judges could follow no rule but the rule of common sense, and the Police Power, translated into plain English, presently came to signify whatever, at the moment, the judges happened to think reasonable.Consequently, they began guessing at the drift of public opinion, as it percolated to them through the medium of their education and prejudices. Sometimes they guessed right and sometimes wrong, and when they guessed wrong, they were cast aside, as appeared dramatically enough in the Temperance agitation.[55]

Even when the courts moved aside, however, most legislatures did not intrude the criminal law into the private life of the alcohol consumer. Even if the constitutional limitations had disappeared, the practical social limitations inhibiting enforcement of such laws remained. Yet these same legislatures were simultaneously imposing severe criminal restraints on the life of a narcotics user. And while the courts were imposing additional obstacles on full enforcement of the alcohol laws against the consumer, they were simultaneously aiding legislative efforts to apprehend and punish that immoral, vicious population of narcotics users.

The third policy pattern suggested by the history of alcohol and narcotics prohibition is that the likelihood of prohibitory drug legislation is increased when the drug is identified with ethnic minorities. Whether motivated by an ideological preference for cultural homogeneity or by outright prejudice, drug legislation may be aimed at the lifestyle of the users rather than at use of the drug. Users of opium were often Chinese; street users of cocaine, and later heroin as well, were often perceived as black and West Indian; intemperate users of alcohol were often Irish, Italian, and German; and later we shall see that users of marihuana were often Mexican and users of peyote were often American Indian.

A related pattern is that drug use or other minority behavior is more likely to be viewed with anxiety (and to be indicted as a "menace") in times of social malaise than in times of social stability and optimism. When the dominant social order is thought to be threatened—by economic woes, by internal disruption of lawlessness, or by external aggression—policy-making is likely to be defensive, lashing out at behavior perceived to be associated with the general societal fears.

CHAPTER II

The Alien Weed

THE PRACTICES of smoking marihuana and of growing it for that purpose filtered into the United States from the south in the early years of the twentieth century. Transported by Mexicans and West Indians, the plant and its intoxicant use encountered a hostile political and social climate. Gradually during the ensuing quarter-century, criminal prohibitions appeared on the statute books of nearly every state where the drug was used. Well into the 1930s, however, marihuana-smoking attracted little concerted attention from the national policy and opinion apparatus, which was deeply engaged in drug matters of much wider social impact than the limited, regional use of this new drug. Thus, the story of marihuana policy in the United States begins as a series of distinctly local tales.

Beginning around 1900 in the towns along the Mexican border and a decade later on the Gulf coast, the practice of marihuana-smoking entered the United States at two independent points. The users in the two areas differed, as did the degree of public awareness of the phenomenon and nature of the public perception. During the twenties the use of the drug spread from these points of entry in two directions, and with two distinct identities: it traveled north and west from the border, taking along an ethnic identity, and north and east from New Orleans, with its identity as a fungible narcotic and enslaver of youth.

Marihuana Crosses the Rio Grande

Political chaos at home and economic opportunity in the United States significantly augmented the migration of Mexicans to Texas and New Mexico at the turn of the century.[1] In Mexican districts of the border towns and in major cities these immigrants continued to smoke and grow marihuana as they had done at home. Cultivation of the plant was a major industry in the vicinity of Mexico City, the mountains of Thalpam, and in surrounding Mexican provinces, and a steady supply of marihuana easily crossed the border into Laredo, El Paso, San Antonio, Nogales, and other border towns and major cities. Laredo was of major importance because it was linked directly to the Mexico City area by the Mexican National Railroad. The demand for the plant was significant enough that in 1917 a United States government investigator reported that several importing firms commercially distributed marihuana to other points in the region, particularly to San Antonio. One company, in business only three months, had five hundred pounds of marihuana in stock at the time of the investigation. Retailers, mostly local grocers, openly advertised.[2]

The demand for "Rosa Maria" was satisfied not only by garden plants and bulk Mexican imports but also by one-ounce packages sold over the counter in drug stores. Since no prescription was required for its purchase, the corner druggist was a useful source of the weed. In fact, a mail-order business grew up; one druggist in Floresville, Texas, sent marihuana by mail to twenty customers in Texas, Arizona, New Mexico, Kansas, and Colorado. Although medical application of the drug was apparently limited by this time, major pharmaceutical houses still manufactured it in "herb" package as well as in tincture and extract form.[3]

Marihuana-smoking was probably a casual adjunct to life in the Mexican community—a relaxant, a folk remedy for headaches, a mild euphoriant cheaply obtained for two cigarettes for a dollar. But within the Mexican community, marihuana had also achieved a potent folklore status which spread to the Americans more quickly than did the drug.

According to contemporary reports, a common Mexican saying "Esta ya ledio las tres" ("you take it three times") referred to the exhilarating effects of three inhalations of marihuana. The first puff was said to induce a feeling of well-being; the second allegedly provoked extreme elation coupled with activity; and the third was reputed to make the smoker oblivious to danger, quarrelsome, delirious, destructive, and conscious of superhuman strength.[4]

A drug with such obnoxious properties soon attracted the attention of the law enforcement officials of El Paso, characterized as a "hot bed of marihuana fiends"[5] where use of the drug was reportedly common not only among Mexicans but among "Negroes, prostitutes, pimps and a criminal class of whites."[6] In response, El Paso passed an ordinance banning sale and possession of the drug in 1914.[7] According to one interested physician who traveled along the border towns around 1920, passage of this ordinance was precipitated by a major fight allegedly involving a marihuana user.[8]

Similar anecdotes were common. One police captain reported three years later:

> I have had almost daily experiance [sic] with the users of [marihuana] for the reason that when they are addicted to the use they become very violent, especially when they become angry and will attack an officer even if a gun is drawn on him, they seem to have no fear, I have also noted that when under the influence of this weed they have abnormal strength and that it will take several men to handle one man where under ordinary circumstances one man could handle him with ease.[9]

The captain of detectives concluded that marihuana produced "a lust for blood," rendering the user "insensible to pain" and capable of "superhuman strength when detained or hindered from doing whatever [he is] attempting to do."[10] The chief of police wondered why the Mexican government did not feed the "marihuana dope" to its armies to get the civil war over with because the soldiers would then fight instead of looting and hunting as they were prone to do.[11]

Actually, marihuana was in common use in the Mexican army. A U.S. Customs officer who served at the international bridge at El Paso and was a self-declared authority on "marihuana fiends" did not think the drug helped the Mexican army much. In his view, marihuana users became irresponsible and strayed aimlessly about. He told the story of a Mexican who suddenly appeared on the bridge and was escorted back to Juarez, but soon returned. At this point the customs officer "noticed [the Mexican's] eyes protruding and...knew that he was under the influence of marihuana." After disarming his captive of a belt of rifle cartridges and an empty six-shooter, the American ordered him to the guard house. When the Mexican refused, he was pushed and knocked to the ground. Upon being informed that the Mexican had committed no offense, the American turned him over to the Mexican consul. The belt of cartridges, however, led the American to continue to search for a rifle. "About half way over the bridge we found his rifle standing up against a post. Later investigation proved that he was a sentry in the Mexican army on duty at the bridge and that under the influence of marihuana [he] had simply started to wander."[12]

American authorities were particularly concerned that the troops stationed along the border under General Pershing in 1916 might become infected with the marihuana vice. When a federal investigator learned from an El Paso druggist that numerous American soldiers had sought cannabis packages upon their return from expeditions across the border, he interviewed almost every military official along the border. All of them denied any knowledge of the practice.[13]

However, an army physician stationed in Texas at this time recalled nine years later: "Mexican laborers were about the only ones I knew of to use it in the United States. They use it, get "hopped up," are picked up by the police who send them [to the hospital] for treatment. We would keep them five or six weeks and send them back. After the guard went down to Mexico and came back, I saw the first white people who smoked the plant. Soldiers who had been on the border smoked cigarettes of marihuana either straight or mixed with tobacco."[14] This hypothesis is further supported by the fact that use of marihuana was prohibited at Fort Sam Houston by order of the commanding general in July 1921.[15]

Apart from its possible infusion into the American military, marihuana-smoking in Texas appears to have been confined primarily to lower class Mexicans. Marihuana use was a lower class phenomenon in Mexico as well; it is therefore of particular interest that several states of the Mexican Republic adopted a restrictive public policy at about the same time marihuana appeared in the southwestern United States. Mexican authorities, even more class-conscious than their American counterparts, were particularly apprehensive about its use in the army, fearing it might contaminate the upper classes. The Mexican aristocracy's position is clearly reflected in a 1917 editorial, translated from a Spanish-language San Antonio newspaper:

[The hemp] plant is terribly noxious when used as a narcotic, from which a dangerous vice is acquired by those who make a

bad use of it, as happens among the lower classes in Mexico. . . .
The men who smoke this herb become excited to such an
extent that they go through periods of near frenzy, and worse,
it is always aggressive as the crimes which have been committed
in garrisons, armories, barracks, and the humble suburbs of
Mexico [attest].
In the South of the United States, this menacing evil has
begun to appear, especially in the army and among the
Negroes. . . .
[T]he authorities . . . [must] uproot this malicious vice in its
incipiency as it is growing even in the army among members of
distinguished families and also as it is happening in Mexico
among young men of good society; this, of course, is doubly
lamentable.[16]

On 15 March 1920 the Department of Public Health of the
Federal Government of Mexico published a "regulation concerning
commerce in products that may be utilized to encourage vices
degenerating the race and concerning the cultivation of plants that
may be employed for such purpose," wherein the "cultivation and
commerce of marihuana" was strictly prohibited.[17]

Class consciousness was a recurrent element in marihuana prohibition even in its infancy. Mexican-American patricians appealed
to sentiments of Negro inferiority, and European-American officials
appealed to sentiments of Mexican inferiority. Most interesting is
the fact that Mexican-American physicians painted a more fantastic
account of the drug's effects than did the El Paso police. Dr. Lopez,
a member of the Association of Military Surgeons of the United
States and former director of the General Hospital in Mexico City,
alleged that smoking marihuana "causes hallucinations of both eye
and ear," rendering the person under its influence "actually crazy
and irresponsible for the time being." "Continued use of the drug,"
he observed, "causes the body to wear away as is the case with
other drug fiends."[18] Dr. Francisco de Ganseca, a graduate of the
National School of Medicine in Mexico City, contended that "mad-
ness is the final result," the drug being "worse than opium as it not
only destroys the life of the person who smokes it, but causes him
to take the lives of others."[19] Another Mexican-American doctor
contended that a person "under [marihuana's] influence may see
a friend and imagine that he is an enemy and kill him."[20]

From all accounts, marihuana use and tales of its destructive effects were prevalent in the border towns of Texas and New Mexico after 1910. One botanist from the U.S. Department of Agriculture noted in 1925 that "the plant . . . is used a great deal . . . in Texas, Arizona and New Mexico, especially by the Mexicans. I have been told that a few years ago two guards in the penitentiary at Tucson, Arizona, were killed by a Mexican, while under the influence of the drug."[21] An army botanist observed that the drug was used by Mexican railroad laborers and by inmates of the prison at Yuma, Arizona, and that a former superintendent of this prison had declared that "under its baneful influence reckless men become bloodthirsty, trebly daring and dangerous to an uncontrollable degree." This same observer quoted an American consul from Nogales who noted in 1911 that use of the drug "causes the smoker to become exceedingly pugnacious and to run amuck without discrimination."[22]

The Mexican marihuana folklore apparently made a deep impression on any American who came in contact with the drug or its alien users. Having no reason to suspect the veracity of such tales, law enforcement officials and local representatives of the Customs and Agriculture departments of the federal government agitated for state and federal legislation to combat the "killer weed." The deputy sheriff of El Paso persuaded a local Food and Drug inspector to bring the matter to the attention of the chief of the Bureau of Chemistry in the federal Agriculture Department, the man with primary enforcement responsibility under the Food and Drug Act. Without any further investigation, the bureaucracy responded with the necessary administrative action: in 1915, after an official request by the secretary of agriculture, the secretary of the treasury issued a decision under the Food and Drug Act prohibiting importation of cannabis for other than medical purposes.[23] (The Act itself required only that any quantity of cannabis contained in a retail product be explicitly designated on the label.)

On the state level, legislation was slow in coming. Marihuana use was still a local problem in the border towns of Texas, and it attracted little statewide interest. Finally, in 1919, the legislature included marihuana in a general statute, modeled after the Harrison Act, prohibiting transfer of certain narcotics except for medical purposes.[24] The law's failure to prohibit possession or use reflected a continuing reluctance, under prevailing constitutional doctrine, to interfere with private (possessory) conduct. The judicial precedent in Texas for such restraint had been set in an alcohol case in 1897.[25] Nevertheless, in 1923 the still hesitant legislators tightened the statute, but only to prohibit possession of narcotics with intent to sell.[26] The 1923 legislation received extremely limited newspaper coverage. In its only direct reference to marihuana, the *Austin Statesman* briefly noted: "The McMillian Senate Bill amended the antinarcotic law so as to make unlawful the possession for the purpose of sale of any marihuana or other drugs. Marihuana is a Mexican herb and is said to be sold on the Texas-Mexican border."[27] The *El Paso Times* did not mention the McMillian Bill before or after its passage.

In the same year New Mexico prohibited sale, cultivation, and importation of cannabis. Mere possession was not expressly prohibited, but anyone found in possession was presumed to have imported the marihuana illegally.[28] This technique was apparently modeled after the federal Narcotic Drugs Import and Export Act of 1922. The Santa Fe *New Mexican*, hometown newspaper of the bill's sponsor, paid scant attention:

> The Santa Fe representative, however, had better luck with his bill to prevent sale of marihuana, cannabis indica, Indian hemp or hashish as it is variously known. This bill was passed without any opposition. Marihuana was brought into local prominence at the penitentiary board's investigation last summer when a convict testified he could get marihuana cigarettes anytime he had a dollar. The drug produces intoxication when chewed or smoked. Marihuana is the name commonly used in the Southwest and Mexico.[29]

Beets and Marihuana in the Rockies

Mexican immigration during the first third of the twentieth century increased enormously; the Bureau of Immigration records the entry of 590,765 Mexicans from 1915 to 1930. Two-thirds of these people remained in Texas. The others settled in states in the Rocky Mountain area, most of them as farm laborers.[30] During this period practically every state west of the Mississippi River passed antimarihuana legislation (see map): California and Utah in 1915; Colorado in 1917; Texas in 1919; Iowa in 1921; New Mexico, Arkansas, Nevada, Oregon, and Washington in 1923; Idaho, Kansas, Montana, and Nebraska in 1927; Wyoming in 1929; South Dakota in 1931; and North Dakota and Oklahoma in 1933.[31] Whether motivated by outright ethnic prejudice or by simple discriminatory lack of interest, the proceedings before each legislature resembled those in Texas and New Mexico in 1923. There was little if any public attention and no debate. Pointed references were made to the drug's Mexican origins, and sometimes to the criminal conduct which inevitably followed when Mexicans used the "killer weed."

Contemporary accounts and official correspondence uniformly suggest that marihuana-smoking was common in Colorado by the late twenties. Senator Phipps of that state manifested his own concern by plaguing the Washington bureaucracy endlessly. He prodded an unenthusiastic surgeon general into issuing a report on the dangers of marihuana and peyote in 1929,[32] and he continually tried to force federal legislation out of a reluctant Bureau of Prohibition (later Narcotics).[33] Although the bureau resisted the senator's pleas for some six years, for reasons we will explain in chapter 3, he did convince them that marihuana use had assumed "noticeable" proportions in Colorado.[34]

In May 1931 the agent in charge of the Denver division of the Bureau of Narcotics reported that marihuana was commonly grown in all the states in his jurisdiction, particularly in Colorado. When he found that the drug was marketed both in cigarette and loose, canned forms, the agent corroborated Phipps's contention that "the use of marihuana has noticeably increased during the past five years,"[35] or since 1926. The Colorado legislature had first prohibited cultivation and sale of the drug in 1917.[36] At that time, judging from the use of the Mexican term "mariguana" and from subsequent newspaper reports, the drug was "used almost exclusively ... by the Mexican population employed in the beet fields."[37] Then, in 1927 the legislature prohibited possession and tightened the restrictions on distribution, raising the penalties for all violations in 1929.

Similarly, in 1929 the Montana legislature amended its general narcotics law to include marihuana, prohibiting use, sale, or possession without a prescription.[38] On seven different days from 24

June to 10 February, the date of the bill's passage, the Butte *Montana Standard* succinctly noted the progress of the bill through a legislature whose attitude was characterized in the 27 January issue:

> There was fun in the House Health Committee during the week when the Marihuana bill came up for consideration. Marihuana is Mexican opium, a plant used by Mexicans and cultivated for sale by Indians. "When some beet field peon takes a few rares of this stuff," explained Dr. Fred Fulsher of Mineral County, "he thinks he has just been elected president of Mexico so he starts out to execute all his political enemies. I understand that over in Butte where the Mexicans often go for the winter they stage imaginary bullfights in the 'Bower of Roses' or put on tournaments for the favor of 'Spanish Rose' after a couple of whiffs of Marihuana. The Silver Bow and Yellowstone delegations both deplore these international complications." Everybody laughed and the bill was recommended for passage.[39]

About the same time, Mexican laborers had begun to appear in Idaho, and the mayor of Boise remarked: "The Mexican beet field workers have introduced a new problem—the smoking in cigarettes or pipes of marijuana or grifo. Its use is as demoralizing as the use of narcotics. Smoking grifo is quite prevalent along the Oregon Short Line Railroad; and Idaho has no law to cope with the use and spread of this dangerous drug."[40] Idaho passed such a law in 1927.[41]

In 1931 the Texas legislature finally prohibited possession of marihuana. By now alcohol prohibition had withdrawn any philosophical barrier to making possession illegal. The *San Antonio Light* reported that: "At last the state legislature had taken a definite step toward suppression of traffic in a dangerous and insanity-producing narcotic easily compounded of a weed (marihuana) indigenous to this section. . . . This newspaper has urged the passage of prohibitory legislation and is gratified that the solons at Austin have acted, even if tardily, in the suppression of traffic in a drug which makes the addict frequently a dangerous or homicidal maniac."[42]

Setting out to enforce the new law by destroying patches of the weed, a local agent emphasized the difficulty of his task. There were a lot of patches to destroy because "consumption of this 'tobacco' has been very heavy among Mexicans and Negroes."[43]

Unexplained Prohibitions: California and Utah

The earliest marihuana prohibitions in the West were adopted by California and Utah in 1915.[44] Satisfactory explanations for these incipient legislative responses remain elusive. On the one hand, it is clear that these prohibitions were directed at a drug with which someone was familiar. In California the drug was specifically added to a preexisting comprehensive antinarcotics package. And the Utah prohibition even extended to possession of pipes for smoking the drug. On the other hand, it does not appear likely that sufficient numbers of immigrants would have arrived in either state by this early date to arouse interest in them and their unusual habits. (There is much evidence of a sizable Mexican colony in Los Angeles fifteen years later.)[45] We can only speculate.

In California it is possible that (Asian) Indian cannabis use inspired the same collision of curiosity and fear which had been aroused by Chinese opium prohibitions a generation earlier. In connection with preparation for the first Hague Conference in 1912, one of the U.S. delegates joined Dr. Wright of the State Department in requesting the inclusion of cannabis in the international accords. Henry J. Finger of the California Board of Pharmacy reported the concern of Californians, particularly in San Francisco, over a "large influx of Hindoos . . . demanding cannabis indica" and their claim that they would attract "the whites into their habit."[46]

In Utah no evidence of local concern has been discovered. Indeed, the proceedings of the General Conference of the Council of Elders reflect a serious concern with the use of drugs, particularly tobacco, during the second decade of the twentieth century, but marihuana was never mentioned.[47] Unsupported conjecture suggests one possible explanation for the prohibition. The United States Supreme Court in 1878 had upheld congressional prohibition of polygamy, rebuffing a Mormon claim that the law inhibited the free exercise of their religion.[48] For the ensuing two decades, the federal government made little effort to enforce the decision. On 6 April 1890 the church reversed its own position, declaring continuation of the practice heretical. Some members of the church were unwilling to accept this capitulation and at Brigham Young's suggestion they moved to Mexico for marital sanctuary and to seek new prospects for conversion. Unfortunately their colonization was inhibited by the civil war and converts were difficult to find. Around 1912 the members of this renegade sect returned to Utah, albeit with only one wife apiece. We suspect they may have also returned with some knowledge of marihuana, which was soon translated into legislation reflecting the traditional aversion of the Mormon church to drug use of any kind.

The Battle of New Orleans

While Mexican immigrants were introducing marihuana to the border states and the Southwest, Caribbean sailors and West Indian immigrants were introducing the habit to ports along the Gulf of Mexico. Although use in the border states remained essentially an alien phenomenon, contemporary accounts suggest that marihuana-smoking became well established among certain segments of the native population in Houston, Galveston, and particularly in New Orleans.

Although there is evidence that some marihuana came to these areas from Mexico by way of Tampico and El Paso, most of it was smuggled in by enterprising sailors from Cuba and other points in the Indies. Around 1925 Dr. Frank Gomila, commissioner of Public Safety of New Orleans, began his campaign for federal legislation to supplement the Treasury Department's ineffectual 1915 ban on importation for nonmedical purposes. He observed that the traffic was quite organized, amounting to thousands of kilograms a year: "The custom was to keep [marihuana] in warehouses or store-rooms for further distribution. It was sold by the wholesaler to the retailer who in turn put the 'weed' through a process known as 'sweating.' The dried leaves and stems were soaked in sugar water and dried on butcher's brown papers."[49]

If Gomila and the newspapers can be believed, the demand in New Orleans in the mid-twenties was so great that the "peddlers" were able to become exceptionally prosperous by dividing the market. One had exclusive jurisdiction over the blacks unloading the fruit boats, another over the lobby in a certain hotel, and so on. Marihuana was, of course, also available at local pharmacies without a prescription before 1919 in Texas and before 1924 in Louisiana.

After that, marihuana had to be bought on the street unless the user could obtain or forge a prescription.

Druggists in Houston reported in 1917 that their marihuana purchasers were no longer predominantly Mexican, but increasingly white—"sporting" women (prostitutes), gamblers, pimps, and "hop heads," some of whom were allegedly "having difficulty in obtaining their usual supply of dope."[50] In Galveston the story was much the same. One druggist characterized his marihuana clientele as "Mexicans, a low class of whites, and East Indians coming off the boats." Another referred to "Mexicans, Negroes, and chauffeurs, and a low class of whites such as those addicted to the use of habit-forming drugs, and hangers-on of the underworld."[51] Gomila suggests that in New Orleans about the same time, the previously unknown practice rapidly became "more and more of common knowledge among the vicious characters of the city."[52]

Different pictures emerge of the marihuana user in El Paso and San Antonio on the one hand and New Orleans and Galveston on the other. In the border towns he was a Mexican laborer, indolent to some, volatile to others. Local authorities were, by and large, unable to generate any significant public or political interest, although there were no political objections to making the Mexican weed illegal.

In the port cities, however, the marihuana user was a "dope fiend," the basest element of American society. He was a narcotics addict, a pimp, or a gambler; she was a prostitute. Marihuana was simply "another narcotic" in a city with a major "narcotic problem." The issue was always open to sensationalism. Even before public attention was excited, however, the prevalence of marihuana use came to the attention of the president of the Louisiana State Board of Health, Dr. Oscar Dowling. On 21 August 1920 he advised the governor of the increasing availability of marihuana, a "powerful narcotic, causing exhiliration, intoxication, delirious hallucinations, and its subsequent action, drowsiness and stupor. . . ." Apparently the drug had come to his attention through the arrest, conviction, and incarceration of a twenty-one-year-old musician convicted of forging a doctor's name to a prescription.[53]

At the same time, Dr. Dowling wrote to the surgeon general of the United States, Dr. Hugh Cummings, to advise him of the increasing traffic in morphine, opium, and marihuana, and to seek federal cooperation. It is interesting that Dr. Dowling was simultaneously involved with federal officials in the effort to close the New Orleans morphine clinics;[54] within a few years, none of the morphine clinics were open, and a maintenance approach to narcotics addiction was to be foreclosed for a half-century.[55]

Very little, however, was done about the marihuana issue until the press seized upon it. In the fall of 1926 the *New Orleans Item* dispatched an army of reporters among the smoking and selling population. A series of articles published by the more widely circulated *Morning Tribune* (both papers were owned by the same publishing company) exposed the immense profits being made peddling "muggles" or "moota" and commented upon the volatile effects of the drug upon its "addicts." It was reported that marihuana "numbs the sense, creates wild fancies and has a hypnotic effect upon the user, making his will easily subordinated to that of others."

What emerged from these articles, however, was not a vision of addicts on the streets and pushers on the docks. Rather, the public was encouraged to believe that the peddlers were men who lurked on playgrounds seeking to entrap young minds. "Over two hundred children under fourteen are believed to be addicted to the marihuana habit," the paper reported, and at least forty-four schools were infected.[56]

Although it was quite clear that the "addicted" children were street-wise youths drawn from the same socioeconomic classes as the adult users, the impact was no less pointed. In those innocent early days of the juvenile court movement, harassed social workers, pastors, teachers, and club women tended to attribute delinquent behavior to any identifiable defect in the physical and social environment—in this case the marihuana menace.

Local policy makers wasted no time. The New Orleans Police Department immediately launched a roundup. They arrested more than 150 persons for violation of a law which had lain dormant for two years.[57] Dr. Dowling reportedly soon circulated "a warning to parents, guardians and teachers of children against this menace."[58] The Women's Christian Temperance Union jumped on the bandwagon, focusing their attacks on the "soft drink" bars which had sprung up all over New Orleans during prohibition: "The soft drink stand and the corner drug store have taken the place of the saloon as a social meeting place. Here is where marihuana and liquors can sometimes be bought."[59]

Beyond these immediate effects, a more substantial result of the local policy reaction in New Orleans was the formation of a tightly knit coterie of New Orleans law enforcement, public health, and social welfare officials, who would carry their antimarihuana campaign to Washington, with ultimate success.

Marihuana Comes to the Big Cities

The West Indies was one source for the marihuana that arrived in the port cities of America. Not long after the practice became established in the Gulf area, it seems to have appeared on a much smaller scale in New York City. During the twenties the commercial traffic which steamed up the Mississippi from New Orleans and Texas also spread Mexicans and marihuana to Chicago, Kansas City, Cleveland, Detroit, St. Louis, and other major commercial centers.

Large communities of Mexican laborers penetrated the industrial region on the southern shore of Lake Michigan during the 1920s. By 1930 the Mexican population in Chicago alone had reached approximately 30,000. Judging from all contemporary accounts, the "white" population, which included many second generation immigrants, exhibited considerable distaste for the new immigrants and their different habits of life. The Mexican customs and police prejudice were a highly cumbustible mixture, apparently resulting both in a disproportionately large number of Mexicans being arrested and in a belief among the "whites" that Mexicans were inherently lawless.[60]

In a 1928 study of Mexican employment in the Chicago-Gary area, economist Paul Taylor found that discriminatory treatment by police was commonly perceived by Mexicans and was supported by available data. One native "white" observed: "The Mexicans get little protection in the courts. The Mexicans are now learning that you must buy justice. The police searched the Mexican houses without warrants (during the Mexican-Polish troubles) and let the crowd hit their Mexican prisoners while they were in custody. The Mexican is in the same position as the Negro in the South. He is always wrong unless there is a white man to speak for him."[61]   The author reported that a high percentage of the Mexican arrests were for disorderly conduct and other "status offenses" which are particularly susceptible to discriminatory enforcement. Alcohol offenses were similarly disproportionate, leading the author to observe, somewhat cynically, that

> Mexicans are politically helpless. To what extent this fact makes them particularly liable to arrest is of course not readily determinable. Hypothetically, however, it is easy to see that a politically dry official could satisfy the drys with a large number of arrests and at the same time avoid offending his wet constituents by arresting Mexicans. In fact, Mexicans, both Mexican- and American-born, are generally conscious of an inferior standing in the eyes of the law.[62]

Finally, Dr. Taylor attributed much of the social prejudice and perception of Mexican lawlessness to simple variations in custom:

> Violation of our legal codes may and often does involve practices which are less serious violations or even no violations at all of the customs and codes prevailing among this class of Mexicans in Mexico. . . . [T]o select a practice of Mexicans which is unquestionably dangerous, but which is no violation of their code, we may refer to the practice of carrying knives. We regard them as concealed weapons. In Mexico the common folk wear knives so habitually as to regard them practically a part of the dress.[63]

It is in this context that we must view the Mexican laborers' use of marihuana or "muggles" which apparently took local officials by surprise in 1927. One law enforcement official reported: "There are about 7,000 Mexicans in Gary, 10,000 in Indiana Harbor and 8,000 in South Chicago. . . . The Mexicans depend on the steel mills, railroads, and construction gangs for employment. Many are drifters when slack labor conditions prevail. . . . [T]wenty-five percent of these Mexicans smoke marijuana. In fact, many of them make their living by raising and peddling the drug."[64]

Such a situation seemed likely to infect the rest of the community. As in New Orleans, reports started to appear that high school students were smoking the weed.[65] Then the dam broke. Since neither state nor federal legislation prohibited sale of marihuana, the local United States attorney declared war, armed with an internal revenue statute prohibiting production and transfer of "a cigarette substitute" on which tax had not been paid. In June 1929 he raided wholesale houses "believed to have disposed of large quantities of marihuana cigarettes, sold to school pupils and other youthful thrill-seekers," and arrested nine men, "most of them Mexicans."[66] At the same time, local officials began to use a statute which prohibited transfer of "any cigarette containing any substance deleterious to health."[67]

The *Chicago Tribune*, lobbying heavily for antimarihuana legislation then pending before the Illinois legislature, breathlessly reported the day-to-day progress of the enforcement activity.[68] Every stall in the legislature earned a banner headline.

> BAN ON HASHISH
> BLOCKED DESPITE
> RAVAGES OF DRUG

In an article appearing in June 1929 the paper noted: "The number of addicts is growing alarmingly according to authorities, because of the ease with which [marihuana] can be obtained. The habit was introduced a dozen years ago or so by Mexican laborers . . . but it has become widespread among American youths . . . even among school children." The specter of substitution was also raised: "There being no legal ban such as makes other drugs scarce, 'loco weed' is cheap. The rush of its popularity in Chicago and all over the country since the oncoming of Prohibition is partly explained by the price of cigarettes, 3 for 50 cents or at most 30 cents apiece." Apparently the bill had been waylaid in a Senate committee by one senator, a druggist from Chicago, who "declared that the seed of the plant is used as birdseed." The *Tribune* was not convinced. They contacted a birdseed seller who disputed the senator's contention, but whatever the senator's reason, he successfully killed the bill.[69]

To place the Tribune's epidemic description in perspective, it should be noted that representatives of the major local pressure groups (the WCTU, the Immigrant's Protective League, and the National Federation of Women Clubs) who became heavily involved in the marihuana issue several years later were essentially unfamiliar with marihuana even after the *Tribune* campaign.

Anticipatory Regulation in the East

Cannabis was produced and dispensed in the United States for medical use throughout the period of the first antinarcotics legislation. The drug was mentioned in the poison laws of nine states,[70] and in the course of bringing the pharmaceutical manufacturers, pharmacies, and physicians under regulatory control, a handful of states had enacted tighter restrictions on cannabis. In 1911 Louisiana prohibited refills of prescriptions containing cannabis or opiates, cocaine, chloroform, or hyoscyamics.[71] Maine (1913), Massachusetts (1914), Vermont (1915), and Rhode Island (1918) all barred the sale of cannabis without a prescription as part of comprehensive regulatory laws.[72]

These early cannabis laws in the East were passed not in response to street use, since the intoxicant use of marihuana had not yet appeared in the Northeast, but rather in anticipation of future problems. The medical establishment in the Northeast was already familiar with the psychoactive properties of cannabis and with literary descriptions of the virtues of hashish. For example, Victor Robinson reported in 1912 on the nature of acute intoxication on the basis of self-administration and observation of ingestion by friends. His report was widely circulated.[73] Among the most moralistic of the antinarcotics reformers there was little doubt that effective elimination of the curse of the "drug habit evil" demanded strict control over any and all potentially intoxicating substances to which addicts might resort once the opiates and cocaine became more difficult to obtain. Several authorities who spearheaded the development of the Harrison Act had even urged the inclusion of cannabis in that act despite the fact that the drug had not yet attracted any habitual users. The State Department's Dr. Hamilton Wright, who coordinated domestic and international aspects of the mushrooming antinarcotic movement, Cornell University's Dr. Alexander Lambert, who later became president of the AMA, and the Agriculture Department's Dr. Harvey Wiley, who had shepherded the Pure Food and Drug Act through Congress, all testified in favor of covering cannabis by federal law.[74]

In response to these reform sentiments, the drug industry vehemently protested, contending that cannabis was an insignificant medicine which had no place in antinarcotics legislation. A 1902 questionnaire to physicians and pharmacists sent by the American Pharmaceutical Association's Committee on the Acquirement of the Drug Habit covered the opiates, cocaine, and chloral hydrate but did not even refer to cannabis. Nor was cannabis included in the committee's 1903 model law which, after revisions, was adopted in 1905 by the National Wholesale Druggists Association (NWDA), the National Association of Retail Druggists (NARD), and the American Pharmaceutical Association. Charles West, chairman of the NWDA's legislative committee, argued in 1910 that "cannabis is not what may be called a 'habit-forming drug.' "[75]

The industry successfully resisted the inclusion of cannabis in federal legislation. But the reformers' purification sentiment easily accounts for the drug's inclusion in the initial Eastern prohibitions, especially after 1914 when the states were pressed to implement the national policies declared in the Harrison Act.This hypothesis is supported by the New York experience.

In January 1914 the New York legislature passed its first comprehensive narcotics statute—the Boylan Bill—which regulated the sale and use of "habit-forming" drugs.[76] The bill did not include marihuana in this classification. A few months later, however, the Board of Health of New York City amended its sanitary code by adding "Cannabis indica, which is the Indian hemp from which the East Indian drug called hashish is manufactured,"[77] to the city's list of prohibited drugs. Reporting this action, the *New York Times* described cannabis as a "narcotic [having] practically the same effect as morphine and cocaine,"[78] and it noted in an editorial that: "The inclusion of cannabis indica among the drugs to be sold only on prescription is only common sense. Devotees of hashish are now hardly numerous enough here to count, but they are likely to increase as other narcotics become harder to obtain."[79]

As late as 1918 a state legislative committee which had exhaustively investigated the narcotics problem in New York did not mention marihuana.[80] Nevertheless, by 1921 at least one writer noted an increase in marihuana use. He sounded the alarm in the title to his work—*From Opium to Hashish*—and raised new fears. Marihuana could be used as a substitute not only for opium and morphine but also for alcohol, which had recently been suppressed by the Volstead Act.[81] Marihuana was not the only focus of the substitution argument, as one commentator had warned in 1919: "Cocaine in particular is in great demand. When prohibition is in force, persons, especially drinkers from compulsion of habit who have been robbed of the daily drink, will naturally resort to cocaine."[82]

By 1923 the *New York Times* referred to marihuana as the city's "latest habit-forming drug" when reporting its exhibition at a women's club meeting.[83] In 1927 the legislature included marihuana in its list of "habit-forming drugs" in a comprehensive narcotics bill.[84] As will be discussed in chapter 4, the 1927 New York law was drafted by an AMA committee; we suspect, therefore, that the inclusion of cannabis was not attributable to any significant increase in use in the city. If marihuana use was increasing, however, it was not attracting attention. During the period from 1914 to 1927 the New York newspapers were replete with articles dealing with narcotic addiction; yet only four brief references were made to marihuana in the *New York Times*.[85] Public concern was focused on drug problems at the time of the 1927 act; yet none of the postenactment comments on the act referred to marihuana.[86]

Probably the best description of the nature of marihuana use in New York about this time appears in a 1930 report by a federal agent on the basis of an undercover survey. He portrayed a small-time, unorganized traffic with a limited ethnic clientele. One user said she "got her supply . . . from Spaniards and East Indians working as members of the crew on boats belonging to the United Fruit Lines and other boat lines touching South American, Mexican and Cuban ports. . . ." Another woman revealed that

> her husband was a steward on the Bull Line Ships running between Cuba, Mexico and South American countries; that the marihuana was purchased by her husband in Cuba and he brought it into the United States in 10 and 15-pound lots, and he could bring in a larger quantity on order ... (and) that she made up the packages of marihuana for sale to the trade, which consisted mostly of Spaniards, East Indians, Filipinos, and a few Americans, both white and colored.[87]

In New York during the first quarter of the twentieth century, a reforming zeal impelled an attack on the narcotics menace, particularly after prohibition. Every intoxicant posed a threat, whether or not its use was common. Judging from contemporary accounts, marihuana use was rare outside areas of ethnic concentration. Thus, the enactment of statutory proscriptions in 1927 was axiomatic and did not constitute a matter of public concern, even within the medical and law enforcement communities.

Local Prohibition: A Legend Disputed

It has become fashionable in recent years to attribute the illegal status of marihuana to the Federal Bureau of Narcotics and its long-time head, Harry J. Anslinger. Such a theory has been particularly popular among those seeking to alter the existing public policy since it implies that what was done by one man is not entitled to the deference which a more broadly based policy would enjoy.

However, the recent public policy emerged in a more subtle, less controversial fashion. Although the federal narcotics bureaucracy, with Commissioner Anslinger at the helm, was to become marihuana's leading antagonist in the mid-thirties, a restrictive public policy toward the drug was well rooted locally before that time. During the "local" phase of marihuana prohibition, lasting roughly from 1914 to 1931, twenty-nine states, including seventeen west of the Mississippi, prohibited use of the drug for nonmedical purposes. (Four more states did so in 1933.)

The most important feature of this initial prohibitory phase is that marihuana was inevitably viewed as a "narcotic" drug, thereby invoking the broad consensus underlying the nation's recently enunciated antinarcotics policy. This classification emerged primarily from the drug's alien character. Although use of some drugs —alcohol and tobacco—was indigenous to American life, the use of "narcotics" for pleasure was not. Evidently, drugs associated with ethnic minorities and with otherwise "immoral" populations were automatically viewed as "narcotics." The scientific community shared this social bias and therefore had little interest in scientific accuracy.

From this instinctive classification of marihuana with opium, morphine, heroin, and cocaine flowed the entire set of factual

Map 1. Marihuana prohibition. Phase one: State legislation prohibiting distribution for nonmedical purposes, 1915-33

Date indicates the year marihuana prohibition was first enacted.

supports on which narcotics prohibition rested. Marihuana was presumed to be addictive, its use inevitably tending to excess. Since its users—Mexicans, West Indians, blacks, and underworld whites—were associated in the public mind with crime, particularly of a violent nature, the association applied also to marihuana, which had a similar reputation in Mexican folklore. Since the nation was preoccupied during the twenties with lawlessness, especially among the foreign born, this association was a strong one.

To the idea of an alien cancer in the social organism was added the inevitable fear that it would spread. In New Orleans, Denver, and Chicago the specter of a doped school population was the cornerstone of the prohibitory effort. And during alcohol prohibition, paralleled by the local phase of marihuana prohibition, it was naturally imperative to suppress a drug which frustrated alcohol users might substitute for their customary intoxicant.

In short, marihuana prohibition was a predictable phenomenon. In states where either Mexicans or the weed had appeared, suppressing its use required no public clamor or citizens' movement; soon after being apprised of its presence, local lawmakers invoked the criminal law, and some also turned to Washington for assistance.

CHAPTER III

Washington Resists the Temptation

THE FIRST CRY to Washington for help in suppressing marihuana came from El Paso. In 1914 the deputy sheriff decided that Mexicans should no longer be permitted to bring any more "loco weed" across the Rio Grande. He had little difficulty persuading local representatives of the federal government to recommend the only available administrative action: a declaration by the secretary of agriculture that importations of cannabis "were being used for purposes other than in the preparation of medicines and that, unless used in medicinal preparations, this drug is believed to be injurious to health."[1] Upon such a declaration, the secretary of the treasury was authorized under the Food and Drug Act of 1906 to deny importation of the drug if it was not intended for medical purposes. On 25 September 1915, after the El Paso recommendation had traveled routinely through all the administrative channels, the treasury secretary in Treasury Decision (T.D.) 35719 so declared; hence all Mexicans who crossed the border with the weed on their person were now guilty of smuggling. In addition, the commissioner of Internal Revenue, in his 1915 report, recommended the inclusion of cannabis in the Harrison Act, reiterating the suggestions of Drs. Lambert and Wright four years earlier. This proposal went virtually unnoticed.

As the history of T.D. 35719 suggests, several branches of the federal bureaucracy were involved in drug regulation. Enforcement of the Harrison Narcotic Act was the responsibility of the commissioner of Internal Revenue until 1927. Then these duties were transferred to a separate Bureau of Prohibition in the Treasury Department.[2] It will be recalled that the Harrison Act was drafted as a tax law rather than an outright regulatory or prohibitory statute in order to accomplish indirectly what Congress believed, probably correctly, it could not do directly—that is, to regulate the possession and sale of narcotics. That the Supreme Court upheld the act as an exercise of taxing power by a slim five-to-four margin in 1919 had a significant bearing on the federal response to marihuana during the ensuing twenty years. In 1930 the narcotics area of the Prohibition Bureau's responsibilities was extracted and transferred to a separate Bureau of Narcotics.[3]

Medical scrutiny and research matters were the responsibility of the surgeon general—also located in the Treasury Department—and his administrative arm, the Public Health Service. Within the Public Health Service, drug matters came within the purview of the Hygienic Laboratory, which later became the National Institutes of Health. In 1929 Congress carved a separate "Narcotics Division" out of the Hygienic Laboratory,[4] and renamed it the "Division of Mental Hygiene" the following year, designating its chief medical officer as an assistant surgeon general.[5] Under the Pure Food and Drug Act domestic regulatory matters were the responsibility of the Bureau of Chemistry in the Department of Agriculture, while direct enforcement of the act's importation restrictions (as well as those under T.D. 35719) was the responsibility of the Bureau of Customs in the Treasury Department.

Dr. Alsberg, chief of the Bureau of Chemistry, dispatched his personal assistant, Reginald Smith, to the Southwest in 1917 to see how T.D. 35719 was working out. Smith's report,[6] based on extensive interviews in eleven Texas cities, is of considerable interest. He found that marihuana was used infrequently for medical purposes—for childbirth, asthma, and gonorrhea—and then only by Mexicans "of low birth." The weed, however, was widely used for smoking by Mexicans and sometimes by "Negroes and lower class whites." Their demands were easily met by local cultivation, street sales, and by grocery stores and drug stores, some of which even advertised their product.

The imported supply, he found, came from two sources: smuggling from Mexico by local entrepreneurs in contravention of T.D. 35719, and distribution by major pharmaceutical houses that imported large quantities and distributed them in bulk form to druggists for over-the-counter sale.

The ardor with which Smith pursued his investigation (judging from the detail in his report, he probably interviewed every druggist in every city he visited) was matched only by the indignation with which he viewed the conduct of the pharmaceutical houses. He asserted that these firms, particularly Parke-Davis, were importing large amounts of the drug and distributing it to retail druggists in bulk or package form, even though they probably knew that physicians did not prescribe it in this form—only in extract or fluid —and that druggists did not use it in the preparation of medicinal compounds. Accordingly, he recommended that an investigation be made to ascertain how much of the drug was being sold by the leading drug manufacturers.

Finding that T.D. 35719 had been totally ineffective in curbing the use and distribution of marihuana and that, when smoked, the drug "is not only injurious to the health of the smoker but often causes him to commit heinous crimes," Smith urged inclusion of marihuana in the Harrison Act. He also recommended that federal authorities advise state officials to prohibit the sale or possession of the drug in bulk or package form.

Despite Smith's urgent pleas, federal authorities were not anxious either to antagonize the pharmaceutical industry or to draw further attention to the questionable constitutionality of the Harrison Act. The border states and New Orleans were left on their own to deal with the killer weed. Washington showed no interest in going beyond the ineffectual declaration of T.D. 35719.

Evidently, Washington had its hands full with the enforcement of the Harrison and Volstead acts. In addition to changing the liquor habits of half of the adult population, the government was attempting to reduce a major addiction problem at home and to lead the cause of international drug control abroad. Whether or not the Harrison Act actually affected narcotics addiction, the "clean-up" psychology prevalent during this period mandated a continuing effort to root out drug use. Study after study was conducted on every level of government. Still there was no evidence of public familiarity with, or official interest in, marihuana outside the border and Gulf regions.

Two major drug studies, one conducted in 1918-19[7] by a special committee appointed by the secretary of the treasury and the other in 1924[8] by the U.S. Public Health Service, did not even mention marihuana. An interesting feature of the first study is the prominence it gave to local liquor prohibition as a cause of drug addiction. The committee speculated that increased sales of narcotics and patent medicines containing opiates in the southern states, where liquor prohibition had long been in effect, supported the thesis that nationwide prohibition would result in an increase in drug addiction. On the international front,[9] the United States had assumed leadership in the control of drug traffic before the Hague Convention of 1912. In an effort to tighten its own restrictions, the government enacted the Narcotic Drugs Import and Export Act in 1922.[10] During the initial fifteen-year life of the Harrison Act, it is not surprising that isolated complaints about marihuana did not receive notice in Washington.

The Stir on Capitol Hill

In late 1928 several congressmen and senators had become interested in marihuana. By this time local authorities and newspapers, particularly in Texas, Colorado, and Louisiana, were drawing attention to the scope of marihuana use. Congressman James O'Connor of New Orleans, having been advised by a constituent on 18 December 1928 that marihuana "is being sold to school children to their great mental and physical injury," inquired of the Bureau of Prohibition whether the sale of marihuana could be prohibited by means other than amendment of the Harrison Act. If not, he continued, "will you prepare the amendment, as I don't want [to] do something that might lead to confusion."[11] Senator Sheppard of Texas was not so hesitant. On his own on 30 October 1929, he offered a bill (S. 2075) to amend the Narcotic Drugs Import and Export Act to include cannabis.

There was also a second reason for the increasing congressional awareness of marihuana. On 19 January 1929 Congress passed a bill authorizing the establishment of two "narcotic farms" for the treatment of persons addicted to the use of habit-forming drugs. In addition to the usual combination of opium and cocoa leaves and their derivatives, the legal definition of "habit-forming drugs" included also "Indian hemp" and "Peyote." For the first time in federal legislation, marihuana was classified with the narcotics.[12]

In the legislative history of the act, Indian hemp is hardly mentioned at all,[13] and its inclusion clearly was not attributable to any documented cases of cannabis "addiction" in the United States. The likely explanation for the language of the 1929 act lies in the greater awareness within official circles of cannabis' status as "another narcotic." This awareness may have stemmed in part from indictments of marihuana in the international forum.

The 1929 act, drafted in the Justice Department, was introduced in the House by Congressman Stephen G. Porter of Pennsylvania, chairman of the House Foreign Affairs Committee. He had been chairman of the United States delegation to the Second Geneva Opium Conference in 1924-25, which had for the first time placed cannabis under international control.

The first mention of marihuana on the international front had come during the preliminary negotiations for the Hague Conference of 1912. In its preparations for this conference, which represented an attempt to deal with the international opium traffic, Italy proposed that the production and traffic in Indian hemp drugs be included as part of the agenda.[14] During the conference itself there was no mention of the drug, and the convention did not include cannabis in its provisions. In addition to the convention, however, the delegates signed a closing protocol supporting a statistical and scientific study of "the question of Indian hemp. . . with the object of regulating its abuses, should the necessity thereof be felt, by internal legislation or by an international agreement."[15] This proposal was not mentioned again until 1923 when the following resolution was passed by the Advisory Committee on Traffic in Opium and Other Dangerous Drugs of the League of Nations:

> IV. With reference to the proposal of the Government of the Union of South Africa that Indian hemp should be treated as one of the habit-forming drugs, the Advisory Committee recommends to the Council that, in the first instance, the Governments should be invited to furnish to the League information as to the production and use of, and traffic in, this substance in their territories, together with their observations on the proposal of the Government of the Union of South Africa.[16]

At the Second Geneva Opium Conference in 1925 the Egyptians led the way by urging that hashish be included within the convention. An Egyptian delegate presented a paper on the effects and use of hashish in Egypt, emphasizing the drug's precipitation of insanity: "The illicit use of hashish is the principal cause of most of the cases of insanity occurring in Egypt. In support of this contention, it may be observed that there are three times as many cases of mental alienation among men as among women, and it is an established fact that men are much more addicted to hashish than women."[17]

The Egyptian proposal was referred for study to a subcommittee which later in the year concluded that the "raw resin is at present of no therapeutic or industrial value"; that it was collected and traded only because it induced intoxication, its "noxious preparations" ultimately causing addiction; and that any galenical preparation was derived from the plant itself rather than the resin. Accordingly, the subcommittee recommended:

> The use of Indian Hemp and the preparation derived therefrom may only be authorized for medical or scientific purposes. The raw resin (charas), however, which is extracted from the female tops of the (plant) . . . not being at present utilized for medical purposes and only being liable to be utilized for harmful purposes in the same manner as other narcotics may not be produced, sold, traded in, etc. under any circumstances whatsoever.[18]

Primarily because the Indian delegation considered enforcement of such an agreement highly unfeasible for "reasons of an administrative and social character," the plenary conference did not ratify the subcommittee's recommendation. Instead, the convention, as adopted by the conference, made internal control applicable only to the galenical preparations (extract and tincture). The rest of its references to the drug were purely hortatory. In Chapter IV of this convention, use of and trade in the resin were not prohibited as the subcommittee had recommended; however, importation and exportation of the resin was subjected to a system of special certificates. Finally, in Article 2, the parties to the convention undertook to "exercise an effective control of such a nature as to prevent the illicit internal traffic in Indian Hemp and especially in the resin."[19]

In terms of international drug control, the substantive impact of the Indian hemp provisions of the convention was modest. Indeed, the convention as a whole was a failure. Led by Congressman Porter, the United States withdrew in February 1925 before the conference concluded, and very few countries ratified the convention. By obligating the signatories to limit the use of mari-

huana to medical and scientific purposes, however, it stamped an
international imprimatur on the classification of marihuana as a
habit-forming drug, the intoxicant use of which should not be
condoned. This is reflected in the fact that Great Britain's marihuana control laws are traceable to the Geneva Convention.
Similarly, the reference to Indian hemp in the "narcotic farm" act
probably stemmed from the drug's inclusion in state narcotics
legislation and in the convention rather than from any perception
that its use posed any significant domestic concern.

Not surprisingly, the inclusion of marihuana in the 1929 act
triggered a number of requests for information from the surgeon
general and the Bureau of Prohibition. For example, Senator
Vandenberg wondered why, if marihuana was a "narcotic," it was
not included in the Harrison and Import and Export acts.[20]

The Bureaucracy Formulates a Game Plan on Marihuana

By the end of 1929 both the Bureau of Prohibition and the surgeon
general's office had received numerous congressional inquiries.
Each asked the obvious question—why not include marihuana in
the basic federal antinarcotics legislation? And S. 2075, as we
noted above, was introduced by Senator Sheppard of Texas. Yet
the narcotics bureaucracy did not wish to amend the Harrison Act
to include marihuana and did not want Congress to pass S. 2075.

The scientific and medical establishment did not object to the
prohibition of marihuana. This is clear from a report of the surgeon
general issued in 1929. Prepared at the instance of Senator Phipps
and in response to the new departures of the 1929 act, Dr.
Cummings' *Preliminary Report on Indian Hemp and Peyote* com-
bines textbook pharmacology and popular myth.

In a brief statement, which will be analyzed in detail in chapter
7, the surgeon general simply summarized the folklore surrounding
the drug. Apart from a methodical elaboration of "The Toxic
Effects of Cannabis Sativa" in language similar to that employed in
the pharmacological literature, the report was notably unscientific
and impressionistic. Habitual users, Cummings noted, "are said to"
develop a delirious rage during which they are liable to commit
violent crimes. Support for this was drawn from the Eastern hashish

myths. Similarly, his report stated without any further elaboration at all that the prolonged use of "this narcotic is said to produce mental deterioration." Finally, the document reflected considerable confusion regarding the drug's dependence liability, noting the absence of the type of physical symptoms associated with dependence on the opiates but attributing marihuana's narcotic and habit-forming nature to the "stimulating effects obtained and the individual satisfaction experienced through the temporary inflation of the personality."

In sum, the surgeon general concluded that marihuana was "definitely" a narcotic, and lent official credence to the notions that it was addictive, criminogenic, and insanity-producing. No firsthand study was either attempted or recommended; the *Preliminary Report* was apparently considered a sufficient study of the situation. In fact, the Narcotics Division dissuaded a pharmacology professor from the University of North Dakota from engaging in any research in May 1930 because "we know all about [marihuana's] physiological, toxic, and pharmacological properties."[21] We have no doubt, then, that there were no scientific objections to the inclusion of marihuana in the basic federal narcotics legislation.

Nor were there any political objections. Because of the local, ethnic nature of the phenomenon, there was no active nationwide political interest in such legislation. But, by the same token, there was no political impediment. In the *Preliminary Report*, Cummings accurately noted that the prohibitory laws enacted in the border states "reflect the state of public opinion along the Rio Grande, both on the American and the Mexican sides, where the majority of people are opposed to use and abuse of this narcotic." As we noted in chapter 2, the popular image of marihuana as a "narcotic" and its social identity with Mexicans, blacks, and whites of bad moral character predisposed criminal legislation.

It is clear that the Public Health Service and the Prohibition Bureau would have preferred to eliminate the smoking of marihuana. Some staff members felt more strongly than others. But there was a *legal* objection to the proposed legislation. Opinion was virtually unanimous that the inclusion of cannabis in the Harrison and Import and Export acts was illogical, possibly unconstitutional, and might even endanger the entire federal legislative scheme which experts viewed as the most effective in the world.

Of the legal objections to amendment of the Harrison Act, the most important related to the medical utility of marihuana. Violation of the Harrison Act arose from the failure to register, pay, or otherwise comply with its provisions taxing legitimate (i.e., medical) transactions. The act rendered all nonmedical traffic illegal. Congress chose to cast this act as a revenue-producing act because, under the prevailing interpretation of the constitutional scheme allocating power between the state and federal governments, only the states had power to regulate directly the practice of medicine, including the local distribution and possession of narcotics. These activities, unless they involved interstate commerce, were beyond the direct legislative cognizance of Congress. So, by using the taxing power Congress was aiming to regulate medical and pharmaceutical practice, not to raise revenues.

When the Supreme Court upheld the act by a five-to-four margin in 1919, it emphasized that the favorable decision depended largely on the fact that the law did produce substantial revenue, notwithstanding its "incidental" effect in restricting narcotic use. But wide variations in potency had by now undermined therapeutic interest in cannabis, and little or no revenue could be derived from a statute purporting to tax legitimate (medical) use of this drug. Thus, as applied to marihuana, this kind of statutory framework would probably have been held unconstitutional. Further, since the Harrison Act itself had been upheld by so narrow a margin, the bureau was not eager for any further litigation in the Supreme Court.

The ease with which marihuana could be cultivated compelled the federal narcotics chiefs also to oppose S. 2075, Senator Sheppard's bill that sought to include cannabis in the Import and Export Act. Since Congress did not have power under prevailing constitutional doctrine directly to prohibit possession of any commodity, it used its jurisdiction over foreign commerce in the Import and Export Act as a means to prohibit local possession in much the same way that it had used the taxing power in the Harrison Act as a means to regulate the distribution of narcotics. Under Section 2f of the Import and Export Act, possession was made *presumptive evidence* of concealment of drugs illegally imported in violation of the act. A. L. Tennyson, the legal adviser to the commissioner of prohibition, contended that such a presumption of illegal importation would be irrational, hence unconstitutional, as applied to marihuana because hemp was so easily grown throughout the United States.[22] As with the Harrison Act, Tennyson was concerned that an attack on Section 2f as applied to marihuana would endanger the presumption as applied to cocaine and opium.

There were dissenting views to this reasoning. One official in the Bureau of Prohibition thought that there were already too many statutes, that some immediate restrictions were imperative, and that both acts should be amended to include cannabis in the definition of "habit-forming drugs."[23]

On 28 June 1930 the narcotics bureaucracy's objection to S. 2075 was transmitted to the Senate Finance Committee by Harry J. Anslinger, in his capacity as secretary to the Federal Narcotics Control Board.[24] The bill then died in committee. But this was not the end of the affair. The narcotics experts had successfully resisted the initial congressional effort to enact federal legislation prohibiting marihuana; but these deliberations had aroused their interest and therefore left an important legacy.

Government experts were now of two minds. Some believed that marihuana use was essentially a local problem in a few areas of the country, that it probably would remain confined, and that federal legislation would not be much help anyway since effective control could only be achieved on the state and local levels. This view, held by the assistant surgeon general in charge of narcotics, by the deputy commissioner of prohibition, L. G. Nutt, and by the legal adviser for the bureau, A. L. Tennyson, is probably best reflected in the bureau's letter dated 25 January 1929, drafted by Tennyson and signed by Nutt, which opposed Senator Phipp's suggested amendment of the Harrison Act:

> [The] evils represented by the abuse of cannabis indica . . . do not appear to be nearly as widespread as those connected with the possession of opium, cocoa leaves or their derivatives, the former being confined to the southwest and midwest states and possibly in some of the larger cities. It is thought that this evil may more properly be met by state and municipal legislation, for which there is more ample fundamental authority. I respectfully venture the suggestion that if the abuse of cannabis indica . . . exists to an appreciable extent in Colorado, the matter be referred to the state legislature for appropriate attention.[25]

Those opposed to federal legislation were also skeptical of the horrors "said to be associated with [marihuana's] abuse" and they were not eager to tangle with the AMA and the pharmaceutical industry, a fate they considered inevitable if tight controls were to be obtained.[26]

Others who were convinced that "abuse of the drug far exceeds its use as a medicine" were inclined to believe the allegations of crime and insanity and hoped to see that the drug was "absolutely outlawed." This would require a three-pronged plan: complete federal prohibition of importation and exportation (by separate statute); federal prohibition of interstate transportation; and comprehensive, uniform state laws restricting or prohibiting growth, sale, and possession.[27]

The important issues raised by these proposals, which were advocated by Anslinger and J. M. Doran, retiring commissioner of prohibition, were whether there was any medical need for cannabis and, if so, whether this need could be met by other drugs. If there was a medical need which cannot otherwise be met, could it be satisfied by domestically grown hemp?

In the course of developing the departmental position on S. 2075, Anslinger had solicited responses to those and related questions. Among the respondents were the American Drug Manufacturers' Association and the American Medical Association. The AMA was not enthusiastic about the prospect of greater governmental interference with the medical profession and the pharmaceutical industry. Also it expressed resentment over the implicit suggestion that physicians and manufacturers were responsible for cannabis "abuse," a charge which had been made quite explicitly by Agriculture's R. F. Smith in 1917.

Dr. William C. Woodward, director of AMA's Bureau of Legal Medicine, did not mince any words in his response. He indicted the arrogance of those in the federal narcotics bureaucracy who could contemplate a wholesale alteration of the legal status of cannabis without consulting all the interested parties in the private sector. He thought he saw a fait accompli and he was very nearly right:

Before your letter was referred to this bureau, it was referred to our Council on Pharmacy and Chemistry, and when it was referred to me, I was informed that that Council had never had occasion to give consideration to the questions you raise. The same might be said to be true generally with reference to this bureau; it has never had occasion to give consideration to most of the questions raised by your letter, and I doubt whether any other agency, public or private, has ever had occasion to do so, unless it be the United States Department of Agriculture and the several analogous departments of the state governments. I presume that you have, of course, communicated with the United States Department of Agriculture, and if you have not communicated with the several analogous state departments, it might be worth your while to do so.

Dr. Woodward's outrage is matched only by his sarcasm:

Undertaking to answer so far as practicable your specific questions, the following information is offered in response to the particular questions propounded by you:

I

What is the quantity of Indian Hemp produced in the United States? Ans. — The American Medical Association has no knowledge with respect to this matter.

II

What is the geographical distribution of the areas where Indian Hemp is grown within the United States? Ans. — The American Medical Association has no information with respect to this matter except such as may be found in books and journals, with which information, it is presumed, you are already familiar.

III

What are the medical needs and uses of the drug or drugs produced from Indian Hemp? Ans. — The answer to this question can be found in standard books on pharmacology and therapeutics, which are available in large numbers in the Surgeon General's library in Washington.

IV

What is the comparative medical value of Indian Hemp as domestically produced and as produced in foreign countries? Ans. — The answer to this question can be found in standard books on pharmacology and therapeutics, which are available in large numbers in the Surgeon General's library in Washington.[28]

In the course of exploring the feasibility of including cannabis in a uniform State Narcotic Drug Act—which the AMA had been working on in earnest since 1922—Dr. Woodward had conducted a survey of the pharmaceutical interests during the later 1920s. To his own amazement, he reported, all but one of the responses challenged the accepted view that cannabis was "habit-forming." Many of the respondents cited a 1925 Canal Zone study which concluded that marihuana presented insufficient danger to public health or safety to warrant its prohibition. No respondents reported any knowledge of the abusive use of pharmaceutical products. They felt that even if this were possible, most cannabis was sold for compound preparations whose abuse would be farfetched, that the medicinal use of cannabis had declined substantially, that its intoxicant use was not enough of a problem to justify the red tape which the medical profession and drug industry would have to suffer should major controls be imposed. They further suggested that the passage of legislation would only call attention to cannabis which might well cause abuse where there was now none. Finally, they believed that attempts to regulate the distribution of cannabis would be completely irrelevant to the control of any illegitimate use because the drug would then "come direct from the soil and not through drug channels."

In their response to Anslinger, the Drug Manufacturers' Association echoed these arguments. The only way to prevent smoking would be to eliminate domestic growth, and the federal government could not do that.[29] But the corollary point, that domestic production was sufficient to satisfy whatever medical need existed, had important implications for federal legislation. Thus, although opposing S. 2075, Anslinger told the chairman of the Finance Committee that "there would be no objection to the enactment of a *separate* measure prohibiting the importation and exportation of this particular drug."[30]

Just about the time of this decision to oppose S. 2075 but not to oppose separate legislation, there was a change in the federal narcotics bureaucracy that was to have a major impact on the course of future marihuana legislation. On 14 June 1930 Congress abolished the Federal Narcotics Control Board, which had been established by the Import and Export Act, and transferred its duties, along with the responsibilities of the narcotics division of the Bureau of Prohibition, to a new Federal Bureau of Narcotics, to be housed in the Treasury Department. The birth of this separate agency, eager to fulfill its role as a crusader against the evils of narcotics, was as important as any other single factor in influencing public policy toward drugs from 1930 to 1968.

Then, on 15 July 1930 Harry Jacob Anslinger was appointed acting commissioner of the new bureau, an appointment that became permanent on 12 August. A man who would single-handedly control U.S. drug policy for three decades, Anslinger had taken a fortuitous route to his new post. Born in 1892 in Altoona, Pennsylvania, Anslinger entered the U.S. Foreign Service as the clouds of war were gathering over Europe. After several postwar assignments to The Hague, Hamburg, and Venezuela, he headed the U.S. consulate in the Bahamas. In this post he prevailed upon British authorities to aid the prohibition experiment then underway at home by halting the bootleg liquor traffic originating in the West Indies.

It was at this point, in 1926, that Anslinger's career took its fateful twist. His diplomatic assistance to the cause of prohibition apparently came to the attention of the Treasury Department, which immediately borrowed his services from the State Department to serve as the chief of the Prohibition Bureau's Division of Foreign Control. In 1929 Anslinger was promoted to the post of assistant commissioner of prohibition and was designated secretary to the Narcotics Control Board. It was in this latter position that he was introduced to the more durable area of narcotics policy and participated in the initial departmental decision-making on marihuana.

Until 1930 federal narcotics policy fell under the jurisdiction of L. G. Nutt, deputy commissioner of prohibition. Nutt would presumably have been in line for an appointment to head the new bureau had it not been for a scandal uncovered in early 1930 involving federal narcotics agents. A federal grand jury found that New York agents had falsified their records, reporting local police arrests as federal arrests; there was also some evidence of collusion between the federal agents and illegal traffickers. In any event, Anslinger took over Nutt's responsibilities in the narcotics division, continuing at the helm of the new bureau.

Soon after the Senate confirmed his appointment on 18 December 1930 Commissioner Anslinger decided that the bureau's first major project should be an active involvement in the drafting of the Uniform State Narcotic Drug Act, an endeavor then in its fourth year. Because prohibition of growth was essential to combating marihuana, the Uniform Act was an ideal vehicle for securing comprehensive state legislation. Also, since the drafting of the Uniform Act could be conducted away from public debate, it seemed the best forum for confronting the medical profession and pharmaceutical industry. The federal aspects of the marihuana plan would be deferred and the case could be presented to Congress "at the appropriate time."[31]

Pressure from Prosecutors

Ironically, soon after this decision was made agitation for federal legislation began to increase among certain private pressure groups, particularly the law enforcement community. Most of the discontent came from New Orleans, where, apparently, it had been ignited by a significant increase in the local crime rate during the late 1920s. Although "payroll and bank guards were doubled," this "did not prevent some of the most spectacular holdups in the history of the city."[32] Probably tied to the widespread violation of alcohol prohibition, the crime increase was nonetheless attributed to the convenient scapegoat, marihuana, and local officials took highly visible steps to implicate the alien drug. A local physician, Dr. Fossier, indicted the "marihuana menace." He surveyed local "experts" in order to document the thesis that "muggle-heads" fortified themselves with marihuana as a prelude to violence. He reported that the local coroner found 125 confirmed users of marihuana among 450 prisoners.[33] On the basis of Fossier's article and the surgeon general's 1929 report, the local district attorney, Eugene Stanley, who had been instrumental in closing the New Orleans morphine clinics a decade earlier, began to campaign for federal marihuana legislation. He circulated a pamphlet drawing heavily on Dr. Fossier's article, and he addressed numerous local organizations. Using the "assassin" myths to set the stage, he offered a sweeping assertion which was to be reproduced in

New Orleans *Times-Picayune*, 5 June 1930

practically every commentary on marihuana published during the 1930s:

> It is an ideal drug to cut off inhibitions quickly. . . .
>
> At the present time the underworld has been quick to realize the value of this drug in subjugating the will of human derelicts to that of a master mind. Its use sweeps away all restraint, and to its influence may be attributed many of our present-day crimes. It has been the experience of the Police and Prosecuting Officials in the South that immediately before the commission of many crimes the use of marihuana cigarettes has been indulged in by criminals so as to relieve themselves from the natural restraint which might deter them from the commission of criminal acts, and to give them the false courage necessary to commit the contemplated crime.[34]

No empirical data were offered in support of this contention. A habit so menacing, he continued, obviously could not be eliminated by local action alone:

> Inasmuch as the harmful effects of the use of marihuana are daily becoming more widely known and since it has been classed as a narcotic by the statutory laws of seventeen American States, England and Mexico, and since persons addicted to its use have been made eligible for treatment in the United States Narcotic Farms, the United States Government will unquestionably be compelled to adopt a consistent attitude towards it, and include it in the Harrison Anti-narcotic Law, so as to give Federal aid to the States in their effort to suppress a traffic as deadly and as destructive to society as that in the other forms of narcotics now prohibited by this Act.[35]

Stanley's campaign did not go unnoticed either locally or nationally. A typical illustration of its success is the following letter to President Hoover from George Doyle, vice-president of Local No. 93 of the Operative Plasterers' and Cement Finishers' International Association, and formerly deputy U.S. marshall of the eastern district of Louisiana:

> I beg to call your attention same time asking your kindly cooperation and assistance to suppress the use of a dirty and dangerous weed commonly known as Marihuana or Muggles. [T]he weed is a product from (Mexico) and has done more harm to the young generation than morphine, opium, or cocaine.

[I]t has an influence of creating false courage amongst our young criminals and bandits and hold up bankrobbers even cold blood murders of recent status of two holdups of brances of the canal bank. [A]s one who is very interested in our community welfare I would ask if you kindly recommend to Congress or some members of the House of Representatives to amend the Harrison narcotics act. . . .[36]

The local press took up the cry. They were quick to imply a causal relationship between marihuana and crime on the flimsiest of evidence. The following 1931 news report was headlined:

CARRIED MARIHUANA

The essential text of the report was:

Robert Jacques, 18, testified . . . that he fired a shot under an "impulse of the moment" which seriously wounded [an acquaintance].
The judge sentenced Jacques to . . . 18 months to 3 years, declaring that "it's time we put a stop to these dangerous impulses."
Jacques was arrested the day after the shooting. . . . A revolver was found in his pocket as were some marihuana cigarettes.[37]

During the height of Stanley's campaign, an FBN agent in the New Orleans division forwarded Stanley's pamphlet to Commissioner Anslinger. He added that Stanley had been trying to mobilize public opinion "to compel the Federal Government to have a law passed with respect to marihuana similar to the anti-narcotics statute."[38] Anslinger was in Geneva, but Acting Commissioner Wood answered that there were many medical and agricultural questions to be resolved before the federal government could consider legislation. It "would be appreciated if the substance of these views were communicated to Mr. Stanley."[39]

But Stanley was not alone. Prohibition's legacy of lawlessness, together with the economic woes of the depression, found an uncertain America drawing into itself; the nation sought to preserve its strength and no longer sap it in the pursuit of diversity. As in previous times of crisis and national anxiety, a latent xenophobia surfaced, as pleas were heard for immigration restriction to reduce both the labor force and the crime rate as well. The perceived relationship between immigrants and crime is reflected in the fact that the National Commission on Law Observance and Enforcement (the Wickersham Commission), appointed by President Hoover in 1929, devoted an entire research volume to a "Report on Crime and the Foreign Born."[40] Much of this volume, in turn, was devoted to an examination of the incidence of criminality among Mexicans.[41] Anti-Mexican feeling was running high; and the Wickersham research was undoubtedly triggered by a widely shared belief that Mexican laborers were responsible for a disproportionate number of violent crimes.[42]

Marihuana, the Mexican loco weed, was a convenient scapegoat once the crime thesis, bolstered by the assassin myth, had been unleashed. Law enforcement officials, in concert with the press, were eager to use it in order to explain increases in crime within their jurisdictions. In many areas of the country the cry went up for bans on marihuana (and sometimes for bans on Mexican immigration). For example, state and federal legislation were said to be necessary to complement the local ordinance recently adopted by the city of Tulsa, Oklahoma. Twin fears were raised—contamination of youth and incitement of crime. A Tulsa county attorney asserted:[43]

> The general use of the drug among young people is making it imperative that the state or the government of the United States take immediate steps to cope with this deadly drug, the dope which is used by murderers.
> . . . . .
> In some eastern cities, it has been learned, the gunman has discovered that the weed offers him something new in the way of courage—courage to kill.
> It is notoriously a fact, authorities point out, that gunmen, who occupy the lowest levels in the ranks of crime, are usually cowards. To undertake murder, they need something to "pep them up." A few whiffs of a marihuana cigarette, mixed with tobacco and he loses all sense of fear.

"Crime is on the increase in Denver," reported the *Rocky Mountain News* on 27 September 1931, and one of the major causes is the "spread of the use of marihuana—the deadly Indian hemp which, during the past year, has virtually supplanted cocaine,

morphine, heroin and opium among drug addicts." The paper had
been so advised by the manager of safety, Carl Millikin.[44] Denver
was fertile ground for the crime thesis. Even in 1929, when marihuana was perceived to be confined to Mexicans, the press did not
hesitate to attribute criminal tendencies to the new immigrants and
their weed. The *Denver Post* gave front-page attention to the
violent death of a young girl, allegedly murdered by her Mexican
stepfather on 7 April 1929. The story was lead news in the *Denver
Post* every day until 16 April, in part because the girl's mother was
white. On the 16th it first mentioned that the accused might have
been a marihuana user. Headlined "Fiend Slayer Caught in
Nebraska [;] Mexican Confesses Torture of American Baby," and
subheaded "Prisoner Admits to Officer he is Marihuana Addict,"
the story relates in full the conclusive evidence:

"You smoke marihuana?"
"Yes."
The Mexican said he had been without the weed for two days
before the killing of his stepdaughter.

On 17 April the story on the Mexican included the following: "He
repeated the story he had told the Sidney Chief of Police regarding
his addiction to marihuana saying that his supply of the weed had
become exhausted several days before the killing and his nerves
were unstrung."[45]

Four days later the governor signed a bill increasing the penalties
for second-offense possession, sale, or production of marihuana.[46]

Naturally a perceived increase in marihuana use in 1931, especially among the young, provided a convenient explanation for an
increase in crime generally and juvenile crime in particular. The
Rocky Mountain News noted: "Marihuana, until a comparatively
recent date, has been used almost exclusively by the Mexican
population employed in the beetfields. Today, however, this deadly
narcotic . . . has found its way into the very heart of society. Boys
and girls of tender years . . . use it to 'get a thrill'; criminals smoke
it to gain courage for their lawless deeds; drug addicts have adopted
it because of its cheapness."

Millikin had no doubt about the ill effects of the weed: insanity
("consumed over any period of time, [it] drives the user insane and

leads to an early grave") and murder ("Full of the drug and the wild dreams that go with it, [the user] is just as likely to commit murder as anything else"). He also had no doubt about the prescription—a feverish publicity campaign to awake the citizenry. Even though marihuana prohibition was already on the books, Millikin emphasized that "countless thousands of Denver citizens know nothing of marihuana or its effects."[47]

An oft-cited article which reiterated the crime and insanity theses during this period appeared in 1932. Written by M. A. Hayes and L. E. Bowery (a member of the Wichita, Kansas, Police Department), the article was published in *The Journal of Criminal Law and Criminology.*[48]

Hayes and Bowery explicitly attributed the introduction and diffusion of the marihuana evil to Mexicans, noting that "so long as it was confined to Mexicans themselves, [it] was not generally noticed." But when it began to spread to "native whites" around 1925 (presumably in New Orleans), it became "a menace of increasing importance and one against which the battle has just begun." From contemporary newspaper accounts, particularly in Kansas, the authors documented their assertion that marihuana use was widespread among students, who preferred the weed to alcohol and had begun to throw marihuana parties. Whether or not use had indeed become so widespread, the description confirms the picture emerging from other contemporary accounts. The justification for further legislation lay not only in the increase in use but also in the effects of the drug itself. The authors contended that marihuana is the most dangerous of all drugs, mainly because of the volatility of the second, or "exhilaration," phase of intoxication, where "the barrier of control over the emotions is lowered and the smoker may commence to boast, shout or dance. Any contradictions or restraint now offered may excite a state of frenzy leading to actions of uncontrollable violence or even murder." As an example, the authors offered a quotation from the chief of detectives of the Los Angeles Police Department, culled from an article in the *Fraternal Order of Police Journal:* "In the past we have had officers of this department shot and killed by marihuana addicts and *have traced the act of murder directly to the influence of Marihuana, with no other motive.* Numerous assaults have been made upon officers and citizens with intent to kill by Marihuana addicts which were directly traceable to the influence of Marihuana."

Also during the exhilaration phase, Hayes and Bowery maintained, the user is capable of "feats of great strength and endurance, during which no fatigue is felt." They suggested that this phenomenon provided a physiological basis for Stanley's claim "that criminals often prime themselves with marihuana before starting on an enterprise, for they lose all sense of fear and are prepared to take any risk." The authors offered further examples from "case studies" compiled from interviews. The following is typical:

> A Mexican, under the influence, while going beneath a railroad viaduct imagined that he saw approaching him, at great speed, a rider on an enormous horse. Dodging behind a column for protection, when he looked out again, he realized that what he had seen was an old woman pulling a small wagon. Going home, despite the fact that his wife had that day given birth to a child, he compelled her to get out of bed and prepare his dinner. Still suffering from the characteristic hallucinations, as she was peeling an onion, he imagined that she was preparing to attack him, and seized a club and hit her in the head with such force that she was knocked unconscious.

During the exhilaration phase, they stated, "sexual desires are stimulated and may lead to unnatural acts, such as indecent exposure and rape." To support this proposition the authors first cited a 1926 *Chicago Herald-Examiner* newspaper account: " 'A Kansas hasheesh eater thinks he is a white elephant. Six months ago they found him strolling alone a road, a few miles out of Topeka. He was naked, his clothing strewn along the highway for a mile. He was not violently insane, but crazy—said he was an elephant and acted as much like one as his limited physique would let him. Marihuana did it.' "

Another of the "case histories" provided the only other "support":

> F, age twenty-two, with a long police record, states that at one time he was a user, but that upon becoming acquainted with the evil, ceased its use. He said further that it caused him to suffer weird hallucinations, and to commit acts he would not normally have considered. F reported several instances of which he claimed to have positive knowledge, where boys had induced

girls to use the weed for the purpose of seducing them. He reports that its use is prevalent among members of the National Guard.

Investigators' note: While he claims to have ceased its use, this young man has all the appearances of a weed-head with the symptoms given by medical authorities.

With respect to the effects of long-term use, the authors felt so little doubt that they provided only one supporting statistic:

It is impossible to fix a definite time in which one becomes an addict. . . . After the chronic use of marihuana "cannabinomania" develops, which in many persons, especially if psychopathic, leads to a loss of mental activity. . . . [E]ach [smoking] experience ends in the destruction of brain tissues and nerve centers, and does irreparable damage. If continued, the inevitable result is insanity, which those familiar with it describe as absolutely incurable, and, without exception ending in death. Statistics show that from seventeen to twenty percent of all males admitted to mental hospitals and asylums in India have become insane through the use of this drug.

The Hayes–Bowery article typifies the allegedly scientific accounts distributed to propagandists, newspapers, and policy makers during this period. Like Stanley's article it did not go unnoticed. Both were frequently cited in judicial opinions and FBN literature.[49]

It should be apparent that the law enforcement community, with ready access to the public print, exerted a major influence on public opinion toward marihuana in the late twenties and early thirties. From an ascending crime rate and anti-Mexican bias emerged a pressure for marihuana prohibition which the FBN chose to divert to the state legislatures. This public opinion process is best illustrated by the FBN response to the two studies of Mexicans and crime prepared for the Wickersham Commission and published in late 1931 in the commission's final volume "Crime and the Foreign Born."

The commission-sponsored analysis of criminal justice data in several regions of the country tended to confirm, in most cases, the overrepresentation of Mexicans in the categories of arrests, convictions, and prisoner populations. These data were interpreted at length by Dr. Paul Taylor, associate professor of economics at the University of California, who accounted for the statistical association in terms of unequal and unfair administration of the law.[50] A further study of "Crime and Criminal Justice Among the Mexicans of Illinois" was contributed by Paul L. Warnshuis, head of the western branch of the Presbyterian Board of National Missions (with headquarters in Denver), whose answers to the question "Is the Mexican really criminally inclined?" reflect the paternalism of one who can find many "natural causes" for the Mexican's many "difficulties in being a law-abiding citizen." Along with differences in custom and manner of life, economic deprivation, and "well-known faults in our system of law enforcement and criminal justice," Warnshuis implicated marihuana: "Those who know the Mexican . . . would be certain to blame marihuana for a portion of the Mexican arrests. . . ."[51]

Warnshuis' views about marihuana, which correlated perfectly with prevailing myths, added legitimacy to the crime thesis. In a passage which came to the personal attention of Commissioner Anslinger,[52] Warnshuis noted:

> There are two other factors which no doubt play no unimportant role in bringing about the arrest of many Mexicans. The first is drunkenness. . . . A second factor is marihuana. In the Southwestern states and in Mexico, marihuana is known as "loco" weed—that is, "crazy"—because of the effect it produces. It is used for making cigarettes, and is not only a powerful drug, but to all appearances renders the user either drunk or crazy. The South Chicago police told of one Mexican who needed four officers to subdue him. It is especially insidious because it causes the brain and nervous system to deteriorate. To what extent it is being used it is impossible to learn, because those using it, like morphine and cocaine addicts, are secretive. Its use is not confined to Mexicans only, for within the past year four youths of other nationalities charged with a series of robberies admitted that they had to get "loaded" with marihuana before they could stage their nightly forays.[53]

Engaged in drafting the Uniform State Narcotic Drug Act, and having some trouble persuading the medical community to include a cannabis provision, Commissioner Anslinger seized on the Wickersham study as grounds for a country-wide ban on the drug. In September 1931 antimarihuana crusaders apparently planted a story in the *Christian Science Monitor* which publicized these isolated marihuana "findings" under the heading:

Drug Used by Mexican Aliens Finds Loophole in U.S. Laws
SPREAD OF GROWTH OF MARIHUANA IN WAKE OF IMMIGRANTS
CAUSES GRAVE CONCERN AT WASHINGTON—EFFECTS DESCRIBED IN
WICKERSHAM STUDIES.[54]

Then, in October, Anslinger attempted to bring public pressure to bear on the commissioners and publicly endorsed the crime thesis (for the first time, as far as we can tell): "Instances of criminals using the drug to give them courage before making brutal forays are occurrences commonly known to the narcotic bureau."[55]

Anslinger's purpose in going to the press at this time is quite apparent. He had decided that there was no legitimate medical use of the drug, that allowing such use would merely open a gigantic loophole in the law, and that, accordingly, the essential first step was for each state to enact a total ban on cultivation, sale, and possession of marihuana. To implement this, the FBN had just proposed such a provision to the Conference of Commissioners for Uniform State Laws. The bureau proposal had been defeated, however, by the medical-pharmaceutical interests. Consequently, Anslinger took his case to the press.

Although at least twenty-five states had prohibitory legislation by this time, the commissioner grossly misstated the alleged inadequacy of state law, contending that only two, California and Texas, had "restrictive legislation." "Elsewhere," he noted, "the situation is shocking, to say the least." Anslinger went on to state, apparently in exaggeration: "I have several stacks of correspondence from various parts of the country urging that some steps be taken by the Federal Government." But he had already determined to resist the growing pressure for federal legislation and to focus instead on inserting an adequate cannabis provision in the Uniform Narcotic Drug Act. Wanting to galvanize the conference of commissioners, but not yet wanting to seek federal legislation, the bureau took a calmly preventive line, as is illustrated by the following official statement which was issued in early 1932:

A great deal of public interest has been aroused by newspaper articles appearing from time to time on the evils of the abuse of marihuana, or Indian hemp, and more attention has been focused on specific cases reported of the abuse of the drug than would otherwise have been the case. This publicity tends to magnify the extent of the evil and lends color to an inference that there is an alarming spread of the improper use of the drug, whereas the actual increase in such use may not have been inordinately large.[56]

Marihuana was a highly dangerous drug, the bureau agreed, but its use was not of such proportions that federal legislation was needed.

CHAPTER IV

The Uniform Act and the Marihuana Compromise

In 1919 the American Medical Association asked the commissioner of Internal Revenue to call a conference to consider better control of traffic in narcotic drugs. Faced with an amalgam of conflicting state laws, the profession was uncertain of its obligations in the matter. The AMA asked that the wholesale, retail, and manufacturing drug interests be among those attending, along with delegates from the medical profession in each state. The proposal received no official or unofficial response either from the commissioner of Internal Revenue or the Bureau of Prohibition. Nevertheless, the AMA, through its own Council on Health and Public Instruction, held a conference in early 1922 during which a uniform state narcotic control law was presented. At another conference the following November there were present fifteen representatives of ten pharmaceutical organizations and two representatives of the medical profession. The draft of a uniform law was approved unanimously. The AMA set out to codify the draft and to send it for approval to each of the constituent organizations.[1] After securing approval, all the associations agreed to pursue enactment first in New York.

One impetus for the American Medical Association's concern was the lack of uniformity among state narcotic laws. A second and equally important concern was the laxity of state enforcement of the narcotic laws.[2] The medical director of the Boston Municipal Court, for example, called for more effective enforcement of Massachusetts' 1917 antinarcotic law:

Our laws aiming at the suppression of morphinism could perhaps be better, but no matter whether they be improved or not, they will not have their maximal efficiency without *adequate appropriations* for their enforcement. Even with the insufficient funds now [1921] available, more could be reached. I understand, for instance, that there is *no special police force* (white squads) entrusted with the detection and arrest of cases of VDL [Violation of the Drug Law] and that officers are very much hampered by not being allowed to follow suspected persons outside their particular districts.[3]

The lack of uniformity[4] and the weakness of state enforcement procedures,[5] together with the growing hysteria about dope fiends and criminality,[6] also converged in prompting several requests outside the medical community for a uniform state narcotic law.[7]

These proposals for drafting a uniform narcotic drug act occurred against the background of two larger movements: the trend toward the creation and dissemination of uniform state laws by the National Conference of Commissioners on Uniform State Laws, a group to which each state sent two representatives appointed by its governor; and the general concern in the late twenties and early thirties with interstate criminal networks, manifested, for example, by the creation in 1930 of the nearly autonomous Federal Bureau of Investigation. Because the concepts of states' rights and narrowly construed federal power were still powerful, an appeal to the national commissioners was the inevitable recourse for those pressing for uniform antinarcotic regulation.

Marihuana Sneaks In and Out

In 1924 the commissioners appointed a committee to draft a uniform narcotic drug act that it could recommend for state adoption. At the 1925 meeting of commissioners, the chairman of the committee reported that he himself had prepared a first tentative draft based on the 1921 New York act, the Washington state legislation, the Harrison Act, and a bill then before the New York legislature. Presumably this bill was the one drafted by the AMA conference after its 1922 meeting. The tentative draft included cannabis in the list of "habit-forming drugs" that could be distributed and used only for medical purposes.[8] The chairman noted, however, that Dr. William Woodward, head of the AMA's Bureau of Legal Medicine and Legislation, with whom he had only recently conferred, had made "some very valuable suggestions." Because the tentative draft had already been printed before he received these suggestions, he requested that it "not be read but be re-committed to the Committee."[9] A second tentative draft was presented in 1928 and again the draft was not discussed at the conference but was recommitted for further study. The second draft was essentially a copy of the 1927 New York statute. It also included cannabis in the class of habit-forming drugs.[10]

The lack of concern on the part of the commissioners themselves with the whole narcotics problem between 1924 and 1928 is reflected in the remarks of the president of the conference. Introducing Dr. Woodward, President Miller said: "In view of the importance of the act I think it would not be amiss to listen to the Doctor for a few minutes, that he may point out to us why it is important. In some of the states we do not recognize the importance because it has not been called to our attention."[11] Nor was the Bureau of Prohibition particularly concerned at this time with the cannabis provision. Deputy Commissioner Nutt, who was in charge of the narcotics division until 1930, commented on the first tentative draft: "With respect to the definition of cannabis indica or cannabis sativa, this office does not feel qualified to make any recommendations as these substances are not included in the Federal Narcotic Laws."[12] Lack of official concern and interest continued to affect the bureau's attitude toward the second tentative draft.[13]

Since neither the commissioners nor the federal narcotics officials were particularly concerned about state and local control of narcotics generally and marihuana in particular, it seems clear that neither was responsible for the inclusion of marihuana in the category of "habit-forming drugs." Rather, it would appear that this substance was included in the first draft because it was "another narcotic" listed in various state laws, particularly in the 1923 Washington statute from which the first draft was drawn. As the second draft was a copy of the 1927 New York act, its presence there is no mystery. It is unlikely that any of the persons involved in the drafting were concerned about marihuana-smoking. At best they might have been aware of its use in a few isolated regions.

Two third drafts were submitted, the first in 1929 and the second in 1930. The initial one closely resembled the second tentative draft, and once again it included cannabis in the category of "habit-forming drugs." Again, the growth, distribution, and possession of cannabis were prohibited except for medical purposes.

Unlike the previous drafts, this one received the full attention of the Bureau of Prohibition's narcotics division, now headed by Harry Anslinger. The bureau's comments on the third tentative draft reflect its emerging policy of supporting action on the state, rather than the federal, level:

> Sub-paragraph 12 covering cannabis sativa and its derivatives does not at present come within the purview of the two principal Federal narcotic laws. However, many complaints have reached this office of the abuse of this form of drug in certain localities. In view of what is understood to be its very limited medical use and its lack of dependability as to potency, query is made whether this drug could not be absolutely proscribed and its limited function as a medicine met by some substitute. From the limited information in possession of this office it is believed that the elimination of the abuse of this drug is a consideration which greatly outweighs that of its possibly very limited medical use, particularly if the latter need could be met by some less potentially harmful substitute.[14]

Like its predecessors, the initial third tentative draft was recommitted for further study.[15]

The other third tentative draft, submitted in 1930, removed cannabis from the category of "habit-forming drugs" and included only a supplemental provision for dealing with the drug.[16] A note following the supplemental section states the reason for this change:

> *Note:* Because of the many objections raised to the inclusion of cannabis indica, cannabis americana and cannabis sativa in the general list of habit-forming drugs, no mention is made of them in other sections of this act. The foregoing section is presented in order to meet the apparent demand for some method of preventing the use of such drugs for the production and maintenance of undesirable drug addiction. It may be adopted or rejected, as each state sees fit, without affecting the rest of the act.[17]

The conference's official record provides no clue as to the sources of the "many objections" to classifying marihuana with the "habit-forming drugs." We should recall, however, Dr. Woodward's sarcastic memorandum to Anslinger and the Federal Narcotics Control Board concerning S.2075 under which cannabis would have been included in the Import and Export Act. In that memorandum, he noted that he had been surveying the pharmaceutical industry and that on the basis of the response, he had reversed his own previous opinion that cannabis was habit-forming.[18] As a result, it seems that Dr. Woodward relegated cannabis to an optional status in the subsequent third tentative draft.

When the conference of commissioners met to consider the second version of the third tentative draft, Judge Deering, chairman of the Committee on the Uniform Narcotic Drug Act, recommended its recommission for further study because the committee had not yet had an opportunity to consult the newly created Bureau of Narcotics. At the time of this conference, 14 August 1930, no one had yet been appointed commissioner of the bureau, although Anslinger was acting commissioner.[19]

After Anslinger became commissioner he moved the bureau into the thick of the drafting process for the fourth and fifth tentative drafts. Involved before only on an advisory basis, the bureau now sought to become an equal partner with the AMA. Anslinger himself felt that had the bureau remained on the sidelines, "a delay of another year would have been the case."[20] In large part, the bureau's involvement provided an antidote to the internecine squabbles developing between the drug industry and the medical profession. Early in 1932, in fact, only a major effort by the Federal Narcotics Bureau and the surgeon general prevented a wholesale battle that clearly would have postponed conference adoption of the Uniform Narcotic Drug Act.

The bureau's involvement converted the cannabis provision from an appendage of little importance to a major bone of contention. Anslinger, having chosen the Uniform Act as the bureau's first priority on the marihuana issue, seems to have decided soon after his ascendency to seek the total prohibition of domestic marihuana cultivation, sale, possession, and even use for medical purposes. The commissioner was convinced that the limited medical use for cannabis was far outweighed by the need to control potential cannabis addiction.[21] The battle lines had formed: Woodward and the pharmaceutical industry advocated optional inclusion of marihuana; the federal narcotics bureaucracy urged not only inclusion but elimination of medical use.

The fourth tentative draft retained the optional cannabis provision, despite Commissioner Anslinger's objections. In all its comments on the fourth tentative draft and the cannabis section, the FBN was most careful to protest its lack of any *official* connection with the issue altogether. Nevertheless, it is clear that inclusion of a strict marihuana provision in a uniform state law was a major part of the bureau's plan. This conclusion is buttressed by a letter from Anslinger to Dr. Woodward urging that the law contain such a provision dealing with cannabis.[22] Unable to convince Woodward, Anslinger took his case to the chairman of the committee. At an evening session before the convening of the full conference of commissioners from 9-12 September at Atlantic City, Commissioner Anslinger and A. L. Tennyson of the bureau met with Judge Deering to discuss the bureau's feelings about the fourth tentative draft, section by section. At this time Commissioner Anslinger stated again the bureau's position regarding marihuana—the bureau felt strongly that inclusion of cannabis in the state law ought to be mandatory. Moreover, the bureau once again urged that the only successful way to deal with the marihuana drug traffic, because of its domestic nature and the easy availability of the weed, was to prohibit the cultivation of the plant altogether and to find some substitute for its limited medical use.[23]

Apparently Anslinger was unable to convince Deering. The fourth tentative draft presented to the conference of commissioners again included only the optional marihuana provision. Anslinger discussed the matter with all of the commissioners. Again he proposed a total prohibition and again he was rebuffed. The conference tentatively approved the fourth draft and directed the committee to prepare a final draft.[24] Commissioner Anslinger then went to the press, wielding the Warnshuis study for the Wickersham Commission linking marihuana, Mexicans, and crime. He hoped public pressure would force the commissioners to take his advice.[25]

The Squabble

Between the Atlantic City conference of commissioners in 1931 and their final conference in October 1932, the bureau found itself not only busily involved in the drafting of the proposed law but also caught in a cross fire of personalities and interests which almost sabotaged the drafting of any Uniform Narcotic Drug Act. In order to understand the bureau's role in this matter, one must first consider the ill-sorted collection of interest groups which had been involved in the drafting of the uniform law over its long history.

The American Medical Association played the dominant role in the drafting process until the entry of the FBN in 1931. Their efforts had been largely responsible for consideration of the Uniform Narcotic Drug Act in the first place. Since 1925 Dr. Woodward, the director of their Bureau of Legal Medicine and Legislation, had single-handedly nurtured the drafting of the act and circulated the drafts to scores of interested persons for their comments. His reversal on the cannabis provision, for example, was precipitated by a survey of pharmaceutical houses. It appears, however, that Dr. Woodward's personal style and the preeminent position of the AMA in the drafting process were resented by the two remaining interest groups—the FBN and the retail and wholesale pharmaceutical associations.

When Commissioner Anslinger, whose relations with Dr. Woodward were clearly uneasy, attempted to assume an active role for the bureau in the drafting process, he found it very difficult to avoid stepping on Woodward's toes. Frustrated by the bureau's formerly inactive role, Anslinger was not quite sure how to handle the situation and tried at first to enter the process informally and gradually. Finally by August 1932 he was so anxious for the bureau to participate in the drafting of the fifth and final draft of the Uniform Act that he wrote to Judge Deering requesting a delay in the committee's consideration (this would grant the bureau an opportunity not only to review the draft prepared by Dr. Woodward but also to redraft and rewrite significant provisions):

> I appreciate fully the necessity for the utmost expedition of this work and am quite anxious that there shall be no untoward delay on the part of this Bureau. . . . I appointed a Committee of Treasury Department lawyers to review Dr. Woodward's draft and, if considered necessary, to redraft such portions thereof to strengthen the measure from an enforcement standpoint. . . .
>
> I had understood after the last Conference in Atlantic City that Dr. Woodward intended to redraft the measure in line with suggestions then made as early as possible after his arrival back

in Chicago. But I believe that due to press of other official duties Dr. Woodward was unable to commence the work until sometime in May of this year. I received the last portion of Dr. Woodward's draft with a letter from him dated July 16, 1932 and the time we have had to review same, in view of the importance of the work, has been comparatively short, as I believe you will agree.[26]

Even within the AMA there was some grumbling about Dr. Woodward's role and his unwillingness to consult other interest groups, particularly the pharmaceutical industry.

The controversy erupted just before the fifth draft was presented. Dr. William Charles White, an influential member of the association, wrote to the president of the AMA, Dr. Olin West, inquiring about the status of the Uniform Narcotic Drug Act and suggesting that a conference be held to include all the leaders of the pharmaceutical profession with some "high official" of the American Medical Association—not Dr. Woodward. "The reason for suggesting someone other than Dr. Woodward is to relieve the situation of a condition which has arisen largely because of his hard labor and intimate association with this problem from the beginning."[27] Dr. West responded:

Frankly I am somewhat surprised at some of the statements offered in your letter with respect to the attitude of Dr. Woodward concerning some phases of the proposed legislation for control of narcotics. . . .

I happen to know that Dr. Woodward has done a great deal of arduous work in an effort to be helpful in drafting 'A Uniform State Law' and I feel very sure that it has not been his intention to antagonize other organizations that are actively interested in this matter. In a spirit of fairness to Dr. Woodward, I shall as soon as possible discuss with him the matters referred to in your letter and I shall be glad to write you again.[28]

Dr. Woodward responded directly to Dr. White in shock and dismay. With respect to the charge that he had been insensitive to the concerns of the pharmaceutical industry and the drug trade, Dr. Woodward protested vehemently:

In the first place, I resent your charge of ignorance and intolerance with respect to the cooperation of manufacturing chemists, pharmacists, pharmaceutical houses, and other groups.

You suggest the importance of consulting such groups as if it were a bright and new idea of your own. As a matter of fact, they have been frequently consulted not only by me, but by the Council on Health and Public Instruction before I assumed my present duties with the American Medical Association.[29]

The pharmaceutical industry itself felt that their interests were considered only peripherally and that they had been excluded from the heart of the drafting process. As one spokesman for the industry put it, Woodward was trying "to limit the consideration of the fifth tentative draft of the AMA Bill to his Association and Judge Deering and his subcommittee."[30] On the other hand, Dr. Woodward and Dr. West detailed numerous instances in which representatives of the drug industry were invited not only to submit comments but also to participate in conferences and drafting sessions. They both strongly argued that the pharmaceutical associations had every opportunity to engage in the drafting of legislation and had failed of their own volition to take advantage of these opportunities. They went on to suggest that in raising this question at this time, the associations were actually trying to block the passage of the final draft, which was scheduled for presentation two months hence.[31] As Dr. Woodward wrote: "In any event, the criticism of my course is so widespread and has reached such important places that I have no doubt whatever that it has been deliberately promoted to serve the ulterior purposes of some interest that is unwilling to be known in connection with the matter."[32]

Finally, Assistant Surgeon General Treadway, seeing the "need to remedy a situation which was getting somewhat out of hand," intervened. Treadway succinctly isolated the perspective of the federal narcotic bureaucracy when he noted:

The attitude of these so-called "vested interests" concerned with the sale, distribution and uses of narcotic drugs have tended to regard Dr. Woodward's attitude in the matter as not talking frankly across the table. One's instinctive reaction toward matters of this sort, especially in the professional field, is to ignore the demands of the "vested interests" and "commercial organizations" who may be interested in the materialistic side of the subject. *Yet I know that certain organizations, unless they are in accord, can balk and defeat any legislation submitted to a state legislature when they have not had the opportunity to air their views* or to come to some previous uniform understanding and agreement.[33] [emphasis added]

Treadway was well aware of the political influence of the pharmaceutical industry, the National Association of Retail Druggists, the Federal Wholesale Drug Association, and the Pharmaceutical Manufacturers' Association, among others, and he tried to smooth things over. A conference of interested parties with the committee was therefore scheduled before the final draft was to be presented to the conference of commissioners.

Despite the controversy that was raging, the Federal Bureau of Narcotics maintained strict neutrality in the Woodward matter. For this reason the bureau was largely responsible for pushing the fifth and final draft to its timely conclusion. While the other interests involved were distracted during the months of July and August 1932, the FBN diligently continued to prepare its comments and a redraft for the preliminary conference.

The Bureau Retreats on Marihuana

Present at this conference on 15 September 1932 were representatives of the Deering committee, the Federal Bureau of Narcotics, the Department of State, the Public Health Service, the American Medical Association, and delegates from the drug industry and other health-related industries and organizations. The final version of the Uniform Narcotic Drug Act was hammered out at this session. The bureau was central to the drafting process, and Commissioner Anslinger made a major effort to involve the drug manufacturers and the wholesale and retail drug trade in it to protect the act from possible subsequent political sabotage.[34] Finally, the conference agreed on a draft to be presented to the national conference in October.

One manifestation of this strategy of accommodation to the pharmaceutical interests was the bureau's modulation of its policy on the marihuana issue. As early as 1929 the American Pharmaceutical Association had objected to the "effort being made by sensationalistic papers to enlarge upon the extended use of marihuana." At that time, the surgeon general had begun to prepare the industry for eventual state legislation.[35] Yet, as Woodward's survey late the same year showed, a consensus of opinion had emerged in the industry that regulation of the distribution of cannabis was wholly unnecessary because the drug was not habit-forming, because medical preparations were not responsible for whatever abuse there was, and because effective control, in any event, depended upon elimination of domestic growth. The industry generally regarded prohibitory legislation as counterproductive. One respondent wrote: "It would seem to me that in regard to regulations, it would be better left exactly as it is today rather than penalize its use thus bringing publicity to it where there is apparently a considerable lack of evidence of its harmfulness." A more cryptic response was, "Absolute Rot. It is not necessary. I have never known of its misuse."[36] The manufacturers of drug products were strongly opposed to the inclusion of cannabis under any criminal regulatory scheme. When the fifth tentative draft was circulated to representatives of the drug industry, one important spokesman said bluntly: "Strike the cannabis section. Section 12. This Section should not be incorporated in this draft at all as the abuse complained of is altogether local and limited to extremely narrow territory."[37]

At the preliminary conference the pharmaceutical industry was not the lone dissenter on the cannabis provision. Spokesmen for the domestic hemp industry also stated its opposition:

> After a lengthy discussion regarding cannabis, Judge Deering stated that the definition as suggested by Dr. Woodward should be made more clear and then it should be left to the Conference to decide whether or not cannabis should be included in the Act. At this point, Dr. Woodward called attention to the report of the United States Public Health Service, dated July 10, 1932, in which the statement was made that 28,000 acres of Indian Hemp were under cultivation in the United States last year.
>
> Mr. Thompson (the Proprietary Association) objected to the inclusion of cannabis in the Act because of the effect it would have on the hemp industry of Kentucky.[38]

The final conclusion reached by all the parties present was: "After considerable comment, it was decided to eliminate Section 12 (Cannabis) and leave it to the Conference of Commissioners as to whether it should be included under the general provisions of the Act."[39]

The bureau had now retreated, it appears, on the marihuana issue and was no longer insisting on the mandatory inclusion of an absolute prohibition. Risking the opposition of the drug industry to the entire act simply was not worth it. Moreover, it was probably felt that the hemp industry could secure deletion of the cannabis provision in some states even if it were included in the draft. Despite the fact that the final decision was to be left to the plenary conference of commissioners, the bureau seems to have given up.

The fifth tentative draft did, however, include a significant change in form which would have important consequences in the decades to come. Although the marihuana provision remained supplemental to the main body of the act, any state wishing to regulate the sale and possession of marihuana was instructed simply to add cannabis to the definition of "narcotic drugs." All the other provisions of the act would then apply to marihuana as well as to the opiates and cocaine. It appears that the Narcotics Bureau felt that this method of amending the act would facilitate the addition of other drugs in the future.[40] As a result of this technical modification, marihuana came to be defined as a "narcotic" in every state. Of equal importance was the fact that this format assured that legislators would not distinguish between marihuana and the opiates in any subsequent effort to increase penalties for "narcotics" offenses.

The proceedings of the plenary conference of commissioners, held on 8 October 1932, do not contain any synopsis of debate on the subject of whether or not cannabis should be included in the act. Predictably, the cannabis provision remained optional, and the commissioners adopted the fifth tentative draft as it had been prepared at the 15 September conference without major change. Indeed, although the anticipatory conflict between and among the medical and drug interests was quite controversial, the proceedings of the National Conference of Commissioners on the Uniform Drug Act are practically devoid of substance.

The only recorded opposition to the adoption of the final draft came from some commissioners who objected to tying the Uniform State Law to the terms of the federal Harrison Act. This last obstacle was overcome by the argument that a number of states already had passed such legislation, so that the states' rights problem need not stand in the way. This brief debate confirms the notion that the act received very little attention, if any, from the commissioners other than those sitting on the committee which drafted it.[41] The act was adopted 26 to 3.[42] No one challenged or even brought up the issue of the designations of the drugs to be prohibited.

CHAPTER V

Marihuana Becomes a "National Monster"

AT THE BEGINNING of the campaign for passage of the Uniform Act in the several states in 1933, marihuana use was not widespread or very much noticed. As we have seen, marihuana use was pretty much confined to the Mexican communities of the southwestern states throughout the twenties. Sometime around 1926, however, use among the black and lower-class white elements of New Orleans emerged along with the propensity toward use by youth in these communities. Later in the decade it appears that use had appeared in the major urban areas, particularly in Chicago, Denver, Tulsa, Detroit, San Francisco, and Baltimore. There is little evidence, however, that the habit was widespread in New York City. Apart from those in the Mexican communities, it appears that the urban users were artists, musicians,[1] medical students, and blacks.[2] It is also possible, of course, that white high school students, primarily from the lower class, had been attracted to the drug in communities where it was available.

Despite the propaganda released by the law enforcement community in the early thirties, the general public was probably largely unaware of the drug, its use, or its alleged effects. Contrary to the picture of a marihuana epidemic conveyed by the propagandists in the early thirties, use at this time probably had stabilized both geographically and demographically. It was still a regional, ethnic phenomenon. Commissioner Anslinger himself observed in late 1937 that "ten years ago we only heard about [marihuana] throughout the Southwest. . . . [I]t has only become a national menace in the last three years."[3]

As Anslinger's comment suggests, there seems to have been a change around the end of 1934. It is hard to determine whether use increased or whether opinion makers—including the press, the FBN, and various other groups—succeeded in increasing public awareness. Whatever its cause, this increased awareness played a

A Trap for a Mad Dog

Copyright. 1932.

New York—Pennsylvania—Rhode Island—California.

These four States have made the Uniform State Narcotic Law a part of their codes, thereby leading the way toward extirpation of the infamous "dope" evil in America.

In the past the Federal Government has carried on against this evil without much State backing. Some States have had effective legislation; others have not. And in the murky "twilight zone" between State and Federal jurisdiction the "dope" traffic has found many a lair.

The Uniform State Narcotic Law is devised to wipe out this "twilight zone." It was written by experts, and approved by authorities on the narcotic problem.

Legislatures meeting in January in more than 30 States should, as a primary public duty, pass the law, and add their States to the honor roll led by New York, Pennsylvania, Rhode Island and California.

Washington Herald, 4 November 1932

significant role in passage of the Uniform Narcotic Drug Act by the states and in the decision of national politicians to seek federal legislation.

The Role of the Federal Bureau of Narcotics

Critics of existing marihuana legislation have frequently attributed the illegal status of marihuana solely to the crusading zeal of the Federal Bureau of Narcotics and especially of its long-time head, Harry J. Anslinger. Some observers have suggested that the bureau's activity was produced by bureaucratic exigencies and the need to expand;[4] others have said the bureau was on a moral crusade;[5] still others have asserted that the bureau believed its own propaganda about the link between criminality and marihuana.[6] While each of these factors may have played some role, it is clear that the bureau did not single-handedly conjure up the idea of banning marihuana use. Since twenty-four states had already undertaken the prohibition of marihuana before the creation of the bureau in 1930, the bureau cannot alone be credited with the pressure to outlaw the drug.

The bureau did, however, play a pivotal part. Although Anslinger suffered a setback during the drafting of the Uniform Act, he set to work at once to secure its enactment by the states, including the optional marihuana provision. There can be little doubt that the bureau's activity hastened the passage of the act by state legislatures and increased public awareness of marihuana. The bureau's primary objective, of course, was adoption of the entire Uniform Act; of particular interest here is its activity regarding marihuana.

Immediately after the commissioners approved the act, the bureau began a comprehensive campaign in the press, in legislative chambers, and in any other forum it could find to gain public support for the act's passage. Perceiving the absence of public awareness of marihuana and wanting to encourage positive action to overcome the drug's optional status, the bureau sought to arouse public interest in marihuana through "an educational campaign describing the drug, its identifications and its evil effects."[7] That the FBN had a difficult task is illustrated by the fact that as late as 1936 it was necessary to show marihuana to the New York police so that they could recognize the growing plant and its dried, smokable form.[8]

A large part of the bureau's activity consisted of intensive lobbying in each legislature before which the act was pending. Anslinger instructed his district supervisors and local agents to campaign actively with state legislators for the passage of the act, urging them to make as many speeches and public appearances as possible to marshal public support. On 19 February 1934, for example, Isabelle Ahern O'Neill, a former Rhode Island state legislator and then New England representative of the FBN, delivered a major address over a Providence radio station calling for that state's legislature to be among the first to pass the Uniform Narcotic Drug Act.[9] Anslinger made numerous speeches and several radio broadcasts throughout the country in an effort to encourage public support for the legislation. In an important strategic decision, the commissioner suggested that his three hundred agents work directly with legislators. They were to discuss in detail the provisions of the act with any legislator who voiced objections and seek to convince him to support the act. Agents were also assigned to assist the floor managers and sponsors of the act in each state's legislature.[10]

Elizabeth Bass, a Chicago agent, was a particularly effective lobbyist and opinion maker. Her sustained activity before such groups as women's clubs and the Women's Christian Temperance Union enlisted a great deal of support. Over and above direct personal appeals to civic groups and legislators by FBN personnel, Anslinger conducted a press campaign across the country to gain the support of different constituencies. He sought editorial support in newspapers[11] and assisted in the drafting of articles for popular magazines.[12] To mobilize the Bar, Anslinger and Tennyson wrote an article for law journals explaining the need for the Uniform Narcotic Drug Act.[13]

Despite all these FBN efforts, the Uniform Act did not fare well in state legislatures at first. By 26 April 1933 only two states had enacted it in full. Twenty months later only seven additional states were in the fold. The state of Indiana so badly mutilated the Uniform Act that the commissioner and the bureau were greatly disappointed with the legislation.[14] As late as March 1935 only ten states had enacted the Uniform Narcotic Drug law. This lack of success led Anslinger to complain: "The representatives of this

Washington Herald, 23 November 1932

Bureau have persistently and patiently worked to overcome the apathy or hostility to the proposed legislation and so far as I have been able to determine the Bureau has been working alone in its nationwide attempt to stimulate interest in bringing about favorable action upon the Uniform State Narcotic Law, at least until very recently."[15]

A number of significant objections emerged in the state legislatures considering the passage of the Uniform Narcotic Drug Act. First among these was the potential cost to the state of enforcing the act. Second, a widely held belief that the Uniform Act would require special licensing of doctors, dentists, and veterinarians provoked concern about the amount of red tape involved. Third, the limit on the amount of exempt preparations which could be sold caused a great deal of technical difficulty with the act. Fourth, many objected to the power of the courts to revoke or suspend licenses to practice medicine or pharmacy. Finally, there seemed to be widespread misunderstanding of the record-keeping requirements of the act. Although these objections were largely administrative, and may well have emanated from the American Medical Association and the Pharmaceutical Association, they nevertheless posed what appeared to the bureau to be serious stumbling blocks to the successful passage of the Uniform Act in most of the states.[16]

The combination of public apathy and administrative resistance dictated a new strategy. The bureau needed to arouse public interest so that the professional objections would seem inconsequential beside a "felt need" of the legislatures. The "marihuana menace" was an ideal concept for such a campaign. Thus, beginning in late 1934, Commissioner Anslinger gradually shifted the focus of the FBN's publicity campaign away from the inability of federal law enforcement agencies to deal effectively with local drug problems toward the need to cope with a new drug menace—marihuana.

From 1932 through most of 1934 very little of the bureau's propaganda was directed toward the supplemental marihuana provision. But by late 1934 the Narcotics Bureau had begun to use the specter of widespread marihuana addiction as a means of calling attention to and gaining support for the Uniform Narcotic Drug Act. When Commissioner Anslinger was asked in 1934 what would be the best way of dealing with the marihuana problem, he replied: "The confusion among the States' narcotic laws today is one of the greatest aids of the illicit traffic in every dangerous drug. It clogs all the machinery of detection, impedes all the processes of prevention and punishment. Put a Uniform State Narcotics Act through every legislature. That will not only cure the worst of the hashish evil; it will help reduce the whole drug evil to a minimum."[17]

The change in bureau strategy is apparent in a comparison of two official statements of Commissioner Anslinger—one made in 1933, the other in 1936. The 1933 statement explained the need for a Uniform Narcotic Drug law and emphasized international obligations of the United States, the need for more effective coordination in law enforcement, and the impact the law would have on the incidence of morphine, cocaine, and opium addiction.[18] In his later statement, however, the commissioner devoted more than half his time to a discussion of the "worst evil of all," the marihuana problem. In the commissioner's words:

> Another urgent reason for the early enactment of the Uniform State Narcotic Act is to be found in the fact that it is *THE ONLY UNIFORM LEGISLATION* yet devised to deal effectively with MARIHUANA. . . .
> There is no Federal law against the production and use of Marihuana in this country. The legal fight against its abuse is largely a problem of state and municipal legislation and law enforcement.
> All public spirited citizens should enlist in the campaign to demand and to get adequate state laws and efficient state enforcement on Marihuana.[19]

In the new strategy Anslinger discarded his previous policy of not officially associating himself or the FBN with the coterie of propagandists on the marihuana issue. Instead, he too tried to popularize the issue through speeches and articles. Indicative of his efforts was "Marihuana: Assassin of Youth," which appeared in the widely circulated *American Magazine* in July 1937.[20] The FBN files contain over fifty letters addressed to the commissioner which say, "your article was the first time I ever heard of marihuana."

In addition to its own attempts to impress the public with the scope of the marihuana menace, the bureau stood ready to assist others in writing about the new evil, whether the intended product was factual reporting or literary fiction. Indeed, in the depression

THE PITIABLE ARMY

Evening Herald and Express, 21 February 1934

era when sensational journalism was a competitive necessity, it was very hard to tell the two apart. One author requested "information . . . as background material for literary fiction which will, in effect, further the fight against the evil. Any facts regarding the narcotic plant marihuana is [sic] especially desired."[21] In response the bureau asserted: "Police officials in cities of those states where it is most widely used estimate that fifty per cent of the violent crimes committed in districts occupied by Mexicans, Spaniards, Latin-Americans, Greeks, or Negroes may be traced to this evil."[22] The FBN supported all efforts, fact or fiction, to arouse public interest in the threat posed by marihuana and its users and to generate support for the otherwise unglamorous Uniform Narcotic Drug Act.

Anslinger's Army

Among the most effective proponents of the Uniform Act was the Hearst newspaper chain. These papers began editorializing in favor of enactment within days after the act was approved by the American Bar Association in October 1932. Dr. Woodward then observed that "the support of the Hearst papers should contribute materially toward procuring enactment of legislation."[23] From then on, the editorial pages of the Hearst newspapers across the country periodically carried declarations of support for the fledgling act. Especially after a combination of hostility and apathy began to bog down the bureau's efforts in the legislatures, Hearst frequently published cartoons and editorials to incite public pressure. And the content of Hearst editorials clearly reflects the bureau's decision to emphasize marihuana. This one appeared on 11 September 1935:

> Much of the opposition to the Uniform State Narcotic Law must be imputed to the selfish and often unscrupulous opposition of racketeering interests.
> But more than half the states have not acted favorably and Commissioner Anslinger has announced that an intensified drive will be made at once to bring the rest into line.
> One thing that the indolent legislatures should be made to understand is that the "dope" traffic does not stand still.

In recent years, the insidious and insanity producing marihuana has become among the worst of the narcotic banes,
invading even the school houses of the country, and the Uniform
State Narcotic Law is THE ONLY LEGISLATION yet devised to deal
effectively with this horrid menace.[24]

One indication of the influence of these articles is a 1937
resolution of a narcotics conference of lawyers, judges, and civic
leaders commending William Randolph Hearst and his newspapers
"for pioneering the national fight against dope."[25]

The Hearst chain was not alone. A Birmingham, Alabama, paper
on 22 August 1935 emphasized the need to control marihuana as a
reason for adopting the act.[26] A *Washington Post* columnist in
September 1934 devoted three quarters of a column to marihuana
with quotes from Anslinger and New Orleans' Stanley urging
adoption of the Uniform Act.[27]

Where this newspaper propaganda was heavy, the legislatures
usually became, in time, aware of the so-called marihuana problem.
In Colorado, for example, the Denver *News* and other papers had
been reporting marihuana horror stories since the late twenties.
This newspaper interest and repeated activity on the legislative
front strongly suggest a public antipathy, which continued unabated into the thirties, toward the Mexicans and their weed. On
4 September 1936 the bureau received a letter from the city editor
of the Alamoosa *Daily Courier*, describing an attack by a Mexican-
American, allegedly under the influence of marihuana, on a girl of
his region. It went on to say: "I wish I could show you what a
small marihuana cigaret can do to one of our degenerate Spanish-
speaking residents. That's why our problem is so great; the greatest
percentage of our population is composed of Spanish-speaking
persons, most of whom are low mentally, because of social and
racial conditions."[28] The FBN volunteered its own cooperation at
once in the paper's "educational campaign to describe the weed
and tell of its horrible effects."[29]

Other large-city newspapers such as the Cleveland *Plain Dealer*[30]
and the St. Louis *Star-Times*[31] kept a stream of antimarihuana
propaganda flowing in the period just before the passage of the
Uniform Act in those areas. In Missouri, especially, local concern
generated by the sensational articles in the *Star-Times* speedily

Reaching Over

For months the illicit narcotic traffic has been reaching over into America from its new bases in the Far East.

International control last year had pretty well broken up the old European and Levantine trade centers from which the "dope" racketeers used to obtain their supplies of contraband.

Since then the Manchukuo Opium Monopoly began to exploit the poppy fields of Jehol and Manchuria as the world's chief sources of opium and its habit-forming derivatives.

Beyond the control of the International Opium Committee, the conscienceless traffickers of the Far East are able to flood America and Canada with cheap smuggled morphine.

Smuggling from the Asiatic regions became a problem in our West Coast ports before we were aware of the dangers.

It is a continuing problem which must be met. The Pacific Coast States must do their part by way of local vigilance and Congress must see to it that the Federal Narcotics Bureau is able to function efficiently.

That means the Federal Bureau must have at all times sufficient funds and sufficient personnel to do its essential work.

Atlanta Georgian, 17 March 1934

pushed the legislature to adopt the Uniform Act. Activity by the press, particularly after 1935 when marihuana "became a menace," played a significant role in generating legislative awareness and support for adoption of the Uniform Act in a number of states.

Marihuana made better copy than the Uniform Act, and a marihuana epidemic made better copy than its isolated use. Thus, it is as unreliable to conclude from increased press coverage that the use of marihuana mushroomed around 1935 as it is to assume from newspaper reports that marihuana caused crime. At the same time, it is possible that use did spread *after* the publicity campaigns, especially among the young. Certainly use increased in New York City in the 1930s, judging from the tremendous expansion in coverage by the *New York Times* beginning in 1935, the evidence supplied by the LaGuardia Commission in its 1944 report, and the leap in enforcement activity.

Another influential participant in the FBN's campaign, especially after the repeal of prohibition, was the Women's Christian Temperance Union. Although the WCTU had distributed a pamphlet on marihuana as early as 1927, the *Union Signal* does not reflect any significant interest either in the Uniform Act or marihuana until 1934. Before that year the "narcotic" receiving the most attention was nicotine. Then the *Signal* contained a plea for passage of the Uniform Act each year from 1934 to 1936 in a special section of the paper observing Narcotic Education Week. The editorial content during these years reflects the change in FBN strategy. The theme in 1934 is the Uniform Act's role in promoting more effective law enforcement. Marihuana is mentioned only once. By 1936 the act is promoted as a necessary concomitant to an active campaign against the marihuana menace.

During 1934 and 1935 Elizabeth Bass, the FBN's agent in charge in Chicago, supplied most of the WCTU's information. Beginning in 1936, however, the *Union Signal* had a direct line to the FBN national office, and from then on every issue contained propaganda on the marihuana menace. Surgeon General Cummings' 1929 report was published, as was every report, statement, interview, or letter from Anslinger. The *Signal* continuously editorialized in 1936 and 1937 for adoption of the Uniform Act, with most attention being devoted to marihuana.[32] Under the auspices of the World Narcotic Defense Association, the president of the WCTU,

Ida B. Wise Smith, gave a speech over the CBS radio network urging public support for adoption of the Uniform Act.[33]

A recurrent theme in the WCTU publications is an increase in use, especially among the middle class and among the young. Elizabeth Bass is reported to have stated in 1934 that "dope parties" were becoming common on Chicago's North Side and that "smoking of marijuana is becoming particularly widespread." The *Union Signal* also printed reports from other federal agents:

> Marihuana-smoking at women's bridge parties has become frequent, "the parties usually ending up in wild carousals, sometimes with men joining the orgies."

> The appalling effects on both body and mind seem no hindrance to its increase of consumption, particularly in the states where there is a large Spanish-American population, says a recent news item in the New York Times. In Western and Southwestern states, it is being sold more or less openly in pool halls and beer gardens and, according to some authorities, is being peddled to school children.[34]

On 20 April 1935 the *Signal* reported that the use of "love weeds" was "growing to appalling proportions, especially among young people" many of whom "come from good homes."[35] Almost a year later the *Signal* noted that Elizabeth Bass and local educators and police officials agreed that marihuana use in Chicago high schools was increasing, with the major source of supply being south Chicago's "Mexican colony."[36] Then in October of the following year the *Signal* cited an article appearing in *Hygeia* to the effect that, in 1937, there were 100,000 "marihuana addicts in the United States, the majority of whom were of high school and college age."[37]

The second major theme of the WCTU literature was that the use of marihuana led to use of heroin, opium, and cocaine. Although inconsistent with the contention that marihuana was the "worst" of the drug evils, and contradicted by Commissioner Anslinger in testimony before Congress in 1937,[38] the WCTU continually emphasized this.[39] It is not surprising since their literature often postulated a similar causal relationship between alcohol and the use of narcotics. Others used the same argument; the safety director of Denver had stated in 1931 that "from liquor to marihuana is but a step."[40]

Minneapolis Star, 11 December 1934

The WCTU literature also stressed the relation of marihuana to crime. In February 1936 the *Union Signal* reported that Commissioner Anslinger had estimated that "fifty per cent of the violent crimes committed in districts occupied by Mexicans, Greeks, Turks, Filipinos, Spaniards, Latin Americans, and Negroes may be traced to the use of marihuana."[41] On 19 September of the same year the *Signal* printed an article by Rex Stewart, a Phoenix attorney, which enlarged upon the Stanley thesis in a manner bearing a striking resemblance to the Mexican "you take it three times" folklore: "A man is dangerous after a whiff or two of marihuana. He doesn't need to smoke an entire cigarette. A few sucking puffs are enough to give him the heart of a lion and make him as resilient to punishment as a rubber ball. He will commit any crime if he is mentally so inclined, and he will take chances he would not dare normally."[42]

Ida B. Wise Smith devoted a major portion of her radio address on the Uniform Act to marihuana and most of that to the criminal impulse of marihuana users. "It creates delusions of grandeur and breaks down the will power and makes the addict ready for any crime, even murder."[43]

Still another of the dramatis personae in the propaganda campaign directed by the FBN was the World Narcotic Defense Association. Led by Admiral Richmond P. Hobson, a native Alabamian and veteran of the Spanish-American War, the association included among its supporters many former government leaders. It commanded a position of moral leadership during the narcotics clean-up campaign, and it had urged adoption of a uniform state narcotic act since the early 1920s. Despite its well-intentioned proposal and its respected public image, however, the WNDA had been excluded from the drafting process of the Uniform Narcotic Drug Act. The federal narcotics bureaucracy and the medical establishment, determined to keep the drafting process out of the public eye, were wary of the extremism of most of the association's propaganda against the drug trade. When the association submitted a draft of its own proposed uniform law in 1927 to the surgeon general, internal hygienic laboratory correspondence noted:

The World Narcotic Defense Association is an outgrowth of two other closely related associations, the International Nar-

Washington Herald, 14 December 1934

cotic Education Association and the World Conference on
Narcotics Education, and it is practically under the same management. The [Public Health] Service has had occasion to call
attention before to the propaganda nature of these associations
and the gross exaggerations of the narcotic situation that they
have made in the name of education.[44]

This skepticism was shared by many reputable doctors and governmental officials. As late as 1 July 1932 an influential doctor in the
American Medical Association observed: "There is a rather pernicious group working under the direction of Mr. Hobson on the
adoption of the law which if utilized and passed by the legislatures
will postpone and complicate uniformity later."[45]

The Federal Bureau of Narcotics did not seem quite so concerned about the bad reputation of the WNDA as many of the
others involved in the drafting process. Nevertheless, the bureau
was eager to quash the draft of the uniform act drawn up by the
association because it feared avid legislators might accept that
draft and thereby undermine the efforts of the Conference of
Commissioners on Uniform State Laws. When the time came to
campaign for passage of the Uniform Narcotic Drug Act in the
various state legislatures, however, Commissioner Anslinger was
willing to seek help anywhere it was offered. The bureau was not
above utilizing the tremendous lobbying network and prestige
offered by the World Narcotic Defense Association.

The association was continually in postal contact with almost
every state legislator in the country.[46] Hobson's name constituted
a stamp of moral approval for the operation. Newspapers editorializing in favor of the act continually noted his leadership in the
narcotics field.[47]

The Hobson group was among the well-financed divisions of
Anslinger's army. In addition to underwriting national broadcasts,
such as that by Ida Smith over CBS, the association distributed
widely a lengthy pamphlet on marihuana in 1936. The following
excerpt reflects the kind of exaggeration the FBN had once dis-
claimed but now embraced:

> The narcotic content in Marihuana decreases the rate of heart
> beat and causes irregularity of the pulse. Death may result from
> the effect upon the heart.

Prolonged use of Marihuana frequently develops a delirious rage which sometimes leads to high crimes, such as assault and murder. Hence Marihuana has been called the "killer drug." The habitual use of this narcotic poison always causes a very marked mental deterioration and sometimes produces insanity. Hence Marihuana is frequently called "loco weed" (loco is the Spanish word for crazy).

While the Marihuana habit leads to physical wreckage and mental decay, its effects upon character and morality are even more devastating. The victim frequently undergoes such moral degeneracy that he will lie and steal without scruple; he becomes utterly untrustworthy and often drifts into the underworld where, with his degenerate companions, he commits high crimes and misdemeanors. Marihuana sometimes gives man the lust to kill, unreasonably and without motive. Many cases of assault, rape, robbery, and murder are traced to the use of Marihuana.[48]

The General Federation of Women's Clubs also contributed energetically to the bureau's cause. Support of the national organization was enlisted by Helen Howell Moorehead, head of the Foreign Policy Association and one of the most respected leaders of the international drug control movement. In January 1936 Acting Commissioner Wood sent the president of the federation a list of states which had not yet passed the Uniform Act and a list of states without marihuana legislation. Following current FBN practice, Wood emphasized marihuana, noting the success of the propaganda campaign which had begun late in 1934: "Public opinion generally is being aroused by the steady accumulation of reports showing the evils attendant upon the abuse of marihuana and of atrocities committed by persons under its influence, and this office looks forward to increased state control over the growth and distribution of cannabis, or marihuana."[49]

The federation wasted no time in educating its membership about the need for the Uniform Act and about the evils of marihuana in particular. A lengthy article appeared in *Clubwoman*, the group's magazine.[50] The chairman of the federation's department of legislation noted: "The situation concerning club women particularly is the accessibility of the frightening, degenerating, marihuana weed, which is rolled in cigarettes . . . and has been playing such havoc with young high school boys and girls."[51] The state and local clubs immediately began to write local legislators

Still a Menace

One year ago the Geneva protocol for international control of narcotics became operative.

For the first time in history civilized nations had combined to outlaw and to combat an age-old scourge of mankind.

The event was celebrated this week in New York City by the World Narcotic Defense Association. And important progress was recorded.

In particular, the Turkish Government officially reported its efforts. A State monopoly has been established there to take medicinal narcotics out of the field of private profits and to prevent the smuggling abroad of habit-forming drugs.

Turkey did this at a great financial loss. One of the world's largest poppy-growing countries, with thousands of peasants living from their poppy fields and much national revenue derived therefrom, Turkey is willingly substituting a sugar industry to support its farmers while reducing and controlling the opium production.

Elsewhere, sad to say, Turkey's progressive example is not followed.

Not only China but also Japan's conquered provinces of Manchukuo and Jehol are fostering opium culture and putting out vast quantities of cheap morphine which reaches our West coast.

Erstwhile rum smugglers use the islands of St. Pierre and Miquelon as a center for contraband shipped to our Atlantic cities, and from Central America tons of "dope" in the last year have entered the South.

The narcotic vices are still a menace to this country as to others.

And, at home and abroad, the fight must go on till it is won.

New York American, 1934

and to conduct educational campaigns for parents, teachers, and children.

Narcotics agents worked closely with the Federation of Women's Clubs in an effort to instill the fear of marihuana among the middle-class women of America. To them, the marihuana "menace" was an unfamiliar abstraction which had to be tied to reality. For example, an FBN agent appeared at a New York meeting with two marihuana plants. They were exhibited at a local flower show:

> Marihuana Plant
> exhibit at
> Flower Show
> of Katrina Trask Garden Club
> Tomorrow, 3 P.M. on at the Casino
> This plant is the cause of a dread menace which is
> being fought by the State Department of Health.
> Public Invited to Show . . . 25 cents[52]

Other groups such as the YWCA, the National PTA, and the National Councils of Catholic Men and Women were all in touch with the bureau, and they were made aware of the bureau's dual aims of "influencing and creating public opinion in favor of the passage of the Uniform Narcotic Drug Act, and awaken [sic] the parents of this country to the increasing danger of the use of marihuana. . . ."[53] Typical of Anslinger's approach to such groups, and perhaps of his own thinking, is his letter to the general secretary of the National Catholic Welfare Council:

> The Act has been and is being opposed in some of the legislatures in session this year by certain "groups" who wage their campaigns under cover. These cliques think that their interest may be negatived by passage of this legislation. Many of the legislatures in session this year will not convene again until 1937. It is, therefore, of the greatest importance to concentrate activities in these commonwealths now. There is no more important or far reaching problem affecting health and morals before the world today than that of narcotic drug control.

> Within the past three years there has been an alarming and almost unbelievable spread of the use of Marihuana, known botanically as cannabis. A cigaret is compounded from the dried, flowering pistillate tops of Marihuana or Indian Hemp, and sold illicitly and insidiously by peddlers to adolescent youths, children in high and grammar school grades. This statement is not exaggerated but is unfortunately true, as the Bureau has legal proof of such malpractice.

When an opium or cocaine habitue has been made, it is
extremely difficult to effect a cure, although this has been done
by scientific medical hospitalization. The case of Marihuana
addicts is well nigh hopeless as the Hasheesh or Marihuana
smoker becomes insane. Favorable action must be taken to prevent the spread of this pernicious weed because its evil consequences are irremediable.

In behalf of the intensive campaign which we are waging for
the adoption of the Uniform Narcotic Drug Act in the 35 state
legislatures, I respectfully request the endorsement of the
National Catholic Welfare Councils of Men and Women for this
necessary and vital legislation.[54]

Marihuana: the Campaign and Public Opinion

The FBN wanted to arouse public opinion against marihuana, and
Commissioner Anslinger enlisted an army of public opinion makers
and legislative pressure groups to accomplish this task. How deeply
into the general public consciousness all these efforts spread the
fear of marihuana is a moot point. But what Anslinger really
wanted was enactment of the Uniform Act along with prohibitory
marihuana legislation in all the states. From this point of view the
campaign was a success, and the adoption of the marihuana strategy
in 1935 was the turning point.

Whether or not widespread public interest actually existed,
public opinion makers influenced legislative opinion and created a
"felt need" for legislation. Because there was rarely any substantive
opposition to the legislation, the job was usually not difficult.
When the marihuana strategy was instituted early in 1935, only
ten states had adopted the Uniform Act. And three of these states
had not included marihuana. Within the next year eighteen more
states adopted the act, and each that had no previous legislation
included marihuana. Minnesota, New Hampshire, and Missouri even
enacted special legislation on marihuana without adopting the
Uniform Act. Certainly the precipitating factor in Missouri was the
campaign waged against the drug by the St. Louis *Star-Times*.

The ease with which legislation was passed once the opinion
makers got started is reflected in the Virginia experience. One of
the first states to pass the Uniform Act, in 1934, Virginia did not
include the marihuana provision.[55] A year later, however, rumors

The Jaws of Death

A slinking thing with hellish sting,
  The reptile known as Dope.
Its poison breath is living death
  Beyond the pale of hope,
And in the blight of endless night
  Its countless victims grope.

In stricken homes the reptile roams
  On hearthstones bare and bleak.
Ambition dies in youthful eyes,
  Slain by the noxious reek.
For Dope is strong and prospers long
  Because the laws are weak.
  By George E. Phair.

Atlanta Georgian, 27 February 1935

began to circulate in Roanoke that school children were using the weed. With the assistance of FBN Agent L. C. Rocchiccioli, the commonwealth's attorney of Roanoke secured a local ordinance against the drug.[56] Rocchiccioli then turned his attention to Richmond, hoping to use the Roanoke experience as a wedge to remedy the deficiency in Virginia's narcotics legislation. He quickly succeeded. A bill, prohibiting sale, possession, and cultivation and providing harsher penalties than did the 1934 act, passed both houses unanimously.[57] After the state senate passed the measure on 29 February 1936, the *Richmond Times-Dispatch* noted:

> Among the bills passed by the Senate was the Apperson measure prohibiting the cultivation, sale or distribution of derivatives of the plant cannabis sativa, introduced as an outgrowth of alleged traffic in marihuana cigarettes in Roanoke. It fixes punishment for violation of its provisions at from one to 10 years in the penitentiary, or by confinement in jail for 12 months and a fine of not more than $1,000 or both.
>
> Charges that school children were being induced to become addicts of marihuana cigarettes and that the weed was being cultivated in and near the city on a wide scale were laid before the Roanoke City Council last year. A youth who said he was a former addict of the drug testified before the Council that inhalation of one of the cigarettes would produce a 'cheap drunk' of several days' duration.[58]

In some respects Colorado, Missouri, and Virginia reflect the typical levels of public awareness and legislative reaction on the marihuana "issue." In Colorado, use by Mexicans had been discussed for many years, and the legislature acted three different times on marihuana before adopting the Uniform Act in 1935. In Missouri, a sudden newspaper campaign precipitated legislation in 1935, and then the "issue" quickly receded. In Virginia, a single story from a single city generated state legislation with no public interest. Of course, there is another point on the continuum also— no use, no interest. When New Jersey, Rhode Island, Oregon, and West Virginia passed the Uniform Act in 1934 and 1935, including the cannabis provision, the major newspapers of Newark, Providence, Salem, and Charleston referred to the Uniform Act only once and to marihuana not at all.[59] Typical of both legislative and newspaper concern about the new law is the following *Charleston Daily Mail* comment:

Map 2. Marihuana prohibition. Phase two: The Uniform Narcotic Drug Act, 1933-37

☐ States that passed Phase I legislation.

▨ States that did not pass Phase I legislation

Date in large type indicates year in which state passed Uniform Narcotic Drug Act (* indicates that state included marihuana provision in Uniform Act). Date in small print indicates that state passed separate marihuana prohibition apart from Uniform Act.

A Narcotic Bill

Inconspicuously upon the special calendar of the delegates—rather far down upon it—is Engrossed S.B. No. 230, lodging specific powers in the hands of state authorities for the control of the traffic in narcotics. It has passed the Senate unanimously. It should pass the House, and its only danger of defeat there is the very real one that it will become lost in the shuffle of adjournment now but a few hours away. The bill goes under the name of the Uniform Narcotic Drug Act and it is just that. Identical measures for the control by the states of illicit traffic on drugs have been passed by other states, notably the Southern group. Its passage here would result in a broad territory in which there are corresponding laws. . . .[60]

All in all, neither narcotic drugs in general nor marihuana in particular were major public issues during the thirties. After the bureau initiated the marihuana strategy in late 1934, sufficient

Hand in Hand

Speaking of the narcotic drug addicts of both sexes in the underworld of our large cities, Homer S. Cummings, Attorney-General of the United States says:

"*They come forth from their apprenticeship equipped with the technique of crime and, as gunmen and killers, are the ready instruments of racketeers and gangsters.*

"*Drug exploitation is a recognized factor in robberies and other crimes of* violence and an integral part of the problem of lawlessness.*"

He added:

"*Both personally and as Attorney-General, I am deeply interested in the enactment of the UNIFORM NARCOTIC DRUG LAW . . .*

"*The Federal Government alone cannot reach this menace. UNIFORM LEGISLATION IS VITALLY NECESSARY.*"

Washington Herald, 3 August 1935

attention was aroused among organized moralist groups to incite legislative adoption of the Uniform Act. Interest in marihuana was still regional, although transient interest had now been aroused elsewhere. Viewed nationally, apathy was the norm. In a sense, however, there was nothing to be concerned about. Use was confined and there was no substantive opposition to overcome. Usually if a person had heard of marihuana, he could be counted on to favor prohibition of this grave evil. In one of the few dissents triggered by the FBN's campaign, a Chicago judge, addressing a women's club meeting, tried to place marihuana in perspective: "My own personal opinion is that the 'Home Medicine Chest' (pain killers and sleep producers) as found in homes such as yours is a greater menace than marihuana. One percent to two percent of cases coming through our Court are 'drug' cases, 20% - 25% are alcoholic. Why don't you Clubwomen frown on such a social evil."[61] Such heresy was atypical. Most of the public which had heard at all of marihuana would have concurred in Anslinger's own characterization of the drug in April 1937: "If the hideous monster Frankenstein came face to face with the monster Marihuana, he would drop dead of fright."[62]

CHAPTER VI

The Federal Bureaucracy Finds a Way

APPREHENSIONS about the constitutionality of federal action and the political influence of the pharmaceutical industry deterred the FBN from seeking federal legislation in 1930 and 1931. The bureau chose to concentrate its energies instead on securing adoption of the Uniform Act, including the cannabis provision, by the state legislatures. Even so, however, Commissioner Anslinger had not ruled out federal legislation "at the appropriate time."

The hesitation of the federal policy makers was not motivated either by philosophical objection or scientific uncertainty. For Anslinger and his colleagues, there was no philosophic issue. Criminal legislation was needed simply because "Indian hemp is used in certain sections for improper purposes, that is to say, for non-medical purposes."[1] It is unlikely that Anslinger ever confronted the question begged by such a statement—the role of social policy with respect to the use of drugs for pleasure or other self-defined purposes. It may be, however, that the magnitude of the evils perceived to be associated with such use—addiction, insanity, and death—superseded this issue. But again, it is unlikely that Mr. Anslinger or his colleagues considered the relationship between crime and sin—in this case the role of the criminal law in protecting the individual from his own folly. Criminalization of consumption-related behavior apparently went hand-in-hand with any curtailment of availability. The government's burden of proof in such a case was merely one of coming forward with some evidence, not one of demonstrating the validity of that evidence. Anslinger at no time felt compelled by policy or circumstance to demonstrate the accuracy of his beliefs about marihuana. The commissioner's hesitant attitude about federal action had nothing to do with limited information regarding the effects of the drug.

Commissioner Anslinger's decision to deflect proposals for a federal law was based instead in bureaucratic considerations—in a desire to protect the FBN's jurisdiction under the Harrison Act. His attitude is reflected in his responses to politicians who urged federal action from 1932 through 1934. Opposing a bill (introduced in 1933) of Congressman Fish of New York to amend the Harrison Act, Anslinger, for example, noted that federal action should be deferred until all the states had acted.[2] A memo from Tennyson, from which Anslinger drew his response, also warned of the possible opposition of "one or two pharmaceutical houses."[3] Meanwhile, however, all FBN agents were directed to refer "all complaints concerning marihuana to [Anslinger] with perhaps the possibility in view of effecting some federal laws at some future data."[4]

The Genesis of the Marihuana Tax Act

That "future date" may have come sooner than even Anslinger had hoped or desired. The occasion was the request, in 1935, for a Treasury Department position on a pair of bills, S. 1615 introduced by Senator Hatch of New Mexico and H.R. 6145 introduced by Congressman Dempsey of New Mexico, to prohibit the shipment and transportation of cannabis in interstate or foreign commerce. This legislation had been part of a three-pronged approach which had been suggested by Anslinger in 1930. The FBN nevertheless recommended that the department oppose both bills because: "There is no evidence of an appreciable degree of interstate traffic in or international traffic toward the United States in cannabis for what may be termed improper purposes. . . . At this time I can see no need for the enactment of [this bill]."[5]

This position was stated by Tennyson and Acting Commissioner Wood while Anslinger was participating in international discussions at The Hague. But when the draft response reached Treasury Secretary Morgenthau's office, the bureau was overruled by Assistant Secretary Gibbons, on the advice of Herman Oliphant, the general counsel of the Treasury Department. The Congress was advised officially over Secretary Morgenthau's signature that "the Department interposes no objections to such proposed legislation. . . ."[6] This was on 13 April 1935.

The tide had turned. Although the Hatch and Dempsey bills did not reach the floor, the "appropriate time" for federal legislation was drawing near. The intriguing question is why: what provoked Assistant Secretary Gibbons to overrule a position taken by the agency with primary responsibility, an agency already campaigning with great fervor against the evil with which the bills dealt, and the agency which itself played such a major role in increasing public awareness of this evil? We can only surmise that political pressure was building for federal action because the FBN and its private army had generated a climate of fear in order to secure passage of the Uniform Act—but the bureau had done its job too well. As Gibbons noted sometime later, in October 1936, "steps should be taken legally or otherwise that will definitely control this product, for if we are to believe a small fraction of what is written, it is frighteningly devastating."[7]

Whether or not Anslinger concurred with Gibbons and Oliphant on the desirability of federal legislation, he undoubtedly preferred to wait until he and Tennyson could work out a full statutory scheme which would not endanger the Harrison Act. After Morgenthau's decision, Tennyson had his legal staff studying alternative ways of "securing valid federal control." He and Anslinger perhaps anticipated legislation some time in 1936. For the time being, however, they wanted no congressional tinkering; and, more important, they wanted no agitation from the lobbying public. In May 1935 Tennyson, aware of the attempts by Helen Howell Moorehead to incite congressional interest, noted that "after discussing it with Mrs. Moorehead, she agreed to postpone further agitating this question until the fall."[8]

The bureau had not found a plan by that fall. But in January 1936 Anslinger convened a conference in New York to consider the matter, and the following month, he presented the secretary's office with what he conceived to be the only constitutionally permissible approach—a treaty with Mexico and Canada with supplementary federal legislation to enforce its terms. One may legitimately wonder what such a treaty would have to do with Congress' power to control domestic traffic in marihuana.[9] To answer this we must review the bureau's apprehensions about amending the Harrison Act or using the Harrison Act model with regard to marihuana.

It will be recalled that there were two constitutional problems with "regulating" marihuana by use of the taxing power, which

Congress had used in the Harrison Act to regulate the opiates and cocaine. First, because the drugs covered by the Harrison Act were almost exclusively imported, the constitutional objection that Congress was regulating production, a local activity, was not germane; instead the main constitutional difficulty under the Harrison Act was that Congress was regulating the medical profession. Marihuana, however, was growing widely as a roadside weed or in gardens or fields all over the country; under these circumstances, effective control would require intensive regulation and/or the prohibition of production, either of which would go well beyond the Harrison Act. The taxing power might not suffice as a shield in this case.

Second, legitimate production of marihuana for medical purposes was decreasing, and the cost of controlling illegitimate growth under the Harrison scheme would far exceed the revenue which might be derived. In such an event—a net loss to the government— the court would not be likely to accept Congress' word that it was exercising the taxing power and probably would not close its eyes to Congress' real motive. Of course, a more limited taxing scheme could be devised, as could schemes simply controlling interstate and foreign commercial activity; but these would not substantially affect the marihuana evil, which required tight control over cultivation and possession. For this reason, Anslinger advised Gibbons that "under the taxing power and regulation of interstate commerce, it would be almost hopeless to expect any kind of adequate control."[10]

How would a treaty with Mexico and Canada allow more effective control? The answer lies in the famous "migratory bird case," *Missouri* v. *Holland* (1920).[11] There, Congress had established open and closed seasons for killing certain birds which migrate between the United States and Canada. In so doing, Congress was regulating a clearly "local" activity; but the Supreme Court had held that this was permissible because the statute was passed merely to implement a treaty between the U.S. and Great Britain executed for the purpose of protecting these birds from extermination. The Court held that as long as legislation is "necessary and proper" for carrying out a valid treaty, Congress could go beyond its usual powers to regulate matters ordinarily reserved to the states.

Cleveland Press, 13 November 1936

Under the FBN's scheme, the United States and its two immediate neighbors would enter into a treaty for the purpose of eliminating traffic in marihuana among the three countries. Each would agree to undertake appropriate steps to serve that objective. Then Congress could pass a statute strictly controlling or prohibiting the domestic cultivation of marihuana.

This scheme seemed sound to Oliphant, the Treasury Department general counsel, and to Assistant Secretary Gibbons; in March 1936 they gave their approval.[12] Representatives from the three governments began to meet, and Canada soon expressed its "entire sympathy" with the proposal. As might be expected, however, Mexico was highly uncertain whether it could effectively carry out the terms of the treaty, and it did not respond so readily.

Six months later Assistant Secretary Gibbons grew tired of the delay. After being advised by the dean of the University of Texas Medical School that "he could absolutely prove that marihuana is a habit-forming narcotic," Gibbons fired a memorandum to Oliphant asking him to find a way to control this "frighteningly devastating" product. He said, moreover, that he simply did not understand the objection to bringing marihuana within the purview of the Harrison Act.[13]

Oliphant, well aware that Gibbons' urgency was aroused by the "rather considerable publicity which the marihuana problem has received," responded that the bureau did have legitimate objections to the amendment of the Harrison Act, that the treaty idea was promising, and that a reply from the Mexican government was expected imminently. He concluded that "we are making real progress toward the achievement of Federal control over a problem which I, like yourself, regard as a major evil."[14]

However, it soon became apparent that Mexico was unwilling to shoulder the domestic hardships which would be required in order to enforce the treaty's terms. Further, the State Department rejected Anslinger's request that the United States participate in a 1936 Geneva Conference only on the condition that any resulting convention require domestic cannabis control. This was in June.[15] It became clear that a federal antimarihuana law would not rest on the treaty power.

But there was no turning back. By the fall of 1936 Oliphant had decided to employ the taxing power, but in a statute modeled after the National Firearms Act and wholly unrelated to the Harrison Act. Oliphant himself was in charge of preparing the bill. Anslinger directed his army to turn its campaign toward Washington.[16]

The Treasury Department did not publicize the fact that it was preparing a bill.[17] Since Congress was also unaware of Treasury's activity, antimarihuana legislation was introduced in both houses at the opening of the first session of the Seventy-fifth Congress in January 1937. The Hatch Bill to prohibit the shipment and transportation of cannabis in interstate and foreign commerce was reintroduced in the Senate, and the Fish Bill to prohibit importation was resubmitted in the House.[18] Later in the session, Congressman Hennings of Missouri introduced another bill that was probably well beyond congressional power at that time. His bill would have prohibited sale, possession, and transportation of cannabis except in compliance with regulations to be made by the commissioner of narcotics.[19]

On 14 April the Treasury Department, having resisted for seven years, finally unveiled the "administration proposal," H.R. 6385, to stamp out marihuana.[20] H.R. 6385 was a tax measure and therefore it ran the risk of invalidation on the two grounds discussed above—intensive control of domestic growth and failure to produce revenue through legitimate enterprises. By employing a separate measure, however, the Treasury Department hoped to avoid contamination of the Harrison Act. The scheme provided in H.R. 6385 was threefold: a requirement that all manufacturers, importers, dealers, and practitioners register and pay a special occupational tax; a requirement that all transactions be accomplished through use of written order forms; and, the imposition of a tax on all transfers in the amount of $1/ounce for transfer to registered persons and a prohibitive $100/ounce for transfer to unregistered persons.

The key departure of the marihuana tax scheme from that of the Harrison Act is the notion of the prohibitive tax. Under the Harrison Act a nonmedical user could not legitimately buy or possess narcotics. To the dissenters in the Supreme Court decisions upholding the act, this clearly demonstrated that Congress' motive was to prohibit conduct rather than to raise revenue. So in the National Firearms Act, designed to prohibit traffic in machine guns, Congress "permitted" anyone to buy a machine gun but

The Devil's Roost

Congressman Hamilton Fish, in a Narcotics Education Week address, declared that eighty per cent of narcotic addicts **BECOME CRIMINALS.**

He said further that thirty-two per cent of the inmates of Federal penal institutions are either addicts or traffickers in **DOPE.**

Nothing could more sharply expose the **DOPE HABIT** as a one-way ticket to a life of crime.

Dope fills prisons, asylums, hospitals and **GRAVES.**

Dope also fills the pockets of dealers, smugglers and peddlers **WITH PROFITS.**

It is the **TRAFFIC** in dope that is the heart of the evil.

The miserable wretches who have already wrecked their lives **may be** beyond hope.

But the criminals who **PREY UPON HUMAN MISERY** are not beyond the penalty of laws properly enacted and properly enforced.

These **MERCHANTS OF MISERY** belong behind prison bars.

America can reduce crime and poverty, and prevent the destruction of thousands of men and women by PUTTING required him to pay a $200 transfer tax and to carry out the purchase on an order form. The Firearms Act, passed in June 1934, was the first act to hide Congress' motives behind a "prohibitive" tax. When the Court of Appeals for the Seventh Circuit upheld the act on 9 November 1936,[21] the stage was set for a Supreme Court test of this technique. The high Court agreed to hear the case on 15 February, it was argued on 12 March, and the Court unanimously upheld the antimachine gun law on 29 March.[22] Oliphant had undoubtedly been awaiting the Court's decision, and the Treasury Department introduced its marihuana tax bill two weeks later, on 14 April 1937.

It is important to understand that these legal intricacies were the essence of the marihuana "issue." There was a recognized need for the federal government to take action forbidden to it under prevailing constitutional doctrine. The legal reality of the marihuana issue was of significantly more interest to the bureaucracy and to the Congress than the scientific and social realities of marihuana use.

H.R. 6385 was introduced in April. In less than four months the Marihuana Tax Act would become law. For the first time since the drafting process of the Uniform Act, the bureau would be called upon to justify its concern about marihuana. Before analyzing the legislative process, it might be wise at this point to examine what the bureau actually knew, thought it knew, or had reason to know about marihuana.

CHAPTER VII

What Was the Marihuana Menace?

MARIHUANA was condemned without a trial. The decision makers did not insist on accurate information, and the policy-making process reflects only the trappings of science. The assumptions that marihuana caused addiction, insanity, and crime were not without serious attack even then; yet the federal narcotics bureaucracy made no serious effort before the decision to seek federal legislation to find out what the drug's effects really were.

The proponents of H.R. 6385 expressed no uncertainty in their public characterizations of marihuana's effects. Yet a collection of world authorities on the cannabis drugs observed in June 1937 that "as to the effects of abuse of cannabis, [available information] still leaves much to be desired."[1] And immediately after the passage of the Marihuana Tax Act, the bureau convened a conference for the purpose of determining the effects of the drug.[2] Even now, thirty years later, alteration of the legal status of marihuana is being resisted on the ground that "we don't know enough" about the effects of the drug. It is, then, reasonable to inquire what the policy makers thought they knew about marihuana during the criminalization period.

Although the British and the French had sponsored a number of investigations and a fair amount of research regarding the psychological, social, and moral effects of cannabis use in India and Africa in the late nineteenth century, it does not appear that these studies were consulted prior to the formulation of T.D. 35719 in 1915. Nor does it appear that any review of the world literature (or even of the English-language literature) preceded the drafting of Surgeon General Cummings' report in 1929.

The Surgeon General's Cursory Report

The *Preliminary Report on Indian Hemp and Peyote*, issued by Surgeon General Cummings in 1929, was the first official statement by the scientific establishment of the United States government on the effects of marihuana. However, by almost any standard more rigorous than that applicable to popular journals, the report is woefully inadequate.

First, an account of the three-phase theory of acute intoxication (exhilaration, delirium, and depression) was drawn from pharmacology texts:

> It produces first, an exaltation with a more or less feeling of well being; a happy jovial mood, usually an increased feeling of physical strength and power; and a general euphoria and variable aphrodisiac is experienced. Accompanying this exaltation is a stimulation of the imagination followed by a more or less delirious state characterized by vivid kaleidoscopic visions, sometimes of a pleasing sensual kind, but occasionally of a gruesome nature. Accompanying this delirious state is a remarkable loss in spatial and time relations. . . . While the delirium is one of degree it gradually merges, if the dose is sufficient, into a state of general motor weakness, fatigue, drowsiness and sleep.

Regarding the effects of habitual use, the report is well hedged; by drawing on popular myth, however, it implicitly implicates the drug. With respect to crime, Cummings noted that "those who are habitually accustomed to the use of the drug are said to develop a delirious rage after its administration during which they are temporarily, at least, irresponsible and liable to commit violent crimes." This proposition is supported only by: "It is sometimes alleged that the murderous frenzy of the Malay, characterized as running 'amok,' is the result of the habitual use of hashish. It is also said that the Mohammadan leaders, opposing the Crusades, utilized the services of individuals addicted to the use of hashish for secret murders. The frenzy produced by the drug led to these persons being called 'haschischin,' 'hashshash' or 'hashishi' from which the modern word 'assassin' is derived."

Regarding the drug's dependence liability, the report reflected the ambiguity which then surrounded the notion of addiction, finding essentially that the drug was habituating although not addicting (or, in current terminology, that it causes psychological but not physiological dependence):

Effects of Habitual Use.

While the effects of the drug are definitely narcotic in nature it is habitually taken for the stimulating effects obtained and the individual satisfaction experienced through the temporary inflation of the personality. No evidence exists that the drug is accumulative in its effect or that a tolerance may be developed through its continued use. . . . The sudden discontinuance of its use . . . does not give rise to any "withdrawal" symptoms such as is seen in opium addiction.

Finally, the report stated that "the prolonged use of this narcotic is said to produce mental deterioration." In short, the surgeon general found that marihuana is a narcotic and its use is addictive, although the physiological attributes of addiction are absent. It may, he felt, cause violent crime and it may cause mental deterioration.[3]

It appears that the Public Health Service had conducted only minimal inquiry in the preparation of this report. The surgeon general had contacted the Federal Department of Health of the Republic of Mexico requesting information regarding, among other things, the number of persons "addicted to marihuana, especially in those regions adjacent to the United States." On-site visits were made to New Orleans and to other southern cities.

In outlook and effect, the Cummings Report is not startling. Since Western medical literature had analyzed the acute effects of the drug for purposes of therapeutic application, this presentation is straightforward. But Western public health investigations had generally not had any reason to study the individual and social impact of repeated use; so this presentation is hedged and heavily laced with unverified representations of the Eastern experience. The approach is not unlike that of contemporary pharmacology texts. The Solis-Cohen and Githens *Pharmaco-Therapeutics* had, for example, commented in 1928:

In certain eastern people . . . perhaps because of continued use, the somnolent action is replaced by complete loss of judgment and restraint such as is seen more often from alcohol. An Arab leader, fighting against the crusaders, had a bodyguard who partook of haschisch, and used to rush madly on their enemies, slaying everyone they met. The name of "haschischin" applied to them has survived as "assassin." The habitual use of cannabis does not lead to much tolerance, nor do abstinence symptoms follow its withdrawal. It causes, however, a loss of mentality, resembling dementia, which can be recognized even in dogs.[4]

What is surprising about the *Preliminary Report* is that it made no reference at all to either of the English-language, government-sponsored studies of cannabis "abuse" then in existence: the multi-volume report of the Indian Hemp Drugs Commission, which studied cannabis use among the native population in India in 1893-94; and the Panama Canal Zone Report of 1925, which studied marihuana use among American soldiers stationed in the Zone. Both of these investigations are inadequate by today's methodological standards; but since they represented the only first-hand research relating to the hypotheses so blandly supported in the *Preliminary Report*, their omission is startling.

The Indian Hemp Drugs Commission Report

The Public Health Service investigators participating in the drafting of the Cummings Report were probably aware of the Indian report since it had been cited in the Canal Zone study and in numerous English-language medical journals. Yet the surgeon general failed to distinguish between moderate use of the drug on the one hand and its excessive use on the other. That the consequences of cannabis' use to the individual as well as to the society differ significantly according to frequency and intensity of use has been a common thread of all recent government reports and was pivotal to the conclusion of the Indian Hemp Commission report as well. The commission summarized its conclusions as follows:

> In regard to the physical effects, the Commission have come to the conclusion that the moderate use of hemp drugs is practically attended by no evil results at all. There may be exceptional cases in which, owing to idiosyncracies of constitution, the drugs in even moderate use may be injurious. There is probably nothing the use of which may not possibly be injurious in cases of exceptional intolerance. . . . Speaking generally, the Commission are of opinion that the moderate use of hemp drugs appears to cause no appreciable physical injury of any kind. The excessive use does cause injury. As in the case of other intoxicants, excessive use tends to weaken the constitution and to render the consumer more susceptible to disease. . . .
> In respect to the alleged mental effects of the drugs, the Commission have come to the conclusion that the moderate use

of hemp drugs produces no injurious effects on the mind. It may indeed be accepted that in the case of specially marked neurotic diathesis, even the moderate use may produce mental injury. For the slightest mental stimulation or excitement may have that effect in such cases. But putting aside these quite exceptional cases, the moderate use of these drugs produces no mental injury. It is otherwise with the excessive use. Excessive use indicates and intensifies mental instability. It tends to weaken the mind. It may even lead to insanity. It has been said by Dr. Blanford that "two factors only are necessary for the causation of insanity, which are complementary, heredity, and stress. Both enter into every case: the stronger the influence of one factor, the less of the other factor is requisite to produce a certain instability of nerve tissue and the incidence of a certain disturbance." It appears that the excessive use of hemp drugs may, especially in cases where there is any weakness or hereditary predisposition, induce insanity. It has been shown that the effect of hemp drugs in this respect has hitherto been greatly exaggerated, but that they do sometimes produce insanity seems beyond question.

In regard to the moral effects of the drugs, the Commission are of opinion that their moderate use produces no moral injury whatever. There is no adequate ground for believing that it injuriously affects the character of the consumer. Excessive consumption, on the other hand, both indicates and intensifies moral weakness or depravity. Manifest excess leads directly to loss of self-respect, and thus to moral degradation. In respect to his relations with society, however, even the excessive consumer of hemp drugs is ordinarily inoffensive. His excesses may indeed bring him to degraded poverty which may lead him to dishonest practices; and occasionally, but apparently very rarely indeed, excessive indulgence in hemp drugs may lead to violent crime. But for all practical purposes it may be laid down that there is little or no connection between the use of hemp drugs and crime.

Viewing the subject generally, it may be added that the moderate use of these drugs is the rule, and that the excessive use is comparatively exceptional. The moderate use practically produces no ill effects. In all but the most exceptional cases, the injury from habitual moderate use is not appreciable. The excessive use may certainly be accepted as very injurious, though it must be admitted that in many excessive consumers the injury is not clearly marked. The injury done by the excessive use is, however, confined almost exclusively to the consumer himself; the effect on society is rarely appreciable. It has been the most striking feature in this inquiry to find how little the effects of hemp drugs have obtruded themselves on observation. The large number of witnesses of all classes who professed never to have seen these effects, the vague statements made by many who professed to have observed them, the very few witnesses who could so recall a case as to give any definite account of it, and the manner in which a large proportion of these cases broke down on the first attempt to examine them, are facts which combine to show most clearly how little injury society has hitherto sustained from hemp drugs.[5]

The Canal Zone Study

Beginning about 1916 and becoming noticeable by 1922, cannabis-smoking became a relatively common diversion among the lower enlisted ranks of the United States Army stationed at various locations in the Panama Canal Zone. Although it is not clear whether the practice was common among native Panamanians, the chief of police of the Canal Zone observed in 1925 that "the plant, by its local names, is well known on the Isthmus and in the various West Indian Islands."[6] This view is supported by the fact that the Republic of Panama prohibited the "cultivation, use and consumption of the herb Kan-Jac" as part of its act prohibiting the distribution and use of opiates and cocaine without a prescription on 3 April 1923.[7]

In any event, use of the drug by army personnel was viewed with some alarm as a threat to military discipline, and in 1923 the commanding general of the Panama Canal Zone Department issued the following order: "Except in the proper discharge of military duty, no Army member of this command will have in his possession or under his control marihuana. . . ." Violation of this regulation was punishable by dishonorable discharge, total forfeitures, and confinement at hard labor for one year.[8]

It appears that the army did not succeed in eliminating a practice that was adopted by succeeding troop arrivals. Difficulties in gathering sufficient proof to convict known marihuana "addicts" resulted in only twenty-seven general courts martial during the period between issuance of the order and 11 December 1925. Administrative discharges, based only on suspicion, were apparently more common. In any event, the army sought to improve the situation by requesting Governor M. L. Walker of the Canal Zone to prohibit the cultivation, sale, and use of marihuana throughout the entire Canal Zone.

In response to this request, the governor, on 1 April 1925, appointed a committee to investigate use of the drug and make appropriate recommendations. Sitting on the committee were its chairman, Colonel W. P. Chamberlain, chief health officer of the Canal Zone, F. E. Mitchell, the district attorney, C. H. Calhoun, chief of the Civil Affairs Division, and Guy Johannes, chief of police. Sitting in an advisory capacity were representatives from the army and navy, and playing active investigatory roles were Dr. A. E. Hesner, the superintendent of the Corozal Hospital for the Insane, and Dr. Lewis Bates, chief of the Board of Health Laboratory.

In marked contrast to the cavalier, uninquiring attitude of the Public Health Service manifested in Cummings' 1929 report, the Canal Zone committee took its job seriously. From the beginning, each of the four members was skeptical that the drug produced the dire consequences that had been attributed to it and insisted that the deleterious effects—violence, insanity, and addiction—be demonstrated affirmatively before prohibitory action would be taken. The day after the committee was appointed, Chief Johannes observed that "there is in various texts and reference books very little information as to the drug effect of the plant. It would appear that there has been very little research. . . ."[9] And Colonel Chamberlain advised the governor that "there is very little information on the subject."[10]

For its prohibitory approach, the military relied primarily on anecdotal testimony of various officers regarding the effects of marihuana use on their enlisted men. For medical support, it appears that the military authorities were relying on Dr. Hesner whose clinical responsibilities, both on the Isthmus and in the United States, placed him in the best position to observe adverse effects on the personality. As has been true whenever marihuana's effects are discussed, persons with the clinical perspective have tended to be more suspicious of the drug than their colleagues. In Dr. Hesner's case this was true; yet he was unable to corroborate the military view from his experience in dealing with the very patients to whom they referred.

To aid the committee's deliberations, Dr. Hesner solicited information from the American consulate general in India, who summarized the Indian Hemp Commission's report; from Dr. M. V. Ball of Warren, Pennsylvania, who was probably one of the country's foremost experts on the subject and to whom we will return in this chapter; and from The H. K. Mulford Company, biological chemists from Philadelphia, the AMA, Parke-Davis, and the attorney general of California.

To supplement the first-hand testimony and the literature review, the committee also sponsored a controlled laboratory experiment on the acute effects of the drug. Dr. Bates conducted three separate "physiological tests of locally grown marihuana" with six, four, and five subjects.[11] By today's standards, the experiment may be regarded as primitive; but this should not cloud the fact that the research was undertaken at all. (Original investigations were not conducted by the surgeon general in 1929, by the Congress in 1937, or by any state in the years between.) Dr. Bates, it should be noted, was aware of the limitations of his experiment: "One question which has been raised and which the Board [of Health] has not investigated and does not find itself in a position to investigate is as to whether the use of marihuana by a considerable proportion of a command over a prolonged period of time has a tendency to lower the moral tone of that command or the efficiency of the soldiers individually."[12]

Having gathered these data, the committee, on 18 December 1925, issued its report (in which the military advisors concurred) to the governor, recommending "that no steps be taken by the Canal Zone authorities to prevent the sale or use of marihuana."[13] The committee determined further that "there is no evidence that marihuana, as grown and used [in the Canal Zone] is a 'habit-forming' drug in the sense in which the term is applied to alcohol, opium, cocaine, etc., or that it has any appreciably deleterious influence on the individuals using it."[14] The committee cited the following findings to support its conclusion:

> The influence of the drug when used for smoking is uncertain and has apparently been greatly exaggerated. Most of the reports appear to have little basis in fact. There is no medical evidence that it causes insanity.

The British commission which investigated the effects of Cannabis indica in India came to the conclusion that it was not a habit forming drug, particularly among Anglo-Saxons, and that most of the effects attributed to it were due to other substances (opium, datura, stramonium, hyocyamus, cantharides, etc.) added to the preparations which were used.

The plants vary in potency, some being almost devoid of the active principle. Certain individuals appear much more suscepti-ble to the drug than others.

Tests with locally grown plants have been carried out by your Committee and have shown no effects which would appear to indicate that a habit was likely to be formed. These experiments have not produced any of the symptoms popularly attributed to the drug. Neither pleasurable sensations nor any acts of vio-lence were observed.

The Health Department of the Panama Canal and the Police Department of the Panama Canal have no knowledge of any ill effects from the use of the drug in the Canal Zone.

The Navy officials on the Isthmus have no records of the use of the drug by its personnel or of any ill effects attributable to it.

The Medical Department of the Army on the Isthmus has no records of any sickness attributable to the use of marihuana.

Two soldiers were treated in Corozal Hospital for mental symptoms which were considered by the Superintendent to be due to marihuana, but the evidence is by no means conclusive that the symptoms in question were due to that drug.

The Judge Advocate of the Panama Canal Department states that twenty-seven soldiers have been tried by general courts martial during the last three years *for having marihuana in their possession*. In seven of these cases the Judge Advocate considers there is evidence in the trial record that there was insubordi-nation or violence, and it is his opinion that the insubordination or violence was due to the use of marihuana. These seven cases represent only one per cent of the total number of cases tried by general courts martial during the last three years.[15]

Why did the Cummings Report not take into account the findings of these reports? Why was it so inadequate measured even by the inadequate data then available? The truth of the matter is that Cummings was under no pressure to be thorough. The use of the drug was regionally and ethnically confined, and there was no constituency interested in a comprehensive medical evaluation. It was easier to conduct a cursory "investigation" and say that cor-roboration existed for prevalent assumptions without committing oneself one way or the other.

Cummings' sketchy *Preliminary Report* was never followed by a more comprehensive report. The surgeon general's staff, which had not been interested from the beginning, apparently dropped the whole subject when Anslinger decided in 1930 not to seek federal legislation. Although Dr. Lawrence Kolb of the Division of Mental Hygiene continued casual inquiry into the subject during the early thirties, the federal narcotics bureaucracy never made any serious attempt to determine the effects of the drug. As we have seen, one researcher was told in May 1930 that the government already knew all about the drug's physiological, toxic, and pharmacologic properties.

The FBN, on the other hand, continued to compile systematic reports from law enforcement personnel in anticipation of eventual federal legislation. These data came from two sources: first, case studies compiled by law enforcement officials allegedly linking marihuana use and violent crime; and second, information gathered by participants in the inquiries of the subcommittee on cannabis of the League of Nations Advisory Committee on Traffic in Opium and Other Dangerous Drugs, on which Anslinger sat.

The net effect of Cummings' report and the Public Health Service's disinterest in marihuana was that the field of official activity with respect to the drug was abandoned to the FBN—a law enforcement agency. In this way the FBN, which, unlike its medical counterpart had developed an interest in the subject, became the federal spokesman on its scientific aspects as well. In this respect, its path was eased by the failure of the Cummings Report to question the assumptions about the drug which then prevailed within the opinion-making institutions: that the drug was addictive, caused deterioration and insanity, and stimulated crime. In the remainder of this chapter we will try to describe the state of knowledge on these assumptions on the eve of the Hearings on H.R. 6385.

Addiction

We have noted that medical expertise was not sought in connection with many of the initial legislative prohibitions of marihuana. However, whenever medical assistance was solicited in the course of the decision-making process during the twenties, the primary issue was generally whether or not marihuana was a "habit-forming drug." The nation's tardy discoveries of the dependence liability of morphine and later of heroin emphasized this factor in legislative determinations and induced a fear that every drug was habit-forming.

During the AMA's preparation of a Uniform Act in the early twenties and the drafting of the 1927 New York legislation, the decision to include cannabis hinged heavily on this factor. Rumor, 1905 vintage, had it that "the smoking of marihuana is a seductive habit. It grows upon a person more quickly and securely than the use of opium or cocaine."[16] But Dr. M. V. Ball, who was engaged in the AMA drafting process, traveled to the Border area in 1922 to verify the tales of its effects and concluded that "there is no evidence worthy of belief that marihuana is a habit-forming weed or drug."[17] After further study in 1925 he objected strenuously to the tendency of policy makers to accept uncritically fanciful characterizations of the drug's effects and to minimize its utility as a therapeutic agent: "There is no proof that cannabis indica extract by itself taken internally or even smoked, causes a habit, and to continue to list it with such habit-forming drugs as morphine, chloral, alcohol, greatly detracts [from] whatever value it might have as a sedative."[18]

The 1929 Narcotic Farm Act had classified marihuana as a "habit-forming narcotic drug." Cummings' *Preliminary Report* denied the existence of the tolerance and withdrawal symptoms associated with opiate addiction, finding instead that the habitual marihuana user became dependent on "the stimulating effects obtained and the individual satisfaction experienced. . . ." The nature of this dependence was not explored; Cummings was apparently postulating something more than habituation, as to tea or candy, for example, but something less than the craving associated with the opiates.

After issuance of the 1925 Canal Zone report, which disputed this thesis and agreed with Dr. Ball, the matter remained under "continuing study" within the Zone's Health Department. Accordingly, Dr. J. F. Siler, Dr. Chamberlain's successor as chief health officer on the Isthmus, wrote the director of the National Institutes of Health in March 1931, asking once again whether marihuana was a "habit-forming drug." A Canal Zone committee to reinvestigate the issue was convened in 1932 and Siler directed its investigations. On the basis of a study of thirty-four soldier-users, he discovered that only 15 percent missed marihuana when deprived of it, and 71 percent stated that they preferred tobacco.[19] This report of the reinvestigation committee in October 1932 was forwarded by Siler to Assistant Surgeon General Treadway. Two months later the secretary of war officially forwarded the report to the secretary of the treasury, stating that the report would remain confidential and would not be made public unless mari-huana-smoking by soldiers in the Canal Zone became of interest to the press.

In 1934 Dr. Walter Bromberg, senior psychiatrist at Bellevue Hospital, distinguished between opiate addiction and "addiction" to marihuana in the same way as did Cummings' 1929 report. Having examined 2,276 felons, he found no tolerance, no physical compulsion, no withdrawal. Instead, the marihuana "user wants to recapture over and over again the ecstatic, elated state into which the drug lifts him. . . .The addiction to cannabis is a sensual ad-diction: it is in the services of the hedonistic elements of the personality."[20]

The notion of marihuana addiction, then, bottomed on the assumption that the drug experience was so pleasurable that the user would grow dependent on it. It is possible that the medical authorities formed this opinion on the basis of the many fantastic accounts describing acute cannabis intoxication appearing in the pharmacology texts as well as in romantic literature. The following, for example, appeared in the AMA *Journal* in 1925:

> The imagination is more untrammeled than in any other form of intoxication, and the intoxicated person, even in the wildest flight of ideas and the most exuberant hallucinations, retains a remnant of reality; he has a dim idea that he is only in a pleasant dream state, and can give more or less sensible answers when addressed. The action generally begins with a feeling of warmth and heaviness in the head, sounds as of rushing water, and a motley of color hallucinations of incomparable beauty. Later on, the ground seems to disappear beneath the feet; there is a feeling of being snatched away from this world; the body, freed from all weight, floats through space in a condition of the greatest physical and psychic well-being, and in alluring dreams, which

for a short time transport Orientals to a paradise endowed with Mohammedan ideals. Sometimes the dreams are of a rapidly changing nature in which tears alternate with laughter, occasionally only of a sad or terrifying character, thus engendering deep depression or giving rise to a desire for destruction and fits of mania. The feeling of pain is lessened, and the sense of touch blunted. The intoxication gradually deepens; there are periods of unconsciousness, and, in conclusion, a deep sleep ensues, from which the subject awakes feeling perfectly well.[21]

In the scientific community, then, the prevalent notion of marihuana "addiction" combined an exaggerated understanding of the acute intoxication with a moralistic opposition to pleasure-seeking. Of course, this ambiguous concept of psychological dependence was not the image claimed by the legislators and general public. Instead, the craving of the marihuana "fiend" was popularly considered either equal to or greater than that of any other "dope fiend."

In some respects the medical experts were playing a semantic game. The use of the term "addiction" was essential for those who, for policy reasons, felt compelled to generalize about the threat posed by the drug itself. This was particularly true in the United States, which had no social history of cannabis use from which to develop a perspective. For public policy reasons, there was a strong need to indict the drug and refer to all users as marihuana "addicts." For some the presence of psychological dependence was enough. Others supplemented this with notions of physical dependence which had very little scientific basis, except perhaps for the heaviest of chronic users. To this approach should be compared the calmer, but no less hard-line, attitude of Dr. J. Bouquet, inspector of pharmacies of Tunis. Judging from the FBN files during this period, a report submitted by Dr. Bouquet to the Cannabis Subcommittee of the League of Nations Advisory Committee on Traffic in Opium and Other Dangerous Drugs on 17 February 1937 played a major supporting role in chrystallizing Commissioner Anslinger's thinking and in providing expert information otherwise lacking in the United States.

Dr. Bouquet did not hesitate to admit that "the addiction engendered by hemp in its various forms is undoubtedly less serious than that produced by chemical narcotics." But he recognized "a form of addiction" with identifiable social causes and adverse social consequences. The essence of the matter is that one becomes addicted if one wants to become addicted, and this depends on the person:

> Only part of the Moslem population of North Africa is given to the regular consumption of hemp to an extent which can be regarded as amounting to drug addiction.
>
> *Hashaishiya* (singular: *Hashaish*) or *Tkarriya* (singular: *Tkarri* or *Tkarli*) are, with rare exceptions, found neither among the nomadic Arabs (tent-dwellers) of the steppes and sub-Saharan region, nor among middle-class dwellers in towns. They are found rather among the sedentary inhabitants of the Southern Oases and among the poorer classes in urban communities: artisans, small traders, workmen, etc. The petty criminal classes, moreover, are ardent devotees of hashish, a fact which has doubtless contributed in great measure to their removal from the ranks of the law-abiding community.
>
> The countryside is far less affected by cannabis addiction than towns and villages: tea addiction is there the most widespread evil. . . .
>
> The basis of the Moslem character is indolence; these people love idleness and day-dreaming, and to the majority of them work is the most unpleasant of all necessities. Inordinately vainglorious, thirsting for every pleasure, they are manifestly unable to realize more than a small fraction of their desires: their unrestrained imagination supplies the rest. Hemp, which enhances and stimulates the power of imagination, is the narcotic best adapted to their mentality. The hashish addict can dream the life he longs for: under the influence of the drug he becomes wealthy, the owner of a well-filled harem, of delightful cool gardens, of a board richly supplied with exquisite and copious viands; his every longing is satisfied, happiness is his! When the period of intoxication is over and he is again faced with drab realities of his normal shabby life, his one desire is to find a corner where he may sleep until a new orgy of hemp brings him back to the realm of illusions.[22]

Although Eastern studies suggested the possibility of slight withdrawal symptoms and the development of a tolerance for chronic users of heavy doses of hashish, the prevailing view within the Western scientific community in 1937 was that physical dependence was not characteristic of cannabis use, certainly not of the less potent mixture of the drug, marihuana. Nevertheless, a compelling, but perhaps unrecognized, public policy need to postulate a form of addiction generated an ambiguous notion of "mental fascination" which was thought to be "particularly compelling" for certain individuals or social classes.[23] This notion was not well understood, but if one substitutes "Mexican" for "Moslem" in Bouquet's explanation of addiction, the basis for the American concept is probably revealed. It was stated quite forthrightly by some and implicitly by others. The key point, however, is that the subtleties of scientific understanding were not communicated to the public. While most hard-line scientists viewed "addiction" as the "least serious aspect of the problem,"[24] the public, in fact, was told that marihuana was the "most alarming" of the "habit-form-ing drugs."

Insanity

On the basis of reports from Egypt and India compiled in the late nineteenth and early twentieth centuries, it was long a common-place assertion that chronic cannabis use ultimately resulted in organic deterioration, psychosis, and insanity. After 1870 it was generally reported that between 30 and 50 percent of the admissions to Indian asylums was due exclusively to the effects of hemp drugs.[25] In 1930 Dhunjibhoy concluded that of the toxic psychoses, hemp was first and alcohol second in degree of incidence.[26] It was stated in 1897 that "in a considerable number of cases in Egypt, hasheesh is the chief if not the only cause of mental disease, although it is doubtful whether hashish insanity can be diagnosed by its clinical characters alone."[27] Testimony before the 1924-25 Geneva Conference subcommittee contained many reports attribu-ting insanity among Egyptians to hashish.

In the international discussions, the causal relation between cannabis use and psychosis was generally assumed on the basis of Egyptian and Indian data. As late as 1937 the chairman of the League of Nations Cannabis Subcommittee "reminded his col-leagues that there was little definite information on [cannabis' effects] apart from the fact that such abuse was known to lead to homicidal mania and insanity."[28]

As Western scientists began to consider the phenomenon in the 1930s, however, doubt was cast on these assumptions. A repre-

sentative of the secretariat of the League of Nations submitted a
report to the Cannabis Subcommittee in 1937:

> The state of acute intoxication normally induced by Indian
> Hemp may, as the result of habitual abuse, particularly in the
> cases of persons predisposed, develop into a genuine and clearly-
> defined state of insanity of longer or shorter duration.
> There are no means of estimating the number of such cases of
> insanity, since even in the most detailed statistics of disease, such
> cases are included in a large group of exogenous psychoses or
> psychoses due to intoxication. It is true that some directors of
> lunatic asylums in Egypt and British India have estimated the
> number of psychoses due to the abuse of hashish at 15% or even
> 30% of all the cases admitted in the course of a year, but it is
> generally held by the experts of Western countries that this per-
> centage must be exaggerated, and that many cases of schizo-
> phrenia are dissimulated under the erroneous diagnosis of toxic
> insanity.[29]

And Dr. Robert Walton, one of the leading antimarihuana
crusaders within the scientific establishment, noted in 1938 that:

> These reports from hospital officials in the Old World
> constitute a very serious indictment of the drug habit. Very
> probably, however, the significance of hemp drugs as a causative
> factor has been exaggerated in most of these interpretations.
> Other similarly placed observers do not attach as much signifi-
> cance to the effects of the habit. Reports from such observers
> are distinctly in the minority although the actual number of
> observers who would minimize the incidence of hemp drug
> insanity is much greater than would be indicated by the number
> of these reports. There is less incentive to publish lengthy disser-
> tations intended to establish a negative or to minimize the
> significance of a given factor. . . . [I]n the Old World there has
> been a numerical preponderance of published opinions to the
> effect that "hemp drug insanity" constitutes a clinical entity.
> On the other hand, some of those equally in contact with the
> conditions there are inclined to discredit any causal relationship
> of this drug vice and insanity. In the United States, a formulated
> conception of hemp drug insanity is generally lacking.[30]

Information from the Eastern countries linking marihuana and
insanity had not been corroborated in the West. The Western under-

standing during the twenties was probably best captured by Dr. Louis Bragman in a 1925 article entitled "The Weed of Insanity." Emphasizing that the Indian Hemp Drugs Commission had shown that, "the habitual use of small quantities [is] not . . . harmful to Easterners," Dr. Bragman focused on "cannabism." The continued "abuse," "misuse," or "over-indulgence" of cannabis, he observed, "may finally lead to mania and dementia." Supporting the title of the article is the following statement: "There is no insanity from over-indulgence in hashish in this country, but it is comparatively frequent in India and Egypt."[31] By the time of the Marihuana Tax Act, Western scientists were also becoming somewhat skeptical of the methodology of these Eastern studies as well.

Crime

The link between crime and marihuana use, on the other hand, was primarily a contribution of the American experience. To the policy makers, the general public, and the international scientific community, the American "experts" delivered substantiation of the hypothesis that marihuana addiction and even acute intoxication caused violent crime and sexual excess.

No small role in this was played by the alleged etymology of the word "assassin." Professor Jerry Mandel has ferreted out the origins and successive perversions of the assassin myth, and the interested reader should consult his article "Hashish, Assassins, and the Love of God," which appeared in the 1966 volume of *Issues in Criminology*.[32] For our purposes, however, it is sufficient to recount the Marco Polo tale "Concerning the Old Man of the Mountain," which is generally considered the origin of the myth:

MULEHET is a country in which the Old Man of the Mountain dwelt in former days; and the name means "Place of the Aram." I will tell you his whole history as related by Messer Marco Polo, who heard it from several natives of the region.

The Old Man was called in their language ALOADIN. He had caused a certain valley between two mountains to be enclosed, and had turned it into a garden, the largest and most beautiful that ever was seen, filled with every variety of fruit. In it were...

palaces the most elegant that can be imagined, all covered with gilding and exquisite painting. And there were runnels too, flowing freely with wine and milk and honey and water; and numbers of ladies and of the most beautiful damsels in the world, who could play on all manner of instruments, and sung most sweetly, and danced in a manner that it was charming to behold. For the Old Man desired to make his people believe that this was actually Paradise. . . . And sure enough the Saracens of those parts believed that it was Paradise!

Now no man was allowed to enter the Garden save those whom he intended to be his ASHISHIN . . . . He kept at his court a number of the youths of the country, from 12 to 20 years of age, such as had a taste for soldiering, and to these he used to tell tales about Paradise. . . . Then he would introduce them into his garden, some four, or six, or ten at a time, having first made them drink a certain potion which cast them into a deep sleep, and then causing them to be lifted and carried in. So when they awoke, they found themselves in the Garden. . . .

When therefore they awoke . . . they deemed that it was Paradise in very truth. And the ladies and damsels dallied with them to their hearts' content, so that they had what young men would have; and with their own good will they never would have quitted this place.

Now this Prince whom we call the Old One . . . made those simple hill-folks about him believe firmly that he was a great Prophet. And when he wanted one of his Ashishin to send on any mission, he would cause that potion whereof I spoke to be given to one of the youths in the garden, and then had him carried into his Palace. So when the young man awoke, he found himself in the Castle, and no longer in that Paradise; whereas he was not over well pleased. He was then conducted to the Old Man's presence. . . . The Prince would then ask whence he came, and he would reply that he came from Paradise! and that it was exactly as Mahommet had described it in the Law. This of course gave the others who stood by, and who had not been admitted, the greatest desire to enter therein.

So when the Old Man would have any Prince slain, he would say to such a youth [as wished to enter Paradise] : "Go thou and slay So and So; and when thou returnest my Angels shall bear thee into Paradise. And shouldst thou die, natheless even so will I send my Angels to carry thee back into Paradise." So he caused them to believe; and thus there was no order of his that they would not affront any peril to execute, for the great desire they had to get . . . into that Paradise. . . . And in this manner the Old One got his people to murder any one whom he desired to get rid of.[33]

Even if we assume that the potion administered to the young men was hashish—Mandel suggests that it was probably opium—the point of the story is that the executioners had never had the drug. It was, in fact, with the promise of paradise that the Old Man induced the political crimes. Nevertheless, throughout the period of marihuana prohibition, medical journals, pharmacology texts, popular articles, official government statements, newspaper reports, and legislative testimony all recounted a version of this tale according to which the executioners were under the influence of hashish at the time the Old Man directed the murders and during the commission of the murders themselves.

The proposition that marihuana intoxication provoked violent conduct by removing restraint and building false courage, the perverted form of the assassin myth, appeared in Cummings' 1929 report,[34] in District Attorney Stanley's influential 1931 piece,[35] and from then on in almost every publication which recounted the evils of marihuana. Typical of disappearance of the basic tale is Fossier's version in 1931. He refers to the followers of the Old Man as a "diabolical, fanatical, cruel and murderous tribe" who "under the influence of hashish . . . would madly rush at their enemies, and ruthlessly massacre everyone within their grasp."[36]

The crime thesis first received concerted attention around 1931, when law enforcement officials in New Orleans, Denver, and other cities with a significant incidence of marihuana-smoking began to attribute a rising crime rate to the effects of the killer weed. In the succeeding four years, however, the FBN did not employ the crime thesis in an active way. When it addressed the alleged relationship between marihuana and crime, the bureau was content simply to cite reports of local authorities. This is not to say, however, that the commissioner was skeptical of the connection. In fact, after the appearance of the Warnshuis Report for the Wickersham Commission, Anslinger seems to have been convinced.[37] Soon thereafter he directed all local agents to forward to him information on local crimes allegedly caused by marihuana.[38]

This information was first used in the international arena. The League of Nations Advisory Committee on Traffic in Opium and Other Dangerous Drugs reconvened the Cannabis Subcommittee in the mid-thirties, and in an early memorandum the committee attributed the renewed interest in expanding the limited coverage of the 1925 convention to "new facts," which had come to the committee's attention in the intervening years. Of overwhelming importance was the "fact" that: "drug addiction owing to the consumption of Indian Hemp and the spread of crime amongst young persons as a result have assumed proportions in the United States of America which have seriously alarmed public opinion and medical circles."[39]

In November 1934 the United States submitted a twelve-page document reviewing "The Abuse of Cannabis in the United States" in response to the committee's request that all governments submit reports outlining the "situation as regards Indian Hemp."[40] Almost eight pages were devoted to a state-by-state review of existing legal controls. Only two of the remaining pages were devoted to the effects of the drug. The section "Toxic Effects" was drawn verbatim from Cummings' 1929 report, except that the following was added: "In cases of prolonged addiction, the somnolent action, however, is replaced by psychomotor activity with a tendency to wilfull violence accompanied by complete loss of judgment and restraint. It is significant that cannabis acts quickly and effectively to cut off inhibitions."

After reproducing the short section from the Cummings Report on "The Effects of Habitual Use" without the myths, Anslinger went on to report to Geneva on the:

Extent to which crimes of violence have been traced to the abuse of Cannabis.
Reports from narcotic officers who have consulted the police in various cities of those States in which the abuse of cannabis is most widespread, are to the effect that marihuana addicts are becoming one of the major police problems. While it is admitted by these officers that marihuana offenses do not show up directly in many cases, they state their estimate to be that fifty per cent of the violent crimes committed in districts occupied by Mexicans, Turks, Filipinos, Greeks, Spaniards, Latin-Americans and Negroes, may be traced to the abuse of marihuana.
A prosecuting attorney in Louisiana states that the underworld has been quick to realize the possibility of using this drug to subjugate the will of human derelicts. It can be used to sweep away all restraint and many present day crimes have been attributed to its influence.
Police officials in the South have found that, immediately before undertaking a crime, the criminal will indulge in a few

marihuana cigarettes in order to remove any natural sense of restraint which might deter him from committing the contemplated acts and in order to give him the false courage necessary to his purpose.

Prosecuting attorneys in the South and Southwest have not infrequently been confronted with the defense that, at the time of committing a criminal act, the defendant was irresponsible because he was under the influence of marihuana to such a degree that he was unable to appreciate the difference between right and wrong and was legally insane.

While the recording by the Federal Government of specific cases of violence as the result of the abuse of cannabis is of comparatively recent date, the records of the Bureau of Narcotics make reference to four cases of a particularly frightful nature:

(1) From California there came a report from the Chief of the Narcotic Enforcement Bureau of that State which is quoted in part: "Marihuana has a worse effect than heroin. It gives men the lust to kill, unreasonably, without motive—for the sheer sake of murder itself. In Eureka, California, a man under the influence of marihuana actually decapitated his best friend; and then comming [sic] out of the effects of the drug, was as horrfied [sic] as anyone else over what he had done."

(2) In Denver, Colorado, agents of the Federal Narcotic Bureau had made arrangements with one Halloway for a purchase from a "plant" of stolen cocaine. It was generally known that Halloway was addicted to marihuana and that a short time before in a restaurant, he had made an unprovoked assault upon a policeman in full uniform who had entered to get a cup of coffee and who had to club Halloway into unconsciousness. Nevertheless, the night before a purchase of cocaine was to be completed, Halloway again resorted to marihuana, ran amok, attempted to shoot his wife, but mortally wounded her grandmother, and after shooting it out with the police officers, finally killed himself.

(3) A short time ago the silence of the State prison at Marquette, Michigan, was shattered by the sound of a fusillade of pistol shots. An hour later, a kindly prison doctor lay dead and beside him lay the trusty who had given his life trying to save his friend the doctor. An investigation developed that arms and ammunition had been smuggled into the prison in the false bottoms of herring containers and that the marihuana from which Tylczak, the murderer of the doctor and trusty, had derived his demoniac courage, had also been smuggled into the prison.

(4)   Within a month after the passage of the Uniform Narcotic Drug Act in the State of Florida, twenty-two arrests were made in the city of Tampa for the sale of cannabis in the form of marihuana cigarettes and in bulk. A short time later, a young boy who had become addicted to smoking marihuana cigarettes, in a fit of frenzy, because, as he stated while still under the marihuana influence, a number of people were trying to cut off his arms and legs, seized an axe and killed his father, mother, two brothers and a sister, wiping out the entire family except himself.

Anslinger's submission of this unscientific, impressionistic "data" reflects the bureau's adoption of the Stanley thesis and the fruits of its three-year effort to gather corroboration for this thesis. So far as we have been able to determine, this was the first time that the bureau had officially propounded this view. In doing so, Anslinger ignored the contrary findings of every scientific inquiry which had been conducted: the Indian Hemp Drugs Commission Report; the 1925 Canal Zone study; the 1932 Canal Zone study together with Siler's 1933 article ("Delinquencies due to marijuana smoking which result in trial by Military Court are negligible in number when compared with delinquencies resulting from use of alcoholic drinks which also may be classed as stimulants and intoxicants".);[41] and the 1934 study of felons by Bromberg, from which he concluded that marihuana was far less responsible for crime than alcohol, that marihuana users tend to be passive in comparison to users of alcohol, and that use of the drug would lead to crime only when consumed by already psychopathic individuals.[42]

The bureau would obviously compile a collectively larger number of such case histories than each local district attorney, and the bureau could also publicize the resulting information more broadly than the local newspapers. The bureau thus began to record all crimes that could be associated with marihuana, and Commissioner Anslinger kept abreast of the situation.[43] Apparently, however, there was some restraining influence in the Treasury Department, for a full-scale propagation of the crime thesis was postponed.

During the first half of 1935 the typical bureau response to requests for information included the commonplace ethnic association: "Police officials in cities of those states where [marihuana] is most widely used estimate that fifty percent of the violent crimes committed in districts occupied by Mexicans, Spaniards, Latin-Americans, Greeks or Negroes may be traced to this weed."[44] (We have been unable to discover the origin of this figure.) During this transition period in FBN policy, a number of key bureaucrats who had long been convinced of the violent tendencies of marihuana users were anxious to collect data from any source. Will S. Wood, acting commissioner while Anslinger was in Geneva, confided to a Virginia prosecuting attorney, for example, that marihuana "has been said to give the user the lust to kill for the sheer sake of murder."[45]

Others in the FBN hierarchy were highly skeptical of the crime thesis. When newspaper accounts began to color bureau responses, A. L. Tennyson, the legal adviser, exerted a restraining influence:

I think we might give [a police official in Waltham, Massachusetts] some information on the subject of cannabis, but please do not go into detail about those examples of murder, etc., allegedly under the stimulus of cannabis. We only have reports on these cases, and I doubt whether we should outline them without having something more definite than we have. We might [say] instead that the drug is understood to have very evil effects if use is long continued or something along that line.[46]

Tennyson was fighting a losing battle. When Anslinger returned from Geneva, the detail and conviction with which the bureau stated the crime thesis for public consumption increased. In April 1936 Anslinger noted:

From time to time, instances are brought to light of acts committed by persons under the influence of or addicted to marihuana, which illustrate the viciousness of this drug. In Colorado, a man under the influence of marihuana attempted to shoot his wife, but killed his grandmother instead and then committed suicide. A Florida youth, while under the influence of the drug, murdered five members of his family with an ax. On November 23, 1935, in Baltimore, Maryland, a twenty-five-year-old Puerto Rican charged with criminally assaulting a ten-year-old girl, entered a plea on grounds of temporary insanity caused by smoking marihuana cigarettes, but was adjudged sane, found guilty, and sentenced to death by hanging. . . .[47]

Anslinger was not satisfied to record newspaper accounts. He began to seek corroborating information even more actively. Quite often his repondents went to unusual lengths to find some hint of a connection with marihuana:

> With reference to our conversation . . . I promised you that I would . . . secure information about the two boys I mentioned to you as having murdered a policeman and stated they did it while under the influence of marijuana.
> I looked over the record . . . but did not find any written statement . . . in which they admitted that they were under the influence of marijuana. However, some of the detectives, who worked on the case [stated] they had told them orally. . . . I am going to . . . the officer in charge of their investigation, and possibly there is something in his records pertaining to this case in which they admit they were smoking marijuana.
> I am going to interview [various detectives] for the purpose of collecting some data about marijuana and the vicious crimes committed by persons under its influence.[48]

Toward the end of 1936, after the final decision to seek federal legislation had been reached, any ambivalence in the attitude of the FBN toward these "atrocious marihuana crime" sketches disappeared. In the course of drafting a reply to *Collier's* Readers Research Bureau, which had requested information regarding "crime as connected with the drug marihuana," Anslinger wrote:

> So far as I know, no student of crime has as yet made any direct study of the relative percentage of violent crime which is attributable to the use of marihuana. Recently, we have received quite a number of reports showing crimes of violence committed by persons while under the influence of marihuana; usually by dramatic methods. I enclose a short summary of some of these incidents which have recently been brought to my attention.
> Apparently many of the users of marihuana are quickly reduced to insanity and to criminal acts; and it is my opinion that the incidents shown in the enclosed summary bear rather eloquent testimony as to the relation of crime with marihuana.
> However, in many of the cases, we are unacquainted with the previous mental and moral characteristics and habits of the persons committing crimes while under the influence of marihuana, so it can readily be seen that a final and conclusive

statement in this regard is not yet in order. In most of the cases under observation, we do not know whether they were psychopaths, neurotics, moral delinquents or normal individuals.

The marihuana problem is of comparatively recent origin in this country, and further investigations, both scientific and statistical, must be made and carefully studied. *In the meantime conclusions must be drawn from the facts at hand, which in themselves are enlightening, as witness the enclosed.*[49]

The enclosure specified thirteen "random" cases including the Baltimore insanity defense case, the Colorado grandmother-suicide, and the Alamoosa sexual assault case. When the draft response was submitted to Gaston, assistant to Secretary Morgenthau, he suggested only that the italicized portion be deleted. Probably he wished to avoid any implication that the administration had already made up its mind on the seriousness of the marihuana "problem" since the drafting of the Marihuana Tax Act had not been completed.[50]

However, once the administration had decided to seek federal legislation, the FBN began to propagate the crime thesis in earnest. Anslinger's 1937 article in *American Magazine*, "Marihuana: Assassin of Youth,"[51] was heavily supported by "marihuana atrocities." Beginning in late 1936 case descriptions allegedly linking marihuana and violent crime, culled "at random from the files of the FBN," began to appear in popular magazines and in the publications of of Anslinger's army, the WCTU, the Federation of Women's Clubs, the American Foreign Policy Association, and the World Narcotic Defense Association.[52] According to Becker and Dickson, the number of articles on marihuana appearing in popular magazines skyrocketed from seven between 1922 to 1936 to twenty-six in 1937. Two-thirds of them either acknowledged or reflected bureau assistance and one-third repeated the marihuana atrocities.[53]

On the eve of the Marihuana Tax Act, there was no scientific support for a significant statistical association between marihuana use and major criminal behavior. There was little evidence of increased motor excitement attending acute intoxication, much less the release of violent tendencies. There was only anecdotal evidence generated by local law enforcement officials and a persuasive belief that the people who used marihuana, Mexicans and other ethnic minorities, represented the antisocial elements in society.

The Scientific Community Muzzles Itself

Many members of the scientific community who were skeptical of the veracity of the claims against marihuana were nevertheless willing to tolerate "a certain necessary degree of sensationalism"[54] to propel enactment of criminal legislation. Treadway, Bromberg, Kolb, Walton, and others were very quiet during the agitation of the thirties. Clearly, they viewed the marihuana phenomenon from both the scientific and the sociological perspectives. But social, not scientific, thinking dictated their policy judgments. For Kolb and Treadway, silence may also have been a requisite of Treasury Department affiliation since the decision to seek federal legislation had been made at the highest levels of the department.

Assistant Surgeon General Treadway's report for the Cannabis Subcommittee of the League of Nations Advisory Committee in early 1937 indicates the scientific perspective:

> Cannabis indica does not produce a dependence such as in opium addiction. In opium addiction there is a complete dependence and when it is withdrawn there is actual physical pain which is not the case with cannabis. Alcohol more nearly produces the same effect as cannabis in that there is an excitement or a general feeling of lifting of personality, followed by a delirious stage, and subsequent narcosis. There is no dependence or increased tolerance such as in opium addiction. As to the social or moral degradation associated with cannabis it probably belongs in the same category as alcohol. As with alcohol, it may be taken a relatively long time without social or emotional breakdown. Marihuana is habit-forming, although not addicting, in the same sense as alcohol might be with some people, or sugar or coffee. Marihuana produces a delirium with a frenzy which might result in violence; but this is also true of alcohol.[55]

The sociological perspective in its most blatant form can be seen in Dr. Fossier's influential 1931 piece: "The debasing and baneful influence of hashish and opium is not restricted to individuals but has manifested itself in nations and races as well. The dominant race and most enlightened countries are alcoholic, whilst the races and nations addicted to hemp and opium, some of which once attained to heights of culture and civilization have deteriorated both mentally and physically."[56]

Although this language may have been a little strong for Fossier's contemporaries, it is certain that the identification of the hemp drugs with alien cultures, and with the lower classes in those cultures, significantly affected the public policy attitude of those for whom adversity of effects was a relevant consideration. Bouquet had attributed "the readiness with which Moslem populations became addicted to use of Indian Hemp to the immemoriality of the custom, the indolence endemic to the 'Moslem character,' and the absence of family life in the Western sense."[57] Similarly, Walton noted that awareness and availability of the drug in the United States were not sufficient in themselves to establish "this sort of popular indulgence." Fixation of "this vice as a folk practice" requires "a reasonably intimate social contact between an uninitiated population and a population which practices the vice"; and a temperament and social condition conducive to the practice. On the first point, Mexican and East Indian immigration posed the threat. With regard to the second, it was said that the vice easily took root "among the idle and unresponsible classes of America." Conversely, the "environmental conditions and social outlook" of the "Kentucky pioneers who cultivated hundreds of tons of hemp with no recorded instances of a perversion of hemp narcotics" represented an "unfavorable medium."[58]

The excising of marihuana use from the social organism was seen quite clearly as a means of rooting out idleness and irresponsibility among deviant minorities. The assertion of the Protestant ethic required drastic measures for marihuana, but not for alcohol, because for sociological, if not pharmacological, reasons the use of marihuana inevitably tended to excess while "civilized" use of alcohol was characteristic of the American middle class. Especially during the depression era, public health experts were apprehensive that increased idleness would spawn increased marihuana use, which would in turn perpetuate further idleness. And since "the vice still flourishes in every country in which it has once been established,"[59] early, decisive action was required.

CHAPTER VIII

Nonchalance on Capitol Hill

THE TREASURY DEPARTMENT went to Capitol Hill to secure passage of the Marihuana Tax Act with an open-and-shut case. Anslinger and his colleagues stressed four points in their testimony before the House Ways and Means Committee and a subcommittee of the Senate Finance Committee: marihuana was a disastrous drug; its use was increasing alarmingly and had generated public hysteria; state legislation had proved incapable of meeting the threat posed by the weed, and federal action was therefore required; and, the government might best act through separate legislation rather than through an amendment to the Harrison Act.

For five mornings in the House and one morning in the Senate, the legislators and bureaucrats convinced one another of the need for this legislation. The selection and questioning of witnesses reflect clearly the consensus among the participants regarding the relative importance of the matters upon which the legislation was predicated. Of primary interest was the question of federal responsibility. The New Deal Congress had been flexing its muscles for four years and resented any suggestion that any "national" problem was beyond its competence. If the Treasury "experts" contended that marihuana was a national menace, then the United States Congress was committed in principle to federal action. The threat of invalidation by the Supreme Court posed the only restraint, and even that issue was rapidly becoming one only of form.

What's Wrong with Marihuana?

The narcotics bureaucracy had no definitive scientific study of the effects of marihuana to present to the Congress. Even so, one might have thought the Treasury Department would have submitted a synthesis of available scientific information, or perhaps would have summoned a number of private investigators or the government's own public health experts to testify about the drug's effects. None of these things were done. No statement was submitted by the Public Health Service. Neither of the government's own public health experts, Drs. Treadway and Kolb, testified, nor did Drs. Bromberg and Siler who had recently published scientific articles on the effects of cannabis in humans.

Instead, the scientific aspects were summarized briefly by the FBN, a law enforcement agency. The bureau submitted a written statement which acknowledged some uncertainty within the scientific community. Then they dismissed it:

> Despite the fact that medical men and scientists have disagreed upon the properties of marihuana, and some are inclined to minimize the harmfulness of this drug, the records offer ample evidence that it has a disastrous effect upon many of its users. Recently we have received many reports showing crimes of violence committed by persons while under the influence of marihuana. . . .
>
> The deleterious, even vicious, qualities of the drug render it highly dangerous to the mind and body upon which it operates to destroy the will, cause one to lose the power of connected thought, producing imaginary delectable situations and gradually weakening the physical powers. Its use frequently leads to insanity.
>
> I have a statement here, giving an outline of cases reported to the Bureau or in the press, wherein the use of marihuana is connected with revolting crimes.[1]

Only the Gomila and Stanley articles were presented to support this statement.[2] Stanley's article cited the Indian Hemp Drugs Commission report, and Gomila cited Bromberg's study, but neither of these reports were themselves presented, nor were the Canal Zone studies. The few hints of uncertainty in the bureau's written statement disappeared in Anslinger's oral testimony.

Mr. ANSLINGER. I have another letter from the prosecutor at a place in New Jersey.
It is as follows:

THE INTERSTATE COMMISSION ON CRIME,
March 18, 1937

CHARLES SCHWARZ,
Washington, D.C.

MY DEAR MR. SCHWARZ: That I fully appreciate the need for action, you may judge from the fact that last January I tried a murder case for several days, of a particularly brutal character in which one colored young man killed another, literally smashing his face and head to a pulp, as the enclosed photograph demonstrates. One of the defenses was that the defendant's intellect was so prostrated from his smoking marihuana cigarettes that he did not know what he was doing. The defendant was found guilty and sentenced to a long term of years. I am convinced that marihuana had been indulged in, that the smoking had occurred, and the brutality of the murder was accounted for by the narcotic, though the defendant's intellect had not been totally prostrate, so the verdict was legally correct. It seems to me that this instance might be of value to you in your campaign.

Sincerely yours,

RICHARD HARTSHORNE.

Mr. Hartshorne is a member of the Interstate Commission on Crime.
We have many cases of this kind.
Senator BROWN. It affects them that way?
Mr. ANSLINGER.   Yes.
Senator DAVIS (viewing a photograph presented by Mr. Anslinger). Was there in this case a blood or skin disease caused by marihuana?
Mr. ANSLINGER. No. this is a photograph of the murdered man, Senator. It shows the fury of the murderer.
Senator BROWN. That is terrible.
Mr. ANSLINGER. That is one of the worst cases that has come to my attention, and it is to show you its relation to crime that I am putting those two letters in the record. . . .
I have a few cases here that I would just like to tell the committee about. In Alamoosa, Colorado, they seem to be having a lot of difficulty. The citizens petitioned Congress for help, in addition to the help that is given them under the State law. In Kansas and New Mexico also we have had a great deal of trouble.
Here is a typical illustration: A 15-year-old boy, found mentally deranged from smoking marihuana cigarettes, furnished enough information to the police officers to lead to the seizure

of 15 pounds of marihuana. That was seized in a garage in an Ohio town. These boys had been getting marihuana at a playground, and the supervisors there had been peddling it to children, but they got rather alarmed when they saw these boys developing the habit, and particularly when this boy began to go insane.

In Florida some years ago we had the case of a 20-year-old boy who killed his brothers, a sister, and his parents while under the influence of marihuana.

Recently, in Ohio, there was a gang of very young men, all under 20 years of age; every one of whom confessed that they had committed some 38 holdups while under the influence of the drug.

In another place in Ohio a young man shot the hotel clerk while trying to hold him up. His defense was that he was under the influence of marihuana. . . .

Senator BROWN. There is the impression that it is stimulating to a certain extent? It is used by criminals when they want to go out and perform some deed that they would not commit in their ordinary frame of mind?

Mr. ANSLINGER. That was demonstrated by these seven boys, who said they did not know what they were doing after they smoked marihuana. They conceived the series of crimes while in a state of marihuana intoxication.

Senator DAVIS. How many cigarettes would you have to smoke before you got this vicious mental attitude toward your neighbor?

Mr. ANSLINGER. I believe in some cases one cigarette might develop a homicidal mania, probably to kill his brother. It depends on the physical characteristics of the individual. Every individual reacts differently to the drug. It stimulates some and others it depresses. It is impossible to say just what the action of the drug will be on a given individual, or the amount. Probably some people could smoke five before it would take effect, but all the experts agree that the continued use leads to insanity. There are many cases of insanity.[3]

Anslinger's testimony was the only information on effects which was presented to the Senate subcommittee.

In the House, Anslinger brought along a representative from the scientific community. Instead of presenting one of the few researchers who had done any significant research into the effects of cannabis on humans, however, the bureau chose a Temple University pharmacologist, Dr. James Munch, whose experience was confined to limited experimentation of the effects of cannabis on dogs. One participating committeeman, Congressman McCormack (later the Speaker), soon realized how little Dr. Munch could contribute, and with his questions began to assume the role of the expert witness on the effects of cannabis in man:

> Dr. MUNCH. In connection with my studies of Cannabis, or marihuana, I have followed its effects on animals and also, so far as possible, its effect upon humans.
>   . . . . .
> Continuous use will tend to cause the degeneration of one part of the brain, that part that is useful for higher or physic reasoning, or the memory. Functions of that type are localized in the cerebral cortex of the brain. Those are the disturbing and harmful effects that follow continued exposure to marihuana. . . .
> I have found in studying the action on dogs that only about 1 dog in 300 is very sensitive to the test. The effects on dogs are extremely variable, although they vary little in their suscepti- bility. The same thing is true for other animals and for humans.
>   . . . . .
> Animals which show a particular susceptibility, that is, which show a response to a given dose, when they begin to show it will acquire a tolerance. We have to give larger doses as the animals are used over a period of 6 months or a year. This means that the animal is becoming habituated, and finally the animal must be discarded because it is no longer serviceable.
> Mr. McCORMACK. We are more concerned with human beings than with animals. Of course, I realize that those experiments are necessary and valuable, because so far as the effect is concerned, they have a significance also. But we would like to have whatever evidence you have as to the conditions existing in the country, as to what the effect is upon human beings. Not that we are not concerned about the animals, but the important matter before us concerns the use of this drug by human beings.
>   . . . . .
> Mr. McCORMACK. I take it that the effect is different upon different persons.
> Dr. MUNCH.   Yes, sir.
> Mr. McCORMACK. There is no question but what this is a drug, is there?
> Dr. MUNCH.   None at all.
> Mr. McCORMACK. There is no dispute about that?
> Dr. MUNCH.   No.
> Mr. McCORMACK. Is it a harmful drug?
> Dr. MUNCH.   Any drug that produces the degeneration of the brain is harmful. Yes; it is.

Mr. McCORMACK. I agree with you on that, but I want to ask you some questions and have your answers for the record, because they will assist us in passing upon this legislation.

Dr. MUNCH. I have said it is a harmful drug.

Mr. McCORMACK. In some cases does it not bring about extreme amnesia?

Dr. MUNCH. Yes; it does.

Mr. McCORMACK. And in other cases it causes violent irritability?

Dr. MUNCH. Yes, sir.

Mr. McCORMACK. And those results lead to a disintegration of personality, do they not?

Dr. MUNCH. Yes, sir.

Mr. McCORMACK. That is really the net result of the use of that drug, no matter what other effects there may be; its continued use means the disintegration of the personality of the person who uses it?

Dr. MUNCH. Yes; that is true.

Mr. McCORMACK. Can you give us any idea as to the period of continued use that occurs before this disintegration takes place?

Dr. MUNCH. I can only speak from my knowledge of animals. In some animals we see the effect after about 3 months, while in others it requies more than a year, when they are given the same dose.

Mr. McCORMACK. Are there not some animals on which it reacted, as I understand it, in a manner similar to its reaction on human beings? Is that right?

Dr. MUNCH. Yes, sir.

Mr. McCORMACK. Have you experimented upon any animals whose reaction to this drug would be similar to that of human beings?

Dr. MUNCH. The reason we use dogs is because the reaction of dogs to this drug closely resembles the reaction of human beings.

Mr. McCORMACK. And the continued use of it, as you have observed the reaction on dogs, has resulted in the disintegration of personality?

Dr. MUNCH. Yes. So far as I can tell, not being a dog psychologist, the effects will develop in from 3 months to a year.

Mr. McCORMACK. The recognition of the effects of the use of this drug is only of comparatively recent origin, is it not?

Dr. MUNCH. Yes; comparatively recent.

Mr. McCORMACK. I suppose one reason was that it was not used very much.

Dr. MUNCH. That is right.

Mr. McCORMACK. I understand this drug came in from, or was originally grown in, Mexico and Latin American countries.

Dr. MUNCH. "Marihuana" is the name for Cannabis in the Mexican Pharmacopoeia. It was originally grown in Asia.

Mr. McCORMACK. That was way back in the oriental days. The word "assassin" is derived from an oriental word or name by which the drug was called; is not that true?

Dr. MUNCH. Yes, sir.

Mr. McCORMACK. So it goes way back to those years when hashish was just a species of the same class which is identified by the English translation of an oriental word; that is, the word "assassin"; is that right?

Dr. MUNCH. That is my understanding. . . .

Mr. McCORMACK. Can you give us any information about the growth in recent years of the use of it as a drug, in connection with the purposes that this bill was introduced to meet?

Dr. MUNCH. You mean the illicit use rather than the medicinal use?

Mr. McCORMACK. Exactly.

Dr. MUNCH. The knowledge I have in that connection is based on contacts with police officers as they collected material, even in Philadelphia. They tell me that until 10 years ago they had no knowledge of it, but now it is growing wild in a number of different places.

I was in Colorado about 3 years ago, going there as a witness in a prosecution brought under the Colorado act in connection with the use of marihuana. The police officers there told me its use developed there only within the last 3 or 4 years, starting about 1932 or 1933.

Mr. McCORMACK. Has there been a rapid increase in the use of marihuana for illicit purposes—and I use the word "illicit" to describe the situation we have in mind?

Dr. MUNCH. It is my understanding that there has been.

Mr. McCORMACK. There is no question about that, is there?

Dr. MUNCH. No, sir; there is not.

Mr. CULLEN. We thank you for the statement you have given to the committee.[4]

The Birth of a Menace

The second component of the bureau's case was the contention that marihuana use had spread alarmingly in recent years, provoking a public outcry. To demonstrate this, the bureau submitted only the 1936 letter from the city editor of the Alamoosa *Daily Courier* and the Gomila article, hardly firm evidence of any such alarming increase.[5] The Congress, however, was neither in the mood nor in a position to question Anslinger's contentions. What did interest legislators, however, was why use suddenly increased in 1935. In both houses Anslinger dismissed the suggestion that drug users turn to marihuana when other drugs are not available:

Senator BROWN. Do you think that the recent great increase in the use of it that has taken place in the United States is probably due to the heavy hand of the law, in its effect upon the use of other drugs, and that persons who desire a stimulant are turning to this because of enforcement of the Harrison Narcotics Act and the State laws?

Mr. ANSLINGER. We do not know of any cases where the opium user has transferred to marihuana. There is an entirely new class of people using marihuana. The opium user is around 35 to 50 years old. These users are 20 years old, and know nothing of heroin or morphine.

Senator BROWN. What has caused the new dissemination of it? We did not hear anything of it until the last year or so.

Mr. ANSLINGER. I do not think that the war against opium has very much bearing upon the situation. That same question has been discussed in other countries; in Egypt particularly, where a great deal of hasheesh is used, they tried to show that the marihuana user went to heroin, and when heroin got short he jumped back to hasheesh, but that is not true. This is an entirely different class. I do not know just why the abuse of marihuana has spread like wildfire in the last 4 or 5 years.[6]

When asked to estimate the number of users, Anslinger reported that the states had made about 800 marihuana arrests, 400 in California alone, the previous year. He suggested that the California authorities had cracked down and that if the other states were more efficient, there would have been more arrests, although he admitted that use probably was not as prevalent anywhere else as in California.[7]

Arrest figures are singularly unhelpful in ascertaining incidence of use, being a function more of enforcement policy, investigative activity, and statistical reporting than of the size of the using population. But even if a significant leap in arrest figures could be taken to indicate increased incidence of use, Anslinger's figures were meaningless. There was no systematic reporting of state arrests, so Anslinger could not possibly have compiled a reliable figure. Even so, he did not present figures for prior years for

And There Should Be No Hope of Parole

New Orleans *Times-Picayune*, 23 September 1937

comparative purposes, and 800 arrests in a year could not have been much of an increase. Some perspective is provided by the fact that in 1970, when statistical reporting was *still* primitive, there were an estimated 200,000 marihuana arrests and perhaps 60,000 were in California.

All in all, Anslinger's bold assertion that marihuana use had markedly increased was entirely unsupported. But that, of course, did not make any difference. Anslinger used the newspaper campaigns of 1935 to paint a credible picture of public hysteria. Just as such propaganda generated interest in the Uniform Act among state legislatures, it created a "felt need" for federal legislation in the Congress, despite the fact that there is no evidence this public hysteria about marihuana really existed on any signficant scale. [8]

The Need for National Legislation

The third component of the bureau's case was that even though every state now had marihuana legislation, local authorities could not cope with the marihuana menace. To support this proposition the bureau offered editorial pleas from the Washington newspapers and Anslinger's testimony that officials of several states had requested federal help. The FBN offered no information on why the states needed help. Was there a major interstate trafficking network which could not be broken by local authorities?

Senator Brown realized the importance of this question and asked Anslinger to "make clear the need for federal legislation. You say the states have asked you to do that. I presume it is because of the freedom of interstate traffic that the States require the legislation." Anslinger agreed: "We have had requests from the States to step in because they claimed it was not growing in that State, but that it was coming in from another state."[9] He presented nothing to support this statement, no letters from local authorities and no investigative reports by FBN agents describing the trafficking apparatus. Although absence of recorded evidentiary support is not necessarily conclusive on this matter, nothing remains today in the FBN's files which would have supported the contention.

The bureau's implicit attitude was that most of the states were not trying very hard to enforce their marihuana legislation, due to either inadequate resources or simple lack of interest. The need for federal legislation did not arise from the limitations imposed by state boundaries but from the inefficiency of state authorities within their own jurisdictions, as perceived by the bureau. If the bureau was given statutory responsibility through a federal law on marihuana, Anslinger hoped to spark state and local enforcement in those jurisdictions which had not yet taken the problem seriously. In the states which had already begun to suppress marihuana—New York, Louisiana, Colorado, and California—the bureau would assist by supplying additional manpower and money.[10]

The congressmen and senators participating in the hearings accepted the bureau's argument. In fact, Senator Brown, chairman of the subcommittee which considered the legislation in the Senate, and Chairman Doughton of the Ways and Means Committee had been thoroughly briefed by the bureau in advance of the hearings. Again and again, Anslinger, Doughton, Brown, and McCormack seemed merely to be reinforcing each others' convictions. There was no probing of the government witnesses. In fact, the government made its case in the House in one session, and the next three sessions were devoted to countering technical objections of the oilseed, birdseed, and hemp industries.[11]

On the last morning of scheduled hearings, however, the final witness introduced some suspense into these otherwise pro forma proceedings. Dr. William C. Woodward, the bureau's sometime ally, appeared on behalf of the AMA to oppose the bill. Dr. Woodward methodically challenged the validity of each of the assumptions upon which the legislation was based, noting again and again that he had no objection to amendment of the Harrison Act. Yet the congressmen were in no mood for the AMA or Dr. Woodward, and they roundly insulted his audacity in daring to question the wisdom of the bill (an attitude that might not have surfaced had Woodward not been standing alone while his medical colleagues stood on the sidelines).

How Dare You Dissent!

Dr. Woodward objected to H.R. 6385 because he believed that its ultimate effect would be to strangle any medical use of marihuana.

Although there were admittedly few recognized therapeutic applications, the bill, in his view, inhibited further research which might bear fruit. He implied that the bill was designed with this objective in mind. Dr. Woodward was, in fact, quite correct in both respects. Anslinger had desired since 1930 to eliminate any medical use, and the Marihuana Tax Act had exactly that effect for thirty years.

It was not characteristic of Dr. Woodward to raise objections without presenting alternatives. He patiently noted that if federal legislation was considered necessary, it could be achieved without sacrificing medical usage by simply amending the Harrison Act. The bureau had drafted the Marihuana Tax Act in secret[12] without consulting him or any other representative of the AMA, and he did not hesitate to point out deficiencies in the bureau's case.

First, he criticized the nature of the testimony in general:

That there is a certain amount of narcotic addiction of an objectionable character no one will deny. The newspapers have called attention to it so prominently that there must be some grounds for their statements. It has surprised me, however, that the facts on which these statements have been based have not been brought before this committee by competent primary evidence. We are referred to newspaper publications concerning the prevalence of marihuana addiction. We are told that the use of marihuana causes crime.

But yet no one has been produced from the Bureau of Prisons to show the number of prisoners who have been found addicted to the marihuana habit. An informal inquiry shows that the Bureau of prisons has no evidence on that point.

You have been told that school children are great users of marihuana cigarettes. No one has been summoned from the Children's Bureau to show the nature and extent of the habit among children.

Inquiry of the Children's Bureau shows that they have had no occasion to investigate it and know nothing particularly of it.

Inquiry of the Office of Education—and they certainly should know something of the prevalence of the habit among the school children of the country, if there is a prevalent habit—indicates that they have had no occasion to investigate and know nothing of it.

Moreover, there is in the Treasury Department itself, the Public Health Service, with its Division of Mental Hygiene. The Division of Mental Hygiene was, in the first place, the Division of Narcotics. It was converted into the Division of Mental Hygiene,

I think, about 1930. That particular Bureau has control at the present time of the narcotics farms that were created about 1929 and 1930 and came into operation a few years later. No one has been summoned from that Bureau to give evidence on that point.

Informal inquiry by me indicates that they have had no record of any marihuana or Cannabis addicts who have even been committed to those farms.

The Bureau of the Public Health Service has also a division of pharmacology. If you desire evidence as to the pharmacology of Cannabis, that obviously is the place where you can get direct and primary evidence, rather than the indirect hearsay evidence.[13]

Woodward noted with regard to the alleged evil effects of the drug, that during the drafting of the Uniform Act, the participants "could not . . . find evidence that would lead it to incorporate in the model act a [marihuana] provision."[14] Dr. Woodward also pointed out that there was no evidence to believe there had been an increase in the use of the drug.

> Mr. McCORMACK. There is no question but that the drug habit has been increasing rapidly in recent years.
> Dr. WOODWARD. There is no evidence to show whether or not it has been.
> Mr. McCORMACK. In your opinion, has it increased?
> Dr. WOODWARD. I should say it has increased slightly. Newspaper exploitation of the habit has done more to increase it than anything else.[15]

Dr. Woodward's most pointed attack was directed against the assumption that federal legislation was needed to control the marihuana habit. He argued that existing state legislation was more than sufficient, if properly enforced, and that if lack of coordination was the problem, that was the FBN's fault. Noting that the FBN already had the authority under its establishing act to "arrange for the exchange of information concerning the use and abuse of narcotic drugs in [the] states and for cooperation in the institution and prosecution of suits. . . ,"[16] he asserted that the bureau had not done its job: "If there is at the present time any weakness in our state laws relating to Cannabis, or to marihuana, a fair share of the blame, if not all of it, rests on the Secretary of the Treasury and his assistants who have had this duty imposed upon them for 6 and more years."[17]

Quoting denials of federal responsibility in the 1929 Cummings Report and Anslinger's 1934 submission to the League of Nations, Woodward observed that "it has only been very recently, apparently, that there has been any discovery by the Federal Government of the supposed fact that Federal legislation rather than state legislation is desirable."[18] In short, Woodward suggested that the federal legislation was contrived and that it would serve no useful purpose beyond that which could be served by the exercise of leadership in the coordinated enforcement of state laws.

Dr. Woodward also contended that the law would be a useless expense to the medical profession and would be unenforceable as well. Since marihuana grows so freely, and every landowner was a potential "producer," whether wittingly or unwittingly, full enforcement would require inspection of the entire land area of the country, a task which would be unseemly for the federal government to undertake.[19] Further, the assumption of federal responsibility would exacerbate the "general tendency to evade responsibility on the part of the states, . . . a thing that many of us think ought not to be tolerated." [20]

Finally, Dr. Woodward wondered why, if federal legislation was considered necessary, the Congress did not simply amend the Harrison Act. To the bureau's argument that such a course would be unconstitutional, he inquired how Treasury's counsel could argue that the present bill was constitutional since the technique was identical. Dr. Woodward's own view was that amendment of the Harrison Act would be constitutional and that such a course would dispel the professional objections which he had raised.[21]

As soon as Dr. Woodward completed his testimony, he was met with objections. First, Congressman Vinson suggested that Woodward was not speaking for the AMA, and he engaged the doctor in a contentious dialogue about the impact of a recent AMA *Journal* editorial which appeared to support the bill.[22] Vinson argued that it reflected AMA policy. Woodward contended that it merely paraphrased Anslinger. Then Vinson embarked on a thinly veiled diatribe against the AMA's opposition to New Deal legislation, suggesting that Woodward's position on H.R. 6385 was the kind of obstructionism which he had come to expect from the association?[23] When the subject turned to the AMA's position on the Harrison Act, Congressman Cooper joined the fray:

Mr. COOPER.   I understood you to state a few moments ago, in answer to a question asked by Mr. Vinson, that you did not favor the passage of the Harrison Narcotic Act, because you entertained the view that the control should be exercised by the States.

Dr. WOODWARD. I think you are probably correct. But we cooperated in securing its passage.

Mr. COOPER.   You did not favor it, though?

Dr. WOODWARD. Did not favor the principle; no.

Mr. COOPER. Are you prepared to state now that that act has produced beneficial results?

Dr. WOODWARD. I think it has

Mr. COOPER. You think it has?

Dr. WOODWARD. I think it has.

Mr. COOPER. You appeared before this committee, the Ways and Means Committee of the House, in 1930, when the bill was under consideration to establish the Bureau of Narcotics, did you not?

Dr. WOODWARD. I did.

Mr. COOPER. And at that time, did you not state that "the physicians are required by law to register in one form or another, either by taking out a license or by a system of registration that is provided for in the Harrison Narcotic Act; they are required to keep records of everything they do in relation to the professional and commercial use of narcotic drugs. To that, I think we can enter no fair objection, because I see no other way by which the situation can be controlled."

That was your view then, was it not?

Dr. WOODWARD. It was; and if I may interject, to that—that same method of regulating Cannabis, insofar as it is a medical problem, tying it in with the Harrison Narcotic Act—I think you will find that our board of trustees and house of delegates will [not] object. . . .

Mr. COOPER. . . . [D]o you state now before this committee that there is no difficulty involved—that there is no trouble presented because of marihuana?

Dr. WOODWARD. I do not.

Mr. COOPER. What is your position on that?

Dr. WOODWARD. My position is that if the Secretary of the Treasury will cooperate with the States in procuring the enactment of adequate State legislation, as he is charged with doing under the law, and will cooperate with the States in the enforcement of the State laws and the Federal law, as likewise he is charged with doing, the problem will be solved through local police officers, local inspectors, and so forth.

Mr. COOPER. With all due deference and respect to you, you have not touched, top, side, or bottom, the question that I asked you. I asked you: Do you recognize that a difficulty is involved and regulation necessary in connection with marihuana?

Dr. WOODWARD. I do. I have tried to explain that it is a State matter.

Mr. COOPER. Regardless whether it is a State or a Federal matter, there is trouble?

Dr. WOODWARD. There is trouble.

Mr. COOPER. There is trouble existing now, and something should be done about it. It is a menace, is it not?

Dr. WOODWARD. A menace for which there is adequate remedy.

Mr. COOPER. Well, it probably comes within our province as to what action should be taken about it. I am trying to get from you some view, if you will be kind enough to give it. To what do you object in this particular bill, in the method that is sought to be employed here?

Dr. WOODWARD. My interest is primarily, of course, in the medical aspects. We object to the imposing of an additional tax on physicians, pharmacists, and others, catering to the sick; to require that they register and reregister; that they have special order forms to be used for this particular drug, when the matter can just as well be covered by an amendment to the Harrison Narcotic Act.

If you are referring to the particular problem, I object to the act because it is utterly unsusceptible of execution, and an act that is not susceptible of execution is a bad thing on the statute books.

. . . . .

Mr. COOPER. I understood you to say a few moments ago, in response to a question that I asked you, that you recognize there is an evil existing with reference to this marihuana drug.

Dr. WOODWARD. I will agree as to that.

Mr. COOPER. Then I understood you to say just now, in response to a question by Mr. Robertson of Virginia, that some of the State laws are inadequate and the Federal law is inadequate to meet the problem.

Dr. WOODWARD. Yes, sir.

Mr. COOPER. That is true?

Dr. WOODWARD. I think that is clear.

Mr. COOPER. And, as you recall, there are two States that have no law at all?

Dr. WOODWARD. That is the best of my recollection.

Mr. COOPER. Taking your statement, just as you made it here that the evil exists and that the problem is not being properly

met by State laws, do you recommend that we just continue to sit by idly and attempt to do nothing?
Dr. WOODWARD. No; I do not. I recommend that the Secretary of the Treasury get together with the State people who can enforce the law and procure the enactment of adequate State laws. They can enforce it on the ground.
Mr. COOPER. Years have passed and effective results have not been accomplished in that way.
Dr. WOODWARD. It has never been done.
Mr. COOPER. And you recommend that the thing for us to do is to yet continue the doctrine of laissez-faire and do nothing?
Dr. WOODWARD. It has never been done.[24]

This exchange captures vividly what was at issue. Dr. Woodward was opposed to federal legislation which, in his view, would impose severe burdens without achieving any benefits. The New Deal Congress, on the other hand, was disposed to legislate on any colorably "national" evil, whatever its scope. It could be said, indeed, that the Congress was psychologically habituated to the enactment of federal legislation. Several minutes later Chairman Doughton began:

The CHAIRMAN. If [marihuana's] use as a medicine has fallen off to a point where it is practically negligible, and its use as a dope has increased until it has become serious and a menace to the public, as has been testified here—and the testimony here has been that it causes people to lose their mental balance, causes them to become criminals so that they do not seem to realize right from wrong after they become addicts of this drug— taking into consideration the growth in its injurious effects and its diminution in its use so far as any beneficial effect is concerned, you realize, do you not, that some good may be accomplished by this proposed legislation?
Dr. WOODWARD. Some legislation: yes, Mr. Chairman.
The CHAIRMAN. If that is admitted, let us get down to a few concrete facts. With the experience in the Bureau of Narcotics and with the State governments trying to enforce the laws that are now on the State statute books against the use of this deleterious drug, and the Federal Government has realized that the State laws are ineffective, don't you think some Federal legislation necessary?
Dr. WOODWARD. I do not.
The CHAIRMAN. You do not.

Dr. WOODWARD. No. I think it is the usual tendency to— —

The CHAIRMAN. I believe you did say in response to Mr. Cooper that you believed that some legislation or some change in the present law would be helpful. If that be true, why have you not been here before this bill was introduced proposing some remedy for this evil?

Dr. WOODWARD. Mr. Chairman, I have visited the Commissioner of Narcotics on various occasions— —

The CHAIRMAN. That is not an answer to my question at all.

Dr. WOODWARD. I have not been here because— —

The CHAIRMAN. You are here representing the medical association. If your association has realized the necessity, the importance of some legislation—which you now admit—why did you wait until this bill was introduced to come here and make mention of it? Why did you not come here voluntarily and suggest to this committee some legislation?

Dr. WOODWARD. I have talked these matters over many times with the — —

The CHAIRMAN. That does not do us any good to talk matters over. I have talked over a lot of things. The States do not seem to be able to deal with it effectively, nor is the Federal Government dealing with it at all. Why do you wait until now and then come in here to oppose something that is presented to us. You propose nothing whatever to correct the evil that exists.

Now, I do not like to have a round-about answer, but I would like to have a definite, straight, clean-cut answer to that question.

Dr. WOODWARD. We do not propose legislation directly to Congress when the same end can be reached through one of the executive departments of the Government.

The CHAIRMAN. You admit that it has not been done. You said that you thought some legislation would be helpful. That is what I am trying to hold you down to. Now, why have you not proposed any legislation? That is what I want a clean-cut, definite, clear answer to.

Dr. WOODWARD. In the first place, it is not a medical addiction that is involved and the data do not come before the medical society. You may absolutely forbid the use of Cannabis by any physician, or the disposition of Cannabis by any pharmacist in the country, and you would not have touched your Cannabis addiction as it stands today, because there is no relation between it and the practice of medicine or pharmacy. It is entirely outside of those two branches.

The CHAIRMAN. If the statement that you have just made has any relation to the question that I asked, I just do not have the mind to understand it; I am sorry.

Dr. WOODWARD. I say that we do not ordinarily come directly to Congress if a department can take care of the matter. I have talked with the Commissioner, with Commissioner Anslinger.

The CHAIRMAN. If you want to advise us on legislation, you ought to come here with some constructive proposals, rather than criticism, rather than trying to throw obstacles in the way of something that the Federal Government is trying to do. It has not only an unselfish motive in this, but they have a serious responsibility.

Dr. WOODWARD. We cannot understand yet, Mr. Chairman, why this bill should have been prepared in secret for two years without any intimation, even, to the profession, that it was being prepared.

The CHAIRMAN. Is not the fact that you were not consulted your real objection to this bill?

Dr. WOODWARD. Not at all.

The CHAIRMAN. Just because you were not consulted?

Dr. WOODWARD. Not at all.

Mr. CHAIRMAN. No matter how much good there is in the proposal?

Dr. WOODWARD. Not at all.

The CHAIRMAN. This is not it?

Dr. WOODWARD. Not at all. We always try to be helpful.[25]

After accusing Dr. Woodward of obstructionism, evasiveness, and bad faith, the committee did not even thank him for his testimony. When the Senate Finance Committee conducted hearings on the bill—now styled H.R. 6906—two months later, Dr. Woodward must have decided to spare himself the grief of a personal appearance. He submitted instead a short letter which stated the AMA's reasons for opposing the bill. [26]

Both committees reported the bill favorably despite Woodward's objections. The Ways and Means report raised the FBN assertions against marihuana to the level of congressional findings:

Under the influence of this drug the will is destroyed and all power of directing and controlling thought is lost. Inhibitions are released. As a result of these effects, it appeared from testimony produced at the hearings that many violent crimes have been and are being committed by persons under the influence of this drug. Not only is marihuana used by hardened criminals to steel them to commit violent crimes, but it is also being placed in the hands of high-school children in the form of marihuana cigarettes by unscrupulous peddlers. Cases were cited at the hearings of school children who have been driven to crime and insanity through the use of this drug. Its continued use results many times in impotency and insanity.[27]

Congressional "Deliberation" and Action

The marihuana "problem" and the proposed federal cure went virtually unnoticed by the general public. Having failed to arouse public opinion on any significant scale through its educational campaign, the Bureau of Narcotics nevertheless pushed the proposed legislation through congressional committees. The committee members were convinced by inaccurate, unscientific evidence that federal action was urgently needed to suppress a problem that was no greater and probably less severe than it had been in the preceding six years when every state had passed legislation to suppress it. The committee was also convinced, incorrectly, that the public was aware of the evil and that it demanded federal action.

The debate on the floor of Congress illustrates the nonchalance of the legislators. The bill passed the House of Representatives in the very late afternoon of a long session. Many members were unfamiliar either with marihuana or with the purpose of the act. When the bill came to the House floor on 10 June 1937, one congressman objected to considering the measure at such a late hour:

Mr. DOUGHTON. I ask unanimous consent for the present consideration of the bill [H.R. 6906] to impose an occupational excise tax upon certain dealers in marihuana, to impose a transfer tax upon certain dealings in marihuana, and to safeguard the revenue therefrom by registry and recording.
The Clerk read the title of the bill.
Mr. SNELL. Mr. Speaker, reserving the right to object, and notwithstanding the fact that my friend, Reed, is in favor of it, is this a matter we should bring up at this late hour of the afternoon? I do not know anything about the bill. It may be all right and it may be that everyone is for it, but as a general principle, I am against bringing up any important legislation, and I suppose this is important, since it comes from the Ways and Means Committee, at this late hour of the day.
. . . . .

Mr. RAYBURN. Mr. Speaker, if the gentleman will yield, I may say that the gentleman from North Carolina has stated to me that this bill has a unanimous report from the committee and that there is no controversy about it.
Mr. SNELL.   What is the bill?
Mr. RAYBURN. It has something to do with something that is called marihuana. I believe it is a narcotic of some kind.
Mr. FRED M. VINSON. Marihuana is the same as hashish.
Mr. SNELL.   Mr. Speaker, I am not going to object but I think it is wrong to consider legislation of this character at this time of night.[28]

On 14 June, when the bill finally emerged on the House floor, four congressmen in one way or another asked that the proponents explain the provisions of the act. Instead of a detailed analysis, they received a statement of one of the members of the Ways and Means Committee which repeated reflexively the lurid criminal acts Anslinger had attributed to marihuana users at the hearings. After less than two pages of debate, the act passed without a roll call.[29] When the bill returned as amended from the Senate, the House considered it again and adopted as quickly as possible the Senate suggestions, which were all minor.[30] The only question was whether the AMA agreed with the bill. Congressman Vinson not only said they did not object, but he also claimed that the Bill had AMA support. After turning Dr. Woodward's testimony on its head, he also called him by another name—Wharton.[31]

The act passed Congress with little debate and even less public attention. Although the Federal Bureau of Narcotics had not sought legislation, the bureau's efforts on behalf of the Uniform Narcotic Drug Act had created a climate of fear which provoked insistent cries for a federal remedy, particularly by a few state law enforcement agents hoping to get federal support for their activities. As a result, the law was tied neither to scientific study nor to enforcement need. The Marihuana Tax Act was hastily drawn, heard, debated, and passed. It was a paradigm of the uncontroversial law.

CHAPTER IX

Marihuana Recession, 1938-1951

IT HAS BEEN POSTULATED by some researchers that the FBN's own desire to expand its jurisdiction ignited passage of the Marihuana Tax Act.[1] Conversely, there is some evidence that Anslinger resisted federal legislation in order to *protect* his bureaucracy. In any event, the act did increase significantly the bureau's area of responsibility. In fact, as Dr. Woodward pointed out to the Ways and Means Committee, the bureau was economically incapable of securing full enforcement of the act. Hemp growing wild all over the country would have to be eradicated. Since medical distribution of the drug had all but disappeared, the contorted revenue-related devices employed in the act (written order forms, registration) bore no relation to the real world; the net effect was that simple possession now became a federal crime. Similarly, all nonmedical transfers, whatever the amount, circumstances, or geographical nature, were also federal crimes. In a sense the Marihuana Tax Act blanketed existing state and local offenses with a coextensive range of federal offenses, all of these governing the same conduct.

Given the breadth of this statutory mandate, what did the bureau do? Anslinger began with a four-pronged enforcement policy when the act was passed:

1. Control of cultivation of the plant for legitimate purposes and eradication of wild growth

2. Pacification of marihuana sensationalism in the press

3. Education of the federal judiciary toward strict application of the law

4. Allocation of federal enforcement resources toward major trafficking rather than petty possession offenses

Crabgrass

The effort to control the legitimate growth and to eradicate the wild growth of marihuana was stymied from the outset. H. J. Wollner, consulting chemist to the Treasury Department, noted at once that "virtually nothing is known concerning the nature of the narcotic principle, its physiological behavior, and the ultimate effect upon the social group." Without some knowledge of the active principle, he went on, it was impossible to establish the presence of the psychoactive substance in a court of law, or to breed a strain which could serve the industrial purpose of cannabis without psychoactive properties.

With respect to "Marijuana: The Weed," Dr. Wollner observed:

> As explained above, the plant marihuana is now growing wild in all parts of the country. It is to be anticipated that as the Bureau of Narcotics more effectively is in control of the legitimate growth, distribution, and use of this plant that the Bureau's attention shall be then directed toward the eradication and control of the wild growing weed.
> To this end it would be desirable to know whether or not the plant kingdom provides other species of plants, which, in respect to marihuana, would possess a weed eradicating character. It would be desirable to explore, in addition, the economics of a variety of weed killers to determine whether these can be practically employed.[2]

The scope of marihuana's growth, the transportability and dormancy of the seeds, and the lack of a highly efficient herbicide all militated against a comprehensive eradication program. The cost of such a program would have been substantial even if success were assured. But the federal government simply was indisposed and unequipped to conduct an acre-by-acre survey of the United States, and no active effort was undertaken. The eradication "program" became a matter of reaction to routine information—letters from farmers who had identified the plant and discoveries of acreage by law enforcement agents. As the bureau's interest in marihuana subsided during the forties, so did the effort to eradicate wild growth. In fact, the federal government encouraged the cultivation of hemp during the war, even though a chemically inactive strain had not been developed, because sources of sisal rope had been severed by Japan's occupation of the Philippines. All over the United States the weed remained plentiful and largely undetected.

No More Hysterics

The sensational accounts of the effects of marihuana in the press reached a crescendo around the time of the passage of the act. Although there had been a continuing debate within the medical and official communities about the prudence of encouraging such propaganda, Anslinger undoubtedly agreed with Dr. Walton's assertion that the situation required a "necessary degree of sensationalism." Walton, Anslinger, Gomila, and others tended to dismiss out of hand Woodward's contention that any increase in marihuana use was directly attributable to curiosity ignited by the press.

After the act, however, Anslinger changed his tune. Especially disastrous from the bureau's point of view was press interest in the same two matters which he had enthusiastically encouraged since 1935: the spread of use among the young, and its relation to violent crime. As propagandist, the bureau had since 1935 magnified use; now, as enforcer, the bureau found it politically expedient to minimize use. The goal was now one of deflecting public attention instead of attracting it.

The same change occurred in regard to the crime thesis. The major point of bureau propaganda against marihuana had long been its evocation of homicidal mania, and one of the primary sources of the bureau's evidence of the relation between marihuana use and violent crime had been the use of marihuana intoxication as a defense in criminal cases. Attempts by defense attorneys in an adversary setting to absolve the defendant of responsibility for his actions had become medical authority for the scientific hypothesis that marihuana use caused crime.[3] This was also of tremendous interest to the press, especially in murder cases. Before the act, Anslinger had been somewhat ambivalent toward use of this defense tactic, but he did not attempt to discourage defense attorneys from asserting it. He was as willing to forward "atrocious crime" propaganda to them as to anyone else. One can well imagine how "useful as well as interesting" such an attorney found Anslinger's "Assassin of Youth" article, and how "gladly" he would pay "any necessary charges" for fifteen copies.[4]

State prosecutors, on the other hand, had been uneasy about the bureau's approach before passage of the act, for the FBN propaganda left very little room for rebuttal. If the *drug*, perhaps even one cigarette, removed all restraint and eradicated any moral distinctions between right and wrong, "temporary insanity" or "irresistible impulse" should relieve the defendant of complete responsibility, especially if possession and use of the substance were not illegal. Yet the state prosecutors were among Anslinger's most potent allies in his campaign to criminalize marihuana. This ambivalence is reflected in the letter which accompanied the gory photograph Anslinger used to tantalize the Senate Finance Subcommittee; to escape the dilemma, the prosecutor attributed the murder to the insidious effects of the drug, but noted that since the defendant's mind was not "totally prostrate," the verdict was "legally correct."[5]

After the act, Anslinger began to think more like a prosecutor than a propagandist. He wanted to put a stop to use of the defense and the hysteria it generated. He discouraged Dr. Munch, who had testified at the House hearings, from testifying on behalf of the defense in such situations.

Anslinger also directed his agents to discourage local officials from playing up any alleged involvement of marihuana with crime to the press. In a complete reversal of FBN policy, agents were now alerted to the problem of yellow journalism.[6] On 11 April 1938 the commissioner told his New York district supervisor that "our present policy is to discourage undue emphasis on marihuana for the reason that in some sections of the country recently press reports have been so exaggerated that interest in the subject has become almost hysterical and we are therefore trying to mold public opinion along more conservative and saner lines."[7] Three days later Anslinger acquainted Dr. Munch with the new perspective:

I believe an article for King Features Syndicate would be bad publicity because of the fact that you cannot be sure as to what changes would be made in your article and your experience will only cause the curious to try it. We are now playing down publicity on marihuana as there are indications that the press has become somewhat hysterical on the subject and that as a number of articles which recently appeared have placed the problem all out of proportion to its present status in the field of narcotic control.[8]

The fact that Anslinger had accepted Woodward's view that sensational reports about marihuana would only lead children and impressionable youngsters to try the drug is also reflected in his revised concept of marihuana education. He came to feel very strongly that educational work should be conducted with considerable discretion so that children could be warned in a way which would avoid arousing their curiosity about this drug. Similarly, when the Foreign Policy Association produced its pamphlet *Marihuana: The New Dangerous Drug*, Commissioner Anslinger was heartened by assurances that the pamphlet would be placed only in the hands of mature adults and that no direct contact would be made with children.[9]

Put Them Away for Good

Immediately following passage of the act, the FBN directed an "educational" effort toward the federal judiciary which emphasized the need for severe sentences for marihuana offenders. Some judges needed no reinforcement. In one of the first cases under the act, a Colorado judge left no doubt about his view: "I consider marihuana the worst of all narcotics—far worse than the use of morphine or cocaine. Under its influence men become beasts, just as was the case with [the defendant]. Marihuana destroys life itself. I have no sympathy with those who sell this weed. In the future I will impose the heaviest penalties. The Government is going to enforce this new law to the letter."[10]

Some months later, however, the district supervisor in Philadelphia reported that he and the U.S. attorney were perturbed because a federal judge had assessed only three years' probation to a reputed marihuana addict. Alleging that judges were unaware of the seriousness of marihuana addiction, he proposed that a conference be called for the purpose of educating judges on the importance of severe sentences to control the marihuana trade.[11]

Anslinger did encourage local "lobbying" efforts and they soon bore fruit. In 1938 the district supervisor for the Maryland, Virginia, and West Virginia areas reported "splendid results" in two recent narcotics cases handled in the western district of West Virginia. The defendants in these cases were given ten- to twelve-year sentences for possession and growth of marihuana. Noting that the judge had been most cooperative in meeting his appeals for severe sentences in marihuana cases, the supervisor pointed out that his agents had spent a great deal of time addressing women's clubs in West Virginia in an effort to encourage public support for severe sentencing practices. Commissioner Anslinger was elated and he pledged to continue his efforts to educate judges to the need for harsh sentences.[12] He wanted more judges to share the view expressed by Judge McClintock in the West Virginia cases: "Anything more infernal than the trade of these people is hard to imagine."

No Big Deal

Without much initial guidance from Washington, FBN agents immediately began to arrest marihuana addicts whom they had formerly either ignored or turned over to state authorities. From 1 October to 31 December 1937 federal agents made 369 seizures totaling 229 kilograms of the drug.[13] In so doing, however, the FBN personnel were only performing duties that state officials could have handled. Thus, on 14 December 1937 Commissioner Anslinger instituted a new policy in a confidential memorandum to all district supervisors:

> The Bureau has noted that a great many marihuana cases of comparative minor nature are being reported.
> Thus far, the courts have shown a very good attitude with regard to the disposition of marihuana cases and we do not wish to bring about a reaction by congesting court calendars with cases of a petty type. It is believed that in a great number of cases if more strenuous efforts were made to ascertain sources of supply, cases which could command more respect in the courts would be developed.[14]

The commissioner hoped that the bureau's role in the enforcement of the Marihuana Tax Act would be to stifle suppliers, large interstate traffickers, and smugglers, while leaving the small possession cases to local authorities. However, several factors served to frustrate this policy. Of primary importance was the fact that marihuana traffic was highly disorganized and there was no national or regional network against which FBN expertise could be brought to bear.[15] Second, the bureau had always exaggerated the incidence of use and the national proportions of the "problem." Use was still concentrated geographically and socioeconomically; commerce in the drug was a casual endeavor, not a major enterprise.

So, despite the commissioner's directive, the bureau's files are replete with reported apprehensions of individuals in possession of minute quantities of marihuana. In fact, in about half of all marihuana cases reported and marihuana arrests made during the few years following passage of the act, the amount of marihuana possessed by the individual was less than one ounce, and no allegation of trafficking or sale was ever made.[16] Once the United States entered World War II, enforcement activity declined substantially; the Bureau of Customs and the FBN together seized only a total of 257 kilograms in 1945.[17]

By this time the bureau had again altered its policy, implicitly if not explicitly. Beginning during the war years, the bureau abandoned responsibility for most marihuana law enforcement to the states. It chose instead to concentrate on the opiates. This policy became particularly firm after the war when narcotics use rose significantly. The bureau became increasingly selective with regard to the marihuana investigations it chose to launch, beginning to concentrate its efforts on the population it conceived to be most heavily involved, ghetto blacks and musicians.

The Jazz Threat

Ever since marihuana had first appeared in the major urban areas in the late twenties, the journeyman musical community had touted its beneficial effect on their performance. Many of the small-time and second-rate musicians who were arrested were heard to say, either at their trial or during the arrest process, that marihuana greatly improved their ability to play hot music and that a law ought to be passed to permit them to smoke marihuana. At the same time, the commissioner's public statements with regard to the role of jazz music and jazz musicians in spreading the marihuana habit to the young often brought him and the bureau in direct conflict with the musical world, especially its newspapers and union leaders.

In February 1938 two men were arrested outside Minneapolis for growing marihuana for the purpose of selling it. The *Minneapolis Tribune* reported that Federal Narcotics Supervisor Joseph Bell had said: "Present day swing music, the Big Apple Dance, and orchestra jam sessions are responsible for increasing the use of marihuana, both by dance band musicians and by the boys and girls who patronize them." According to the *Tribune*, Bell went on to say, "the tempo of present day music [seems] to do something to the nerves. [The] boys and girls . . . seem to think they need a stimulant for their nerves."[18] The story prompted Sidney Berman, editor of a music magazine *Orchestra World* to complain to Commissioner Anslinger that "this is a rather serious charge against the popular orchestra field which we represent and we would appreciate further clarification on the subject."[19] In response, Anslinger averred that the quotation from the *Minneapolis Tribune* had been made by the two men who had been arrested and not by Agent Bell. In his own report to Commissioner Anslinger, however, Bell emphasized that, in his experience, many jazz musicians used marihuana and that the two men apprehended attested in detail to the fact that jazz musicians and jazz music were spreading a marihuana culture among the young.[20]

In January 1941 the president of the Detroit Federation of Musicians announced on the front page of the union's official organ, *Keynote*, that "drastic action" had been taken to curb marihuana use among the ranks: "Any member found guilty of the use of marihuana or on proof that a member uses same, such member shall immediately be expelled from membership."[21] Wondering if smoke meant fire, Anslinger immediately directed his Detroit agents to determine the extent to which local musicians were engaged in the act of purveying marihuana among themselves or to others. Although the union resolution turned out to be largely precautionary,[22] a subsequent arrest uncovered a large marihuana ring which had regularly sold quantities of the drug to bands traveling through or playing engagements in Detroit.[23]

Four weeks later a Los Angeles newspaper report that two local musicians who had been killed in an automobile accident had marihuana cigarettes in their pockets[24] prompted another letter to Anslinger from Berman of *Orchestra World*. He wondered whether the commissioner knew how much marihuana the musicians had or where they had gotten it.[25] Anslinger replied that he was unable to comment on pending cases, although he noted in his personal file that "musicians appear to be among the principal users of marihuana [and] a shock quote in *Orchestra World* may serve to jolt these people to the dangers of the use of this weed."[26]

A steady stream of such events together with the recession in the narcotics enforcement business during the war years provoked a major escalation in Anslinger's crusade against musicians in 1943. On 7 September the commissioner called for a nationwide roundup. He told all his field agents:

> Because of increasing volume of reports indicating that many musicians of the swing band type are responsible for the spread of the marihuana smoking vice, I should like you to give the problem some special attention in your district. If possible, I should like you to develop a number of cases in which arrest would be withheld so as to synchronize these with arrests to be made in other districts.
> Please let me know what are the possibilities along this line in your district.[27]

As it turned out, the possibilities were slight. Most of the agents reported that there were few cases involving any big name musicians and that most of the smaller, less well known part-time musicians had already been arrested and their cases processed. Nevertheless, Anslinger kept alive the idea of a national roundup of jazz musicians throughout the 1940s. Each time a musician was alleged to smoke marihuana, particularly if his group were well known or had a large following among young people, the commissioner would send letters to all agents urging them to prepare a number of cases so that a nationwide, synchronized arrest could be executed.

One such incident was a birthday party for Tommy Dorsey during the fall of 1944, which ended in a major brawl. One of the guests, a Mr. Hall, testified before the California State Grand Jury that Dorsey had hit him and also smoked "the wrong kind of cigarettes." Apprised of this testimony, Anslinger urged his local agents to interview Hall and to encourage the state's attorney to determine whether Dorsey or members of his band might be involved with the use of marihuana. At first Hall was reluctant to say anything, and the prosecutor, not anxious to anger his only witness, asked the FBN to defer its investigation until the assault case was closed. The agents persevered, however, and finally they were permitted to interview Hall. He was unable to recall anything about the use of marihuana at the Dorsey party, and he said that he had never stated that Dorsey was in any way connected with marihuana. Stymied, the bureau dropped its investigation of the Dorsey band.[28]

Contributing to the bureau's heightened interest in the musical community was the conviction that musicians were draft dodgers. The marihuana laws thus became a tool for supporting the war effort. The commissioner asked the Selective Service System to prepare a list of musicians whose alleged marihuana use had exempted them from the draft. The list contained the names of many prominent musicians of the time, including Thelonius Monk. Anslinger had his agents prepare from this list an additional one designating the orchestras with which the rejectees were associated. These groups, of course, did not necessarily have any connection with marihuana; nevertheless, bands associated with the following entertainers and programs found their way into the official investigative files of the bureau: Louis Armstrong, Les Brown, Count Basie, Cab Calloway, Jimmy Dorsey, Duke Ellington, Dizzy Gillespie, Lionel Hampton, Andre Kostelanetz, the Milton Berle program, the Coca-Cola program, Jackie Gleason, and the Kate Smith program. As a result of these compilations, Anslinger wrote to his district supervisors on 19 December 1944:

> I have in mind such cases as that of———. . . . Not only is this man not in the Army where he belongs but he brazenly tells us that he is able to maintain an almost constant supply of marihuana. I am transmitting a schedule prepared in the file room here which shows some of musicians (and their orchestral connections) who have been rejected by the military as marihuana users.
>
> I wish you would study this and give any suggestions which you may have for dealing with the law violations upon which these men appear to be capitalizing.[29]

Such efforts were doomed, Anslinger soon discovered, by the unwillingness of anyone inside the jazz world to become an informant.[30] On the whole the bureau's musicians crackdown during the war netted only itinerants or musicians of little fame. Much hearsay about big names such as Louis Armstrong, Sarah Vaughn, and Buddy Rich was gathered, but nothing ever came of it.[31] After the war, however, the bureau's interest intensified. Commissioner Anslinger recommended to the under secretary of the treasury on 22 November 1948 that the following letter be sent to the head of the federation to which any person convicted of a narcotics violation belonged:

Arrests involving a certain type of musician in marihuana cases are on the increase. The following are few of the many cases cited as examples: [names omitted].

As you know, some of these musicians acquire following among juveniles. We are all familiar with the type of hero worship in which the juvenile is a slavish imitator of the things good or bad which are done by the object of his admiration.

In my opinion, there is a real juvenile delinquency threat in the marihuana antics of these persons. We, of course, are using all of the limited law enforcement facilities at our command.

I am bringing this situation to your attention because I feel that you might suggest ways in which your organization could assist in eliminating the anti-social activities of this segment of the musician profession. Hoping you can assist us in suppressing this abuse, I am Cordially H. J. Anslinger.[32]

Under Secretary Foley scrapped the idea because of its vagueness and the likelihood that it would raise a public outcry. He also doubted that the American Federation of Musicians would go along voluntarily.

The same year Anslinger observed before the House Ways and Means Committee: "We have been running into a lot of traffic among these jazz musicians and I am not speaking about the good musicians but the jazz type."[33] This broadside provoked an outcry from the musical profession to the effect that jazz music was good music and only a very small segment of jazz musicians had ever been alleged to have been involved with marihuana. *Downbeat* magazine called for a public apology.[34]

The commissioner tried another tack three years later. He proposed that the Department of State cancel the passports of musicians who had at any time been involved in a court proceeding relating to marihuana. Three musicians were singled out for particular scrutiny, one of them Thelonius Monk. This idea surfaced in the course of a casual conversation in Europe between an FBN agent and a prominent music personality. The musician observed that jazz music was becoming popular in Sweden and France and that the indigenous jazz musicians were emulating Americans not only in their musical tastes but also in their smoking habits. He also noted that the traveling American musicians were the only source of marihuana for their European colleagues. Despite Anslinger's contention that passport revocation would avoid embarrassment in the international arena, the Treasury Department rejected the scheme as too vague. It appears that the under secretary of the treasury felt that the allegations against the musicians were not sufficiently supportable to merit communication with the Department of State.[35]

In 1937 Anslinger had made the case for federal marihuana legislation, a matter that had been considered within the narcotics bureaucracy since 1930. He had convinced a willing, uninterested Congress that federal expertise and power were necessary to curb an emerging national menace which the states were unable to control. Public opinion, he had alleged, had been aroused by an alarming increase in use of a disastrous narcotic weed which grew wild all over the country and was purveyed to school children and criminals by an organized interstate trafficking network.

Between 1938 and 1951 Anslinger defused the public "furor" that the bureau had helped create and then discovered that he could not eradicate the weed—which Woodward had predicted— and that there was no organized interstate traffic in the drug. Thus, the federal government had flexed its muscles to no avail; there was no opponent in the ring. This potent legislation—which had been so urgently needed—was ultimately turned upon a selected group of users who offended the FBN commissioner for reasons quite apart from their marihuana use. A law rooted in prejudice against one social group had become an instrument of prejudice against another.

CHAPTER X

The Marihuana Mystery:
Science, 1938-1951

THE SCIENTIFIC COMMUNITY was highly uncertain of the effects of the drug at the time national marihuana prohibition was achieved. This ambiguity was never perceived as an impediment to criminalization; yet it was never readily acknowledged either to the public or to the lawmakers. No group which opposed the law and might have insisted on facts rather than speculation had access to public opinion.

The narcotics bureaucracy was well aware that the state of knowledge about marihuana in 1937 contrasted sharply with scientific understanding about opiates in 1914 and alcohol in 1919 when similar national action had been taken. The FBN was eager to dispel this uncertainty, both to facilitate enforcement and to preclude subsequent criticism. Six months after the passage of the Marihuana Tax Act, the consulting chemist of the Treasury Department detailed gaps in scientific knowledge and encouraged Anslinger to commission research. Emphasizing "that virtually nothing is known concerning the nature of the narcotic principle, its physiological behavior, and the ultimate effect upon the social group,"[1] Dr. Herbert Wollner contrasted the present situation with that prevailing at the time the Harrison Act was passed. In 1914, he pointed out, the scientific community understood how the opiates worked and what their effects were on humans. The behavior of addicts, the physical addiction produced by continued use, and the psychochemical character of the drugs were all sufficiently well understood to permit regulation and administrative control "with clarity and understanding." With marihuana, he observed, lack of understanding as to the nature of the active principle of the drug and consequently the impact of the drug on the physiology and psychology of its users made sensible regulation impossible.[2]

Several months later Wollner convinced Anslinger that it would be desirable for experts "to collate their results (in scientific investigations) and observe the direction of parallel investigations conducted by other investigators in related fields."[3] A Marihuana Conference was convened on 5 December 1938 in Washington to analyze the need for research on "questions relating to the agricultural, chemical, pharmacological, sociological, economic and industrial phases of the problem."[4] The minutes of the conference record the presence of several acknowledged American experts on cannabis. Yet, the discussion continuously reflected the fact that uncertainty about the active principle and the inability to standardize doses for research precluded understanding and permitted only conjecture. For example, Wollner stated:

> The situation is as bad in the chemical literature as it is in all of the other phases.
> I should certainly be within the reasonable bounds of correctness when I guess that ninety per cent of the stuff that has been written on the chemical end of Cannabis is absolutely wrong, and, of the other ten per cent, at least two-thirds of it is of no consequence. . . .
> I think if all the research work done so far were dumped together by a group of chemists, or if they started out today on this investigation, that they would be exactly the same as they are now inside of six months; that is, all of the information which we have which is very little, could be accumulated in six months.[5]

Each professional group at the conference summed up what little was suspected by investigators in their fields about the effects of marihuana. There was only one significant substantive interchange among the participants, a strong disagreement between Anslinger and Dr. Walter Bromberg, senior psychiatrist at Bellevue Hospital in New York, on the relation between marihuana and crime. Drawing on his study of marihuana users in the New York courts (which would be published the following year), Bromberg concluded that "the extravagant claims of defense attorneys and the press, that crime is caused by Marihuana addiction, demand careful scrutiny."[6] This assertion was challenged immediately by the commissioner. He repeated many of the incidents allegedly relating marihuana to crime that he had culled from the files of the bureau. In response Bromberg called for "a Commission (to) be appointed to examine the matter scientifically...."[7] Anslinger quickly changed the subject.

So far as we can tell, the interest in research generated by this conference soon dissipated. The chemists and pharmacologists quietly continued to search for the active principle, but the bureau's interest was limited to agricultural questions which touched enforcement of the law: eradication, and the development of an inactive strain of hemp. Anslinger viewed all new studies of the effects of the drug on man as potential threats. He preferred to rest on the prevailing ignorance. Neither the Public Health Service nor the bureau sponsored any concentrated research. During the ensuing decade private investigators engaged in ad hoc research with the bureau serving as an informal storehouse. As a result the law enforcement agency became the public's arbiter of scientific arguments and debates, functioning as a filter through which scientific research had to pass on its way to the public. Inevitably, the bureau promoted public attention for those scientific studies which supported the law enforcement stance and either ignored or, as in the case of the La Guardia Report of 1944, openly attacked those with which it did not agree.

A variety of technical articles, studies, and books on marihuana were published from 1938 to 1950.[8] Most had significant methodological defects, which recent commentators have identified, but their existence, not their validity, is of interest here. Although a complete review is beyond the scope of this book, let us now examine the general thrust of the most widely circulated literature, as well as the official response, pertaining to the three theses upon which policy makers had relied during the criminalization period: addiction, insanity, and crime.

Addiction

Despite the general consensus within the American scientific community in the 1930s that marihuana users did not evidence the tolerance and withdrawal symptoms characteristic of physical addiction, Commissioner Anslinger harbored his own doubts at least into the forties. At the 1937 hearings the following was characteristic:

Senator BROWN. I want to bring out one fact that you have not touched upon yet. As I understand it, marihuana is not a habit-producing drug, at least to the same extent that opium is, for instance. It is somewhat easier to break the habit in the case of marihuana than it is in the case of opium smoking?

Mr. ANSLINGER. Yes, you have stated that correctly, Senator. It is a very difficult matter to break the opium habit. However, this habit can be broken. There is some evidence that it [marihuana] is habit-forming. The experts have not gone very far on that.[9]

In 1938 an internal Treasury Department research summary refused to distinguish at all between cannabis and the opiates.[10]

For the most part, however, the debate during the forties centered on the notion of psychological dependence, which had surfaced in the thirties.[11] For some this notion was axiomatic. The Public Health Service's Kolb, who had now succeeded Treadway as assistant surgeon general in charge of the Division of Mental Hygiene, noted in 1938 that the "marihuana addict deprived of his drug merely has a hankering for it."[12] But the assistant dean of the Rutgers College of Pharmacy explained the same year that "if four or five cigarettes are smoked daily, a small average for a cigarette smoker, the user would soon become an addict and a danger to society. It is the smoker's desire to keep in 'high,' which eventually makes him a slave to the Mexican Reefer."[13] Another observer noted in 1939 that marihuana gives rise to a craving which may very easily lead to the habitual use of drugs.[14] Probably the consensus, then, is best captured by Bromberg's comment in 1939, which reiterated his conclusion five years earlier:

> In the main, American authorities support the view that marihuana is not a [physically] habit-forming drug. Asiatic and European writers are not in accord with this opinion. . . . The most one can say on the basis of ascertainable facts is that prolonged use of marihuana constitutes a "sensual" addiction, in that the user wishes to experience again and again the ecstatic sensations and feelings which the drug produces. Unlike addiction to morphine, which is biochemically as well as psychologically determined, prolonged use of marihuana is essentially in the service of the hedonistic elements of the personality.[15]

During the forties few attempts were made to examine critically the presumed existence of psychic dependence. In 1942 Allentuck and Bowman concluded that habituation to cannabis was not as strong as that to tobacco and alcohol.[16] The La Guardia Committee concluded in 1944 after a clinical study that there was no compelling urge to use the drug. They found that users encountered little or no difficulty when they were forced to discontinue it.[17] One researcher observed in 1946 that subjects who had smoked seventeen cigarettes a day for thirty-nine days reported some difficulty after abrupt withdrawal, but they exhibited no behavioral changes.[18]

The failure of scientific investigation to demonstrate any significant behavioral indication of addiction was reflected in the bureau's de-emphasis of this issue in its public statements. The observation of arrestees also motivated agents to report that "marihuana is not habit-forming and no discomfort is manifested when a user is cut off from his supply."[19] During the forties the bureau made only occasional reference to marihuana "addicts," and it did not single out the addictive property of the drug as one of its major dangers.[20] It should be noted, however, that the FBN did not make a public concession on this point until forced to do so by the testimony of Dr. Isbell during the Boggs Act Hearings in the 1950s.

Insanity

Despite the skepticism of the scientific community, Commissioner Anslinger left no doubt at the hearings about the relation between marihuana and mental deterioration and insanity. Nor did Dr. Munch, who never once during the course of the hearings acknowledged the obstacles that he discussed at the Marihuana Conference: ignorance of the active principle and lack of standardization.

Two studies in the forties examined long-term users with respect to mental deterioration and they found no such result. A study for the La Guardia Committee utilized quantitative measures, including verbal and abstract tests, on a sample of seventeen chronic users. The researchers concluded that the subjects "had suffered no mental or physical deterioration as a result of their use of the drug."[21] Freedman and Rockmore reached the same conclusion in 1946 on the basis of their examination of 310 army personnel whose average period of use was seven years.[22]

A few efforts were made during the early forties to determine whether the alleged marihuana psychosis, so often described in Eastern literature, existed in American users. Drawing from a total of thirty-one cases of "psychosis" following marihuana use, Bromberg differentiated in 1939 between temporary reactions during acute intoxication and toxic psychosis. In fourteen subjects, the condition lasted from a few hours to several days. In eight of these cases, the reaction occurred during the first experience with the drug. Bromberg concluded that "no permanent effect is observable by psychiatric examination after the effects wear off. . . ." In the seventeen cases of toxic psychosis, lasting from weeks to months, Bromberg found that the toxic picture was generally "superimposed on a basic functional mental disturbance, such as schizophrenia." He also raised the possibility that "the drug experience might occasionally represent the incipient stage of a functional psychosis" in predisposed individuals, although "countless persons use marihuana without the development of an observable mental condition."[23]

From their 1942 study Allentuck and Bowman concluded that "marihuana will not produce a psychosis *de novo* in a well-integrated, stable person," although it might precipitate a functional psychosis in predisposed individuals.[24] In the La Guardia Committee's study of seventy-seven subjects, only nine "psychotic" episodes occurred. Six were clearly of the acute variety, lasting only a few hours. The other three were considered inextricably related to conditions other than the marihuana experience.[25]

After this small flurry of activity, general disinterest set in everywhere, except in the FBN. Even in the countries of the East, the number of insanity-hemp reports decreased precipitously after 1930.[26] Yet Anslinger continued to believe in the relationship between marihuana and insanity, and he continued to seek documentation. In 1943 he directed all agents to be on the lookout for relevant information. Pursuant to this directive, one supervisor requested his agents to canvas state and local hospitals for information regarding "mental derangement of patients caused by continued use of marihuana." They found none.[27]

In his own mind, Anslinger continued to rely on the early Asian and African literature, and he became very defensive about the importance of noncorroborative Western studies. For example, Dr.

Loewe had experimented with cannabis and dogs in 1940. He found only an impairment of muscular coordination: "The dogs show no apparent excitement, anxiety or other emotion. . . ."[28] Dr. Wollner, well aware of the official position, specifically warned the Cornell professor of "the importance of not making statements to news-papermen from which erroneous inferences could be drawn."[29] Similarly, Anslinger vociferously denounced a study by Dr. Salazar-Viniegra, one of the leading authorities in Mexico, whose specialty was social medicine.[30] Dr. Salazar-Viniegra was convinced that marihuana was a fairly benign pharmacological entity and that individual reactions were governed in major part by social factors, particularly the power of suggestion. Moreover, "the suggestive load and the ideas which surround marihuana are formidable and have accumulated during the course of time. Marihuana addicts, journalists and even doctors have been the ones charged with trans-mitting the legend from generation to generation."[31] A major factor in the popular imagination, he observed, is the assumption

[t]hat marihuana 'renders insane' and that the mental disturb-ances which it produces are permanent, being responsible for a large percentage of the inmates of [mental institutions]. The common people are not the only ones who divulge these false-hoods; even the psychiatrists do it, spreading their statements, considerably enlarged and changed, to the newspapers, which are the most powerful means of propaganda.[32]

On the basis of his clinical observation of patients whose mental disturbances had been attributed to marihuana, Dr. Salazar-Viniegra refuted the separate existence of a "marihuana psychosis." There was no evidence in many cases that mentally ill patients had used the plant, and in others use was incidental, infrequent, and of small amount. The doctor also concluded that the symptoms bore little relationship to marihuana. Generally they composed a mental picture common to most inmates of mental asylums.[33]

With support from Dr. Bouquet, Commissioner Anslinger dis-missed Dr. Salazar-Viniegra's contentions out of hand. He called him "a man obviously without any experience in the narcotic problem."[34] Bouquet remarked that if the Mexican was right, then all scientists who have worked on the cannabis problem since 100 A.D. "should have their heads examined."[35] It should be noted, parenthetically, that Anslinger's conflict with Dr. Salazar-Viniegra extended well beyond marihuana. At the latter's suggestion, the Mexican government was then, in 1939, considering establishing clinics for dispensing a month's supply of opiates to addicts. As we noted in chapter 1, the Prohibition Bureau's enforcement of the Harrison Act successfully halted medical attempts—through private practitioners and clinics—to dispense opiates to drug-dependent persons for purposes of maintaining their addiction. According to the official view, this activity was not a legitimate medical practice since addicts were criminals, not sick persons. The debate about the proper public policy in this connection was raging once again, and Anslinger had no patience with anyone who seriously considered the maintenance approach.[36]

The FBN continued to link marihuana and insanity through the forties despite mounting evidence to the contrary. As late as March 1950 the bureau circulated Anslinger's own "Criminal and Psychiatric Aspects Associated with Marihuana" as the leading work in the field.[37]

Crime

Despite the skepticism of most scientific researchers throughout the thirties, the alleged link between marihuana and crime was the mainstay of the bureau's propaganda effort to secure passage of the Uniform Act in 1934-35, of its testimony before Congress to secure the Marihuana Tax Act in 1937, and of its public stance in the forties. Dr. Bromberg forcefully brought his doubts to Commissioner Anslinger's personal attention at the Marihuana Conference in late 1938, but Anslinger ignored the doctor's warnings. Anslinger personally had adopted the crime thesis in 1931, and he became increasingly convinced of its validity over the next five years. He became fully committed to it in 1936 and he nurtured and propagated it from 1936 to 1939. The press was saturated with the fruits of FBN endeavors,[38] a phenomenon which overshadowed the recurrent criticism of Drs. Kolb and Bromberg.

For example, Professor George C. Schicks, assistant dean of Rutgers College of Pharmacy, contributed "Marihuana: Depraver of Youth" to the March 1938 issues of the *Druggist Circular*. On the crime thesis Schicks wrote:

The person may be very susceptible to suggestion. There may be a strong urge toward the commission of criminal acts. The addict at this stage is dangerous. He may commit the most violent or shocking of crimes and not know what he is doing. Finally, he falls into a stupor or deep sleep, wakens the next morning without a hangover, and perhaps realizes for the first time some unfortunate act he has committed. Fortunately, all excessive users of Cannabis do not commit crime, but more cases of crime as a result of the drug action are being reported.[39]

Anslinger was very pleased. He felt that this article was "the best thing we have recently seen."[40] Similarly, in a letter to the bureau's district supervisor in San Francisco, Anslinger acknowledged receipt of a newspaper report that one woman had stabbed another while under the influence of marihuana, noting that "this is just another example of what a person will do while under the influence of that drug."[41]

Since the crime thesis rested entirely on the bureau case reports, Anslinger knew very well that continued corroboration depended on his efforts. Even after passage of the Marihuana Tax Act, he continued to use his agents as propaganda resources. In Circular Letter no. 458, labeled "Marihuana and Criminal Conduct," the commissioner requested all supervisors to send him any data from newspapers or other local sources which suggested a causal connection between marihuana use and the commission of any criminal act.[42]

Despite his continued search for examples of such a connection, Anslinger did not seek to publicize the results, having chosen to reduce public anxieties which he had formerly incited. He also continued his attempts to suppress the insanity defense. Of particular importance was his effort to silence Temple University's Dr. James C. Munch.

Dr. Munch had testified for the bureau at the hearings on the Marihuana Tax Act for good reason; he unhesitatingly linked marihuana with violent crime. The FBN solicited the testimony and Commissioner Anslinger had personally arranged for Munch's appearance before the committee.[43]

Munch's willingness to testify was not limited to legislative proceedings. Immediately after passage of the Marihuana Tax Act, he appeared on behalf of the defense in two of the most famous trials of the period. In the first, Ethel "Bunny" Sohl was tried in January 1938 in Newark, New Jersey. She and another woman were alleged to have murdered a bus driver during a robbery of his bus. Throughout Ethel Sohl's trial, it was claimed that she had smoked marihuana minutes before the robbery. Her attorneys, associated with one of New Jersey's most prestigious law firms, decided that since five eyewitnesses had seen the defendant shoot the bus driver, the only way to save her from the electric chair was to maintain a defense of temporary insanity based on her marihuana use.

Sohl testified during the course of the trial that marihuana made "wrong seem right" and that she was forced under the influence of the drug to do "fantastic things." Following her testimony, Dr. Munch was called by the defense as an expert on marihuana. Dr. Munch testified that the use of marihuana was directly connected with criminal impulses and could make a person unaware of the difference between right and wrong. Ethel Sohl was ultimately convicted of first-degree murder, but the jury did recommend life imprisonment rather than the death penalty. Commissioner Anslinger was convinced that the reason for the jury's leniency was the credence which it had given Dr. Munch's testimony. At the commissioner's instance, an agent interviewed Ethel Sohl in prison. He reported that in his opinion "the commission of this crime by Ethel Sohl was not due to the use of marihuana but that such defense was conceived by her attorney in an effort to free her or lessen her punishment."[44]

Then on 7 April 1938 Dr. Munch testified in the even more notorious case of Arthur Friedman, age twenty-one, who was on trial in New York with five other defendants for murdering a police detective. The *New York Post*, in a story headlined "Prof Flies High and Crashes, All on Wings of Marihuana," reported:

"After the first one I puffed," said a wizened, scholarly little man on a General Sessions witness stand today, "I thought I had wings. Great big blue wings—and I was flying all around the world."

The court and the jury trying five youths for the murder of a police detective cocked curious eyes on Professor James Clyde Munch of Temple University.

"After the second one," he went on, "I was depressed. I thought I had been spending 200 years at the bottom of an ink bottle."[45]

Anslinger immediately wrote to his New York district supervisor, Garland Williams, asking him to convey to Dr. Munch the bureau's displeasure at his testimony.[46] Anslinger was very angry:

I warned Dr. Munch not to testify in this case unless he was absolutely certain that the drug had been used by the defendant prior to the commission of the crime. In the past, we have afforded Dr. Munch considerable cooperation and he has likewise reciprocated.
What I would like to know is whether it was definitely established that the boys smoked the drug before the crime. Possibly the District Attorney can give you some information on this point. I am very anxious to know whether Dr. Munch in spite of my admonition proceeded with his testimony before he was absolutely certain that the drug had been used. I want this information so we may be able to determine our future relations with Dr. Munch.[47]

Agent Williams immediately contacted Dr. Munch to relay Anslinger's message. At the same time, Williams assigned a New York City Narcotics inspector to discuss the case with the two prosecutors to determine whether or not Arthur Friedman had definitely smoked marihuana before the commission of the crime. The district attorneys stated that they had no knowledge that Friedman had been a marihuana user until the defense showed up with two of the defendant's friends claiming that he had used two marihuana cigarettes on the night of the crime. Then, the inspector reported,

Dr. Munch got on the stand and put up a perfect defense for this man who murdered the cop and the two District Attorneys are very sore about it. They think Munch is a representative of the Bureau of Narcotics and wonder why the Commissioner sent him up there. According to the statements of the District Attorneys, Dr. Munch got up on the stand and stated he was an advisor to the Commissioner of Narcotics, Treasury Department, and advisor to the Congressional Committee to prepare the Marihuana Bill and that he furnished most of the information for it.[48]

Anslinger was now irate. He requested Dr. Munch to give a specific and detailed statement of the qualifications he had presented at the trial and, in particular, what connection, if any, he claimed to have with the Federal Bureau of Narcotics.

Munch repented. In a letter of 19 April 1938 he stated that he never assisted defense attorneys in making a claim of temporary insanity unless he was convinced that the defendant indeed used marihuana and would not escape his punishment on account of the defense. Moreover, the doctor continued, he had made every effort to keep his connections with the Federal Bureau of Narcotics from being disclosed at the trial. Finally, he assured Commissioner Anslinger that he would appear in no further murder trials and that he would not lend his assistance to insanity defenses based on marihuana.[49] A few days after receiving Dr. Munch's letter, Commissioner Anslinger spent some time studying the transcript of Munch's testimony in the Friedman case. He identified eight instances in which the testimony was in his view either in error or purposefully misleading, and he circulated his observations to his supervisors, not only to guide the bureau in its future relations with Dr. Munch but also to facilitate rebuttal in the event that Dr. Munch testified in any future cases.

The Munch experience illustrates the dilemma posed by the bureau's previous position on the relationship between marihuana intoxication and crime. It no longer served the government's purposes to allege, as had been done in the Marihuana Tax Act Hearings, that a few marihuana cigarettes incited a violent frenzy. Probably with some pressure from Dr. Kolb,[50] the bureau reexamined the scientific issue and now propagated a refined view that "no general rule could be evolved" since the "physiological effects of marihuana are variable." However, the bureau did maintain that in a substantial number of cases the user did lose control during the intoxication and might then impulsively commit violent acts.[51]

Even this view was difficult to sustain during the forties because study after study refuted it. In 1939, on the basis of review of the records of 16,854 criminal offenders in the psychiatric clinic of the New York County Court of General Sessions, Bromberg confirmed his 1934 conclusions: He found only sixty-seven marihuana users, of whom but six were charged with violent crimes and the remainder with property crimes. He commented: "[I] t was found in general that early use of the drug apparently did not predispose to crime. No positive relation could be found between violent crime and the use of marihuana in the cases observed in the Psychiatric Clinic. No cases of murder or sexual crimes due to marihuana were established."[52]

A 1938 survey of "colored prisoners" in Eastern State Penitentiary in Philadelphia revealed that "in none of these prisoners had there been any evidence that marihuana was a factor in their crimes."[53] In an effort to reconcile this conclusion with cases in the Stanley and FBN reports, the author added that most of those cases "have been very incompletely reported, since we do not know what other factors may have entered into their acts of violence."[54] Allentuck and Bowman (1942),[55] Freedman and Rockmore (1946),[56] and Bromberg again (1946)[57] all disputed the crime thesis, while two studies of marihuana use in the military in 1944 and 1945 found a high incidence of minor criminal behavior among the marihuana users in an overwhelmingly antisocial study population.[58]

The antagonism now developing between the FBN and the scientific community is reflected in the controversy generated by the Allentuck and Bowman paper, which had been published in the *American Journal of Psychiatry* in 1942. In the fall of that year, Assistant Surgeon General Kolb participated in a discussion of this paper during which he characterized the lay literature of the thirties as "fantastic" and "alarmist," noting that "the uninformed [were thereby] led to believe that modern civilization [was] about to disappear because of the drug." He praised the return to scientific moderation reflected by Allentuck and Bowman's 1942 work. He stated, with respect to the crime thesis in particular, that:

> It is reassuring to find from the careful study that Dr. Allentuck has made that the alarm about the relation of marihuana to crime is unfounded. The drug, like most other intoxicants, is taken mostly because it produces a sense of ease and finally sleep, but on its way to this final result there is a peculiar, bizarre type of intoxication with release of inhibitions. One of my cases said, "I can see to the bottom of things and solve problems much better." Other cases have a vivid sense of happiness for short periods. Some become alarmed during one stage of their intoxication, others become hilarious and noisy. It can

readily be seen that a drug which produces all these effects, if used as widely as alcohol is used in this country, might be like alcohol and a very important contributing cause to crimes of various kinds.[59]

Dr. Kolb did disagree with Allentuck and Bowman's suggestion that marihuana might prove beneficial in the treatment of opiate addiction. Yet, the editorial writers of the *Journal of the American Medical Association* echoed Dr. Kolb's sentiments and ratified this aspect of the "careful study" as well.[60]

Commissioner Anslinger was more than a little disturbed by the implications of the Allentuck and Bowman paper, and by the AMA's approval. Since Allentuck was director of a pending clinical study under the auspices of the La Guardia Committee in New York City, he knew there was more to come. He wasted no time in denouncing the Allentuck and Bowman study and the AMA itself.[61] He also solicited a rebuttal by his long-time ally, Dr. Bouquet.[62]

When the La Guardia Committee's report was published in late 1944, the crime thesis was dealt its most devastating blow. In September 1938 the Mayor of New York, Fiorello La Guardia, was prompted by the widespread marihuana propaganda to request advice from the New York Academy of Medicine. Having determined that existing knowledge was inadequate, the academy recommended a two-part study, one to determine the scope and impact of marihuana use within the city of New York, and another to ascertain the drug's effects on humans on the basis of a controlled laboratory study. The mayor agreed and authorized the academy to appoint a blue ribbon committee of thirty-one scientists to make the sociological and clinical studies. Many authorities welcomed the appointment of the committee, which launched its research in 1939. Dr. Kolb, for example, observed: "In view of the misinformation and alarm that has gotten abroad about marihuana, it is important to have a competent group like the Mayor's Committee to study this drug and present the real facts."[63] The sociological study was conducted by a team of New York policemen who reported directly to the committee. The clinical study was performed by Drs. Allentuck and Bowman, using as subjects seventy-seven volunteer prisoners who were observed in a city hospital ward.

The La Guardia Report was finally released late in 1944, six years after the appointment of the committee. There has been some speculation, which we have been unable to confirm or deny, that the FBN tried to suppress the report after the Allentuck publication. Together with its findings disputing the prevalent assumptions linking marihuana with insanity and addiction, the report undercut the crime thesis, finding that the drug was "not the determining factor in the commission of major crimes" and that "juvenile delinquency [was] not associated with the practice of smoking marihuana."[64]

Having been berated by the bureau two years earlier for its endorsement of the Allentuck and Bowman paper which previewed the committee's report, the AMA *Journal* now cast its lot with Anslinger. A stinging indictment of the Mayor's Committee appeared in an April 1945 editorial, which vehemently defended the crime thesis. After questioning the methodological validity of experiments with confined criminals, the editorial writer erroneously looked to Dr. Kolb for support: "Kolb, nationally known addiction expert, after reading the report stated, 'one may say of such a drug that, if it were abused as alcohol is abused, it might be an important cause of crimes and other misdemeanors.' " Of course, the 1942 remark by Dr. Kolb to which the *Journal* referred had actually endorsed the committee's ultimate finding, and the quoted portion reflected only a caveat applying to any widely used intoxicant.

In tone and content the AMA's editorial espoused the FBN's position on the La Guardia Report. Judging from subsequent collaboration between Anslinger and this *Journal*, we have little doubt that the words themselves are Anslinger's:

For many years scientists have considered cannabis a dangerous drug. Nevertheless, a book called "Marihuana Problems" by the New York City Mayor's Committee on Marihuana submits an analysis by 17 doctors of tests on 77 prisoners and, on this narrow and thoroughly unscientific foundation, draws sweeping and inadequate conclusions which minimize the harmfulness of marihuana. Already the book has done harm. . . .

The book states unqualifiedly to the public that the use of this narcotic does not lead to physical, mental or moral degeneration and that permanent deleterious effects from its continued use were not observed on 77 prisoners. This statement has already done great damage to the cause of law enforcement. Public officials will do well to disregard this unscientific, uncritical study, and continue to regard marihuana as a menace wherever it is purveyed.[65]

Drs. Walton[66] and Bowman[67] immediately endorsed the report and objected to the *Journal*'s editorial, while another physician, whose own work had been cited in support of the AMA's attack, entered a qualified dissent.[68] Apprehensive about the growing consensus within the scientific community against the crime thesis, Anslinger had successfully forged a wedge between the AMA and the acknowledged experts. As a direct result, the La Guardia Report sank quietly into oblivion.

In short, despite the accumulation of adverse data, the bureau held tenaciously to the crime thesis. Whenever any corroboration came to his attention, Anslinger seized it eagerly, magnifying its import along the way. For example, in a series of studies in India between 1939 and 1942[69] Dr. Chopra determined that the incidence of detected crime was higher among cannabis users than among the general population. At most, of course, this statistical correlation confirms the fact that Indian cannabis users were found predominantly among the same lower class population that exhibited the highest incidence of criminal conduct. Moreover, the major conclusion in Chopra's study was that violence was less common with marihuana users than with alcohol users. Nevertheless, Anslinger suggested in a letter to the AMA *Journal* that these data disproved the La Guardia Committee's findings.[70]

All Quiet on the Western Front

The public interest in marihuana use had subsided substantially during the early and mid-forties, and there was only limited interest in marihuana research within the scientific community. The sporadic exchanges were of little interest to anyone other than the participants. Even the La Guardia Report, which provoked such intense debate within the "marihuana community," received little attention outside it. Marihuana was no longer a "menace" in the United States.

With legislation already on the books and the eye of the press no longer trained on the issue, the Western scientific community generally coalesced around several propositions: dependence on marihuana, if it existed at all, related more to the motivation of the user than to the action of the drug; severe adverse psychological reactions seemed to be associated with the personality of the user rather than the precise action of the drug; and there was very little reliable evidence for any link between marihuana use and aggressive behavior or violent crime. On occasion scientific observers even questioned the public policy toward marihuana as well. The *Military Surgeon* editorialized in 1943: "It is the writer's considered opinion that the smoking of . . . cannabis is no more harmful than the smoking of tobacco. It is further considered that the legislation in relation to marihuana was ill-advised, that it branded as a menace and a crime a matter of trivial importance."[71]

The Federal Bureau of Narcotics combated this skepticism within the domestic scientific community by attempting to polarize that community and by relying heavily on Eastern investigations. There were muffled dissents within the ranks by government public health officials and even among its own agents,[72] but the bureau held the line, quietly and firmly, during the forties.

The 1950s: Along for the Ride

THE PUNITIVE APPROACH to narcotics use and dependence reached its zenith in the 1950s. After the relative quiet of the war years, there was reportedly an increase in opiate use in the late 1940s, and the public began to be concerned with the spread of narcotic addiction, particularly among young persons. In these days when public panic was aroused by "scares" of many kinds, the call for harsher penalties against drug users and sellers was soothing. Marihuana, too, was caught in the turbulence of this era. Although earlier assumptions about the drug were no longer commonplace, congressional furor was aroused by the new assertion, rejected by Commissioner Anslinger in 1937, that the use of marihuana inevitably led to the use of harder drugs. This new rationale for marihuana prohibition was to provide the basis for a continual escalation of penalties for marihuana use throughout the decade.

The new legislation came in two waves. In 1951 Congress passed the Boggs Act,[1] which increased penalties for all drug violators. For the first time in federal criminal legislation, marihuana and the "narcotic" drugs were lumped together, since the act provided uniform penalties for the Narcotic Drugs Import and Export Act[2] and the Marihuana Tax Act.[3] The states followed the federal lead. Then, in 1956 Congress passed the Narcotic Control Act, escalating the penalties still further. Once again the states responded in kind.

The Problem in 1951: Increased Narcotic Use

The assistant to the United States attorney general commented on the earliest draft of the new narcotic legislation: "We have been concerned to note the increase of narcotic violations in the New Orleans area and in certain other localities."[4] The hearings before the subcommittee of the House Ways and Means Committee and the floor debate leave no doubt that the Boggs Act was motivated by a perceived increase in narcotic use in the period 1948 to 1951. Testimony and evidence from a wide variety of sources indicated an abrupt and substantial increase in use and probably dependence, especially among teenagers, between 1947 and 1951. Senator Kefauver stated at the 26 June 1951 session of the hearings: "Illegal drug use has reached epidemic proportions according to information secured by this committee from different parts of the country. One of the most alarming aspects is the reported increase in addiction among the younger generation, some of school age."[5] And the *New York Times* reported Commissioner Anslinger's observation that "the present wave of juvenile addiction struck us with hurricane force in 1948 and 1949, and in a short time had the two Federal hospitals bursting at the seams."[6] Young people under twenty-one suddenly comprised a substantial part of the addict population. One witness, a fifty-seven-year-old addict who had started smoking opium around 1912, stated at the hearings that he had never seen significant use of drugs by young people until recently. He theorized that marihuana was probably the cause of the wave of youthful addiction.[7]

Congressman Boggs, speaking during the congressional debate on his bill, enunciated a concern that was reflected in many other quarters. After noting that there had been a 24 percent increase in arrests for narcotic violations between 1949 and 1950 and a 70 percent increase between 1948 and 1950, Congressman Boggs stated: "The most shocking part about these figures is the fact that there has been an alarming increase in drug addiction among younger persons. In the first six months of 1946, the average age of addicted persons committed . . . at Lexington, Kentucky, was 37-1/2 years. Only three patients were under the age of 21. During the first six months of 1950, only four years later, the average had dropped to 26.7 years and 766 patients were under the age of 21. . . ."

After remarking that "we need only to recall what we have read in the papers in the past week to realize that more and more younger people are falling into the clutches of unscrupulous dope peddlers . . .,"[8] Boggs inserted in the record eleven newspaper and magazine articles dated between 2 May and 16 July 1951.[9] The

Washington *Evening Star* on 16 July, the day of the debate, carried a story on the results of a mayor's committee report on drug addiction in New York City. According to the newspaper: "Between 45,000 and 90,000 persons in New York City are using illicit dope. . . . Based on the city's population of 7,835,099, that would be one out of every 87 or one out of 174 persons." The paper indicated that the report showed an increase in addiction among teenagers, and it called for more severe penalties for dope sellers and for wholesale revisions of federal and state penal statutes relating to sale.

An article in the 25 June 1951 issue of *Time* magazine related New York City School Superintendent William Jansen's statement that one out of every 200 high school students in the city was a user of habit-forming drugs. The article went on to describe "the alarming increase in dope consumption" in other major cities and the ease with which school children obtained narcotics. Another article in the Washington *Evening Star* on 12 June 1951 contained statements by a member of the staff of the attorney general of New York to the effect that between 5,000 and 15,000 of New York City's 300,000 high school students were drug addicts. To supplement these figures the articles included the testimony of witnesses describing their own acts of prostitution and thievery, the loss of educational opportunities, the death of addicts from "hot shots," the horrors of withdrawal, and a wide variety of other aspects of opiate dependence.

The Solution: Harsher Penalties

The congressional hearings, investigations, and debates also reveal the official and public consensus as to the solution to the epidemic —harsher penalties. It was repeatedly argued that the federal judiciary had abetted the increase in opiate use by assessing insufficient terms of imprisonment to narcotics offenders. For example, Congressman Harrison of Virginia, after noting that narcotics law violations had been increasing only in those jurisdictions where federal judges had failed to impose adequate sentences on recidivists, stated: "Where the judiciary is abusing its discretion, it is the duty of the lawmaking body to limit the discretion in order that the public may be protected."[10] Perhaps Commissioner Anslinger best described the prevailing climate when he observed in a statement later quoted on the floor of the House: "Short sentences do not deter. In districts where we get good sentences the traffic does not flourish. . . . There should be a minimum sentence for the second offense. The commercialized transactions, the peddler, the smuggler, those who traffic in narcotics, on the second offense if there were a minimum sentence of five years without probation or parole, I think it would just about dry up the traffic."[11]

Congressman Boggs had embodied such a remedy in a bill introduced in 1950 to increase penalties for all drug offenses, providing mandatory minimum sentences for all offenders. The bill did not reach a vote in 1950, but in the following year the Senate's Kefauver Committee (Special Committee to Investigate Organized Crime in Interstate Commerce) adopted this approach as one of its own recommendations.[12] When Boggs reintroduced his bill in the House, he affirmed its principal purpose: "to remove the power of suspension of sentence and probation in the cases of second and subsequent offenders against the narcotics and marihuana laws, and to provide minimum sentences. . . ."[13]

To support the contention that mandatory minimum sentences were necessary and that judicial discretion in the matter must be limited, the Federal Bureau of Narcotics had conducted a penalty survey in 1950.[14] The bureau concluded from this survey that the average sentence for a narcotics violator in 1950 was 23.1 months in jail, slightly less than the average length of sentence for a narcotics violator in a similar study conducted by the bureau in 1935. To the fact that average length of sentence had not changed much since 1935, the bureau contrasted the increase in the number of narcotics violators from 1947 to 1951 and also the increase in narcotics recidivism since 1935. From the study the bureau also demonstrated that the average length of sentence for narcotics violators was markedly less than for violators of the Federal White Slave Act and the Federal Counterfeiting Act. This comparison was particularly important in the quest for harsher penalties since it was generally assumed that heavy penalties had deterred kidnapping, white slave trading, and counterfeiting. Commissioner Anslinger, for example, wrote an Oregon state senator in 1951: "You no doubt know that Senator Dirksen has introduced a bill in the U.S. Congress which could provide the death penalty for peddling narcotics to minors. This has our complete endorsement. If all the states would pass similar legislation, this action together with the passage of the Dirksen bill would eliminate narcotics peddling to youths just as the Lindbergh Law practically eliminated kidnapping."[15]

Indeed, the bureau and several representatives in Congress toyed for some time with the idea of imposing death penalties for certain types of narcotics violations. In particular, Commissioner Anslinger and the bureau continued throughout the early fifties to support the "Dirksen bill" in Congress. In addition, Congressman Clemente of New York introduced a bill that would have assessed the death penalty for any violation of the Narcotic Drugs Import and Export Act.[16] Only somewhat more reticent, Congressman Edwin Arthur Hall of New York would have slapped dope peddlers with minimum sentences of 100 years.[17]

By comparison, the Boggs bill smacks of leniency. The consensus was indeed overwhelming that harsh sentences, mandatory in some cases, would strangle the drug traffic. This no-nonsense approach also appealed to the general public. One Californian wrote the commissioner: "As a citizen and veteran (of both World Wars) I strongly support your request for legislation to impose life sentences on narcotics peddlers. In fact, I would go further and urge nothing less than death sentences for these vicious enemies of society."[18] Several of the most influential newspapers, particularly in the Washington area, also joined the public call for harsher penalties. The *Washington Post* on 12 August 1951 urged: "The other, complementary approach is to deal ruthlessly with the peddlers of narcotics. These are criminals of the ugliest and most dangerous type. In localities where they have been given severe sentences, there has been a notable drop alike in the availability of drugs and in addiction."[19] To the same effect is a 5 October 1951 editorial in the Washington *Evening Star* entitled "Make It Hot for Them Here Too."[20] The bulletin of the St. Louis Medical Society added: "It is high time that the law makers reexamine relative values. If spies, saboteurs, and other traitors to our country can be given life sentences, then those who would sabotage the children upon whom the nation's future depends should be given life sentences."[21]

The new hysteria over narcotic drugs emerged at the same time as a similar concern with the international menace of communism. On one level the two phenomena were parallel, reflecting the collective psychology of the period—fear—and the consensus response —fortification. A spy was behind every tree and a narcotics peddler right behind him; the threat from without was matched by that from within. When issues are so easily defined, uncomplicated remedies leap to the fore. For the communist menace, military strength and a willingness to use it; for the drug menace, harsh penalties and a compulsion to assess them. This was no time for subtlety.

These two phenomena were also related on another level. The two sinister characters behind the tree were perceived to be one and the same. In an article headlined "Dope's Flow Said to Have Red Backing," the *Los Angeles Times* quoted the chief of that city's Police Department: "Communists in Europe and Asia are directing, in part, the flow of narcotics into the United States."[22] Political cartoons and commentaries quite often attributed increased drug traffic to the efforts of Chinese Communism to dominate and demoralize American youth.

The FBN no longer had to carry the burden of raising the public ire against the drug evil, but Commissioner Anslinger himself frequently illustrated the difficulty of enforcing the narcotic laws by asserting that often, after the bureau had rounded up a group of violators in a major drug ring, the first ones prosecuted were released from jail before the last ones were tried.[23] Naturally, the bureau once again enlisted Anslinger's army in the lobbying effort for passage of the Boggs Act. The FBN files clearly reflect the assistance of the Women's Christian Temperance Union, the General Federation of Women's Clubs, and the National Congress of Parents and Teachers.

Although there was no debate among the various participants in the legislative process about the need for harsher penalties, some voices were sporadically raised against the idea of mandatory minimum sentences. Deprivation of judicial discretion during the sentencing process was a significant departure from basic precepts of Anglo-American jurisprudence. Thus, during the drafting process before the second Boggs bill was introduced, a representative of the legislative section of the Treasury Department objected to a provision in the previous bill which would have imposed mandatory minimum sentences on *all* offenders, including first offenders. He argued that such a provision was unwise as a matter of policy and would serve only to arouse judicial hostility to the bill.[24] This provision was ultimately eliminated in the Kefauver recommendations and in the parallel Boggs bill.

At the time of the debate on the bill, the only significant opposition came from Congressman Cellar. He thought that the mandatory minimum sentence provision, now only for second and subsequent offenders, would be unjust to addicts. But the majority opinion was clearly that mandatory minimum sentences were necessary to insure the punishment of peddlers.[25] In response to Cellar's contention that young addicts would be subjected to long prison terms because of the loss of judicial discretion in sentencing, Congressman Jenkins stated: "The enforcing officers will always have sympathy for the unfortunate consumer, especially if he is harmless. These enforcing officers are going to protect the little boys and girls. They are not going to drag the high school boys and girls before the criminal courts until they know that they are collaborating with the peddlers."[26]

Boggs presented a more reasonable justification for mandatory minimums: "[I] t is not the intention of the legislation to affect a teenager or any such person who has possession of narcotics. But the gentleman also knows that if we try to make a distinction between possession and peddling that we immediately open the law to all types of abuses."[27]

This was no time for subtle distinctions. The policy makers wanted to hit squarely with a big stick. The Boggs Act passed both houses with overwhelming majorities on 2 November 1951 and provided uniform penalties for violations of the Narcotic Drugs Import and Export Act and the Marihuana Tax Act:

First offense	2 - 5 years
Second offense	5 - 10 years
Third and subsequent offenses	10 - 20 years
Fine for all offenses	$2,000

The relatively low fines reflected a congressional belief that monetary penalties were an insignificant deterrent.[28] Under the central provision of the act, the ameliorative judicial devices of probation, suspension, and parole were no longer available for persons convicted for a second or subsequent offense.

It is plain that the Boggs Act was directed in large part at the federal judiciary. Although the bench had not mounted any concerted lobbying effort during the legislative process, it is not surprising that the judges were indignant after passage of the act. The director of the U.S. Bureau of Prisons, James V. Bennett, who had unsuccessfully opposed the act during the hearings and debates, now tried to arouse the judges at the judicial conference of the Fifth Circuit in 1954.[29] Arguing that the act impaired the separation of powers doctrine upon which the nation's entire political system is based, Bennett suggested that the federal bench establish regional committees to reexamine the Boggs Act and to make recommendations. Bennett's incessant claim that "the Boggs Bill was passed due to hysteria"[30] irritated both Commissioner Anslinger and Congressman Boggs. For this reason FBN agents were detailed to follow him from conference to conference to make reports on what he said and to whom.[31]

The Fifth Judicial Circuit appointed the committee Bennett suggested, and on 27 May 1954 the district and circuit judges of the United States Fifth Circuit unanimously recommended the amendment of the federal narcotics law to remove provisions for mandatory minimum sentences.[32]

This and similar actions by the federal bench were met with immediate counterattacks by Commissioner Anslinger and Congressman Boggs. Shortly after the announcement of the Fifth Circuit decision, Commissioner Anslinger wrote: "It is surprising indeed that this recommendation by these judges should be adopted in New Orleans where shocking narcotic traffic was remedied, for the most part, by the application of the Boggs Act and similar heavy penalties under state legislation." This was released together with Congressman Boggs' own statement against the judges: "I cannot imagine a more shortsighted recommendation." He continued: "Anyone who has studied the narcotics trade and has seen the pitiful effect in countless homes throughout this nation from youths to the very old must recognize that this is one of the most vicious things in our country."[33]

The judiciary was whistling in the dark. Opposition to the removal of their traditional discretion in sentencing ran counter to a strong public preference for harsh penalties for drug violators. For example, one man wrote to Drew Pearson: "A judge who gives a suspended sentence or an insufficient sentence to a narcotic dealer, I would say should be automatically deprived of his judgeship and himself imprisoned."[34]

Marihuana and the Boggs Act

Public and congressional attention was focused on opiate use, not on marihuana. Although there is some evidence that marihuana use had increased concurrently with the use of opiates during the late forties,[35] nothing was made of this in the press. Nonetheless, right from the beginning of the drafting process, all federal drug statutes were to be covered by the new uniform penalties. The Marihuana Tax Act was part of the federal matrix; so it went in. Of course, under the 1937 "findings" no distinction would have been justified.

The persistence of the old myths, despite the evolving consensus within the scientific community, is cogently illustrated by a comment delivered from the bench by a New Jersey trial judge as he sentenced a marihuana seller to seven years in the penitentiary in March 1951:

Marihuana has been called the spawn of the devil. Marihuana destroys all sense of moral responsibility, and for that reason marihuana addicts commit crimes with no sense of regret, shame or responsibility. Marihuana has no therapeutic value whatever. It has been responsible for the commission of crimes of violence, of murder, and of rape. Those are major tributaries that flow from the use of marihuana. It has no value of any kind. It is a fungus growth that comes right from the bowels of Hell. Each cigaret is a stick of dynamite. Half a dozen of them smoked—no girl is safe walking the streets with a man under the influence of this devilish drug. Young girls raped, people murdered—that is the story of the highway of marihuana. A Marihuana peddler, or a man that peddles any drugs, should be punished, and the only way to punish him is to send him to the penitentiary for a long term.[36]

There had now been two decades of such visceral indictments. But 1951 marked the long-postponed entry of science into marihuana's legal history. The policy makers were finally acquainted with the consensus that had developed within the American scientific community since the mid-thirties. In a paper filed as an exhibit to the hearings[37] on the Boggs Act, Dr. Harris Isbell, director of research at the Public Health Service Hospital in Lexington, Kentucky, exploded the traditional rationale. He stated that marihuana was not physically addictive, although he paid lip service to the psychological dependence hypothesis.[38] Acknowledging the possibility of "temporary psychosis" in "predisposed individuals," Isbell otherwise disputed the crime and insanity thesis. Before the Kefauver committee in the Senate he testified that:

[M]arihuana smokers generally are mildly intoxicated, giggle, laugh, bother no one, and have a good time. They do not stagger or fall, and ordinarily will not attempt to harm anyone.
It has not been proved that smoking marihuana leads to crimes of violence or to crimes of a sexual nature. Smoking marihuana has no unpleasant after-effects, no dependence is developed on the drug, and the practice can easily be stopped at any time. In fact, it is probably easier to stop smoking marihuana cigarets than tobacco cigarets.
In predisposed individuals, marihuana may precipitate temporary psychosis and is, therefore, not an innocuous practice with them.[39]

Despite this testimony, the legislators approved greatly increased penalties for marihuana users. The reason was simple. Since Congress was seeking to excise heroin use from the social organism, marihuana, no longer important in itself, was assigned a new role:

Mr. BOGGS. From just what little I saw in that demonstration, I have forgotten the figure Dr. Isbell gave, but my recollection is that only a small percentage of those marihuana cases was anything more than a temporary degree of exhiliration. . . .
Mr. ANSLINGER. The danger is this: Over 50 percent of those young addicts started on marihuana smoking. They started there and graduated to heroin; they took the needle when the thrill of marihuana was gone.[40]

Many others—doctors, crime prevention experts, and police and narcotic bureau officials—testified to support the link between marihuana use and ultimate heroin addiction.[41] Congressman Boggs himself summed up this novel danger of marihuana in one of the few statements which even mentioned marihuana in the House floor debate: "Our younger people usually start on the road which leads to drug addiction by smoking marihuana. They then graduate into narcotic drugs—cocaine, morphine, and heroin. When these younger persons become addicted to the drugs, heroin, for example, which costs from $8 to $15 per day, they very often must embark on careers of crime . . . and prostitution . . . in order to buy the supply which they need."[42]

In the Senate, Chairman Kefauver noted that marihuana use was increasing among the nation's youth as it poured across the Mexican border, beginning the process of addiction: "The path to addiction ran practically the same throughout the testimony from young addicts. In their own vernacular . . . they say they go from sneaky Peter to pot to horse to banging. In ordinary language, this describes the popular sequence—drinking wine, smoking 'reefers' or marihuana cigarettes (sometimes starting at the age of 13 or 14), then sniffing or 'snorting' heroin, finally injecting it directly into the vein."[43]

Specifically rejected by Commissioner Anslinger in 1937, the stepping-stone rationale became, in 1951, the cornerstone of official marihuana doctrine. Earlier contentions to the same effect by law enforcement authorities, international experts, and the WCTU had been either unnoticed or ignored.[44] Its sudden acceptance as official dogma had an interesting consequence.

Marihuana had been medically defined as a narcotic drug in the twenties; from this fact its statutory nexus with the opiates had been drawn. However, despite its comparison to the opiates, cannabis still retained its own distinct, although equally menacing, identity. Once the myths had been dispelled, the substantial pharmacological disparity between marihuana and the opiates became clear; indeed, the new rationale was premised on marihuana's being something of a "weak sister" in the family of abusable drugs. Yet this differentiation did not trigger a public policy review because of a paradoxical twist.

Under the stepping-stone rationale, marihuana no longer had its own identity. Because its primary ill effect was now thought to be a role in opiate addiction, marihuana became inextricably bound to the opiates from a political and legal standpoint as well. It is not surprising, then, that the causal link, once drawn, has persisted for two decades, earning the official imprimatur of President Nixon in 1971. The passage of the Boggs Act marked a significant shift in the rationale for marihuana's illegal status and that status became more entrenched by its causal association with the opiates.

The Sky's the Limit

Even while the Boggs Act was still pending in Congress, the Narcotics Bureau encouraged the states to modify their existing narcotic and marihuana legislation to enact "penalties similar to those provided in the Boggs Bill [which] would be of material assistance in the fight against the narcotic traffic."[45] Seventeen states and the territory of Alaska responded by passing "little Boggs Acts" by 1953 and eleven other states increased their penalties by 1956. Two of the latter group, Ohio and Louisiana, enacted penalty provisions that were substantially more severe than those passed previously in any jurisdiction. The Ohio law, approved 16 June 1955, provided a twenty- to forty-year sentence for the sale of narcotic drugs. The Louisiana measure, adopted the following year, provided severe prison sentences without parole, probation, or suspension for the illegal sale, possession, or administration of a narcotic drug. The sentences ranged from a five-year minimum to a ninety-nine-year maximum.[46]

Whether because use had decreased or because the propagandists had accomplished their mission, public agitation about the narcotics problem reduced considerably after the Boggs Act was passed.

Meanwhile, however, the continuing debate about the appropriate public policy toward narcotic addiction surfaced again, and during the four years following the Boggs Act, a number of professional groups and individual experts began to call for a re-examination of the entire legislative approach. The American Bar Association created a special committee on narcotics in 1954; the following year the American Medical Association recommended that Congress fully review the Harrison Act and the FBN's enforcement policy. The perennial issue of heroin maintenance received considerable discussion in an atmosphere much calmer than that which prevailed in 1951.[47]

ASSAULT WITH INTENT TO KILL

Arlington County, Virginia, *Daily Sun*, 19 March 1955

As a result of this activity, the Senate passed a resolution on 18 March 1955 authorizing the Senate Judiciary Committee "to conduct a full and complete study of the narcotics problem in the United States, including ways and means of improving the Federal Criminal Code and other laws and enforcement procedures dealing with possession, sale, and transportation of narcotics, marihuana and similar drugs."[48] During the next eighteen months this subcommittee, chaired by Senator Price Daniel of Texas, conducted numerous hearings all over the country. In January and April 1956 the Daniel Subcommittee issued two brief reports, on trafficking and treatment, both of which proposed to tighten rather than alter the existing system.[49]

The Daniel Report was more of the same. It proposed that penalties for drug offenses be increased again, that further discussion of proposed opiate clinics be halted, and that all drug addicts be removed from society so they could no longer spread "this contagious problem." In the House, Congressman Boggs was now chairman of the Ways and Means Subcommittee on Narcotics; in close cooperation with Anslinger, his subcommittee developed a similar series of recommendations.

Without significant debate or public interest, except among the groups which the FBN had always counted on for support, Congress subsequently passed the Narcotic Control Act of 1956.

Perhaps more than any of its predecessors, the Narcotic Control Act was a child of the FBN. Together with Senator Daniel and Congressman Boggs, Anslinger was able to resist the growing pressure for reevaluation. Almost every provision in the new act was designed to supplement the tools at the bureau's disposal to detect, arrest, and incarcerate drug users. This legislation thus represents the high-water mark of the punitive approach to drug use begun on the federal level during the 1920s. The penalties for drug offenses were now escalated for the final time on the theory that the end of the nonmedical use of narcotics could thereby be assured.

Interestingly, the efficacy of still higher penalties was not uniformly accepted within the FBN; the deputy commissioner suggested that more severe penalties might press grand juries not to indict and the petit juries not to convict in drug cases. Anslinger rejected this view. He felt strongly that more severe penalties were imperative if society was to be rid of its present peddlers and if new entrants into the narcotics business were to be deterred.[50]

Map 3. Marihuana prohibition. Phase three: Increase in penalties, 1950-61

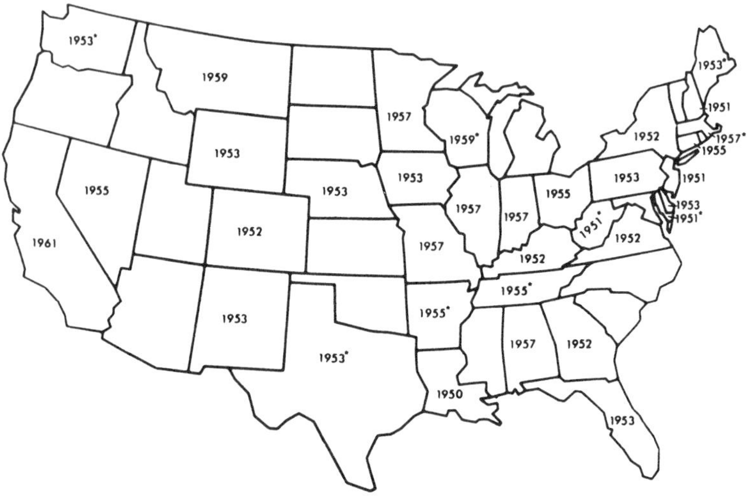

Date indicates year in which state adopted mandatory minimum penalties for possession (* indicates that court had authority to apply lesser penalty for first offenders).

There was little dissent in the Congress from the proposition that harsher penalties were the means to eliminate the illicit use and sale of all drugs.[51] In the Boggs Subcommittee hearings, in fact, it was felt that harsher penalties were the *only* way to deal with the narcotic law violations.[52] The subcommittee felt that educational programs on the evils of narcotics should not be instituted in the schools for fear of exciting the curiosity of young people.[53]

In addition to facilitating enforcement of narcotics laws through a number of ancillary provisions, the Narcotics Control Act established the following penalties:

Possession	*Minimum Sentence*
First offense	2 years
Second offense	5 years
Third and subsequent offense	10 years
Fine	$20,000

Sale	*Minimum Sentence*
First offense	5 years
Second and subsequent offense	10 years
Sale to minor by adult	10 years

Probation, suspension of sentence, and parole were made unavailable to all except first offenders in the possession category.[54]

Even though a few of the act's provisions dealt specifically with marihuana, the legislators paid even less attention to marihuana than they had in 1951. The established precedent of classifying marihuana with the opiates and cocaine resulted in a further increase in marihuana penalties and a proliferation of marihuana offenses. Few legislators recognized that marihuana was in any way different from the physically addictive opiates.[55] The stepping-stone hypothesis had cemented that link.

During the Daniel Committee Hearings, Anslinger emphasized the new rationale, but gladly agreed when his questioners revived the old assumptions about marihuana:

Senator DANIEL. Now, do I understand it from you that, while we are discussing marijuana, the real danger there is that the use of marijuana leads many people eventually to the use of heroin, and the drugs that do cause them complete addiction; is that true?
Mr. ANSLINGER. That is the great problem and our great concern about the use of marijuana, that eventually if used over a long period, it does lead to heroin addiction. . . .
Senator DANIEL. As I understand it from having read your book, an habitual user of marijuana or even a user to a small extent presents a problem to the community, and is a bad thing. Marijuana can cause a person to commit crimes and do many heinous things; is that not correct?
Mr. ANSLINGER. That is correct. It is a dangerous drug, and is so regarded all over the world. . . .

After noting that cannabis had no therapeutic advantages and that it "might cause insanity," Anslinger found himself disputing the crime thesis:

Senator WELKER. Mr. Commissioner, my concluding question with respect to marijuana: Is it or is it not a fact that the marijuana user has been responsible for many of our most sadistic, terrible crimes in this Nation, such as sex slayings, sadistic slayings, and matter of that kind?
Mr. ANSLINGER. There have been instances of that, Senator. We have had some rather tragic occurrences by users of marijuana. It does not follow that all crimes can be traced to marijuana.

There have been many brutal crimes traced to marijuana. But I would not say that it is the controlling factor in the commission of crimes.

Senator WELKER. I will grant you that it is not the controlling factor, but is it a fact that your investigation shows that many of the most sadistic, terrible crimes, solved or unsolved, we can trace directly to the marijuana user?

Mr. ANSLINGER. You are correct in many cases, Senator Welker.

Senator WELKER. In other words, it builds up a false sort of feeling on the part of the user and he has no inhibitions against doing anything; am I correct?

Mr. ANSLINGER. He is completely irresponsible.[56]

Only once during the floor debates on the House and Senate versions of the bill was the subject of marihuana as a separate substance even raised. Senator Daniel advised his colleagues what marihuana was exclusively in terms of the stepping-stone concept: "[Marihuana] is a drug which starts most addicts in the use of drugs. Marihuana, in itself a dangerous drug, can lead to some of the worst crimes committed by those who are addicted to the habit. Evidently, its use leads to the heroin habit and then to the final destruction of the persons addicted."[57]

One provision of the act reveals a curious lapse of memory between 1937 and 1956 regarding the origins of marihuana. Congress finally got around to amending the Import and Export Act, creating a new offense of smuggling marihuana, and mere possession was made sufficient evidence to convict the possessor of knowingly receiving or concealing imported marihuana. This presumption was based on two suppositions—that marihuana traffic depended upon importation from Mexico and that possessors were likely to be aware of that fact. Even in 1956 such findings were dubious.[58] Commissioner Anslinger estimated that 90 percent of all marihuana in the country had been smuggled from Mexico, since 90 percent of all federal seizures were of Mexican marihuana.[59] But this statistic was grossly misleading. The FBN had practically abandoned the responsibility for marihuana control to increasingly effective state narcotics squads and to the customs agents.[60] It was only natural that federal figures, taken alone, would suggest a high percentage of importation. Furthermore, the commissioner's conclusion was inconsistent with an essential premise of the Tax Act[61] and with other materials presented to the Congress,[62] all of which emphasize the large degree of domestic cultivation of marihuana.

As to the possessor's knowledge of the drug's source, the underlying assumption was that there was an organized trade pattern and that each user knew where his drug came from. But marihuana was then no more than a casual adjunct in the lives of unemployed or menially employed members of racial minorities in city centers.[63] Such a class of people, especially the young and black minorities, could hardly be assumed to know the original source of the drug. The presumption, which was ultimately declared irrational by the United States Supreme Court, might have been valid if applied to recently immigrated Mexicans,[64] but certainly to no one else.

Never widely used or known, marihuana had now been fully integrated into the narcotics legislation of every state in the Union and of the national government. Possession of the drug, even for one's own use, was a felony everywhere, and the user was subject to long periods of incarceration as punishment for his indulgence.

CHAPTER XII

The Collapse of the Marihuana Consensus

FOR FIFTY YEARS a latent social consensus supported the nation's marihuana laws. This marihuana consensus was buttressed by a number of ideological and descriptive propositions. The belief that marihuana was a "narcotic" drug was of primary importance. The statutory definitions of marihuana in most states codified this, especially after the passage of the Uniform Act. In other states and in federal legislation, penalty provisions were based upon it. In legal status and in the legislative mind, marihuana was indistinguishable from the opiates and cocaine.

Marihuana prohibition rested in large part on the essential premise of the narcotics policy that use inevitably became abuse. The view that narcotics users were incapable of moderation was reflected in the overwhelming urge to refer to marihuana users as "addicts" and to postulate a strong psychological compulsion for use even if no physiological compulsion existed. There was also a predisposition to attribute other dysfunctional effects to marihuana. Policy makers were inclined to look for high incidences of mental deterioration, psychosis, and violent crime.

Another essential condition of the marihuana consensus was the demography of that portion of the population using it. Because it was used primarily by insulated ethnic minorities, Mexicans and blacks, the drug was always associated with the lowest levels of the socioeconomic structure. This had several important consequences. First, since the user populations were associated in the public mind with crime, idleness, and other antisocial behavior, a causal relationship between marihuana and such behavior seemed evident. Second, since these insulated minorities had no access to the policy-making and public opinion processes, hypotheses supporting this consensus went unchallenged. Sharing the basic public policy predisposition, the medical and scientific communities felt no particular need to study the drug and its effects, especially after cannabis was removed from the U.S. pharmacopoeia. The little research which was conducted tended to undercut prevailing beliefs, but these inconsistencies remained unpublicized because there was no constituency interested in revealing them. The narcotics bureaucracy was also, of course, inclined to suppress them.

Final support for the marihuana consensus came from ideological factors reflected in American public policy during the first six decades of this century. Resting on society's interest in individual productivity and its preference for cultural homogeneity was a legislative tendency to inhibit any personal behavior thought to be incompatible with society's best interests. Two world wars, the depression, several recessions, the Korean conflict, and a cold war, kept the nation on the defensive. There was little tolerance for personal deviance. The notion that there was a sphere of personal activity immune from governmental scrutiny lost its constitutional footing. Legislatures continually sought to compel sexual, sensual, and even intellectual orthodoxy. As increased geographic mobility, institutional growth, and mass communications gradually loosened the capacities of nonlegal institutions—the family, church, schools—to regulate behavior, society relied more and more on the legal system, and the criminal law in particular, to symbolize and enforce the dominant order.

The Challenge

Beginning in the mid-sixties, the marihuana consensus evaporated, as each of its essential supports wobbled and fell away. The drug's sudden attraction to the nation's university population was of primary importance. Although marihuana arrests and seizures had hit their all-time low point in 1960,[1] by 1967 use of the drug was associated in the public mind with life on the campus. This new class of users, regardless of its size, had direct access to the public opinion process because it was drawn from the middle and upper socioeconomic brackets. As a result, this new use pattern incited a broad social awareness of the drug and awakened in the scientific and medical communities a new interest in research.

It is difficult to account entirely for this new interest in marihuana and to pinpoint exactly when it began. In all likelihood marihuana use may have been the most visible by-product of the merger of several different social and political movements in the mid-sixties. Perhaps the most specific of these was the national publicity given the LSD experimentation at Harvard University by Drs. Leary and Alpert in 1963. As a growing segment of the academic fringe began to preach consciousness-expansion, student attention and curiosity in the Northeast became focused on drugs and drug use.

At the same time, the so-called psychedelic movement was launched on the West Coast, particularly in the San Francisco area. Tom Wolfe has described the role of author Ken Kesey and his "Merry Pranksters" in this movement and its attendant subculture. As the Haight-Asbury scene and the West Coast drug culture attracted interest in the press, student curiosity across the country was aroused, as was that of the intellectual avant-garde in Greenwich Village and similar urban communities.

A much more pervasive social development influencing the interest in marihuana was a general loosening of restraints imposed by the legal system on behavior with "moral" overtones. Beginning with the widely acclaimed civil rights movement of the early 1960s, proceeding through the free speech movement, the antiwar movement, and the ecology movement, the decade was characterized by protest and civil disobedience. Martin Luther King's appeal to the higher moral law and the righteousness of his cause made a deep impression on the national conscience, piercing most deeply the souls of the country's youth. The civil rights movement weakened the moral force of the law as an institution by illustrating the evil which could be codified by secular authorities. This tendency was exacerbated, particularly among those in college, by the Vietnam escalation, which began in 1965. Disobedience of the marihuana laws may have been a convenient offspring of the protest attitude. Marihuana, of course, was ready-made for such a symbolic use, having been miscast in the past and being so easily aligned against the establishment's own alcohol.

Whatever its genesis, the change in use patterns immediately affected a number of conditions upon which the marihuana consensus rested. Most obvious was the challenge to the drug's classification as a narcotic. The revelation that marihuana was substantially *different* from the opiates and cocaine made a major impact on public attitudes. The substitution of other labels such as "dangerous drug" or "hallucinogen" did not negate this impact; nor did the initial judicial conclusions that the legislature could legitimately classify marihuana as a "narcotic" even though it was not technically accurate to do so.[2] That marihuana was substantially different immediately dissipated the application of the narcotics consensus.

The scientific propositions attending the application of the narcotics consensus to marihuana had always been assumptions tied to broader social perceptions of the using class. But these assumptions no longer coincided with social expectations when use of the drug was taken up by society's privileged classes. The basic proposition that use inevitably became abuse was quickly challenged. It was as important to the drug's new advocates to emphasize that it was not "addictive" as it had been for its foes to maintain that it was. This society's fear of drug dependence had by now reached the level of moral antipathy, and marihuana's innocence in this regard was an important revelation, even though the information had been available from the earliest prohibitory days. Similarly, the causal relationships between marihuana and crime, idleness, and incapacitation were now more difficult to maintain. The new users were not "criminals" or social outcasts. They were sons and daughters of the middle and upper classes. In short, when the consensus against marihuana lost its sociological support, it immediately lost its scientific support as well.

The continued vitality of its ideological support had also become debatable. Whereas society formerly imposed severe restraints on the individual's personal and social conduct in order to reap the benefits of his economic and political independence, another view was winning an increasing number of adherents. Under this view economic and political institutions have become increasingly omnipotent; the individual is increasingly dependent on the system rather than the system being dependent on him. Increasing numbers of individuals view themselves as cogs in the massive, impersonal, technological machine, the controls for which are beyond their grasp. Consequently, it is argued, a higher value must be placed on personal fulfillment in the noneconomic, nonpolitical sphere. A new emphasis must be placed on personal identity and the individualized, deinstitutionalized pursuit of happiness. Concurrently, as economic productivity demands less of each individual's time and energy, and the workweek continues to shorten, a leisure ethic is emerging. From the perspective of productivity, the argument goes, society has less and less economic interest in what the individual does with his leisure time.

During the mid-sixties this ideological development was manifested in laws and judicial decisions upholding the individual's right to differ—intellectually, spiritually, socially, and sensually. Concurrently, a renascent emphasis on individual privacy appeared. As an incredibly sophisticated technology continually expanded society's control over the individual, he began to insist that the wall around his private life be fortified. The courts responded, proscribing official snooping and invalidating laws interfering with familial decision-making—abortion, contraception, miscegenation—and with private sexual conduct.

A related trend, well underway during the sixties, was de-emphasis of the criminal law as a means of social control. Increasing numbers of legal scholars and social scientists were beginning to indict the process of "overcriminalization" under which the sphere of criminal conduct had been too broadly drawn. Of particular interest are offenses committed in private, by consenting individuals, such as drug offenses. The view that the criminal law was not the only, or even the best, way for society to express its disapproval of certain behavior was certainly a notion foreign to early twentieth-century policy makers.

A new class of users, revived scientific interest and debate, lively public interest, and fundamental ideological crosscurrents all combined to undermine the marihuana consensus in the mid-sixties. This is not to say, however, that the law was no longer defensible or defended—only that conflict replaced consensus. For the first time in its fifty-year history, marihuana prohibition encountered an operating public opinion process.

Retrenchment

A public policy so deeply rooted as marihuana prohibition does not wither away in the heat of debate, especially when it is embodied in criminal law and is thus presumed to circumscribe socially harmful and immoral activity. In this case the immediate tendency was to retrench and lash out at marihuana use. The uneasiness with which the dominant social order viewed the political and racial disruption of the mid-sixties contributed to this reaction. Violent demonstrations and urban riots threatened to tear the society apart physically, while an emerging "hippie" counterculture threatened to do so spiritually by overtly rejecting the prevailing value system and by "dropping out" of society altogether.

Since it was associated with misguided young, marihuana easily became a symbol of these wider social conflicts. A new stereotype of the marihuana user was substituted for the old. From the establishment's side, defense of marihuana prohibition and enforcement of the law was one way to assert the vitality and superiority of the dominant system and thereby extirpate the "permissivists" and "revolutionaries" who aimed to topple that system. Not surprisingly, the marihuana laws were often used selectively as a vehicle for removing radical irritants from the body politic and lazy hippies from the streets.

But the symbolism of the marihuana prohibition was Janus-faced. As we have suggested, marihuana-smoking was an attractive way for the alienated counterculture to taunt the establishment and flout its laws. For the New Left, the drug's illegal status—which put large numbers of young people on the wrong side of the criminal law—was a useful recruiting agent. Some radical leaders went so far as to *oppose* reduction in penalties for marihuana possession because they felt severe penalties aided their recruiting efforts by making marihuana users outraged against the society that overreacted so strongly to a nonexistent danger. Perhaps the best statement to this effect was made by Jerry Rubin, one of the Chicago Seven, in a speech in Charlottesville, Virginia, on 6 May 1970, when he said: "Smoking pot makes you a criminal and a revolutionary—as soon as you take your first puff, you are an enemy of society."[3]

The official retrenchment characterizing the 1965-68 period was led by the law enforcement community. Official propaganda shifted its emphasis away from concerns engendered by the old user population to those associated with the new. The FBN continued to propagate the crime thesis—complete with the kind of anecdotal support used in the old days[4]—but most official spokesmen characterized the problem in terms of public health rather than public safety. The emerging view regarded the marihuana user as a troubled, emotionally unstable individual. Psychological dependence, amotivation, alienation, and an inevitable tendency to use other drugs became the cornerstone of official doctrine.

Within the medical community, increasing numbers of physicians and public health experts were becoming uncomfortable with the official line. But once marihuana became politicized, authoritative medical spokesmen were aware that their statements would be wielded in the rhetorical battle; they therefore employed extreme caution, emphasizing what might be true as well as what was. For example, the World Health Organization (WHO) Expert Commission on Addiction Producing Drugs, which abandoned the terms "addiction" and "habituation" in favor of "drug dependence," reviewed cannabis' effects in 1965. After noting that cannabis use did not induce physical dependence and that chronic use could result in psychic dependence, the commission carefully identified the locus of concern:

> For the individual, harm resulting from abuse of cannabis may include inertia, lethargy, self-neglect, feeling of increased capability, with corresponding failure, and precipitation of psychotic episodes. Abuse of cannabis facilitates the association with social groups and subcultures involved with more dangerous drugs, such as opiates or barbiturates. Transition to the use of such drugs would be a consequence of this association rather than an inherent effect of cannabis. The harm to society derived from abuse of cannabis rests in economic consequences of the impairment of the individual's social functions and his enhanced proneness to asocial and antisocial behavior.[5]

As in this excerpt medical experts generally distinguish between experimental and chronic use, between use and "abuse." For example, the AMA Council on Mental Health and Committee on Alcoholism and Drug Dependence emphasized that American marihuana use was generally experimental or intermittent use of weak cannabis preparations, and that the medical hazard involved in this situation is low compared to that associated with chronic heavy use.[6] Yet, this distinction was generally omitted in dissemination to the public by FBN spokesmen who continually cited both the WHO and AMA reports in support of more drastic propositions. Well into 1968 the FBN held firm against the "permissivist" onslaught, keeping in touch with Dr. Munch (who continued to affirm the relationship between marihuana and crime), insisting that marihuana was a "highly dangerous substance with inherent physical dangers" and maintaining that marihuana users should continue to be felons.[7]

In any event, a common theme within both the medical and law enforcement communities was that marihuana-smoking was a chemical cop-out, suggestive, at least, of underlying psychological instability. For example, one medical expert noted that in the West, marihuana seems to "possess a particular attraction for certain psychologically and socially maladjusted persons who have difficulty conforming to usual social norms."[8]

Dr. Robert Baird, director of the Haven Clinic in New York City's Harlem, observed in 1969 on the basis of his experience with heroin addiction: "Anyone who smokes marihuana, whether it be a doctor, lawyer, nun, priest, who has to use grass already has a mental problem. They are taking it to escape reality, to get high, to relax. I do not care what euphemism you want to employ, they are mentally ill."[9]

Officialdom had very little faith in the nation's young. In their view the entire generation was unstable. Henry Giordano, Anslinger's successor as commissioner of Narcotics, hated "to think what the problem might have been if there had been no marihuana controls. In today's ever-growing hedonistic society, it is obvious the results would have been disastrous."[10] On another occasion, Commissioner Giordano postulated that legalization of marihuana would mean the decline of the American system. "I can just imagine," he opined, "all of our youth spending the rest of their days high on marihuana, and I do not know what our society would come to if that were the case."[11] Although Giordano may have been a little more apprehensive than his official colleagues, it is clear that the marihuana retrenchment was motivated in large part by generational conflict.

In response to the contention that young people are capable of rational choices, the bureau's chief counsel had this to say:

Even if we were to accept the snobbish proposition that the children of our colleges today possess a superior sense of moral intelligence and are better able to deal sensibly with drugs, and even if we were to conclude that marihuana affects only the weak and the vulnerable, since when has our society stopped being concerned about a minority? The very purpose of many of our health laws is the protection of minorities. I am not impressed that a law student with a high I.Q. does not obtain a reaction from taking two or three puffs on a marihuana cigarette. I am concerned over the consequences of making the drug readily available in a society containing millions of persons predisposed to impulsive and aggressive behavior.[12]

Meanwhile, in the laboratories and on the campuses medical researchers were gradually permitted to seek answers to the basic scientific questions. This effort was methodologically facilitated in 1966 when Δ9THC, the active principle in cannabis, was synthesized, and then in 1967 when its pharmacological effects were demonstrated.[13] Young researchers like Andrew Weil of Harvard were anxious to perform clinical human studies, and the National Institute of Mental Health was inundated with requests to approve and fund marihuana research. Apart from pharmacological research, social scientists unleashed an entire arsenal of questionnaires on a new social entity: the "marihuana user." Any new research had an interested audience and, depending on its policy implications, immediate critics.

Having defaulted for forty years, the scientific community no longer had the luxury of time and precision. The public wanted answers, and official spokesmen wanted the right ones. The FBN chief counsel made this quite clear in 1968:

> The real damage being done in this crisis of confidence is that some scholarly men are more willing to attack the marihuana controls than to justify them: that these persons are more concerned with deriding the public officials who are charged with enforcing the laws than in helping them prevent drug abuse; and that they are more interested in rationalizing the use of marihuana than in presenting reasons for controlling it.[14]

There was thus an inherent conflict in the interests of researchers and the interests of the government. This collision was most intense during 1967-68 when the FBN and NIMH struggled to develop procedures for selecting the "right" research applications, thereby demonstrating the government's interest in seeking the truth while minimizing the risk of embarrassing results. Tod Mikuriya, who was in charge of NIMH's marihuana research in 1967, has described the atmosphere:

> None of the DHEW employees wanted to offend any of the Bureau of Narcotics police. One also had to worry about antediluvian congressional types that had it in their power to smite us mightily where it hurt—right in our appropriation. The result was sectional review committees, which are ostensibly selected for their professional positions and pedigrees, but are really picked for their low risk liability for offending others. Understandably, the research approved and funded by their recommendation could not help but reflect this ethic of inoffensiveness. For fiscal years 1968 and 1969, NIHM grantees in the area of marijuana research include nine animal studies, twenty-eight social voyeuristic designs, ten chemical experiments, four pharmacological studies and only two clinical human studies.[15]

Law enforcement officials were not stemming the tide alone. Legislators would not budge, and the courts had no trouble "presenting reasons for controlling" marihuana when the prohibition was challenged. In fact, the retrenchment period is best exemplified by a twelve-day evidentiary hearing held before a Massachusetts Superior Court judge on the question of whether or not marihuana was rationally classified as a narcotic. In defense of two Philadelphia youngsters charged with possession, conspiracy, and possession with intent to sell, Attorney Joseph S. Oteri challenged the constitutionality of the Massachusetts law, parading numerous scientific witnesses before the bench. With the close cooperation of the FBN,[16] the prosecution solicited a similar array of expert witnesses in support of the law. The challenge failed; in the end, the presence of Science on the witness stand made absolutely no difference.

The key legal factor in a determination of marihuana's constitutional status is who has the burden of proof—the legislature or the user. In most situations the courts presume that the legislature has acted rationally, and that it had factual reasons for its actions. In this country's constitutional system, such a presumption of rationality is essential; it is the mortar in the wall separating the judicial from the legislative functions. Without it, the judiciary would be reviewing everything the legislature does and the courts would become nothing more than superlegislatures immune from the popular will. But the legislature is not always entitled to this presumption. In situations where legislative action on its face adversely affects the fundamental constitutional rights of the individual—such as freedom of speech, freedom of religion, or the right to vote—the legislation is presumed to be unconstitutional and the burden is on the state to show a compelling reason why these rights must be abridged or overridden. In an institutional sense the judiciary is the guardian of individual liberties and scrutinizes any alleged interference with care.

If marihuana-smoking is not thought to involve a fundamental right, then the legislation prohibiting its use is presumed to be rational. The burden rests upon the individual to disprove every possible hypothesis that marihuana is harmful. But this is impossible, all drugs being harmful in one way or another and many questions about marihuana remaining unanswered. If, on the other hand, marihuana-smoking is perceived to involve a fundamental right, the legislature must show a compelling reason for suppressing its use. But this is probably impossible as well, because cause-effect relationships are difficult to establish, the effects of the drug are variable, and its social impact is speculative. Once the question regarding allocation of the burden of proof is resolved, therefore, the role of science is simply to provide evidence, not to dictate the answer.

Both sides in the Massachusetts case rightly considered their case a major battleground for the new marihuana controversy. A Colorado trial judge had taken evidence on the effects of marihuana in 1965 and had declared the law unconsitutional. He was reversed on appeal.[17] After the twelve-day parade of witnesses, Judge Tauro ruled against the defendants, to the FBN's glee.[18] Since the judge did not think marihuana-smoking involved any fundamental rights, he presumed the legislation to be rational. He found abundant data to corroborate the legislative determination that marihuana was dangerous and deserving of suppression. His reasoning, however, drawn as it was from 1967 scientific opinion, mirrors the prevailing official dogma. His central finding was: "The ordinary user of marijuana is quite likely to be a marginally adjusted person who turns to the drug to avoid confrontation with and the resolution of his problems. The majority of alcohol users are well adjusted, productively employed individuals who use alcohol for relaxation and as an incident of other social activities."[19]

Of major concern to Judge Tauro was the alleged propensity of marihuana users "to neglect their health and that of others in their care and to submit to a life of indolence." Use of the drug, he noted, "allows them to avoid resolution of their underlying problems rather than to confront them realistically." The new sociological support for the official retrenchment in the mid-sixties was that the nation's youthful marihuana users were sick and that use of the drug probably would make them sicker.

As in Massachusetts, where Judge Tauro's decision was affirmed by the Massachusetts Supreme Court, consitutional challenges were easily rebuffed by the courts of other states.[20] Because any comment departing from the official line would have been suicide for an elected officeholder, marihuana reform won no friends in the political arena either.

Defense of the status quo rested on two policy-making propositions. Having become suddenly aware of the imperfection of much of the data on the effects of the drug, FBN and AMA spokesmen began, in 1968, to emphasize what we did *not* know: no change should be made in public policy toward a drug whose long-term effects were unknown.

No longer in a position to oppose research as they had done for thirty years, both the bureau and the AMA employed a tactic of selective dissemination in support of the status quo. The official experts to whom the public turned for guidance applauded, published, and circulated research studies that tended to affirm the drug's potential for harm and either ignored or challenged any studies that minimized its harmfulness.

The leaders of the law enforcement and medical communities were playing a waiting game; they gave the distinct impression that they thought the problem would eventually evaporate. All it would take was patient dissemination of information that the drug was not harmless, as so many of its most outspoken advocates contended. For example, Commissioner Giordano noted in 1967, "we may soon hope to have the full dangers of marihuana revealed to the public."[21]

The official waiting game also rested on the policy-making proposition that the government did not have any burden since the law was already on the books. The notion was continually expressed that no change should be made unless marihuana was proven *harmless*.

This position echoed that being taken in the courts. In its judicial context, of course, this approach manifests a deference to the political process: the judiciary defers to legislative judgment because, under the American system of government, it is the role of popularly elected officials to sift the evidence and assign proper weight to the scientific and normative elements of the marihuana controversy. Instead, however, the opinion makers in the political process were refusing to confront the issue head-on; they were using a judicial presumption as a rhetorical device for refusing to reassess the status quo.

If all psychoactive drugs used for nonmedical purposes were held to the "illegal unless proven harmless" standard, use of them all would be illegal. All drugs can be used to excess and no psychoactive substance is harmless. The point comes into clearer focus if we ask what the public policy response would have been if marihuana, a previously unknown drug, suddenly appeared on the scene in 1965 at the level it then achieved and among the populations it then attracted. To defend any action to restrict it, the government would be called upon to justify its actions in the same way it had felt obliged to do in 1937. But since use of the drug had already been declared illegal in 1937, the law carried weight of its own, and officials felt little affirmative obligation to justify it.

Naturally, the rhetorical nature of this argument did not escape the challengers, who immediately countered with the alcohol comparison. Although harmful in at least every respect that marihuana might be, alcohol use was not criminal; in fact, its use was permitted and in some ways encouraged by the government. How then, the challengers contended, could the government justify criminal penalties for marihuana use?

As late as April 1968 Giordano was responding officially to this argument in a manner which could have been written thirty years earlier: "The purpose of the present drug laws is to prevent the incorporation of additional debilitating vices within our culture. The fact that other dangerous drugs, alcohol and tobacco, are not prohibited is irrelevant. This attitude may offend logic, but it results in the conservation of human values, and logic may be offended in such a cause."[22]

Any breach in the wall of official retrenchment during this period was fraught with political risk. For example, some officials in the Department of Health, Education, and Welfare began to question the official position in the fall of 1967. Advisory panels from the Food and Drug Administration and the National Institute of Mental Health were directed to make recommendations on the subject to the secretary of HEW, John Gardner. During this fact-finding process, Dr. James Goddard, the head of FDA, apparently became convinced of the need for legal action. He circulated his views unabashedly within the department, and even the FBN was aware of his position. The deputy commissioner of the FBN recorded in October that Dr. Goddard felt that "there should be no penalty for possession of marihuana, only for sale or distribution." He also felt "that the use of alcohol is a far more serious problem than is marihuana" and that "we might in ten years see marihuana legalized."[23] Needless to say, this view anguished Goddard's FBN counterparts.

In October Dr. Goddard reportedly told student gatherings at the University of Minnesota in response to the inevitable comparison: "Whether marihuana is a more dangerous drug than alcohol is debatable. I don't happen to think it is."[24] After this statement was widely publicized, cries for the doctor's resignation were immediately heard on Capitol Hill, and the *Wall Street Journal* noted the "political peril" attending these observations.[25] To explain his heresy Dr. Goddard was summoned to congressional committees three times in one week.

Whether or not Dr. Goddard was misquoted, as he has alleged, the reported remark undoubtedly reflected his views. In his "clarifications" of his previous statement, he noted that both alcohol use and marihuana use were serious problems, and that both were dangerous; alcohol for its damage to the mind and body, and marihuana for its legal consequences and possible long-term physical dangers. Nonetheless, he continued to advocate a relaxation of penalties for marihuana use, stating in an interview with *New Republic*: "I'm interested as a physician in changing the penalty for possession. I don't think we ought to be making felons out of our college students. This is a drug in widespread use today."[26]

Dr. Goddard was an official maverick. The policy-making community did not accept this view for several years. It certainly was unwilling to consider his preferred scheme, which was the removal of *any* penalty from possession for personal use. In the confidential memorandum prepared for Secretary Gardner, leaked to the *Wall Street Journal*, Goddard recommended that marihuana be reclassified under federal law, being brought within the Drug Abuse Control Amendments (DACA) of 1965.[27] Under DACA the FDA's Bureau of Drug Abuse Control had authority to control illicit traffic in the "dangerous" drugs (barbiturates, amphetamines, and hallucinogens, including LSD). Penalties under DACA were considerably more lenient than those under the Narcotic Control Act of 1956, which included marihuana. In particular, there was no penalty for possession of dangerous drugs for personal use. Goddard thought that marihuana should be classified as a "mild hallucinogen," under DACA, and that jurisdiction over it should thereby be transferred from FBN to FDA.

Although this proposal never received an official HEW imprimatur, it mirrored both a jurisdictional squabble and a substantive conflict. That conflict was clearly manifested in Commissioner Giordano's testimony on 15 November before the House Government Operations Subcommittee: "If there is no criminal sanction against possession of marihuana, many people will regard this as tacit approval of its use."[28]

Without stern penalties, he declared, marihuana use would "go through the roof." To Dr. Goddard's argument that LSD users were not criminalized, Giordano asserted that Congress should remedy that inequity by imposing penalties on possession of LSD, not by relaxing penalties for possession of marihuana.

Within a few months Congress had done just that.[29] Dr. Goddard's position that marihuana penalties were too harsh, which would become official orthodoxy a year later, had been rebuffed and he had resigned from government service. Retrenchment continued.

Another example of the fate of official dissent occurred on the state level. In 1966 the California legislature launched a major effort to reform its criminal code. Following tradition, the legislature relied on the legal academic community for the basic drafting, appointing six reporters to assist the Joint Legislative Committee to Revise the Penal Code. One of these reporters was John Kaplan, professor of law at Stanford Law School and a former assistant U.S. Attorney. As reporter he devoted much of his energy to the drug laws and the marihuana laws in particular. After more than two years of study and soul-searching, the reporters unanimously circulated a preliminary draft on marihuana in early 1969, recommending the withdrawal of the criminal penalty from possession for personal use. Shortly thereafter the Joint Legislative Committee fired the six reporters and replaced them with a prosecutor from the attorney general's office. After his dismissal, Professor Kaplan gathered the available information and published it, appealing in his word, to a "tribunal of higher resort."[30]

Respectability and Retreat

While the establishment symbolized its concern about the young generation by defending the marihuana laws, use of the drug nonetheless continued to spread. As more novice marihuana users reported no ill effects from its use, more students tried it, and in turn those who used it and enjoyed the drug began to "turn on" those who had not. By 1970 some campuses reported that over 70 percent of the student body were users.[31] Most observers and surveys estimated that about 50 percent of the nation's college population had tried marihuana.[32] Meanwhile, use of the drug was spreading beyond students to the young professional classes in the cities[33] and later to blue-collar youths. Marihuana became popular with many soldiers because the drug was readily available and widely used in Vietnam. On their return they introduced the practice to still wider segments of the population.

During the last few years of the sixties, then, marihuana use became less identified with any particular class or age. Dipping further into the teenage population and touching increasing numbers of the twenty-five to thirty-five-year-old group, experimental and recreational use of the drug touched all classes of society. By 1970 the *Wall Street Journal* found substantial marihuana use among young professionals and considerable evidence of marihuana use on the job in the New York City area.

As this trend continued, it became a popular sport to try to estimate the total incidence of use among Americans. Dr. Stanley F. Yolles, former director of the National Institute of Mental Health, testifying before a Senate subcommittee in 1969, said: "A conservative estimate of persons in the United States, both juveniles and adults, who have used marihuana at least once, is about eight million. And may be as high as twelve million people."[34] Other estimates in the late 1960s ran as high as twenty-five million users.[35] Although all the polls suffered from methodological flaws, it was generally accepted that use continued to increase into the seventies.

Meanwhile, of course, marihuana-smoking had become the most widely committed crime in America, with the possible exception of speeding on the highways. Reporting the marihuana arrests of Robert Kennedy, Jr., and R. Sargent Shriver, Jr., Walter Cronkite noted: "This case is not unusual; more and more parents across the nation find themselves going to court with their children on drug charges. It's becoming an incident of modern living."[36] It has been estimated that approximately 200,000 persons were arrested for possession of marihuana in 1970.[37]

Marihuana-smoking was no longer associated entirely with radical politics and the hippie lifestyle. In fact, both these social phenomena had probably declined after 1968, and the public anxiety that had characterized the retrenchment period had also receded. Instead, public attention had been turned increasingly to the legal consequences of marihuana use. In September 1970, for example, *Newsweek* headlined its cover story with the question "Marihuana: Time to Change the Law?"[38] Despite the retrenchment rhetoric, uncertainty—about the effects of the drug, and particularly about the propriety of prosecuting and incarcerating its users—now dominated public opinion.[39] Information regarding the harmfulness of marihuana was now less important than information regarding the harmfulness—or costs—of the marihuana laws. The public began to hear a lot about misallocation of enforcement resources, arbitrary prosecution, questionable police practices, and disrespect for law. Instances of political pot prosecutions and convictions were documented in the press. One of the most notorious was the thirty-year sentence meted out by a Texas court to black militant Lee Otis Johnson for giving one joint to an undercover agent. At the time of his conviction in 1968, Johnson headed the Houston chapter of the Student Nonviolent Coordinating Committee (SNCC). His conviction was subsequently reversed in 1972 by a federal district court.[40]

Opponents of the marihuana laws also argued that it was the marihuana *laws*, not marihuana itself, which could lead to "harder stuff" by compelling the marihuana user to secure his drug in an illicit marketplace. Most potent, however, was the challengers' contention that no possible harmful drug effect could justify the social cost of criminalizing the otherwise law-abiding young. Anthropologist Margaret Mead contended that marihuana prohibition was "damaging our country, our laws and the relations between young and old."[41] An otherwise cautious AMA expert committee statement in 1968 pleaded for differential legal approaches for "the occasional user, the frequent user, the chronic user, the person sharing his drug with another, and the dealer who sells for profit." Of "particular concern," the AMA experts emphasized, "is the youthful experimenter who, by incurring a criminal record through a single thoughtless act, places his future career in jeopardy. The lives of many young people are being needlessly damaged."[42]

The retreat had begun. The law enforcement community began to compromise the law, and the legislatures began to change it. The medical community gradually became willing to state the facts, abandoning the uneasy defensiveness of the retrenchment period. The underlying policy issues still remained unresolved, but the waiting period was over.

Local police and prosecutors no longer enforced the letter of the possession laws. By 1969 it was common knowledge in Washington, D.C., and New York City that possession of marihuana would draw attention only if it was flaunted.[43] Harsh criminal treatment of marihuana possession was no longer supported by a social consensus, and the legal system gradually adjusted. Informal diversions and increasing numbers of prosecutorial dismissals weeded out many—perhaps half—young users from the criminal justice system.[44]

While law enforcement authorities were molding their own procedures to the realities of widespread marihuana use, particularly in large cities, the courts had begun by 1969 to take a new view of the propriety of harsh sentences in those marihuana cases which reached the courts. Some judges publicly questioned the prudence of the existing law and pleaded for legislative relief.[45] By 1971 only 13 percent of the judges responding in an opinion survey indicated that they would incarcerate an adult for possession of marihuana; only 4 percent said they would jail a minor.[46] Naturally, heavy sentences in marihuana cases earned attention from the press, and the New Jersey Supreme Court converted the common practice to a rule, forbidding the lower courts in that state from incarcerating anyone for first-offense possession of marihuana.[47]

By 1969 many of society's major institutions of social control had softened their stances on marihuana use. Educators, parents, and physicians deserted the law; and many judges and prosecutors adjusted to the new realities. Finally, the legislators began to respond. By the beginning of 1970 twenty-one states had reduced the penalties for possession of marihuana. This trend continued during 1970, as eleven more states acted (see map). There was something very hesitant about all of this, however, as many states merely restored to the judiciary the sentencing flexibility that they had taken away in the fifties.

A typical example of the tokenism of the penalty-reduction phase of marihuana's legal history is the Virginia experience. On 24 February 1969 a twenty-year-old ex-University of Virginia student, Frank P. LaVarre, was arrested in a Danville, Virginia, bus station while en route to Atlanta from Charlottesville, Virginia.[48] In his possession were four plastic containers of marihuana, valued at $2,500, plus smaller amounts in a tobacco pouch and a shoe. Refusing to "cooperate" by disclosing the names of all university students whom he knew were using drugs, LaVarre's bond was set at $50,000.

Following a plea of guilty to possession of marihuana, LaVarre was sentenced on 31 July 1969 to twenty-five years in the state penitentiary, five years suspended, and fined $500. The sentencing judge admonished him, "Now I want to say to you, young man, that you still have time to mend your ways and make a useful citizen out of yourself."[49] Presumably this meant that under Virginia law LaVarre, "who had never so much as stolen a hubcap,"[50] would be eligible for parole in five years.

Although the trial was reported on the front page of the *Richmond Times-Dispatch*, the conscience of the Virginia citizenry was not awakened until several months later when an article in *Life* magazine used the LaVarre case as an illustration of the nation's antiquated and inhumane drug laws. One suspects that all this publicity embarrassed the people of Virginia[51] and fostered general agreement that marihuana penalties were far too harsh.[52] This was clearly the belief of the governor, who pardoned LaVarre on 2 January 1970, placing him on five years' probation. This act was noted nationally[53] and applauded locally.[54] The existing law was criticized and reform was urged.[55]

The Virginia General Assembly responded and a subcommittee of the House General Laws Committee held hearings.[56] At these hearings the legislators as well as the experts generally agreed that drug laws should be aimed primarily at dealers and should allow more leeway "for youngsters caught following a current fad."[57] Testimony also indicated that many persons arrested were never prosecuted because some commonwealth's attorneys felt that even the minimum penalty for unlawful possession was too great.[58] Many of the legislators believed that lighter penalties would encourage more uniform enforcement of the law.

In response the general assembly enacted a comprehensive drug control measure to replace the old Uniform Narcotic Drug Act; this new law was signed by the governor on 5 April 1970.[59] The penalty for first-offense possession of marihuana was reduced to a misdemeanor punishable by a fine of not more than $1,000 or confinement in jail not to exceed twelve months, or both. However, a second- or subsequent-possession offense was to be rewarded by imprisonment in the penitentiary for between two and twenty years or, at the discretion of the jury or the court sitting without a jury, confinement in jail up to twelve months and a fine of not more than $10,000.[60]

The legislature thus combined light sentences for first-offense possession with extremely tough ones for second and subsequent violations. One legislator summed up the reason for this distinction: "This misdemeanor penalty on the first offense will straighten out most of the kids fooling with it . . . make them stop and think . . . scare them. . . . The ones who are really hooked on it will be back . . . we'll get them on repeat business [and imprison them upon a a second offense]."[61]

The penalty-reduction phase was well underway at the state level by 1971, although the Virginia experience illustrates that policy makers were not yet questioning the fundamental assumptions underlying the existing policy. They were simply tinkering with that policy in order to ameliorate its excesses.

Meanwhile, a similar development was taking place at the federal level. Of substantial importance in this regard was a reorganization of the federal narcotics bureaucracy. In 1968 the FBN was removed from the Treasury Department and the Bureau of Drug Abuse Control was removed from HEW to form jointly a new Bureau of Narcotics and Dangerous Drugs (BNDD) in the Justice Department. The influx of HEW personnel not tied to past FBN policies moderated the tone of the federal response. Within months BNDD was publicly espousing an enforcement policy aimed only at major trafficking, not at possession.[62]

As at the state level, the agitation was building in the Congress for reduction of federal marihuana penalties. This pressure coincided with a broader movement to restructure federal drug laws in general. The need to overhaul the federal response had become increasingly apparent as the sixties wore on. In the first place, the diverse governmental interests in drug control, having evolved in a piecemeal fashion over a half-century, had never been rationalized. A patchwork of regulatory, revenue, and criminal measures had strewn jurisdiction among numerous federal agencies. In addition, the Supreme Court had, in 1969, invalidated some of the contorted presumptions and other awkward devices through which Congress had originally extended federal jurisdiction over the drug area.[63]

It had been apparent for some twenty years that congressional power to regulate interstate and foreign commerce could be employed to prohibit or regulate possession and distribution of drugs, and the Drug Abuse Control Act of 1965 had been premised on the commerce clause. Consequently, full abandonment of the revenue charade was long overdue. Finally, the need for modernization of the drug laws merged with an even broader attempt to rationalize the entire federal penal code. The National Commission on Reform of the Federal Criminal Laws had been established by Congress in 1966 to "review . . . the statutory and case law of the United States which constitutes the Federal system of criminal justice . . . [and] to make recommendations for revision and recodification. . . ."[64] By 1969 the commission had generated a "working paper" which identified the governmental interests in drug control and drafted a statutory scheme integrating all controlled drugs.[65]

U.S. Government Printing Office, 1970

A second aspect of federal law which had been subject to increasing attack during the sixties was the penalty structure, particularly the draconian mandatory minimum sentences levied by the Boggs and Narcotic Control acts. Within six years three presidential commissions had pleaded for sentencing discretion: the President's Advisory Commission on Narcotic and Drug Abuse of 1963 (Prettyman Commission), the President's Commission on Law Enforcement and the Administration of Justice of 1967 (Katzenbach Commission), and the National Commission on the Causes and Prevention of Violence of 1969 (Eisenhower Commission). There can be little doubt that these recommendations were finally adopted in 1970 in part because of the political imperative then attaching to reduction of marihuana penalties.

Beginning in the spring of 1969 and continuing for the ensuing eighteen months, several committees of the Congress conducted a multitude of hearings on drug control. The final result was passage of the Comprehensive Drug Abuse Prevention and Control Act in October 1970.[66] (The drug control part of this measure was called the Controlled Substances Act.) In addition to integrating all controlled substances in a uniform regulatory framework, abandoning mandatory minimum sentences and reducing "simple" possession of all drugs to a misdemeanor, this act established a National Commission on Marihuana and Drug Abuse to conduct a year-long formal, authoritative study of marihuana.

The Nixon Administration had introduced its initial version of the "Controlled Dangerous Substances Act" on 15 July 1969.[67] In most respects the proposed bill retained the penalty structure of the old laws, and even increased penalties for hallucinogen violations, which had been relatively light under DACA. However, the attorney general intimated some flexibility in the first round of hearings, noting that the penalty provisions did not reflect the administration's "definitive opinion."[68] When it appeared that the Congress no longer had the stomach for harsh penalties for users, the administration revised its bill, proposing misdemeanor penalties for simple possession and abandoning mandatory minimums for all offenders except "professional criminals."[69] This brought the administration's bill in line with a similar bill introduced by Connecticut's Senator Dodd, whose subcommittee on juvenile delinquency was conducting the hearings for the Committee on the Judiciary. Comparison of the Dodd bill with early drafts of the administration bill strongly suggests that Senator Dodd had actually introduced an earlier version of the administration's measure.

The Senate passed the Controlled Dangerous Substances Act in February 1970.[70] The House, after a jurisdictional squabble between the Ways and Means and Interstate and Foreign Commerce committees—a dispute reflecting the chaotic structure of the old laws—passed what had now become the Comprehensive Drug Abuse Prevention and Control Act of 1970. With regard to penalties there was some variation between the House and Senate bills. For example, S. 3246, in recognition of the social realities of marihuana use and distribution, treated casual transfers as the functional equivalent of possession; under the House version, any distribution was a felony. Also, the House version assessed higher penalties for importation (smuggling) than for trafficking, while the Senate measure drew no similar distinction.

By far the most important variation between the two measures, however, related to the respective roles of the departments of Justice and Health, Education, and Welfare in the scheduling, classification, and reclassification of controlled substances. Since the scheduling decisions have implications for penal law as well as regulatory control, this issue symbolized the continuing conflict between scientific and law enforcement perspectives on drug control.

Under the new statutory scheme employed in both bills, all previously controlled substances were classified in a series of schedules according to their abuse potential, known effect, harmfulness, and level of accepted medical use. (As enacted, the act includes five schedules.) For example, substances in Schedule I, having high potential for abuse, no accepted medical use, and a lack of accepted safety for use under medical supervision, are subject to the most stringent regulatory controls. Conversely, Schedule IV substances, having a low potential for abuse relative to substances in Schedule III, currently accepted medical use, and limited dependence liability, are subject to the least stringent controls. With some exceptions, criminal penalties for possession or distribution outside the regulatory framework also follow the classification hierarchy.

The variation between the House and Senate measures related to the procedure for classifying future drugs and rescheduling drugs previously controlled. Under the Senate measure this responsibility rested with the attorney general, who was required only to "request the advice" of the secretary of HEW and of a scientific advisory committee in making his decision. He was not required to follow this advice despite the fact that the various criteria require primarily scientific and medical judgments. The Senate rejected an amendment by Senator Harold Hughes of Iowa that would have made the recommendations of the "advisors" binding on the attorney general.[71] Under the House version, however, the secretary's recommendation not to schedule a new drug was binding on the attorney general and his recommendation as to rescheduling was binding as to medical and scientific matters.

The importance of this issue, which was ultimately resolved in conference in favor of the House version, extended well beyond marihuana. However, the marihuana issue may have played a pivotal role in the final result. Congressional interest in reducing penalties responded directly to political and social imperatives; this development was neither tied to nor premised upon a reconsideration of the scientific and ideological issues. But neither the Congress nor the administration could ignore these questions; they could only postpone them.

Uncertainty and conflict still characterized discussion among experts about the effects of marihuana. Accordingly, the administration chose to perpetuate the classification of marihuana with drugs that were recognized to be more dangerous; marihuana appeared in Schedule I with heroin and LSD. Congress meekly deferred to this judgment, but all of the participants seem to have anticipated a change after "the facts were in." The importance of who was ultimately to make the decision was reflected clearly by Senator Dodd: "After the last set of hearings the testimony on it was so conflicting . . . that it was impossible for me to really make up my own mind about it. I don't know how anyone could legislate in such an atmosphere. The law enforcement people pretty generally took the view that it is dangerous, addictive, very harmful and ought to be dealt with very severely; while the medical, scientific and educational community pretty generally took the view that this was not quite so."[72]

The committee report on the House bill noted:

The Committee requested recommendations from [HEW] concerning the appropriate location of marihuana in the schedules of the bill, and by letter of August 14, 1970, the Assistant Secretary for Health and Scientific Affairs (Roger O. Egeberg) recommended "that marihuana be retained within Schedule I at least until the completion of certain studies now underway."

In addition, . . . the bill provides for establishment of a Presidential Commission on Marihuana and Drug Abuse. The recommendations of the Commission will be of aid in determining the appropriate disposition of the question in the future.[73]

Since this possible rescheduling could be accomplished by administrative action, marihuana's legal status depended heavily on the review mechanism built into the Controlled Substances Act. The key question, then, was "who decides?" In this respect the resolution of the House and Senate conflict over scheduling responsibility would determine the administrative decision maker. But an interim fact-finding process was contemplated by all concerned, including the attorney general.[74]

CHAPTER XIII

Science, Marihuana, and Politics

THE MARIHUANA CONSENSUS had collapsed completely by the end of 1970. That use of the drug had so easily been translated into a political symbol assured that no substitute would be quickly achieved. Some thoughtful observers saw no prospect of improvement until American society came to grips with the fundamental social and philosophical issues regarding consumption of *all* psychoactive substances. Others contended that social necessity would itself dictate substantial changes in marihuana policy, whether or not fundamental issues were confronted and whether or not a replacement consensus was achieved. In this view the politics would continue to dominate the rhetoric, but institutional imperatives would dictate policy.

Under the former view objective fact-finding was an essential predicate to rational policy-making, and so long as ideological factors interfered with the scientific process, policy-making would continue to be chaotic. Under the latter view, fact-finding was irrelevant to outcome, although it might continue to be the lightning rod for political dialogue.

Either view is consistent with the evolution of the marihuana issue during 1971-72. The fact-finding process continued to be politically charged; indeed, the pressure for authoritative scientific determinations had made the very selection of the fact-finder an important political issue.

Who Should Be the Fact-Finder?

From the outset of congressional consideration of drug control in the late 1960s, the marihuana discussion did not center on appropriate penalties—almost every witness agreed that penalties should be reduced but not eliminated; instead, attention was generally focused on how and when the government ought to issue a definitive report on the scientific and public policy issues involved. About the same time that the administration introduced the Controlled Dangerous Substances Act, legislators of both parties introduced legislation in both houses to establish a presidential commission on marihuana. Spearheading the movement in the House was Congressman Koch of New York, who garnered 60 co-sponsors for his bill, which was joined in the hopper by four others. Senator Moss introduced a companion measure in the Senate.[1]

The lot of the presidential commission had not been a happy one during the 1960s. Reports issued by commissions on crime (Katzenbach, 1967), civil disorders (Kerner, 1968), violence (Eisenhower, 1969), campus unrest (Scranton, 1970), and pornography (Lockhart, 1970) burdened library shelves, testifying collectively to the political limits of enlightenment. Despite this poor record, many legislators considered the marihuana issue a matter of some urgency and sought an intensive investigation covering all aspects of the problem. They felt further that if the report were to be credible and authoritative, the issuing body would have to be independent, wearing the "mantle of a Presidential Commission with all that suggests and recommends."[2]

The administration was not in such a hurry. It is no accident that the commission approach, sponsored most enthusiastically by legislators of liberal persuasion, was viewed skeptically by an administration that had staked out a conservative position on the drug issue. Marihuana had by now become a political issue on which the liberals were committed to change. In such circumstances "expert" commissions often function as expedient detours, postponing direct confrontation; yet, because expert panels tend to be drawn from the intellectual class, their recommendations frequently coincide with liberal ideology. Thus, Congressman Koch and his colleagues had good reason to seek commission fact-finding, and the Nixon Administration had equally good reason to be suspicious of this approach.

Beyond the political dimension, divergent views on the appropriate fact-finder also stemmed from disparate views concerning which facts were being sought. Each side propounded the need to establish the facts as a predicate for rational decision-making. But each side was also aware that the fact-finder would make significant decisions simply by selecting which facts were important. Thus, advocates of change, including the sponsors of the commission legislation, were anxious for an authoritative body to explode specific myths—crime, addiction, insanity, death, progression to other drugs—and had no doubt that an objective study would aid their cause. The defenders, on the other hand, were looking for more generalized findings—that marihuana was a "dangerous drug," that it was a public health concern, and that its use could have adverse consequences for both the user and society.

Newsweek, for example, reported in September 1970 that Attorney General Mitchell hoped that "a national study commission on marihuana (similar to the Surgeon General's investigation of smoking)" will turn up sufficient negative evidence about marihuana's effects "to allow youth to resist peer pressure to use the drug. It can be a dangerous and damaging drug. . . . I think we'll find physical and chemical evidence of that." For example, Mitchell reportedly continued, "a commission could make clear the distinction between addiction—I think most everyone agrees this is not an addictive substance—and dependency. A kid gets into steady use of marihuana. After a while he gets less of a charge from it, and this psychological dependency causes him to move on to the harder stuff . . . we have to get proof that it does create this dependency."[3]

Thus we see the critical importance of choosing the fact-finder. It was evident, in other words, that a fact-finder who wanted to whitewash marihuana could do so simply by saying what it does *not* do. On the other hand, a fact-finder looking for harm, as was the attorney general, could probably find it.

Another dimension of this conflict was officialdom's increasing discomfort with the medical-scientific orientation of the marihuana debate. Throughout the retrenchment period official spokesmen had submerged the philosophical, social, and legal issues, placing all their eggs in the health basket. Factors such as the drug's toxicity, acute effects, genetic effects, dependence liability, and long-term psychological and physiological effects had been officially assigned a pivotal role in the social and legal policy decision. As Mitchell's comments suggest, it was felt that at least in some of these areas research would indict marihuana as a "dangerous" drug, and that would be the end of it. In some respects the challengers themselves had abetted this response. They could have presented philosophical and social arguments more persuasively than could the government, but they generally failed to do so during the retrenchment period. Instead, they often aided the government's case by contending that marihuana was "harmless."

By the end of the decade the debate was beginning to change direction. The harmless/dangerous charade was joined by more fundamental issues. The challengers relied more and more on philosophical and social arguments, and officialdom, having become uneasy with the medical orientation, was also turning to a socio-cultural defense. When asked what his position would be if a study were to "come out favorably for marihuana," the attorney general responded: "Why *should* we use it when it has no redeeming value? The desire of someone to get out of this world by puffing on marihuana has no redeeming value. There is no rhyme or reason to it."[4] In addition to such normative considerations, government authorities now recognized that a prohibitory policy was best premised on speculation about the adverse impact on the public health if marihuana use were to become widespread. Such considerations, difficult to convey in the first instance, would be impossible to resurrect in the aftermath of headlines such as "Pot Relatively Harmless" or "Occasional Use of Pot Harmless." Thus, the administration wanted a fact-finder it could rely upon to concentrate on the long-term social impact of marihuana use.

Another objection to the commission approach, maintained vociferously within NIMH, was that definitive answers—even from the medical orientation—could not be provided in one or two years. Studies of the effects of long-term use had never been conducted and were just being fielded. A commission, according to this view, would have to emphasize the unknown and therefore could not provide a definitive report; and if it did not emphasize the unknown, the nation might suffer irreversible damage, as the tobacco experience illustrated. Congressman Beister of Pennsylvania expressed the danger: "My apprehension is [that] we may explore the unknown with a target date of one year with a small group of people and achieve a resolution which pretends to say there is no longer an unknown when in point of fact there may continue to be a great one."[5]

Congressman Beister and others were worried about the "human factor in the equation." That same "special impact" sought by the commission's proponents might cause incalculable social damage if the commission were incorrect or imprudent. It would offer "a fresh retreat for those who choose to use marihuana, saying that this does not hurt."[6]

Politicians were being pressed for answers. Some thought they knew what the answers would be and wanted to establish them in a credible way; others thought they also knew but preferred not to hear them. But the vast majority of politicians and certainly the general public were confused. Contradictions about specific drug effects abounded in reported research and official statements, and this uncertainty had been aggravated from 1965 to 1968 when most official medical spokesmen had maintained a judicious silence. In this connection Congressman Claude Pepper chastized the surgeon general in September 1969, noting that "one of the especially alarming and confusing aspects of this entire controversy is the fact that the relevant agencies of our Federal Government have generally remained silent in the face of a most heated debate." Recalling that Dr. Goddard and Dr. Roger Egeberg, assistant secretary of HEW for Health and Scientific Affairs, had expressed personal, nonofficial views that "the criminal laws relating to marihuana are unrealistic and unenforcible," Pepper accused the executive branch of taking "an ostrich-like approach to the problem, [being] more inclined to ignore the issues than to discuss them."[7]

By the fall of 1969 the government's top medical spokesmen had broken their official silence. Drs. Egeberg, Stanley Yolles (Director of NIMH), and Jesse Steinfeld (soon to become surgeon general) each noted the mythology surrounding marihuana and the disutility of the existing law. Dr. Yolles was most outspoken: "I know of no clearer instance in which the punishment for an infraction of the law is more harmful than the crime itself. . . . To equate [marihuana's] risk—either to the individual or society—with the risks inherent in the use of hard narcotics is—on the face of it—merely an effort to defend the indefensible, established position that has no scientific basis."[8] Dr. Yolles then read the following chart:

Marihuana

Fable	Fact
1. Marihuana is a narcotic.	1. Marihuana is not a narcotic except by statute. Narcotics are opium or its derivations (like some synthetic chemicals with opium-like activity).
2. Marihuana is addictive.	2. Marihuana does not cause physical addiction, since tolerance to its effects and symptoms on sudden withdrawals does not occur. It can produce habituation (psychological dependence).
3. Marihuana causes violence and crime.	3. Persons under the influence of marihuana tend to be passive. It is true that sometimes a crime may be committed by a person while under the influence of marihuana. However, any drug which loosens one's self-control is likely to do the same and relates primarily to the personality of the user.
4. Marihuana leads to increase in sexual activity.	4. Marihuana has no aphrodisiac property.
5. Marihuana is harmless.	5. Instances of acute panic, depression, and psychotic states are known, although they are infrequent. Certain kinds of individuals can also become over-involved in marihuana use and can lose their drive. We do not know the effects of long-term use.
6. Occasional use of marihuana is less harmful than occasional use of alcohol.	6. We do not know. Research on the effects of various amounts of each drug for various periods is underway.
7. Marihuana use leads to heroin.	7. We know of nothing in the nature of marihuana that predisposes to heroin abuse. It is estimated that less than 5% of chronic users of marihuana go on to heroin use.

8. Marihuana enhances creativity.	8. Marihuana might bring fantasies of enhanced creativity but they are illusory, as are "instant insights" reported by marihuana users.
9. More severe penalties will solve the marihuana problem.	9. Marihuana use has increased enormously in spite of the most severely punitive laws.
10. It is safe to drive while under the influence of marihuana.	10. Driving under the influence of any intoxicant is hazardous.

Despite such candor, political restraints were still apparent. In contrast to their rhetoric, none of these physicians recommended a public policy more drastic than reduction of penalties. (In fact, Dr. Yolles had apparently broken the ranks; his strong position on marihuana penalties reportedly earned him a dismissal.)[9]

The government physicians also opposed creation of a commission. Dr. Yolles insisted that "there are some things we already know about marihuana in spite of the fact that many people are not willing to accept the knowledge."[10] Instead of establishing another commission, he argued, Congress should "direct NIMH to conduct research and make a basic determination on marihuana."[11] Senator Dodd included such a mandate in his bill.

But Congressman Koch and his colleagues did not think this was sufficient. "There is already feeling," he said, "that the intergovernmental agencies have not told the truth."[12] Recognizing that studies must often be evaluated and reconciled, commission proponents such as Congressman Gude of Maryland insisted on the independence of a body "that is not answerable to the Executive or committed to a political position. . . . I don't think you can achieve this independence with an interdepartmental study."[13]

The administration finally succumbed to the pressure for an expert panel, but proposed that it be appointed jointly by the attorney general and the secretary of HEW instead of by the president. John Ingersoll, director of BNDD, was pressed hard by the House Judiciary Subcommittee members to explain why. He could not do so to their satisfaction. Undoubtedly, the administration was seeking lower visibility, increased control, and greater flexibility in appointments.

Interestingly enough, one witness was suspicious of the political controls attaching to presidential appointees as well. Rutgers University's Dr. Helen Nowlis, who was later prevailed upon to head drug abuse education programs for the Office of Education, was afraid the president would select "a lot of law enforcement people ... [who] will not face the critical issues."[14] To decrease political pressure, she would have diffused the appointing authority; but having come "reluctantly ... to the conclusion that commissions tend to be more political than scientific or expert," she would have dispensed with the idea altogether; instead she would have decriminalized possession of marihuana immediately.[15]

Congress ultimately diffused fact-finding responsibility. First, it enacted the "Marihuana and Health Reporting Act" in July 1970 mandating HEW to report annually on the health consequences of marihuana use.[16] Several months later the House version of the Comprehensive Drug Abuse Prevention and Control Act provided for a bipartisan National Commission on Marihuana and Drug Abuse to be composed of thirteen members, nine to be appointed by the president and four by the Congress. The commission was to spend the first year of its two-year life on marihuana only. The Senate accepted this provision.[17]

The federal government would speak with many voices, but it would speak at last.

The Politics of Fact-Finding

The designation of public fact-finders did not depoliticize the marihuana issue. In fact, initiation of a fact-finding process may have tightened the political screw. For example, the commission's independence was brought into question immediately after its appointment in early 1971.

President Nixon's selections were not greeted kindly by advocates of reform. "Its average age is 'an old 54,' " one commentator noted. "The only pair of sideburns are snowy white, the youngest member is a 37-year-old cop, (Mitchell Ware, then superintendent of the Illinois Bureau of Investigation), and its second youngest, 40-year-old Mrs. Joan Ganz Cooney (executive producer) of ' Sesame Street' is in touch with a clientele somewhat below pot-blowing age."[18] The commission's medical experts, Drs. Dana Farnsworth, Maurice Seevers, Henry Brill, and Thomas Ungerleider were attacked for their deep AMA "establishment" roots and for holding firm preconceived notions. The independence of the commission's chairman, former Pennsylvania Governor Raymond Shafer, and of SMU Law School Dean Charles O. Galvin was questioned on the ground that federal judgeships might hang in the balance of commission deliberations.[19] A Midwest educator, President John Howard of Rockford College, rounded out the presidential appointees. Finally, the commission's staff director Michael Sonnenreich—formerly deputy chief counsel of BNDD and leading protagonist of the Controlled Substances Act—was accused of being an administration tool.[20] This was a "stacked deck" in the eyes of the reformers.

The president himself got into the act at a May Day 1971 press conference six weeks after the commission began its work. In answer to a questioner who pointed out that his own White House Conference on Youth had voted to legalize marihuana, the president replied: "As you know, there is a Commission that is supposed to make recommendations to me about this subject, and in this instance, however, I have such strong views that I will express them. I am against legalizing marihuana. Even if the Commission does recommend that it be legalized, I will not follow that recommendation."[21]

Some weeks later the president elaborated on the reason for his "strong feelings" when, in the context of a discussion of heroin addiction, he noted the need for

> a massive program of information for the American people with regard to how the drug habit begins and how we eventually end up with so many being addicted to heroin. . . .
> In that respect, that is one of the reasons I have taken such a strong position with regard to the question of marihuana. I realize this is controversial. But I can see no social or moral justification whatever for legalizing marihuana. I think it would be exactly the wrong step. It would simply encourage more and more of our young people to start down the long, dismal road that leads to hard drugs and eventually self-destruction.[22]

After these remarks, which received considerable attention in the press, the commission chairman defensively contended that the president had expressed a "personal opinion," and that the commission in no way felt bound by it.[23] Some commentators were not so kind to President Nixon. Joseph Kraft, for example, accused the president of "trying to enhance his own popularity by taking a stand against unpopular habits practiced by an unpopular group," and urged him to "rise above the battles of domestic politics," "keep an open mind and wait for more information from the Marihuana Commission."[24] Hedging their bets on the likely outcome of the commission's deliberations, the proponents of change used the president's statement to impugn the panel's credibility, thereby laying the groundwork for later undercutting any unfavorable commission findings or recommendations.

For the six years during which the marihuana controversy had raged, truth was a highly subjective commodity. Science was but a means to an ideological end, as each research study was publicized immediately by the researchers themselves or by the combatants in the rhetorical struggle. Pending authoritative, objective fact-finding, this development reached a crescendo in May 1971.

On 19 April the American Medical Association issued to the press advance copies of a forthcoming *Journal* article by two Philadelphia psychiatrists, Harold Kolansky and William Moore, entitled "Effects of Marihuana on Adolescents and Young Adults." Accompanying the article was an editorial sigh of relief reflected in the following AMA statement: "The attached paper . . . presents the first real evidence based on good research of the harmful effects of marihuana. Heretofore, medicine has been able to say only that there was no good evidence of harm from smoking pot. Now we have some evidence."[25] The Kolansky-Moore conclusions then appeared prominently in national news magazines, on network news programs, and in newspapers throughout the country.[26]

The response was immediate and predictable. One criminal court judge in Miami, Florida, reportedly stated that he was now satisfied that marihuana had been proven harmful, and accordingly he would no longer be lenient with the drug's users; henceforth, marihuana offenders would all go to jail.[27] Since their article was of considerable interest to policy makers, the Marihuana Commission invited the two doctors to testify at public hearings to be held in May.[28] And advocates of legalization scurried about furiously to prepare a suitable rebuttal before the subversive "findings" could settle into the public consciousness.

Drs. Kolansky and Moore described thirty-eight patients, ages thirteen to twenty-four, whom they had seen in the course of their private practice between 1965 and 1970. These individuals, who all used marihuana moderately to heavily but had not' used other illicit drugs, "showed an onset of psychiatric problems shortly after the beginning of marihuana smoking; these individuals had either no premorbid psychiatric history or had premorbid psychiatric symptoms which were extremely mild or almost unnoticeable in contrast to the serious symptomatology which followed the known onset of marihuana smoking."[29]

Having stipulated that the patients were normal prior to marihuana use, the authors concluded that the "serious psychological effects," including apathy, confusion, and passivity, shown by all patients had been caused by their marihuana use: "Our study showed no evidence of a predisposition to mental illness in these patients prior to the development of psychopathologic symptoms once moderate-to-heavy use of cannabis derivations had begun. It is our impression that our study demonstrates the possibility that moderate-to-heavy use of marihuana in adolescents and young people without predisposition to psychiatric illness may lead to ego decompensation ranging from mild ego disturbance to psychosis."[30]

These findings had been widely publicized, and Drs. Kolansky and Moore testified that they had received hundreds of letters from practicing psychiatrists reporting similar clinical observations and confirming their conclusions. Yet, the authors had not anticipated the criticism to which they would be subjected by virtue of having deposited their controversial views in the public forum.

Drs. Kolansky and Moore were accused by fellow psychiatrists of publicity-seeking, bias and preconception, methodological naivete, and insufficient experience in the area of psychoactive drugs. Not once, however, did their colleagues question the authors' clinical observations. This is an extremely important point. Kolansky and Moore had anticipated criticism because their conclusions were based on clinical experience rather than controlled laboratory experimentation. In fact, they were so conscious of this possibility that they reversed the argument: "We are aware that claims are made that large numbers of adolescents and young adults smoke marihuana regularly without developing symptoms or changes in academic study, but since these claims are made without the necessary accompaniment of thorough psychiatric study of each individual, they remain unsupported by scientific evidence."[31]

Challenging neither the clinical method nor the authors' observations, an impressive array of experts unanimously dismissed the conclusions drawn from these observations. Of course, objectivity in drawing hypothesis from experience—whether clinical or experimental—had always been the casualty in the marihuana controversy. The Kolansky-Moore incident epitomized this issue.

Psychiatric experts in the drug field unanimously concluded that their Philadelphia colleagues had shown only an association between marihuana-smoking and mental illness, not a causal relationship. No less an authority than Dr. Bertram Brown, who succeeded Stanley Yolles as director of NIMH, noted in testimony before the Marihuana Commission:

> I must say that we must always be cautious about any one study and the implications drawn from such a study, a point we've made over and over again.
>
> More specifically, let me make a rather fundamental point. . . .Let us assume that "X" study—not the one you are going to hear—showed that 50 people who smoked marihuana had an acute psychotic paranoid breakdown with homicidal tendencies. Let's assume that for a moment, the worst possible outcome.
>
> I think if you are dealing with a university or a population sample of a million or 10 million or 4 million, you can find 30 or 40 of anything.
>
> I hasten to say, for example, that if you look carefully, you might find 30 or 40 college students who graduate Phi Beta Kappa, summa cum laude, who use marihuana three or four times a week for their four years. But nobody goes looking for that particular phenomenon.
>
> And the reason I make that point is to show how any one study must be seen in the context of the total problem, from an epidemiological or sample point of view.[32]

A professor of psychiatry and pharmacology at Johns Hopkins, Dr. Solomon Snyder,[33] observed that

> [all] Drs. Kolansky and Moore have shown is that some marihuana users have mental illness. From their study it is not at all possible to ascribe a cause and effect relationship.
>
> I do not know whether or not the heavy use of marihuana can lead to emotional disturbance. However, it is quite clear that the

type of case report study reported by Drs. Kolansky and Moore is not capable of providing the information that would enable one to draw any conclusion as to the dangers of marihuana.[34]

Other commentators, whose own opinions about marihuana prohibition were on record, tried to account for the authors' obliviousness to methodology. Joel Fort, one of the earliest proponents of marihuana reform,[35] was most outspoken:

> No drug, whether aspirin, alcohol, or marihuana is harmless or affects everyone in the same way; and a pathological frame of reference (traditionally applied by doctors and particularly psychiatrists) as opposed to a normative or naturalistic one can make any phenomenon including intercourse, a tennis match, or drinking alcohol seem sick or abnormal. One-dimensional viewing with alarm out of context is an unfortunately common human behavior widely practiced by politicians, ambitious physicians, and others seeking instant headlines and rescue from often well-deserved obscurity. I could write the scenario on marihuana for the next decade; a damaged chromosome here, a psychotic reaction there, impotency, violence, promiscuity, dropping out; and less often, inherent pleasure, aphrodisia, health, and harmlessness. A review of the available biographical and publications data (about Kolansky and Moore) combined with their own statements in the article in question show that they are both in their late 40s, practice child psychoanalysis in affluent suburbs, have never worked in the field of mind-altering drugs, took five years to collect the small sample of 38 "patients" (19 each) reported on in the article, saw them one or two times (presumably for fifty minutes) without any previous or future contact, and have as their previous "scientific" publications: "Treatment of a three year old girl's severe infantile neurosis" and "Bee sting in the case of a ten year old boy in analysis."[36]

Dr. Norman Zinberg, who conducted some of the first controlled experimental studies on the acute effects of marihuana in man,[37] was more subtle:

> Each case begins by saying that the patients began by smoking marijuana and then moved on to homosexuality, enormous promiscuity, paranoid psychoses, delusions and so on, without further question as to causal relationship. There is no effort in this article to describe *how* marijuana brings these changes about. When Drs. Kolansky and Moore move into more specific psychological terms, they talk in terms of severe decompensation of

the ego. How does marijuana bring that about? They do not describe any specific mechanisms although they continue to state in several places in the article that this severe decompensation of the ego is the direct result of the "toxic" effect of cannabis. Further, there is considerable confusion in this article between the neurological and the psychological. It is hard for me to imagine that if marijuana were toxic per se to any specific part of the nervous system including the brain, we would not see frequent reports of neurological disturbances with 12 to 20 million regular smokers.[38]

Finally, Dr. Lester Grinspoon, whose *Marijuana Reconsidered*[39] was published earlier in 1971, placed Kolansky and Moore in a wider perspective:

All in all this paper is, from a scientific point of view, so unsound as to be all but meaningless. Unfortunately, from a social point of view it will have great significance in that it confirms for those people who have a hyperemotional bias against marijuana all the things that they would like to believe happen as a consequence of the use of marijuana and in turn it will enlarge the credibility gap which exists between young people and the medical profession. I am convinced that if the American Medical Association were less interested in the imposition of a moral hegemony with respect to this issue and more concerned with the scientific aspects of this drug this paper would not have been accepted for publication.[40]

Ideological factors undoubtedly influenced the Kolansky-Moore interpretations of their data. Suggesting that clinicians as a class may be especially susceptible to "ideological selection of certain classes of facts," sociologist Erich Goode has carefully documented the traces of bias and "overt moralism" which Kolansky and Moore in particular wove "throughout a supposedly detached clinical study." In Goode's view, "it is only because the authors . . . accept the common sense and taken-for-granted assumption that marijuana is harmful that their case descriptions are believed to be meaningful. To accept the validity of their data as demonstrating the medical pathology of marijuana use, it would be necessary to believe in these conclusions beforehand. To an unbiased observer, all they demonstrate are the prejudices of Kolansky and Moore."[41]

Perhaps shell-shocked by the vehemence of these criticisms of the Kolansky-Moore article (and of itself as well), the editorial

board of the *Journal of the American Medical Association* thereafter published a full critique of the "study."[42]

Fact-Finding at Last

The Kolansky-Moore episode ushered out the most unruly phase of
marihuana prohibition. By the end of 1971 most of the facts were
on the table; the medical experts, still cautious from the standpoint of social policy, had begun to speak up. Then the official
governmental fact-finders simultaneously confirmed these facts in
early 1972. NIMH issued its second annual *Marihuana and Health
Report*[43] in February, and the Commission on Marihuana and
Drug Abuse issued its report— *Marihuana: A Signal of Misunderstanding*[44]—in March. These events did not de-fuse the political
aspects of the marihuana issue, but as to science, at least, consensus
had finally replaced conflict. The rhetoric now began to center on
the underlying social issues.

Who Uses Marihuana and How Often?

The commission estimated that 24 million Americans had used
marihuana at least once. The NIMH estimate was more conservative—between 15 and 20 million. Both reports estimated that about
half of these individuals had simply experimented with the drug
out of curiosity and given it up. Another 40 percent of the "ever-
users" continue to use the drug but on an intermittent basis—once
a week or less—for recreational purposes. A small percentage of the
more frequent users (about 2 percent of the ever-using population)
use the drug more than once daily. (The commission's second
report, in March 1973, reported that 26 million Americans had
tried marihuana and that 13 million continued to use the drug.)
    Both reports noted that use of the drug was continuing to in-
crease, spreading to all socioeconomic and occupational groups, but
emphasized that use was highly age-specific. Of all the ever-users,
about half were in the sixteen to twenty-five age bracket. Both
reports estimated that 44 percent of those persons currently in
college or graduate school had used marihuana at least once.

Why Do People Smoke Marihuana?

Both reports dispelled the retrenchment stereotype of marihuana users as sick, emotionally maladjusted persons. Instead, both documents considered experimentation with and recreational use of the drug (thereby encompassing perhaps 90 percent of the ever-users) to be a social phenomenon. The NIMH report stated: "It is well recognized that marihuana use, like much other illegal drug use, occurs first in a social group, is supported by group norms, and functions as a shared social symbol. . . . The spread of marihuana through different segments of the society is aptly viewed as an example of adoption of an innovation." [45]

The commission put it this way:

> The most notable statement that can be made about the vast majority of marihuana users—experimenters and intermittent users—is that they are essentially indistinguishable from their non-marihuana using peers by any fundamental criterion other than their marihuana use. . . .
>
> Experimentation with the drug is motivated primarily by curiosity and a desire to share a social experience. [E]xperimenters are characteristically quite conventional and practically indistinguishable from the non-user in terms of life style, activities, social integration, and vocational or academic performance. . . .
>
> The intermittent users are motivated to use marihuana for reasons similar to those of the experimenters. They use the drug irregularly and infrequently but generally continue to do so because of its socializing and recreational aspects. . . .
> [For them] marihuana smoking is a social activity. [46]

Both fact-finding bodies did suggest that the marihuana-using behavior of the heavy users is more likely to be symptomatic of underlying emotional difficulties, and that these individuals are most likely to be multi-drug users as well.

Acute Effects

As to the acute physical toxicity of marihuana, the commission found:

No conclusive evidence exists of any physical damage, disturbances of bodily processes or proven human fatalities attributable
solely to even very high doses of marihuana.

. . . . .

[M] arihuana is a rather unexciting compound of negligible
immediate toxicity at the doses usually consumed in this country.

. . . . .

Experiments with the drug in monkeys demonstrated that the
dose required for overdose death was enormous and for all
practical purposes unachievable by humans smoking marihuana.
This is in marked contrast to other substances in common use,
most notably alcohol and barbiturate sleeping pills.[47]

The NIMH report noted that "acute toxic physical reactions to
marihuana are relatively rare," and that "evidence from acute
toxicity studies in animals and human case reports of overdose
seems to indicate that the ratio of lethal dose to effective dose is
quite large and is much more favorable than that of other common
psychoactive drugs such as alcohol and barbiturates."[48]

With regard to acute mental effects, the commission stated:

The immediate effect of marihuana on normal mental processes
is a subtle alteration in state of consciousness probably related
to a change in short-term memory, mood, emotion and volition.
This effect on the mind produces a varying influence on cogni-
tive and psychomotor task performance which is highly individualized, as well as related to dosage, time, complexity of the task
and experience of the user. The effect on personal, social and
vocational functions is difficult to predict. In most instances, the
marihuana intoxication is pleasurable. In rare cases, the experience may lead to unpleasant anxiety and panic, and in a
predisposed few, to psychosis.[49]

The NIMH report echoed this finding:

It seems clear that marihuana use can precipitate certain less
serious adverse reactions, such as simple depressive and panic
reactions, particularly in inexperienced users. However, non-drug
factors may be the most important determinants in these cases.
In addition, there is some reason to believe that it may precipitate psychotic episodes in persons with a preexisting borderline
personality or psychotic disorder. There is considerable similarity
in clinical description between the "acute toxic psychoses" reported in the Eastern literature and the acute psychoses described

in a number of Western reports. All seem to occur primarily after heavy usage which is greater than that to which the individual is accustomed. These psychoses have some characteristics of an acute brain syndrome. They seem to be self-limited and short-lived if the drug is removed. Some reports have described a more prolonged psychotic course after such an initial acute phase, but the possibility of other psychopathology in these cases has not been ruled out. [50]

Long-Term Effects

Both the Marihuana Commission and NIMH emphasized the paucity of research regarding the effects of long-term use of marihuana. Truly reliable findings would have to await controlled longitudinal studies with matched samples of long-term heavy users and non-users. The American experience is too recent to have deposited a sufficiently large population of long-term heavy users. Consequently, initial data must be gathered from studies of the heavy hashish-using populations in Jamaica, Greece, Afghanistan, and other cannabis-origin countries. Yet the vastly different standards of medical care and economic development in these countries make the data extremely difficult to evaluate in terms of cause and effect.

As to the long-term effects on the body of intermittent or moderate use (once a day or less), both reports found no disturbing evidence. The commission stated on the basis of an experimental study of Americans who had used the drug intermittently or moderately on an average of five years: "No significant physical, biochemical or mental abnormalities could be attributed solely to their marihuana smoking."[51] NIMH concluded from "both Eastern and Western literature" that there was "little evidence at this time that light to moderate use of cannabis [over a long term] has deleterious physical effects. Almost all reports of physical harm from cannabis use are based on observations of moderate to heavy, chronic use of the drug."[52]

On the basis of preliminary findings from studies of long-term heavy hashish users in Greece and Jamaica, both reports indicated that nothing disturbing had yet appeared other than the chronic bronchitis and respiratory problems associated with heavy smoking of any substance. Mild liver injury and decrement of pulmonary lung function had been associated with heavy marihuana use in some studies, but no conclusions were justified. The *Marihuana and Health* Report warned in this connection, however, that

[t]he difficulty of proving a causal relationship between chronic use of any drug and a resulting illness should be kept in mind. Observation for many years is often necessary with heavy reliance on epidemiologic and statistical methods. The recent example of the role of cigarette smoking in certain illnesses illustrates many of the problems involved. For these reasons it is likely to take many years before the full story on possible physical effects from chronic use of marihuana will be complete.[53]

As to the effect of long-term, heavy use on mental functioning, NIMH concluded that: "At the present time evidence that marihuana is a sufficient or contributory cause of chronic psychosis is weak and rests primarily on temporal association. Further epidemiological and controlled clinical studies are necessary in order to clarify this important issue."[54]

The Marihuana Commission concluded from the Eastern data that:

The incidence of psychiatric hospitalizations for acute psychoses and of use of drugs other than alcohol is not significantly higher than among the non-using population. The existence of a specific long-lasting, cannabis-related psychosis is poorly defined. If heavy cannabis use produces a specific psychosis, it must be quite rare or else exceedingly difficult to distinguish from other acute or chronic psychoses.

Recent studies suggest that the occurrence of any form of psychosis in heavy cannabis users is no higher than in the general population. Although such use is often quite prevalent in hospitalized mental patients, the drug could only be considered a causal factor in a few cases. Most of these were short-term reactions or toxic overdoses. In addition, a concurrent use of alcohol often played a role in the episode causing hospitalization.[55]

In this connection, it is instructive to note the NIMH commentary on the Kolansky and Moore article:

In a widely publicized report, Kolansky and Moore described behavior problems, suicide attempts, sexual promiscuity and psychoses in 38 adolescent psychiatric patients who used marihuana. They attributed all of these problems to marihuana use and on the basis of retrospective information felt that there was no evidence of prior psychopathology. This study illustrates the difficulty in interpretation of attempts to establish a causal role for marihuana using retrospective analysis, biased sampling, and ignoring the prevalance of psychopathology in a comparable population.[56]

Similarly, both reports noted some concern about the persistent suggestions in both Western and Eastern literature that marihuana use caused an "amotivational syndrome" involving lethargy, instability, social and personal deterioration, and loss of interest in activities other than drug use. Nonetheless, both reports concluded that a causal relationship between heavy cannabis use and this syndrome had not been established. NIMH, for example, observed that:

The relevant question would seem to be whether or not the regular use of marihuana at a level below chronic intoxication may bring about personality changes through mechanisms other than the immediate pharmacological effects of the drug.

. . . . .

Sociological factors add to the problems of interpretation since much drug use is associated with a youth counterculture which often rejects the more conventional orientation. The fact that heavy marihuana users may have a high incidence of pre-existing psychopathology raises the question of whether or not any decreased interest and motivation observed in them may be a function of the psychopathological condition rather than of the drug. Therefore, the question of whether or not there exists a causal relationship between cannabis and an amotivational syndrome or only an associative relationship remains to be answered.[57]

Genetic Damage

Neither the commission nor NIMH found, in the commission's words, any "reliable evidence . . . that marihuana causes genetic defects in man."[58]

Dependence Liability

The two reports also agreed that marihuana use does not induce physical dependence and, in the commission's words, that "no torturous withdrawal syndrome follows the sudden cessation of chronic, heavy use."[59] NIMH noted that Eastern studies have suggested a psychological dependence in heavy users, but that U.S. studies using much lower doses for shorter time periods had not found any such evidence.[60] The commission noted in this connection that: "Although evidence indicates that heavy, long-term cannabis users may develop psychological dependence, even then the level of psychological dependence is no different from the syndrome of anxiety and restlessness seen when an American stops smoking tobacco cigarettes."[61]

Progression to Other Drugs

Each report devoted many pages to the alleged causal relationship between marihuana use and use of other drugs, and each affirmed the clear correlation between increasing frequency of marihuana use and use of other illicit drugs. But both reports concluded that the relationship was definitely not a causal one, and that the overwhelming majority of marihuana users use no other illicit drug.

NIMH concluded: "While heavier marihuana use is clearly associated with the use of other drugs as well—those who use it regularly are far more likely than nonusers to have experimented with other illicit drugs—there is no evidence that the drug itself "causes" such use. More frequent users are likely to find drug use appealing or to spend time with others who do so or in settings where other drugs are readily available."[62]

The commission meandered through the statistical maze surrounding the issue, noting:

If any one statement can characterize why persons in the United States escalate their drug use patterns and become polydrug users, it is peer pressure. Indeed, if any drug is associated with the use of other drugs, including marihuana, it is tobacco, followed closely by alcohol.

. . . . .
The overwhelming majority of marihuana users do not progress to other drugs. They either remain with marihuana or forsake its use in favor of alcohol. In addition, the largest number of marihuana users in the United States today are experimenters or intermittent users, and 2% of those who have ever used it are

presently heavy users. Only moderate and heavy use of marihuana is significantly associated with persistent use of other drugs.
. . . . .
Marihuana use per se does not dictate whether other drugs will be used; nor does it determine the rate of progression, if and when it occurs, or which drugs might be used.
. . . . .
Whether or not marihuana leads to other drug use depends on the individual, on the social and cultural setting in which the drug use takes place, and on the nature of the drug market.[63]

Crime

Both reports dismissed the crime thesis. NIMH equivocated a little: "There continues to be little evidence that marihuana use in itself causes criminal behavior. It is still questionable whether marihuana tends to loosen inhibitions and encourage immoral behavior, and whether marihuana tranquilizes users and thus deters violence."[64]

The commission was quite direct:

The weight of the evidence is that marihuana does not cause violent or aggressive behavior; if anything, marihuana generally serves to inhibit the expression of such behavior. Marihuana-induced relaxation of inhibitions is not ordinarily accompanied by an exaggeration of aggressive tendencies.
. . . . .
In essence, neither informed current professional opinion nor empirical research, ranging from the 1930's to the present, has produced systematic evidence to support the thesis that marihuana use, by itself, either invariably or generally leads to or causes crime, including acts of violence, juvenile delinquency or aggressive behavior. Instead the evidence suggests that sociolegal and the cultural variables account for the apparent statistical correlation between marihuana use and crime or delinquency.[65]

What Do the Findings Mean?

The Marihuana Commission had been assigned a broader role than simply assessing the individual health consequences of marihuana use. To place this information in its wider social context, the commission generalized its findings for purposes of social policy. First and foremost, it concluded that marihuana use in contemporary American society is not a problem. "From what is known now about the effects of marihuana," the commission concluded, "its use at the present level does not constitute a major threat to public health." [66] This conclusion was based primarily on the fact that "there is little proven danger of physical or psychological harm from the experimental or intermittent use of the natural preparations of cannabis."[67] This, of course, includes 90 percent of those persons who have ever used the drug.

"The risk of harm," the commission continued, "lies instead in the heavy, long-term use of the drug, particularly of its more potent preparations." And that risk, of course, was itself of uncertain dimensions since the commission's major concern—the psychological consequences of long-term heavy use—remained speculative. Since the at-risk population is no more than half a million, at present, the public health orientation counsels a concern for prevention: "A significant increase in the at-risk population could convert what is now a minor public health concern in this country to one of major proportions." [68]

The Dam Breaks: The Authorities Recommend a Change

Together, the Marihuana Commission Report and the HEW Report finally debunked the marihuana myths. Turning its attention to social and legal policy, the commission recommended that American society adopt a policy of seeking to discourage marihuana use, while concentrating primarily on the prevention of heavy and very heavy use.[69] With regard to the law, the commission urged that the criminal sanction be withdrawn from all private consumption-related activity, including possession for personal use and casual nonprofit distribution. As far as commercial activities were concerned, however, the commission rejected a regulatory (alcohol model) approach, preferring instead to retain the prohibitory model. About the same time (February 1972), Dr. Bertram Brown, director of NIMH remarked in a press conference attending release of the second *Marihuana and Health* Report that he, too, opposed "legalization" but favored "decriminalization" of marihuana use.[70] In so doing, Dr. Brown maintained a stance he had first taken a year earlier— one which was a bit more liberal than that espoused by his colleagues in the executive branch.[71] For example, Surgeon General Steinfeld refused to endorse the commission recommendations, and Dr. Jerome Jaffe, director of the White House Special Action Office for Drug Abuse Prevention (SAODAP), refused to say anything at all. Yet both men privately agreed with the commission approach.

The commission's disenchantment with the possession penalty rested on both philosophical and practical arguments. First, the report took cognizance of "the nation's philosophical preference for individual privacy" and the "high place traditionally occupied by the value of privacy in our constitutional scheme," and noted that possession penalties in the "narcotics" area represented a departure from tradition. "Accordingly," the commission contended,

[w]e believe that government must show a compelling reason to justify invasion of the home in order to prevent personal use of marihuana. We find little in marihuana's effects or in its social impact to support such a determination. Legislators enacting Prohibition did not find such a compelling reason 40 years ago; and we do not find the situation any more compelling for marihuana today.[72]

Then the commission recited the practical costs and functional disutilities associated with prohibition of possession. Selective enforcement, selective prosecution, frustration of other social control institutions, misallocation of resources, collision with constitutional limitations, and disrespect for law among the young, overwhelmingly outweighed the minimal "deterrent" and symbolic values of the possession laws. In essence, law enforcement authorities had already adopted a passive containment policy aimed only at indiscretion; in the commission's view, such a result could be achieved more honestly, artfully, and fairly without the possession penalty.

The commission approach had its own symbols, of course. The commission labeled its scheme "partial prohibition" in an attempt to avoid the implication that it was urging the "legalization" of marihuana use. More important, under the commission's proposed scheme, criminal liability would still attach to public activities, such as use, possession of more than one ounce, and distribution of any amount. Finally, any amount of marihuana possessed in public would be contraband—this was the most concrete symbol of the discouragement policy. All in all, these recommendations were clearly designed to ameliorate only the worst excesses of a prohibitory scheme while retaining the trappings of illegality.

The game of symbol selection was played out in a footnote, where five commissioners qualified their assent to the decriminalization scheme.[73] Three members of the commission (Congressmen Rogers and Carter and Attorney Mitchell Ware) thought "contraband" was not a potent enough symbol; they would have levied a civil fine on anyone possessing any amount of marihuana in public, even if for their own use. Senators Hughes and Javits, on the other hand, would have removed a larger sphere of consumption-related conduct from the criminal law:

> The contraband device, the not-for-profit sale, and public possession of some reasonable amount which should be presumed to be necessarily incident to private use should all be removed from the ambit of legal sanction. To do so would be to strike down "symbols" of a public policy which has never been adequately justified in the first instance. Such steps would in no way jeopardize the firm determination of the Commission that the use of marihuana ought to be discouraged.

Politics was not an irrelevant consideration in this game of symbols. Four of the footnote dissenters were federal legislators and the fifth was also a political figure. For the benefit of their respective constituencies, the two liberal senators staked out a position slightly to the left of the commission, while the two Southern congressmen insisted on being slightly to the right.

It is also interesting to note that the commission *unanimously* rejected the regulatory alternative (legalization). Numerous critics of the Marihuana Commission Report have detected in this fact a compromise to secure unanimity on a decriminalization recommendation or to escape the shackles of the president's May Day statement.[74] Others have seen it instead as a reflection of the basically conservative composition of the panel. In any case, the commission's rationale *is* classically conservative—solicitous of the prevailing order and wary of disruption of the social fabric. The rejection of legalization was premised entirely on preventive considerations: avoidance of cultural dislocation and social conflict and prevention of a public health problem. The commission did not rule out a regulatory approach at some later time. Instead, in an aside well hidden in the report, the commission noted:

> Our doubts about the efficacy of existing regulatory schemes, together with an uncertainty about the permanence of social interest in marihuana and the approval inevitably implied by adoption of such a scheme, all impel us to reject the regulatory approach as an appropriate implementation of a discouragement policy at the present time.
>
> Future policy planners might well come to a different conclusion if further study of existing schemes suggests a feasible model; if responsible use of the drug does indeed take root in our society; if continuing scientific and medical research uncovers no long-term ill effects; if potency control appears feasible; and if the passage of time and the adoption of a rational social policy sufficiently desymbolize marihuana so that availability is not equated in the public mind with approval.[75]

Politics and Symbolism

Among national politicians the Marihuana Commission Report provoked predictable reactions. Two days after the report was issued, President Nixon expressed his continuing preference for the status quo: "I oppose the legalization of marihuana and that includes sale, possession and use. I do not believe you can have effective criminal justice based on a philosophy that something is half-legal and half-illegal."[76] Both the commission and NIMH had expressed the hope that the factual issues would be neutralized in the continuing public debate about marihuana policy. The president complied with this request by confining his objection only to the commission's policy recommendations. He noted that this was the "one aspect" of the report with which he disagreed, adding that "it is a report which deserves consideration and it will receive it." President Nixon did not indicate explicitly whether this meant he now had rejected the stepping-stone hypothesis which he had publicly embraced the year before.

The commission, in response to the president's statement, pointed out that there was ample precedent in American law for a partial prohibition scheme, and that this was actually the traditional way of dealing with sumptuary behaviors: the criminal sanction extends to the gambling entrepreneur, not the gambler; to the distributor of pornographic material, not the private consumer; to the person who sells alcohol and tobacco to underage consumers, not the youths themselves. And the commission also recalled that during alcohol prohibition, it was the bootlegger, not the individual consumer, who was the criminal. [77]

Other administration officials were more vociferous in their opposition to the commission's recommendations. BNDD's Director Ingersoll noted that removal of the criminal sanction from marihuana and other drugs would mean the fight against drug abuse had been "lost altogether." He added, somewhat obliquely: "It is our duty not only to protect the public in the streets from vicious criminals but to protect the public from harmful ideas."[78] Vice-President Agnew thought it was "wrong of us to in any way encourage the use of marihuana." The commission's recommendations "frightened" him, he said, "because no nation in world history has ever legitimated the use of marihuana." Use of the drug in Eastern countries, he noted further, "has really debilitated those societies."[79]

Throughout the country law enforcement officials condemned the report, either ridiculing what they perceived to be a logical inconsistency or lambasting the commission and its findings. For example, Mayor Frank Rizzo of Philadelphia, former police commissioner of the nation's fourth largest city, stated that "somewhere, sometime, we're going to have to clear the cobwebs from the minds of do-gooders who write reports like this." He was "absolutely opposed to sanctioning the private smoking of marihuana," he said, because in his "experience, marihuana has been only a vehicle to the use of harder drugs."[80]

Mayor Rizzo was of the same mind as Harry Anslinger, who branded the commission's recommendations "terrifying," predicting that their adoption would have "very serious national repercussions." If society were to allow "smoking in secret without any penalty," he explained, "then I think in a couple of years we'll have about a million lunatics filling up the mental hospitals and a couple of hundred thousand more deaths on the highways—just plain slaughter on the highways." [81]

On the other side of the political spectrum, liberal public officials from both parties welcomed the Marihuana Commission Report. Senator Percy of Illinois, a Republican, agreed that "substantial public use of marihuana, coupled with the fact that research to date has uncovered relatively few harmful effects to the individual or society" justified removal of criminal penalties. He hoped that this society would now deal "honestly" with the marihuana issue on the basis of the "evidence and sound conclusions of the Commission."[82] Senator Muskie, Democrat from Maine, said he supported the commission's "progressive approach."[83]

The "acceptable middle ground" embodied in the commission's recommendations appealed to Senators Percy and Muskie. But the "middle ground" of "decriminalization" was not yet perceived by all politicians to be "acceptable," a realization which had some effect on the presidential campaign of South Dakota Senator George McGovern. All of the Democratic and Republican candidates had been polled on the marihuana issue by the National Organization for Reform of the Marijuana Laws (NORML), a Washington-based lobby funded primarily by the Playboy Foundation. Together with Senators Humphrey, Muskie, and Hartke, New York City Mayor Lindsay, former Senator McCarthy, Congressman McCloskey (California), and Congresswoman Chisholm (New York), Senator Mc Govern expressed support for decriminalization. With regard to legalization, all but McCarthy, Chisholm, and McGovern backed off.[84] The South Dakota senator had also publicly expressed his inclinations toward legalization. [85]

When the Democratic nomination fight heated up in the late spring, McGovern's candor on the marihuana issue, as well as on other civil libertarian matters such as amnesty for draft resisters and legalized abortion, came back to haunt him. First, Senator Jackson and later Senator Humphrey labeled their rival as "the Triple A candidate," a proponent of "acid, amnesty and abortion." "Acid" of course referred to nothing more than the senator's stand on marihuana, and reflected the persistent attempt to associate marihuana law reform with approval of all drug use. Pretty soon, en route to his party's nomination, the candidate retreated and began urging only a "reduction of harsh penalties" for marihuana use.

Well before the McGovern episode, Republican Senator Dominick of Colorado had exclaimed: "Coming out for legalized pot is like putting your head right on the chopping block. . . . I think this (Commission) Report is two years ahead of itself. What is needed is a massive selling job across the country because anybody who proposes something like this is really headed for trouble right now."[86] The marihuana issue dropped out of the presidential campaign.

There were those, of course, who did not want the issue to recede. The advocates of legalization had mixed reactions to the Marihuana Commission Report. John Kaplan, law professor and author of *Marijuana: The New Prohibition,* hailed the decriminalization proposal as a "step in the right direction" although an insufficient one. He added: "I think Nixon did his best to appoint a Commission which was biased toward his views against the legalization of marihuana, but I am overjoyed to see they gave him an honest Report."[87] Lester Grinspoon, Kaplan's alter ego from the medical profession and author of *Marijuana Reconsidered,* was not so kind. He lambasted the commission for its writing style, "sermon-like tone," inconsistencies, and "wishful thinking." Acknowledging that the commission deserved "credit" for moving the marihuana issue "in the right direction," Grinspoon nevertheless thought it had "produced only, at most, a half a loaf," and he thought he knew why:

> After my testimony before the Commission last May (1971) . . . I got the impression that [one of the commissioners] saw as an important aspect of the Commission's task that of finding a policy which offended the fewest people. Indeed, the Commission in its surveys did much to learn how people thought and felt about marihuana. The only way I can reconcile some of the inconsistencies in its report is to believe that its policy recommendations derive not solely from medical, psychological, and social considerations, but as well from the political reality.[88]

Some advocates were not so disrespectful of the "political reality." The two major lobbying organizations both praised the commission. AMORPHIA, based in California, had been formed in 1969 by Michael Aldrich, one of the original proponents of legal marihuana. Upon release of the Marihuana Commission Report, Amorphia applauded "the greatest single step in alleviating a 40 year accumulation of official myths and falsehoods in this area." As to politics, the group noted that decriminalization is a "politically inescapable step in reeducating the public," although "completely untenable as a long-term policy."[89]

Similarly, NORML, which had been bankrolled by the Playboy Foundation in January 1971, praised the commission for "taking a courageous step in light of the prevalence of misinformation and fear" and promised to lobby for the decriminalization scheme, "in every way possible."[90] NORML had not always been so appreciative of the commission. In the early days when marihuana advocates were sniping at the commission's credibility, NORML was a fledgling group attempting to establish some clout of its own. Its executive director, Keith Stroup, requested an opportunity to testify before the commission at its initial hearings in Washington. He was told by Michael Sonnenreich, the commission's staff director, that the commission was carefully selecting a group of experts in the area to present all viewpoints. Since the commission could make available only a limited number of slots, he did not think NORML would be an appropriate choice. When Stroup countered with the possibility that former Attorney General Ramsey Clark might be willing to represent the group, Sonnenreich viewed this as publicity-hunting, noting that the reform viewpoint would be adequately represented without the former attorney general.

Stroup reported these events to muckraking journalist Jack Anderson, who called Sonnenreich and then printed the story.[91] Ultimately, the commission did call Clark, who claimed that he had no intention of representing NORML and did not desire to testify. For the remainder of the commission's first year, Stroup— who did testify at a later public hearing—carefully scrutinized commission activities, freely predicting that the commission would recommend nothing more substantial than a further reduction in penalties.

By March 1972 when the Marihuana Commission Report was issued, NORML had gotten its feet on the ground and realized the political importance of the panel's recommendations. Naturally, the group did wish the commission had gone further:

The Commission did balk at setting up a regulatory scheme. They reasoned that to do so would serve to institutionalize marijuana use at a time when they were still hoping marijuana would prove a mere fad and disappear. It is on this point we most strenuously disagree. There is absolutely no evidence that marijuana use will disappear. In fact, it has been around for centuries, and its popularity continues to grow at a great rate in this country. It appears likely that marijuana use will be as much a part of our future culture as will the use of cigarettes and even the Commission recognizes that if this is the case, then a regulatory scheme, with controls over the drug and who gets it, would be preferable. This is why NORML favors legalization. We believe the Commission is aware of this inherent weakness in their report, but chose to avoid the possible political repercussions of such far reaching recommendations. We regret this failure.[92]

The Politics of Repeal

Legislators everywhere had held the marihuana issue at arms' length pending a definitive scientific determination of marihuana's harmfulness. Publication of the Marihuana Commission Report in the spring naturally loosed an army of marihuana reformers on the state houses. Despite the addition to their ranks of the former deputy director of BNDD, John Finlator,[93] the going was rough. This was, after all, a political year, and the summer adjournments came without any reform.

The penalty reduction phase of marihuana prohibition had been all but completed in 1971. In that year sanctions were ameliorated by fifteen states that had not already done so in the three previous years and were reduced even more by fourteen other states. By the end of 1971 only three states (Texas, Pennsylvania, and Rhode Island) maintained mandatory felony penalties for possession, although four other states (California, Arizona, Mississippi, and Nevada) allowed prosecution as a misdemeanor or a felony in the discretion of the prosecutor.[94]

Meanwhile, bills that would have reduced possession penalties were actually defeated in New York and California.[95] The New York measure was defeated in face of endorsement by the governor, the state District Attorney's Association, and a state Advisory Commission on Drugs. In California, the proposed reduction of possession to a nondiscretionary misdemeanor passed the general assembly before it was defeated in the senate.

Despite the Marihuana Commission Report, the political obstacle to substantial legislative change of the marihuana laws was still a formidable one. Senators Hughes and Javits and Congressman Koch

Map 4. Marihuana prohibition. Phase four: Reduction of penalties for possession for personal use, 1967-73 (June)

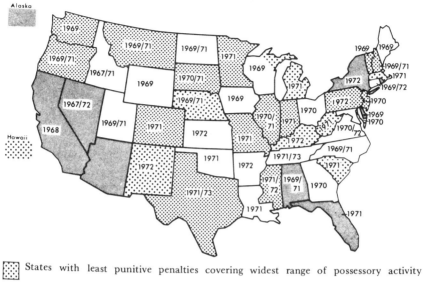

States with least punitive penalties covering widest range of possessory activity

States that have classified possession of at least one ounce as a misdemeanor

States that have classified simple possession as a misdemeanor without amount limitations

States with most punitive penalties for possessory activity

introduced identical decriminalization measures in both houses of Congress. No action was anticipated and none was taken. An attempt by a Special State Committee in Texas to force reconsideration of the marihuana issue aborted when the governor would not open the call of a special legislative session beyond budgetary issues.

The only exception to the political stalemate in 1972 was not too surprising: on 16 May the city council of Ann Arbor, Michigan, a city of 110,000 and home of the sprawling 34,000-student University of Michigan, enacted an ordinance setting a $5 fine for use, possession, or sale of marihuana.[96] Under a ruling by the Michigan attorney general localities are permitted to deviate from the state penalty structure upon a demonstration of "special circumstances." That Ann Arbor is a special location is clearly established by the fact that the ordinance was passed by a six-to-five majority coalition composed of four Democrats and two members of the Human Rights Party (aged twenty-two and twenty-six).[97]

Outside Ann Arbor, however, a legislative consideration of the merits—rather than the politics—of decriminalization was impossible until 1973. In response, reformers sought to bypass the legislative process altogether—through the judiciary, through administrative action, and by appealing directly to the people.

We noted earlier that appellate courts had become restless about the marihuana laws during the retrenchment and penalty-reduction phases, but had refused to invalidate them on constitutional grounds. In 1971, however, two state courts and a federal court held that it was unconstitutional to classify marihuana as a narcotic, and several judges in Illinois, Michigan, and Hawaii concluded that the marihuana possession penalty was itself unconstitutional.[98]

The vehicle for such a declaration is the right of privacy on which the Supreme Court based its 1965 decision invalidating Connecticut's prohibition of the use of birth control devices, its 1969 decision overturning prohibitions of the private possession of obscene literature, and its 1973 decision severely limiting the function of antiabortion statutes.[99] If the right of privacy is thought to be involved, the burden of proof is shifted to the government to demonstrate a compelling state interest in intruding into the private lives of marihuana smokers. Whatever the merits of such an argument from the standpoint of constitutional jurisprudence, it is appealing to those courts who are otherwise inclined to overturn the marihuana laws. The reformers have correctly surmised that the judiciary is unlikely to remain oblivious to perceived injustices under the marihuana laws, especially if the political process does not respond. Such a judicial perspective motivated the American Civil Liberties Union to launch a full-scale attack on the marihuana laws in early 1972.

At the administrative level, NORML, together with the American Public Health Association and the Institute for the Study of Health and Society, petitioned BNDD to remove marihuana from the list of controlled substances under the CSA, thereby legalizing it under federal law. There was, of course, no possibility that BNDD would do so. As an alternative, the petitioners asked that marihuana be removed from Schedule I (with heroin and LSD) and placed in Schedule V together with over-the-counter preparations such as codeine cough syrups. In that event, all nonmedical marihuana distribution and use would be a misdemeanor. BNDD refused even to accept the petition for filing on the ground that the CSA rescheduling procedures do not apply when control of a substance is required by United States obligations under international law in effect at the time the CSA was passed.[100] Since the United States was obligated to control marihuana by the Single Convention on Narcotic Drugs of 1961, administrative action was, under the bureau's reasoning, impossible. NORML's appeal to the U.S. Court of Appeals was pending when this book went to press.[101]

The challengers also went to the people. In a move initiated as an "educational tool" in the summer of 1971, the leaders of the California Marihuana Initiative collected 382,095 signatures on an initiative petition placing the following proposition on the ballot in November 1972:

No person in the State of California 18 years of age or older shall be punished criminally, or be denied any right or privilege, by reason of such person's planting, cultivating, harvesting, drying, processing, otherwise preparing, transporting, or possessing marijuana for personal use, or by reason of that use.
This provision shall in no way be construed to repeal existing legislation, or limit the enactment of future legislation, prohibiting persons under the influence of marijuana from engaging in conduct that endangers others.

Support by Amorphia and NORML, together with the Commission's endorsement of a similar decriminalization scheme, raised the hopes of the CMI organizers. Their effort had gained political respectability over the course of a year and "Proposition 19" was endorsed by the Los Angeles Democratic Central Committee, the California Bar Association, the San Francisco Bar Association, and the Los Angeles County Grand Jury. CMI leaders felt that decriminalization was inevitable: "If we lose this time, we will keep trying until we get it passed."[102] CMI did lose—by a 2 to 1 margin—although it actually *passed* in San Francisco County and got 49 percent of the vote in Marin County and 38 percent in Santa Clara and San Mateo Counties.[103]

Similar initiative campaigns in Arizona, Florida, Oregon, Washington, and Michigan were aborted for lack of signatures. In Arizona, where 23,000 of the required 40,000 signatures were obtained, Senator Barry Goldwater noted that the decriminalization proposal would not have had a chance on his state's ballot anyway: "Pot is like gambling. People in my state have voted down legalized gambling at least six times, even though most people like to gamble. I think the only chance for new marihuana laws is through the legislatures."[104]

Senator Goldwater's remark and the CMI defeat highlight an important point. Repeal of a criminal law by political action is a rare occurrence. Disapproval by one generation of a particular behavior, once embodied in a criminal prohibition, fixes a deep imprint on the attitude of those that follow. As long as the dominant social group continues to disapprove the behavior, however mildly, removal of a criminal proscription is unlikely; for it is perceived that removal of the symbol of disapprobation will symbolize an approval of the behavior itself. And this will be true regardless of the social costs of the criminal law or whether the law is enforced at all. Perpetuation of unenforced criminal sanctions against fornication, adultery, homosexuality, and gambling are illustrative of the potency of symbols.

Criminal prohibitions have been successfully repealed by political action only when the dominant group no longer disapproves of the behavior (gambling); when the behavior is so widespread and visible that enforcement becomes intolerable, and must be replaced by some overt regulation (alcohol prohibition); when the moral premise underlying societal disapproval can be neutralized by counteracting social benefits (abortion, gambling); or when the law may be changed without attracting public attention(homosexuality).

On the marihuana issue, as Senator Goldwater implied, the dominant social group simply could not bring itself to remove the symbol of disapproval. Through formal reduction of penalties and emergence of enforcement desuetude, the most excessive social costs of prohibition were slowly being minimized. Yet, since 200,000 persons a year were still being arrested for possession of marihuana, these costs had not been eliminated. Pointing in the long run for some formal regulation of distributional activity, the reformers aimed in 1972 to generate the necessary changes in public opinion to support a new consensus. They viewed decriminalization as a major step in this regard because a willingness to remove the symbolic possession offenses would itself reflect a weakening of social antipathy toward use of the drug. If this were true, the final step in the reform program, adoption of a regulatory model, would be easy.

Public opinion does not change overnight, however, as the CMI illustrated. Many opinion makers and professional groups such as the National Council of Churches, the National Education Association, the American Public Health Association, and the New York State Bar Association endorsed decriminalization. When the National Coordinating Council on Drug Information polled its membership, which includes groups like the American Legion and the Boy Scouts, it found that substantially more than half its 133-member organizations *officially* favored either decriminalization or legalization.[105] The Consumers Union sponsored and published a study by Brecher that recommended a regulatory approach.[106]

Among editorial writers and columnists, a healthy proportion endorsed the commission proposals, including the *New York Times*, *Newsday* (Long Island, New York), the *San Francisco Examiner* and the *San Francisco Chronicle*, the *Miami News*, the *Louisville Times*, the *Wall Street Journal*, the *Knoxville News-Sentinel*, the *Chicago News*, the *Minneapolis Star*, the *Portland Oregonian*, the *Birmingham Post-Herald*, the *Philadelphia Inquirer*, the Washington *Evening Star*, and the *Cincinnati Enquirer*.[107] Others, including the *Charlotte* (N.C.) *Observer* and the *St. Louis Post-Dispatch*, preferred a regulatory model and accused the commission of compromise.[108] Of particular interest in this regard was the strong endorsement of William F. Buckley, Jr., and several other commentators from the *National Review*, who urged "American Conservatives [to] revise their position on Marijuana."[109]

Despite the breadth of reform sentiment in the press, the possession penalty was too firmly entrenched to be uprooted so suddenly. A small percentage of editorial opinion, particularly in the South, branded the Marihuana Commission Report and its decriminalization proposal "worthless" and "permissive," alleging, for example, that it was "tantamount to encouraging and sanctioning use" of the drug.[110] A more common thrust of editorial opinion opposing the proposed policy was to question its logic and plead

instead for further reduction in penalties.[111] Of this group, only
the *Los Angeles Times* faced the symbolism issue head on, acknowledging that the symbol carried its costs and proposing
desuetude instead:

> Should legal restrictions on private use of the drug ... be
> eliminated entirely? We think not, first because scientific evi-
> dence about marijuana's dangers remains inconclusive, second
> because such a move might well encourage a spread in use. The
> real legal issue, it seems to us, is how vigorously should existing
> prohibitions be enforced.
> . . . . .
> The best approach would seem to be a pragmatic one, to
> regard private marijuana smoking essentially as one of those
> "victimless crimes" where social harm is slight or nonexistent,
> where interference by authority is not really necessitated by any
> demonstrable threat to the community. What an individual
> chooses to do in privacy is his business alone, provided no harm
> is done to others. That choice may not be wise, or likely to win
> moral approval, nor is there need to sanction it by law. But
> neither is there need for interference by authority, and in the
> case of private marijuana smoking, that ought to be the
> practice.[112]

In its editorial statement opposing "Proposition 19" several months
later, the *Los Angeles Times* recommended "pragmatism, tolerance
and caution":

> The passage of Proposition 19 would be a major shift in social
> policy for the state. We believe such decisions ought to be
> made more carefully, and frankly, more reluctantly. The spread
> of drugs in America is of major concern. Perhaps marihuana can
> some day be separated from the terrible hard drugs, and made
> legal, like alcohol. But the linkage between pot smoking and
> hard drugs, though discounted, is not disproven. We don't
> believe the state ought at this point to encourage a more casual
> attitude toward drugs in general.[113]

Thurman Arnold, a renowned legal philosopher, once observed
that laws proscribing adultery and other consensual sexual conduct
"are unenforced because we want to continue our conduct, and
unrepealed because we want to preserve our morals."[114] A sixty-
year association with the narcotics, venality, and crime had imbued
marihuana use with presumptive immorality. The incidence (26

million) of use had wrenched marihuana free of heroin and weakened community antipathy; but the stigma of impropriety remained. After all marihuana *was* a *drug*; its use was not *as* immoral perhaps, but it was immoral nonetheless. As the various justifications for marihuana prohibition were stripped away (crime, progression, health), only the anxiety remained—a tenacious resistance to what appeared to be a substantial change in values.

This resistance was naturally strongest within the most "established" groups in the nation's professional establishment. Soon after publication of the Marihuana Commission Report, both the AMA and the ABA took floor votes on the marihuana issue. The process and outcome within these professional organizations mirrored the state of marihuana decision-making within the larger society. First, expert committees within each group issued reports proposing the elimination of criminal penalties for possession, as had the Marihuana Commission. Adoption of committee recommendations by the houses of delegates of these groups is normally a pro forma matter. On the marihuana issue, however, each house functioned as a political arena and the delegates acted as members of the larger body politic: they each adopted "compromise" resolutions endorsing further reduction of penalties, confirming continuing symbolic importance of the criminal prohibition for possession.

The AMA Council on Mental Health and Committee on Alcoholism and Drug Dependence, acting jointly, issued its first statement on marihuana since 1968. It will be recalled that officialdom relied heavily on the 1968 statement during the retrenchment and penalty-reduction periods. In the new statement, "Marihuana-1972," which was adopted on 28 April 1972, the committees summarized the findings by NIMH and the commission, and then addressed the "legal status of marihuana":

> The Council on Mental Health and the Committee on Alcoholism and Drug Dependence *concur with the conclusion of the National Commission on Marihuana and Drug Abuse* that the dangers of marihuana do not justify a social policy of punishment for the user of the drug. Although further research is needed, especially into the long-term effects of chronic heavy use, at the present time scientific evidence does not justify the punitive legislation in effect.

The Council and Committee concur in the following points as well: possession of marihuana for personal use and transfer of insignificant amounts should not be criminal acts; marihuana use in public should be prohibited; and a plea of marihuana intoxication should not be a defense in any criminal proceeding. In view of the need for further research, and the possibility of some deleterious effects on the user and on society at large which could constitute a major public health problem, the Council and Committee also agree that a policy of discouragement is prudent.[115]

After making some minor changes, the AMA Board of Trustees approved the marihuana statement and voted to submit it to the House of Delegates. On 20 July, after forty-five minutes of discussion, the house rejected the committee recommendation, apparently determining that such action would condone the use of marihuana. The medical writer of the *Los Angeles Times* noted cryptically that "there was no debate over those parts of the report which in general stated that the use of small amounts of marihuana has no known harmful effects." Instead of the committee statement the house adopted the following language:

This AMA House of Delegates does not condone the production, sale or use of marihuana. It does, however, recommend that the personal possession of insignificant amounts of that substance be considered at most a misdemeanor with commensurate penalties applied. It also recommends its prohibition for public use; and that a plea of marihuana intoxication should not be a defense in any criminal proceeding.

In view of the need for further research, and the possibility of some deleterious effects on the user and on society at large which could constitute a major public health problem, the Council and Committee agree that a policy of discouragement is strongly advocated.[116]

The ABA experience was similar. On 21 April 1971 the commission requested the president of the ABA to communicate the organization's views on the marihuana issue.[117] In response, President Edward L. Wright noted that the association "has not adopted any formal policy statement through its Board of Governors or House of Delegates." Instead, he requested the various committees that were considering the area to inform the commission of their views.[118]

On 9 July 1971 the Committee on Alcoholism and Drug Reform of the ABA Section on Individual Rights and Responsibilities recommended unanimously

> . . . the removal of all criminal penalties for the possession of marijuana. We suggest that the distribution of marijuana be regulated along the lines presently employed for the sale of alcohol. Licensing provisions should be used to ensure that the drug is not sold to children, and that other standards are met. If a less drastic reform is preferred we would urge the commission to retain criminal penalties (in reduced form) only for selling (for profit). There is simply no basis for employing the criminal sanction, with its threat of imprisonment, against people who, at the very worst, are harming themselves.[119]

Three weeks later the Committee on Drug Abuse of the Section on Criminal Law unanimously adopted a somewhat more restrained resolution:

> RESOLVED, That because the individual and social costs resulting from imposition of penalties for simple possession of marihuana substantially outweigh the harm caused to the individual and society as a consequence of the use of marihuana, Federal, State, and Local penalties for simple possession of marihuana should be eliminated; and
> BE IT FURTHER RESOLVED, That casual distribution of a small amount of marihuana be handled in the same manner as simple possession; and
> BE IT FURTHER RESOLVED, That the Commission on Marihuana and Drug Abuse consider the feasibility of licensing the distribution of marihuana, in lieu of imposing penalties, in order better to control its use.[120]

The commission cited these views in support of its recommendations.[121] Then, in preparation for the ABA convention in August 1972, the full Section on Individual Rights and Responsibilities recommended in February that the House of Delegates adopt the following resolution:

> RESOLVED, That, because the individual and social costs resulting from existing laws punishing personal use or simple possession of marijuana substantially outweigh any benefits derived, federal, state, and local laws punishing personal use or simple possession of marijuana should be repealed; and,

BE IT FURTHER RESOLVED, That consideration be given to the feasibility of regulating the use of marijuana by licensing its distribution.[122]

In the floor debate on the Section resolution, proponents stressed the alcohol analogy and the social costs of a widely violated criminal proscription. They further emphasized that adoption of a decriminalization recommendation would not mean the ABA approved marihuana use. In response, opponents insisted that marihuana use led to the use of other drugs. Like the AMA, the ABA finally adopted by voice vote a compromise resolution. Offered by New York City U.S. Attorney Whitney North Seymour, it read:

RESOLVED, That because the individual and social costs resulting from some existing laws punishing personal use and simple possession of marijuana substantially outweigh any benefits derived, federal, state and local laws punishing personal use or simple possession of marijuana should be overhauled and present excessive criminal penalties should be eliminated.[123]

The Last Straw: Fear for the Future and a New Steppingstone Thesis

After a temporary hiatus for the 1972 national elections, the social realities continued to erode the symbolic importance of the marihuana laws. In March 1973 the Washington, D.C., Mayor's Advisory Committee on Narcotics Addicition, Prevention, and Rehabilitation recommended immediate decriminalization and even urged congressional consideration of a federally operated regulatory scheme.[124] Two months later, the Texas legislature replaced the most severe marihuana law in the country with a substantially more lenient one.[125] Interestingly, a respectable segment of the Texas legislature even espoused decriminalization, a reform which had previously been recommended by a special senate committee.[126] In July Oregon became the first state to remove criminal penalties from possession when it reclassified possession of up to one ounce as a "violation" subject to a $100 civil fine.

Lawyers' groups also spoke out during the Watergate-preoccupied summer of 1973. In April the committee which drafted the Uniform Controlled Substances Act proposed to amend it by decriminalizing private possession of marihuana for personal use as well as casual nonprofit distribution. In August that proposal was adopted 42-7 by the Committee of the Whole of the National Conference of Commissioners on Uniform State Laws. (An earlier motion that would have killed the amendment was defeated 33-15.) And the very same week, the ABA House of Delegates resolved, by 122-70, that "there should be no criminal laws punishing the simple possession of marihuana by users."

Meanwhile, of course, the forces defending the status quo began to regroup. The counterattack was characterized by vitriolic attacks on the commission and selective citation of studies suggesting the perils of marihuana use. Using tactics reminiscent of the 1930s, several self-proclaimed experts marshaled the moral energies of such stalwart groups as the Leadership Foundation[127] to hold back the tide of marihuana reform. One Berkeley physician, an assistant director of Donner Laboratory, dismissed the commission's report as "a political document written by the staff who are obviously 'potheads,' " and asserted that even the occasional use of marihuana causes brain damage.[128] Similarly, an East Coast psychiatrist, characterizing the Marihuana Commission Report as "the worst hoax ever perpetrated upon the American Public in the name of Science," contended that any relaxation of the marihuana laws would refill the nation's mental hospitals with an entire generation of brain-damaged marihuana smokers.[129]

Such self-styled protectors of the national health relied heavily on a December 1971 publication in *Lancet*, a leading British medical journal, which attributed cerebral atrophy to regular marihuana use.[130] Even though the *Lancet* editors published a lengthy caveat in the same issue[131] and the authors' attribution of cause was questioned, disputed, or ridiculed by virtually every American authority, this study was widely publicized[132] and has remained in the forefront of antimarihuana rhetoric.

Interestingly enough, the author of the most comprehensive defense of strict marihuana control policy to emerge in recent years was exceedingly skeptical of the British report. In *Marihuana: Deceptive Weed* Dr. Gabriel Nahas of Columbia University's College of Physicians and Surgeons found substantial cause for alarm in the pharmacological properties of Δ9THC, but he insisted that any causal relationship between clinical symptoms, cerebral atrophy, and marihuana use was premature until "confirmed on a much larger sample of marihuana users (at the exclusion of other drugs)."[133] Although Dr. Nahas attributed serious psychotoxic effects to Δ9THC, his opposition to significant marihuana law reform (apart from "more human legislation") rests squarely on the crucial sociocultural question: what marihuana means in American society and what its use is likely to mean tomorrow. In his view, Western society faces a drug-induced watershed:

> It is deceptive to consider marihuana intoxication as a youthful fad, similar to many which have occurred in the past. Marihuana intoxication among the affluent youth of today is part of the pandemic toxicomania which has developed in the second half of this century in the Western world dominated by Anglo-Saxon technology.
>
> Drug taking is symptomatic of the dissatisfaction and the craving for fulfillment of disillusioned youth seeking new values. Such fulfillment cannot be found in any lasting way through any type of intoxication. To make marihuana, or any other hallucinogenic drug, available will in no way solve the social malaise which has beset the youth of America and its Western allies.
>
> One may also wonder how long a political system can endure when drug taking becomes one of the prerequisites of happiness. If the American dream has lost its attraction, it will not be retrieved through the use of stupefying drugs. Their use only delays the young in their quest to understand the world they now live in and their desire to foster a better world for tomorrow.[134]

In contrast to the reformers' insistence that the marihuana question not be intertwined with general "drug" issues, and especially that it be freed from its link to heroin, the proponents of existing policy adamantly refused to regard marihuana policy in isolation. Marihuana use is both symbol and precursor of their worst fears about tomorrow. In their view, the fate of the American way of life (indeed, of the free world) hangs in the balance of marihuana policy:

> The orderly and continued development of a number of very powerful political systems which have emerged in the past 60 years require from their people life styles which are drug free. These systems, especially those in the East, have gained great political and economic power and their influence is more and more felt throughout the world. One should therefore expect

that the efforts to achieve control of stupefying drugs, including *Cannabis*, will continue in the years ahead in some of the most powerful and dynamic countries of the world, with or without America. And it is hard to envision how a drug-consuming, pleasure-oriented society will be able to face the challenge which these countries have thrust upon the Western world.[135]

That is what marihuana means to Dr. Nahas. It is also what it means to President Nixon—holding the line against the forces of permissiveness which threaten to overrun America. In October 1972, when the president declared "drug abuse" to be "America's public enemy number one," he pledged to "work unceasingly to halt the erosion of moral fiber in American life," to hold vigilant watch against the "endlessly drugged *Brave New World* which... could conceivably become our world a few years in the future," and not to cater "to the way-out wants of those who reject all respect for moral and legal values."[136] In announcing his battle plan against crime and drugs several months later in March 1973, the president made it "perfectly clear" that marihuana use was one of these "way-out wants." After reminding his radio audience that drug abuse remained "public enemy number one," the president noted:

> In recent days, there have been proposals to legalize the possession and use of marihuana [referring to the Washington, D.C., Mayor's Advisory Committee]. I oppose the legalization of the sale, possession or use of marihuana. The line against the use of dangerous drugs is now drawn on this side of marihuana. If we move the line to the other side and accept the use of this drug, how can we draw the line against other illegal drugs? Or will we slide into an acceptance of their use, as well? . . . . There must continue to be criminal sanctions against the possession, sale or use of marihuana.[137]

Disregarding the circularity of the president's argument (Marihuana is an illegal drug. We must hold the line against illegal drugs. So marihuana must remain illegal.) he was no longer emphasizing what marihuana itself would lead to, but what reforming the marihuana laws would lead to. [138]

This, then, is a portrait of marihuana prohibition in 1973. Political conflict has replaced consensus. One side, fearing for the future and numbed by the pace of social change, identifies marihuana use pharmacologically (steppingstone, brain damage), psychologically (amotivation), sociologically (the youth of tomorrow), and morally with the decline of the American way. The other side, insisting that marihuana use be viewed on its own terms, finds no reason to speculate about tomorrow or engage the question of values; in their view doubt about the future cannot justify the costs of the present laws. Competing with the vision that marihuana law reform might ultimately affect the balance of power in the world is the more optimistic approach of the Marihuana Commission. After exploring the normative and attitudinal aspects of marihuana use, an area it termed the impact on the "dominant social order," the commission concluded:

> Viewed against the background of the profound changes of recent years in the fields of economics, politics, religion, family life, housing patterns, civil rights, employment and recreation, the use of marihuana by the nation's youth must be seen as a relatively minor change in social patterns of conduct and as more of a consequence of than a contributor to these major changes.
> When the issue of marihuana use is placed in this context of society's larger concerns, marihuana does not emerge as a major issue or threat to the social order. Rather, it is most appropriately viewed as a part of the whole of society's concerns about the growth and development of its young people.
> In view of the magnitude and nature of change which our society has experienced during the past 25 years, the thoughtful observer is not likely to attribute any of the major social problems resulting from this change to marihuana use. Similarly, it is unlikely that marihuana will affect the future strength, stability or vitality of our social and political institutions. The fundamental principles and values upon which the society rests are far too enduring to go up in the smoke of a marihuana cigarette.[139]

*   *   *

For obvious reasons, this book ends in the middle of a sentence. We had originally intended to terminate our narrative with appointment of the commission, in itself an important historical event. But as time crept over an unfinished manuscript, further consideration made us realize that American marihuana prohibition had passed completely through one phase (fact-finding) and had entered another (political) within one short year. In describing these events, we have reported our perceptions without the benefit of reflection or historical hindsight. Perhaps someone will take another look several years hence and place the events of the last two years in historical perspective.

The history of American marihuana prohibition is not yet complete. The consensus on which that policy was based has disappeared, and the policy itself is accordingly under review. This is not to say that the policy will be repealed and replaced, at least in the immediate future. But for the first time in its fifty-five-year social history, marihuana is the subject of a concerted policy-making process. In the epilogue we will sketch briefly what we think that policy ought to be. And we will attempt to do so with the lessons of history well in mind.

Epilogue

HISTORICAL DETACHMENT was by definition impossible in writing this book. We do not doubt that our opinions, molded by the present social context, have colored our interpretations of an earlier one; but we did strive for objectivity and hope we have attained it. In these final few pages, we intend to bring these historical observations to bear on contemporary policy-making, and to discuss their implications for the future.

We noted at the outset that this book would begin and end at the same spot—with American society struggling inconsistently with the value-laden issues raised by psychoactive drug use. Throughout the sixty-year period described in these pages, neither philosophy nor science have been shapers of drug policy; instead, the central influence on government action has been the social context—political, economic, and cultural. Amorphous social forces, peculiar to time and place, have shaped both the drug-using behavior of individuals and groups and the wider social response to that behavior. Philosophical and ethical principles may dictate whose needs *ought* to prevail; but the thus far unpredictable forces of history dictate whose needs ultimately *will* prevail.

This is the lesson of the marihuana story. There are no villains, no heroes; only depressions, wars, laws, customs, prejudices, symbols, social values, fears, crime statistics, underemployment, campus riots, youthful alienation, and creaking bones in a social system.

And of course there are naturally-occurring, mood-altering substances to which man has always turned to satisfy his many needs. Because of the special capacity of these substances to influence behavior, every society tends to resist the use of a previously unfamiliar one for self-defined purposes. The intensity of the resistance tends to be determined by the attitudes of the dominant social group toward the using group, the prevailing perceptions of the drug-effect, and the evaluations of these effects in terms of the extant normative system.

When marihuana use seeped across the border early in the twentieth century, the only prerequisite to its prohibition was official notice. The effects of the drug were irrelevant: it was used by a voiceless immigrant group associated with antisocial behavior in general and violent crimes in particular; it was enshrouded in legend—from East and West; and it appeared just after a wave of pharmaceutical and alcohol prohibitions had washed over a haphazard system of distribution. Given the contemporary social context from 1915 to 1930, marihuana prohibition was a foregone conclusion and, indeed, was supported by a latent public consensus.

By the same token, however, if use of marihuana—a previously unknown drug—had suddenly appeared on the American scene in 1970 among the same population and on the same scale it has now achieved, prohibition would not even be considered. The drug is used privately as a social drug, with shared ritual and meaning, among a broad spectrum of the American teenage and young adult populations. For the most part, use of the drug has not been associated with visible antisocial behavior. If marihuana had no past, the issue would be whether some form of government regulation would prove beneficial to the users or to the public coffers. And even then the using population would insist that any restrictive action be tailored narrowly to achieve a specific governmental purpose.

This is not the case, of course. Marihuana use in the 1960s confronted a system of criminal prohibition which carried its own meaning as defined in another time. Decades of classification as a narcotic, the presumptive immorality attaching to felonious conduct, and the implication of addiction, crime, and insanity had instilled in the public consciousness a fear of marihuana unjustified by the demonstrable effects of its use. But that fear, and its codification by law, is an integral part of the present social context, and it cannot be ignored in either shaping or predicting policy.

The Meaning of Marihuana's Past

History has woven a web around the use of marihuana. In our opinion, public reluctance to modify or eliminate marihuana

prohibition in 1973 is based on attitudes molded by two generations of illegality, together with the societal ambivalence toward
self-defined drug use which has prevailed for a century. The
narcotics consensus supporting twentieth-century "drug" policy
was founded on exaggeration. Any use of any so-called "narcotic"
drug was thought to propel the pleasure-seeking user toward a
drug habit or addiction that in turn would result in crime, slothfulness, and immorality. Because of this widely shared image, the
fused concepts of "narcotic" and addiction constituted the organizing principle of drug policy. Formal application of this concept
to marihuana was initiated by the "narcotic farm" act of 1929,
which included Indian hemp in the list of "habit-forming drugs,"
and was reaffirmed by the legislation of the 1950s that linked
marihuana use to heroin use. (The prospect of therapy is what
ultimately gives the concept of habit-formation meaning under the
1929 act; yet few "cannabis addicts" have been identified in the
public health hospitals in Lexington, Kentucky, and Fort Worth,
Texas, since they opened in the thirties.)

The youthful drug use of the 1960s, particularly the substantial
experimentation with marihuana and hallucinogens like LSD,
demonstrated that social disapproval was not tied to "addiction"
alone (and hence was not synonymous with the term "narcotics"
either). Although the "narcotics" consensus remained, it no longer
supported marihuana prohibition. For this reason, American society
was forced to confront the inconsistencies in its dualistic policy
patterns—alcohol and "drugs." In our view, fundamental reconsideration of drug policy is now in order. In particular, a new
organizing principle must emerge to supplant the misplaced emphasis on addiction, and policy makers must evaluate the role of
individual responsibility in psychoactive drug use. The nation
might easily defer such reconsideration by reforming marihuana
policy, the policy most in need of change and the drug least likely
to make a social difference. By the same token, however, popular
reluctance to alter marihuana policy clearly reflects apprehensive-
ness that such a move might in itself signify a fundamental
reconsideration and imply societal "surrender" in the war against
drug abuse.

We see then how marihuana has been trapped by its past; use of
the drug has assumed cosmic meanings which have little to do with

the ethical questions raised by psychoactive drug use and even less to do with health. One need not reject the Protestant ethic either to embrace or condone marihuana use. The intoxicant property of marihuana cannot honestly be distinguished from that of alcohol in terms of this society's moral and social acceptance of recreational drug use. Individual and public health would probably suffer from use of marihuana (and other drugs as well) no more under any other control system than is true under the present one. In sum, the issue is no longer the properties of marihuana—the ethics or effects of its use. The pivotal question instead is the meaning of marihuana policy.

In the first place, retention of marihuana prohibition, an afterthought of the narcotics consensus, has come to symbolize the nation's battle against "drug abuse," the most recent euphemism for disapproved drug use. ("Drug abuse" emerged as the replacement symbol for "narcotics" because it rallies the public to an undefined cause; who could possibly be *for* the abuse of drugs?) In an era characterized by increased use of many drugs, "holding the line" on marihuana is an essential element of the "hard-line" strategy.

But how is marihuana related to use of other drugs? The recent flurry of official fact-finding has undoubtedly convinced the public that marihuana is not identical to other illicit substances, a matter which has been on the official record at least since the fifties. (Indeed, one important by-product of the marihuana debate has been to reverse the tendency to exaggerate the detriments of the "illegal drugs" and to minimize those of the "legal" drugs. Alcohol, for example, has been placed in proper perspective, and the reformers have been forced to retract their initial comparisons between marihuana and alcohol.)

Even without direct identification as a "narcotic," marihuana's indirect association through the steppingstone, or escalation, hypothesis was always a salient feature of the narcotics consensus, although this theory was not officially adopted until the 1950s. Particularly during the last decade, voluminous data have been amassed to interpret the meaning of the statistical association between use of marihuana and use of other drugs. Yet the experts generally agree that the relationship is not causal and reflects non-drug factors. Indeed, marihuana's reputation as a first step on the road to addiction (or to the drug culture) is entirely a function of its legal history. Alcohol and tobacco are significantly more heavily associated with marihuana use than marihuana use is with use of any other drug. Yet the legal prohibition itself defines the terms in which the question is asked: which substances are drugs of "abuse" and are therefore relevant to the escalation hypothesis? Society's continuing concern about use of opiates and about a drug-using lifestyle is foisted on marihuana simply because it is generally the first illicit drug to be used (as distinguished from the first drug to be used illicitly—which would include alcohol and tobacco).

In these and other ways, the debate centers on what marihuana use really means. The reformers now link marihuana to alcohol not to compare their effects (if anything, this is risky business in light of the nine million alcoholics and multitude of alcohol-related deaths), but to establish familiarity; it's not that alcohol's good, but that it's American. So it should be with marihuana— nothing will change apart from the details of the drug-using ritual and the nature of being "high." By contrast, the opponents of reform view marihuana use as something fundamentally different: as either part of or contributor to a pattern of events which will modify the essence of American life—for the worse, in their opinion. Some of them seek to prove their point by searching for immediate ill effects in the laboratories and clinics—marihuana leads to heroin or to amotivation or to promiscuity. But the more thoughtful opponents are not really talking about tomorrow, but the days after tomorrow. They are convinced that marihuana use is a substantial departure from customary conduct and that the drug-using behavior of future generations will be severely disruptive of the social order if effective preventive action is not taken now. For them, marihuana symbolizes fundamental social changes.

The Merits of Reform

We cast our lot with the reformers. In so doing, we suspect we side with the inevitable; but more important, we believe that these laws are indefensible and therefore *ought* to be changed.

We are convinced that logic, science, and philosophy have had almost nothing to do with the evolution of drug policy. The social

structure will ultimately adjust to the realities of drug-using behavior. America will become comfortable with marihuana, and the
laws will vanish in practice if not in form. This process is already
underway. Nonetheless, the marihuana debate has revealed widespread dissatsifaction with the contemporary approach and has
initiated a search for general principles upon which an orderly,
consistent drug control policy can be based. From this perspective,
then, we will summarize what we think marihuana policy *ought*
to be.

In general terms, we believe that this nation ultimately should
adopt a social policy of official neutrality toward the recreational
use of marihuana, but should seek to discourage its heavy or
otherwise irresponsible use. As an integral part of this official
stance, all of the major institutions of society, including the
government, should strive to minimize all forms of social and
economic pressure that tend to encourage the use of psychoactive
substances, including alcohol as well as marihuana. Similarly, in
implementing this social policy, the government should establish
a mechanism for controlling the availability of marihuana which
does not institutionalize the economic incentives for perpetuating
and proselytizing its use.

In this connection, we endorse a regulatory model (or "legalization"), but we do *not* endorse the "alcohol model"; indeed the
legal channels of marihuana distribution should *not* resemble those
now employed for alcoholic beverages. The drug should be distributed through a government controlled or regulated monopoly.
Under no circumstances should product competition be permitted.
To prevent the government from having a vested interest in widespread use, the drug should be taxed primarily as a control device,
not as a revenue-raising device. No advertising or other commercial
inducements should be permitted. The drug should be available at
the retail level only on conditions that emphasize to the user the
psychoactive properties of the substance and the risks of its use; in
this regard, pharmacies might be useful retail outlets. Appropriate
age limitations should be established and enforced against careless
distributors, albeit with the understanding that adolescent experi-
mentaton is inevitable. Potency controls should be utilized to
differentiate among various substances to be available and to inform the consumer; preparations high in THC should not be made

available at the outset but should be marketed, if at all, only to meet demonstrated demand. Such a regulatory scheme should be established with a minimum of fanfare and an abundance of caution.

It has not been our purpose in this book to advocate a regulatory approach to marihuana use; accordingly, we have aimed here only to sketch a public policy which will be suitable over the long term. We do not urge its immediate adoption. If we have become advocates, our cause is reform—a reformed public posture toward what we regard as a matter of minor public consequence. At the moment the fact of reform is more important than its details. We should also emphasize that reduction of penalties can no longer be regarded as reform. As long as personal possession of marihuana is a crime, the law is indefensible; as long as a person can be arrested for use of marihuana—whether he is punishable by a $100 fine or by one day in jail—the narcotics consensus will be exerting dead-hand control over marihuana policy.

In concluding that the law ought to be reformed, we do not rely primarily on science—although marihuana use clearly poses less risk to either physical or mental health than use of any other major psychoactive substance including alcohol. In our view, the current tendency to devise a continuum of drug control schemes and penalties based on a scale of drug effects is misguided. It ties the law directly to science when the basic questions raised by drug use are answerable in social rather than pharmacological terms.

Nor do we rely on any generally applicable ethical principle relating to drug use—although we do believe that experimental and recreational marihuana use are perfectly consistent with the principle that individuals should not behave in a way that could substantially impair their capacity to realize their human potential.

Nor do we join so many other reformers in relying on the libertarian political philosophy of John Stuart Mill, holding that the government has no authority under any circumstances to intervene in essentially private matters such as drug consumption. We do believe, however, that marihuana prohibition is not supportable when the state has the burden of justifying interferences with personal liberty, as it must in a free society professing limited government.

Nor do we rely on pragmatism, by which we mean the supposedly value-neutral cost/benefit approach which is now so much in vogue; without a normative scale and a system of evaluative weights, the act of balancing yields purely subjective results weighing apples (the potential dangers of marihuana use) against oranges (the costs of having a prohibition). Of course, our subjective weighing would consider the costs outrageous and the benefits purely speculative.

The most compelling reason for modification or elimination of marihuana prohibition lies in its disastrous impact on the law as an institution. In this century American society has turned to law, particularly the criminal law, to serve a multitude of functions. An attitude has evolved that any behavior offending a prevailing sentiment should be punishable by law. As a result, the legal system has been overextended until its value as a symbol has been magnified beyond its capacity to absorb disobedience. When the law is so readily employed as a symbol of disapproval, it will be easily wielded as a symbol of oppression. When a society so frequently relies on the legal system to control behavior, it will inevitably debase and weaken the influence of those institutions with the greatest capacity to mold desirable conduct.

The marihuana laws manifest the crisis of law that this society now faces. No criminal law can be fairly or effectively enforced unless it commands a popular consensus. Yet, the marihuana consensus evaporated as soon as the prohibition encountered the rigors of public dialogue. This is not to say that prohibition lacks the support of a popular majority. Our point is that the utility or propriety of a criminal law is not measured in votes but in shared values. Price controls and other regulatory activities derive their legitimacy from the support of a majority, however transient; but outright criminal prohibitions, particularly those involving private behavior, derive their legitimacy from congruence with more enduring normative precepts. The fact that one-third of the voting population of a major state actually registered electoral *opposition* to marihuana prohibition definitively establishes the evaporation of the marihuana consensus. All other evidence establishes that uncertainty dominates the vast center of public opinion, while an increasingly smaller fraction of the public affirmatively supports the current prohibition. Undoubtedly, marihuana prohibition does not command the minimum amount of public support necessary to sustain and reinforce a criminal prohibition.

As a result the law suffers disobedience and ridicule. The criminal justice system operates unfairly and without confidence. And the moral force of the criminal law wanes with each undetected or unenforced violation. Criminal justice simply cannot be achieved when conviction of a crime is perceived to be an injustice not only by the defendant but by large segments of the public and by the participants in the system itself.

Our society normally employs the criminal justice system to apprehend and punish those persons who have committed certain classes of acts which the general society believes to be deserving of punishment. We then utilize discretion at various points in the system to mitigate the implications of this presumptive judgment. Thus, depending on the culpability of the individual offender, we may forego prosecution or avoid a punitive sentence. Where the marihuana laws are concerned, however, the presumption has become precisely the opposite. Since the larger society generally does not view its marihuana offenders, who are overwhelmingly young, as morally culpable and deserving of punishment, the effort is now made to select from the 250,000 persons who are arrested each year, those few who should *continue* to be processed through the system.

Our police, our prosecutors, and our courts—sworn to uphold and enforce the laws of this nation—have been confronted with a population of lawbreakers alien to the ordinary process of the criminal justice system. Thus, the system has responded by contorting itself. The discretion ordinarily exercised—whether or not to arrest, whether or not to prosecute, whether or not to convict, and whether or not to incarcerate—has been employed to determine which of these unlikely defendants should remain in the system: and as the need for discretion increases, so does the likelihood of selectivity and inequality.

The punitive instinct simply is not there. In most cases effort is directed not at securing the symbol of wrongdoing—the conviction—but instead to avoid stigmatizing the youthful or otherwise unlikely offender with a criminal record.

The criminalization of marihuana consumption has severely wounded the legal system and has eroded the public confidence in criminal justice, which confidence is the essence of respect for law. For this reason the first priority of marihuana reform must be to repeal the prohibitions of possession for personal use, casual non-profit distribution and other consumption-related behavior. In our view, the resulting scheme of "partial prohibition" (as the marihuana commission called it) is defensible—certainly over the short run. Nothing less than the decriminalization of possession will constitute sufficient reform; even then, this would only bring marihuana prohibition in line with the precedent of alcohol prohibition, during which forty-three states refused to intrude the criminal law into the life of the consumer.

To state it the other way, although we would prefer more fundamental reform, we do believe that policy makers may *rationally* continue to prohibit, by criminal law, commercial distribution and other profit-making activities, and thereby resist any of the adversity that might conceivably be associated with widespread marihuana use. We believe that the state may legitimately take an organic view of the society, one which is not tied to use patterns at the present time, and may anticipate the effect of legal and social changes in the future. Unlike the decision regarding the desirability of a criminal sanction at the user level, individual privacy and freedom of choice are not directly affected in this context. The key issue here is not the imposition of the law onto private behavior, but rather the preferable mode of availability of the drug. A prudent social policy planner would be remiss if he did not carefully speculate what any given social development might mean in the future for the entire social fabric. He need not rest his decision on the present but may anticipate, speculate, and be judicious.

Under this approach the refusal to legalize and regulate distribution of marihuana would be based primarily on *preventive* considerations, considerations not rooted in logic but in experience. The marihuana commission's recommendations reflect the basic conservatism expressed by Dr. Paton in his foreword to Dr. Nahas' defense of marihuana prohibition: "In discussing Cannabis and social policy, a major effort of the imagination is needed. If legislation is introduced which facilitates its use, one must try to assess how, in subsequent decades, the pattern of use would change, particularly in frequency, quantity and potency; and then one must try to assess the medical and social consequences for our own society."

In this connection, we emphasize that the legal environment has an extraordinarily blunt impact on the patterns of consumption of any social drug. The law is incapable of distinguishing among the patterns of drug-using behavior, and is therefore incapable of discriminating between harmless conduct on the one hand, and intensified or compulsive drug use on the other. Nor can the law be viewed in a vacuum, as an independent influence on decisions to initiate, continue, or terminate forbidden behavior.

These truths are particularly crucial to the details of marihuana reform. On the one hand, the criminal sanction for possession has probably embued marihuana with a symbolic attraction far exceeding its psychoactive virtues. Removal of this unnecessary and counterproductive prohibition might de-emphasize what is now a symbolic social issue, and let natural social forces take their course. There is fairly strong evidence that if this were to happen, marihuana use, after an increase of use among the curious but heretofore reluctant, would eventually taper off. On the other hand, a sudden decision to institutionalize availability of the drug through a regulatory scheme—no matter how strong society's disclaimers and discouraging labels might be—might initially serve to encourage people to use the drug when they would not otherwise do so. This might not have been the case fifty years ago and might not be so five years from now. But it is probably true today. The very leap from an eliminationist, prohibitory policy to a scheme of regulation might imply social approval.

For this reason, we do not urge *immediate* adoption of a regulatory scheme. We prefer evolutionary reform. Right now, decriminalization is a mandatory step. Nothing less will free the legal system of 250,000 criminals whom society wishes not to punish. Over the long term, however, decriminalization will not be enough. The preventive rationale is persuasive (and practical) as long as marihuana is so heavily laden with social meaning. After some other behavior emerges as the cutting edge of social change, marihuana use should be addressed on its own terms. Only then will it finally have been freed of the continuing effects of past policy. Only then can social and legal policy be formulated to comport with the public interest rather than the public imagination.

Notes
Selected Bibliography
Citations to Marihuana Laws
Index

Notes

Unless otherwise noted, the letters, memorandums, and other unpublished materials may be found in the files of the Drug Enforcement Administration, formerly the Bureau of Narcotics and Dangerous Drugs (BNDD). Permission to study these records was graciously granted by John Ingersoll, director of BNDD during the period of research.

In some instances, the identifying information regarding specific memorandums or letters was incomplete; however, most of the materials appear in a series of chronologically ordered files labeled "Subject—Marihuana." In addition, many of the published materials may also be found in the library of the Drug Enforcement Administration, ably and kindly managed by Mrs. Jane Zack.

Prologue

The introductory historical summary of cannabis use was drawn from four sources: L. Lewin, *Phantastica, Narcotic and Stimulating Drugs*, trans. P. H. A. Worth (London: Kegan Paul, 1931), pp. 107-23; R. Walton, *Marihuana: America's New Drug Problem* (Philadelphia: Lippincott, 1938), pp. 1-26; R. Blum, *Society and Drugs* (San Francisco: Jossey-Bass, 1969), pp. 61-84; L. Dewey, "Hemp," in *U.S. Department of Agriculture Yearbook, 1913* (Washington, D.C.: GPO, 1913), pp. 283-345.

Chapter I

1. H. W. Lee, *How Dry We Were: Prohibition Revisited* (Englewood Cliffs, N.J.: Prentice-Hall, 1963), p. 16.

2. The tobacco information in this chapter was drawn from J. L. McGrew, "History of Tobacco Regulation," *Marihuana: A Signal of Misunderstanding*, First Report of the National Commission on Marihuana and Drug Abuse, Appendix (Washington, D.C.: GPO, 1972), I, 513-30.

3. J. E. Brooks, *The Mighty Leaf: Tobacco Through the Centuries* (Boston: Little, Brown, 1952), pp. 215-16.

4.   See generally D. Musto, *The American Disease: Origins of Narcotic Control* (New Haven: Yale Univ. Press, 1973); D. W. Maurer and V. H. Vogel, *Narcotics and Narcotic Addiction* (Springfield, Ill.: Thomas, 1954); C. Terry and M. Pellens, *The Opium Problem* (New York: Prentice-Hall, 1928), p. 66.

5.   Terry and Pellens, p. 69.

6.   Stanley, "Morphinism," *Journal of Criminal Law and Criminology*, 6 (1915), 588.

7.   See the resolution of the Narcotics Control Association of California calling for stricter laws regulating prescriptions and prescription order forms (*Journal of Criminal Law and Criminology*, 13 [1922], 126-27).

8.   Brill, "Recurrent Patterns in the History of Drug Dependence and Some Interpretations," in *Drugs and Youth*, ed. J. R. Wittenborn (Springfield, Ill.: Thomas, 1969), p. 18.

9.   Terry and Pellens, pp. 76-82.

10.   S. H. Adams, *The Great American Fraud* (Chicago: Press of American Medical Association, 1907).

11.   The earliest surveys of drug use employed a methodology much less sophisticated than those conducted after 1914. The later studies, however, suffer from a time lag and from several built-in biases. Taken together, these surveys adequately describe the contours of the phenomenon under consideration. The earliest attempt at a compilation of addiction figures was undertaken by Marshall, "The Opium Habit in Michigan," *Michigan State Board of Health Annotated Reports* (1878), pp. 61-73. From questionnaires sent to doctors, Marshall found 1,313 users of opium or morphine and concluded that there were some 7,763 addicts in the state. Dr. Charles Terry later concluded that if Marshall's figures were representative, total incidence of addiction in the United States in 1878 was 251,936 (Terry and Pellens, p. 15). Marshall was unable fully to take into account the fact that the incidence of opiate use was much higher in the cities than in the rural areas he studied; accordingly, his figures might have underestimated the extent of addiction in the state.

In a similar study of Iowa in 1884, J. M. Hull found 5,732 addicts which, if representative, would reflect a national addict population of 182,215 (Hull, "The Opium Habit," *Iowa State Board of Health Biennial Report* [1885], pp. 535-45, quoted in Terry and Pellens, pp. 16-18).

In 1900 the author of a Vermont study sent 130 questionnaires to various druggists in an attempt to determine the monthly sales of various drugs. His 116 replies indicate that 3,300,000 doses of opium were sold every month, or enough for every person in Vermont over the age of twenty-one to receive 1 1/2 doses per day (Grinnell, "A Review of Drug Consumption and Alcohol as Found in Proprietary Medicine," *Medico-Legal Journal*, 23 [1905], 426, quoted in Terry and Pellens, p. 25). A researcher in 1915 found 2,370 registered addicts in Tennessee and put the national addict population at between 269,000 and 291,670 (Brown, "Enforcement of the Tennessee Anti-Narcotic Laws," *American Journal of Public Health*, 5 [1915], 323-33, quoted in Terry and Pellens, pp. 27-29).

The first post-Harrison Act study, and perhaps the most reliable of all research during this period, was done by Lawrence Kolb and A. G. Dumez of the United States Public Health Service. Utilizing previously computed statistics together with information regarding the supply of narcotics imported into the United States, these authors concluded the addict population never exceeded 246,000 (Kolb and Dumez, "The Prevalence and Trend of Drug Addiction in the United States and Factors Influencing It," *Public Health Reports*, May 1924).

At the same time the Narcotic Division of the Prohibition Unit of the IRS estimated that there were more than 500,000 drug addicts in America (Narcotic Division of the Prohibition Unit, Bureau of Internal Revenue, Release, 4 May 1924, quoted in Terry and Pellens, p. 42, n. 25).

For more recent estimates of drug addiction in America, see W. B. Eldridge, *Narcotics and the Law*, 2d rev. ed. (Chicago: Univ. of Chicago Press, 1967), pp. 49-103; A. Lindesmith, *The Addict and the Law* (Bloomington: Indiana Univ. Press, 1965), pp. 95-134; *Drug Abuse and Law Enforcement* (Cambridge, Mass.: Arthur D. Little, 1967); M. Nyswander, *The Drug Addict as a Patient* (New York: Grune & Stratton, 1956), pp. 1-13.

With regard to the gender of opiate users at the turn of the century, 803 of the 1,313 addicts in Marshall's Michigan study were females and only 510 were males (Terry and Pellens, p. 11). In the Florida study, 228 were men and 313 women (ibid., p. 25). Of the 2,370 registered addicts in the Tennessee study, 784 were men and 1,586 were women (ibid., p. 27). A modern observer has concluded that there were at least as many and probably twice as many women addicts as men during this period. O'Donnell, "Patterns of Drug Abuse and Their Social Consequences," in *Drugs and Youth*, p. 64. For the last thirty years, male addicts have probably outnumbered female addicts by four or five to one (ibid).

Of the 228 men included in the Florida study, 188 were white and 40 black; of the women 219 were white and 94 black. At that time the white and black populations in Jacksonville were equal. Of those covered in the Tennessee study, 90 percent were white (Terry and Pellens, pp. 25, 28).

With regard to class, see Eberle, "Report of Committee on Acquirement of Drug Habits," *American Journal of Pharmacy*, Oct. 1903. "While the increase is most evident with the lower classes, the statistics of institutes devoted to the cure of habitués show that their patients are principally drawn from those in the higher walks of life" (ibid., quoted in Terry and Pellens, p. 23).

12.   H. Kane, *Opium-Smoking in America and China* (New York: Scribner's, 1882), quoted in Terry and Pellens, p. 73.

13.   For general information on Progressivism and on the intellectual climate of the early twentieth century, see M. Curti, *The Growth of American Thought*, 2d ed. (New York: Harper & Row, 1951), pp. 555-716; G. Mowry, *The Era of Theodore Roosevelt* (New York: Harper & Row, 1958); L. Hartz, *The Liberal Tradition in America* (New York: Harcourt, 1955), pp. 288-355; A. Link, *Woodrow Wilson and the Progressive Era* (New York: Harper & Row, 1954); H. May, *The End of American Innocence* (New York: Knopf, 1959); R. Hofstadter, *The Age of Reform* (New York: Knopf, 1955).

14.   Quoted in Curti, p. 233.

15.   J. Higham, *Strangers in the Land: Patterns of American Nativism, 1860-1925* (New Brunswick: Rutgers Univ. Press, 1955).

16.   The "Philadelphia Press," in *Public Opinion*, 5 (1888), 432, quoted in Higham, p. 63.

17.   Edward A. Ross, quoted in Higham, p. 110.

18.   U.S., Treasury Department, *State Laws Relating to the Control of Narcotic Drugs and the Treatment of Drug Addiction* (Washington, D.C.: GPO, 1931), hereafter cited as *State Laws* (1931). The first drug legislation enacted in eight states outlawed the administering of a narcotic drug to any person with the intent to facilitate the commission of a felony. These states were California (1872), Idaho (1887), New York (1897), North Dakota (1883), Pennsylvania (1901), South Dakota (1883), Utah (1876) and Wisconsin (1901) (ibid., pp. 1-2). Twenty-two states made education legislation their first laws concerning the drug problem (ibid., p. 2).

19.   See Wilbert and Motter, *Digest of Laws and Regulations in Force in the United States Relating to the Possession, Use, Sale, and Manufacture of Poisons and Habit-Forming Drugs*, U.S., Treasury Department, Public Health Bulletin no. 56 (Washington, D.C.: GPO, 1912), hereafter cited as *State Laws* (1912). States which prohibited the operation of or presence in an opium "den" or joint were: Alaska, Arizona, Connecticut, Idaho, Iowa, Minnesota, Missouri, Montana, New Mexico, New York, North Dakota, Ohio, Pennsylvania, South Dakota, Utah, and Wyoming. In addition, New Jersey empowered its city councils to take similar action. Four states, all in the West, prohibited the possession or smoking of opium or the possession of opium pipes: California, Nevada, South Dakota, and Washington. See also *State Laws* (1931), pt. 3.

20.   Ex parte Yung Jon, 28 F. 308 (D. Ore. 1886) at 312.

21.   See generally Musto, *The American Disease.*

22.   Terry and Pellens, pp. 84-87.

23.   Stanley, "Morphinism."

24.   See generally Musto, pp. 91-120; Eldridge, *Narcotics and the Law*, pp. 5-6.

25.   *State Laws* (1912), pp. 34-41.

26.   Ch. 3915, 34 Stat. 768 (1906). See Terry and Pellens, p. 75.

27.   U.S., Congress, House, Committee on Ways and Means, *Hearings on the Importation and Use of Opium*, 61st Cong., 2d sess., 1910.

28.   38 Stat. 785 (1914), as amended, 26 U.S.C. §§ 4701-36 (1964). For an excellent analysis of the genesis of the Harrison Act, see Musto, pp. 54-69.

29.   See, e.g., *Hammer* v. *Dagenhart*, 247 U.S. 251 (1918).

30.   *Linder* v. *United States*, 268 U.S. 5, 18 (1925).

31.   *United States* v. *Doremus*, 249 U.S. 86 (1919). The four dissenters asserted that "the statute was a mere attempt by Congress to exert a power not delegated, that is, the reserved police power of the States" (ibid., at 95). It is interesting to note in contrast that a subsequent congressional attempt to regulate child labor through the taxing power was invalidated in *Bailey* v. *Drexel Furniture Co.*, 259 U.S. 20 (1922).

32.   As Musto has pointed out in *The American Disease*, prevailing opinion among policy makers tended to oppose the dispensing of narcotics to habitués or addicts. Habitual use was to be avoided, and when it occurred, it was to be terminated. As of 1912, for example, ten states prohibited the dispensing of narcotic drugs to habitual users (*State Laws* [1912], pp. 34-41).

33.   U.S., Congress, House, 63rd Cong., 1st sess., 1913, H. Rept. 23, p. 2.

34.   Compare Musto, *The American Disease*, with R. King, *The Drug Hang-Up: America's Fifty-Year Folly* (New York: Norton, 1972), pp. 15-68.

35.   Although contemporary estimates of the size of the addict population varied widely, most researchers have concluded that the total probably never exceeded 250,000. See n. 11 and sources cited in Musto.

36.   In fact, one government report estimated in 1918 that 240,000 addicts were under the direct care of physicians (Terry and Pellens, pp. 68f.; U.S. Department of Treasury, Special Committee of Investigation, *The Traffic in Narcotic Drugs* [Washington, D.C.: GPO, 1919], p. 3).

37.   R. King, "Narcotic Drug Laws and Enforcement Policies," *Law and Contemporary Problems*, 22 (1957), 113, 124-26; King, "The Narcotics Bureau and the Harrison Act," *Yale Law Journal*, 62 (1953), 736; Note, "Narcotics Regulation," *Yale Law Journal*, 62 (1953), 751, 784-87.

38.   Kolb, "Factors That Have Influenced the Management and Treatment of Drug Addicts," in *Narcotic Drug Addiction Problems*, ed. R. Livingston (Washington, D.C.: GPO, 1963), pp. 23, 26.

39. Compare *State Laws* (1931) with *State Laws* (1912).
40. *United States* v. *Jin Fuey Moy*, 241 U.S. 394, 401 (1916).
41. Pub. L. no. 227, 67th Cong. (26 May 1922).
42. E. Cherrington, *The Evolution of Prohibition in the United States of America* (Waterville, Ohio: The American Issue Press, 1920), pp. 80-81, 135-45, 176-84, 280-84, 320; Safely, "Growth of State Power Under Federal Constitution to Regulate Traffic in Intoxicating Liquors," *Iowa Law Bulletin*, 3 (1917), 221-22.
43. J. H. Timberlake, *Prohibition and the Progressive Movement* (Cambridge: Harvard Univ. Press, 1963), pp. 34-38.
44. Higham, p. 263.
45. J. P. Gusfield, *Symbolic Crusade* (Urbana: Univ. of Illinois Press, 1963).
46. U.S., Congress, Senate, 66th Cong., 1st sess., 18 Aug. 1919, S. Rept. 151.
47. See *Sheet* v. *Lincoln Safe Deposit Company*, 254 U.S. 88 (1920); *United States* v. *Cleveland*, 282 F. 249 (1922); *Shoemaker's Petition*, 9 F.2d 170 (1925).
48. A. Corcoran, "Possession Under the State Prohibition Laws," *Marihuana: A Signal of Misunderstanding*, Appendix (Washington, D.C.: GPO, 1972), II, 1185-97.
49. In 1904 Ernst Freund, quoting from an article on "personal liberty" in the *Cyclopedia of Temperance and Prohibition*, noted: "Even the advocates of prohibition concede that the state has no concern with the private use of liquor. The opponents of prohibition misstate the case by saying that the state has no right to declare what a man shall eat or drink. The state does not venture to make any such declaration. . . . It is not the private appetite or home customs of the citizen that the state undertakes to manage, but the liquor traffic. . . . If by abolishing the saloon the state makes it difficult for men to gratify their private appetites, there is no just reason for complaint'" (E. Freund, *The Police Power, Public Policy and Constitutional Rights* [Chicago: Callaghan, 1904], p. 484).
50. National Commission on Law Observance and Enforcement (Wickersham Commission), *Report on the Enforcement of the Prohibition Laws of the United States*, report no. 2 (1931; reprint ed., Montclair, N.J.: Patterson Smith, 1968), pp. 6-7.
51. *A New English Dictionary on Historical Principles*, 6 vols., ed. J. A. H. Murray (Oxford: Clarendon, 1908); *The National Medical Dictionary*, 2 vols., ed. J. S. Billings (Philadelphia Lea Bros., 1890); *Dictionaire De Medescine*, ed. P. H. Nysten (New York: Ballienre et Fils, 1858); *The Century Dictionary*, ed. W. D. Whitney (New York: Century, 1897); *Lexicon of Medicine and the Allied Sciences*, 4 vols., ed. H. Power and L. W. Sedgwick (London: The New Sydenham Society, 1892).
52. Compare *Lexicon of Medicine and the Allied Sciences* with *The Century Dictionary*.
53. Ex parte Yun Quong, 159 Cal. 508, 514, 114 P. 835, 838 (1911) quoting lower court opinion; citations omitted).
54. E.g., Bronaugh, "Limiting or Prohibiting the Possession of Intoxicating Liquors for Personal Use," *Law Notes*, 23 (1919), 67; Rogers, "Life, Liberty & Liquor: A Note on the Police Power," *Virginia Law Review*, 6 (1919), 156; Safely, "Growth of State Power," 221; Vance, "The Road to Confiscation," *Yale Law Journal*, 25 (1916), 285.
55. B. Adams, *The Theory of Social Revolutions* (New York: Macmillan, 1913), p. 94.

Chapter II

1. The Bureau of Immigration recorded the entry of 590,765 Mexicans into the United States between 1915 and 1930. Of these, upwards of 90 percent in each year were to be resident in the twenty-two states west of the Mississippi, and more than two-thirds were to reside in Texas alone. Information compiled from Tables, Immigrant Aliens, by States of Intended Future Residence and Race on Peoples, published annually from each fiscal year from 1915 to 1930 in *Commissioner General of Immigration Annual Report*.

2. "Report of Investigation in the State of Texas, Particularly along the Mexican Border, of the Traffic in, and Consumption of the Drug Generally known as 'Indian Hemp' or *Cannabis Indica*, known in Mexico and States Bordering on the Rio Grande as 'Marihuana'; Sometimes also referred to as 'Rosa Maria,' or 'Juanita,' " filed by R. F. Smith to Dr. Alsberg, chief of the Bureau of Chemistry, United States Department of Agriculture, 13 Apr. 1917, pp. 10-12, in Federal Bureau of Narcotics files (hereafter cited as "1917 Investigation").

3. Ibid., pp. 13-15.

4. M. V. Ball, "Marihuana: Mexican Name for Cannabis, Also Called Loco Weed in Certain Parts of Texas," May 1922, in the "Report of Committee Appointed by the Governor of the Canal Zone, April 1, 1925, for the Purpose of Investigating the Use of Marihuana and Making Recommendations Regarding Same and Related Papers" (Balboa Heights, Canal Zone), pp. 55-60. (The Canal Zone Report is an unpublished document hereafter cited as "Canal Zone Report," 18 Dec. 1925. The related Papers are a group of heretofore unpublished documents, hereafter cited as "Canal Zone Papers," which may be found in the National Archives. A copy of these materials is on deposit with the University of Virginia Law Library in Charlottesville, Va. Page references are to the latter copy, which has been ordered chronologically and paginated by the authors.)

5. "1917 Investigation," p. 9.

6. Ibid., p. 13.

7. Ibid., p. 9.

8. Ball, "Marihuana: Mexican Name for Cannabis."

9. "1917 Investigation," p. 36.

10. Ibid., p. 37.

11. Ibid., p. 35.

12. Ibid., pp. 38-39.

13. Ibid., p. 9.

14. Testimony of Dr. Hesner before Committee on Use of Marihuana, 5 Dec. 1925, "Canal Zone Papers," p. 31.

15. W. E. Safford, economic botanist, to Dr. E. R. Hodge, chemist, Medical Department, U.S. Army, "Canal Zone Papers," pp. 106-7.

16. "1917 Investigation," pp. 17(d)-17(e).

17. Mexico, Department of Public Health, "Regulations Concerning Commerce in Products That May Be Utilized to Encourage Vices Degenerating the Race, and Concerning the Cultivation of Plants That May Be Employed for Such Purpose," 15 Mar. 1920, "Canal Zone Papers," pp. 130-32.

18. "1917 Investigation," p. 176.

19. Ibid., p. 29.

20. Ibid., p. 30.

21. Paul C. Standley, associate curator, Division of Plants, Smithsonian Institution, to Mr. Holger Johansen, 18 June 1925, "Canal Zone Papers," pp. 15-16.

22. Safford to Hodge.

23.   Treasury Decision 35719, 25 Sept. 1915.

24.   Texas, *General Laws* (1919), ch. 150, pp. 277-79, at 278.

25.   Ex parte Brown, 38 Tex. Crim. 295, 42 S.W. 554 (1897) (alternative holding).

26.   Texas, *Special Session Laws* (1923), ch. 61, pp. 156-57.

27.   *Austin Statesman*, 19 June 1923.

28.   New Mexico, *New Mexico Laws* (1923), ch. 42, secs. 1-2, pp. 58-59.

29.   *The New Mexican* (Santa Fe), 31 Jan. 1923.

30.   See n. 1, supra.

31.   *State Laws* (1931), pp. 44, 48, 112, 194, 200, 306. See citations to map.

32.   L. C. Nutt, deputy commissioner, to J. K. Caldwell, Department of State, 11 May 1929.

33.   See, e.g., L. C. Nutt to Senator Phipps, 25 Jan. 1929 and 4 June 1930.

34.   *Marihuana* (Evanston, Ill.: National Women's Christian Temperance Union Pub. House, 1928), p. 1 (hereafter cited as WCTU, *Marihuana* [1928]).

35.   L. R. McQuillin to commission, 22 May 1931.

36.   Colorado, *Colorado Laws* (1917), ch. 39, p. 120; ch. 66, p. 186.

37.   *Rocky Mountain News* (Denver), 27 Sept. 1931.

38.   In 1927 the Montana Legislature had included marihuana in the general narcotics statute (Montana, *Montana Laws* [1927], ch. 91, sec. 1, p. 324). The 1929 bill extracted marihuana from the statute, creating separate offenses for use, sale, or possession of marihuana without a prescription (Montana, *Montana Laws* [1929], ch. 6, p. 5).

39.   *Montana Standard*, 22 Jan. 1929, p. 3, col. 2.

40.   WCTU, *Marihuana* (1928), p. 3.

41.   *State Laws* (1931), p. 98.

42.   *San Antonio Light*, 4 May 1931 (editorial).

43.   Agent-in-charge to commissioner, 26 Aug. 1931 and 9 Sept. 1931.

44.   *State Laws* (1931), p. 289.

45.   P. S. Taylor, "Crime and the Foreign Born: The Problem of the Mexican," National Commission on Law Observance and Enforcement (Wickersham Commission), *Report on Crime and the Foreign Born*, report no. 10 (Washington, D.C.: GPO, 1931), pp. 201-15 (hereafter cited as Taylor, "Crime and the Foreign Born," *Wickersham Report*, no. 10).

46.   H. J. Finger to Dr. Hamilton Wright, 2 July 1911, in *Preliminary Inventories*, no. 76, Records of United States Participation in International Conferences, Commissions and Expositions, no. 39, "Correspondence of Wright with Delegate Henry J. Finger, 1911" (Washington, D.C.: National Archives, 1955), quoted in Musto, "The Marihuana Tax Act of 1937," *Archives of General Psychiatry*, 26 (1972), 101-8.

47.   See General Conference of Council of Elders, 6-9 Apr. 1911 (remarks of President Anthon H. Lund); 5-7 Apr. 1912 (remarks of Elder Hyrum M. Smith); 4-6 Oct. 1913 (remarks of President Joseph F. Smith, Elder David O. McKay); 4-6 Apr. 1914 (remarks of Elder Herbert J. Grant, Elder David O. McKay), Salt Lake City.

48.   *Reynolds v. United States*, 98 U.S. 145 (1878).

49.   F. R. Gomila and M. C. Gomila Lambow, "Present Status of the Marihuana Vice in the United States," in *Marihuana: America's New Drug Problem*, ed. R. Walton (Philadelphia: Lippincott, 1938), p. 29.

50.   "1917 Investigation," pp. 72-79.

51.   Ibid., pp. 80-84.

52.   Gomila and Lambow, p. 29.

53.   Dowling to governor of Louisiana, 21 Aug. 1920, United States surgeon general's files.

54.   Dowling to Acting Surgeon General Periz, 3 Dec. 1920; Treasury Department Report on Investigation of Narcotics Dispensory Programs, 25 Mar. 1921. (In the files of the surgeon general for the period 1921-23.)

55.   See generally A. Lindesmith, *The Addict and the Law* (Bloomington: Indiana Univ. Press, 1965), pp. 135-61; King, "Narcotic Drug Laws and Enforcement Policies," *Law and Contemporary Problems,* 22 (1957), 124-26.   For a savage contemporary attack on the clinic system by a well-known supporter of the law enforcement strategy, see Stanley, "Narcotic Drugs and Crime," *Journal of Criminal Law and Criminology,* 12 (1921), 110.

56.   Gomila and Lambow, pp. 29-31; WCTU, *Marihuana* (1928).

57.   WCTU, *Marihuana* (1928).

58.   Ibid., p. 1.

59.   Ibid., p. 3.

60.   Taylor, "Crime and the Foreign Born," *Wickersham Report,* no. 10, pp. 220-35.

61.   Ibid., pp. 230-31.

62.   Ibid., p. 238.

63.   Ibid., pp. 239-40.

64.   Memorandum from Arthur E. Paul, chief, Chicago Station, Food, Drug, and Insecticide Administration, U.S. Department of Agriculture, to chief, Central District, 27 June 1929, p. 4.

65.   Ibid., p. 1; *Chicago Tribune,* 3 June 1929.

66.   *Chicago Examiner,* 22 June 1929.

67.   *Chicago Examiner,* 19 June 1929.

68.   *Chicago Tribune,* 17 Oct. 1929; see also *Chicago Tribune,* 1 July 1928, where an article entitled "New Giggle Drug Puts Discord in City Orchestras" reported that marihuana addiction was common among local musicians. The paper noted that marihuana "is an old drug but was generally introduced into the country only a few years ago by the Mexicans. It is like cocaine. In the long run, it bends and cripples its victims. A sort of creeping paralysis results from long use."

69.   *Chicago Tribune,* 3 June 1929.

70.   *State Laws* (1912), pp. 18-19.

71.   Ibid., p. 124.

72.   Ibid., pp. 34-41.

73.   V. Robinson, "An Essay on Hasheesh: Historical and Experimental," *Medical Review of Reviews,* 18 (1912), 159-60, 300-312. Dr. Robinson's essay was reprinted in book form by E. H. Ringer of New York in 1912 and appeared in a second edition in 1925.

74.   U.S., Congress, House, Committee on Ways and Means, *Hearings on Importation and Use of Opium,* 61st Cong., 3d sess., 14 Dec. 1910 and 11 Jan. 1911.

75.   Ibid., 11 Jan. 1911.

76.   New York, *New York Laws* (1914), ch. 363, p. 1120.

77.   *New York Times,* 30 July 1914, p. 6, col. 12.

78.   Ibid.

79.   *New York Times,* 30 July 1914, p. 8, col. 4.

80.   New York, Senate, Joint Legislative Committee to Investigate the Laws in Relation to the Distribution and Sale of Narcotic Drugs, *Final Report* (Albany, 1918), Doc. no. 35.

81.   Simon, "From Opium to Hash Eesh," *Scientific American,* Nov. 1921, pp. 14-15.

82. Weber, "Drugs and Crime," *Journal of Crime and Criminology*, 10 (1919), 370.

83. *New York Times*, 11 Jan. 1923, p. 24, col. 1.

84. New York, *New York Laws* (1927), ch. 672, p. 1695.

85. In addition to the Women's Club demonstration noted at n. 59, supra, the *New York Times* (29 Dec. 1925, p. 10, col. 7) reported that the drug had been banned in Mexico. One year later, the paper reported the results of the Panama Canal Zone study on the effects of marihuana, noting the investigator's conclusion that no legislation was necessary to prevent sale or use of the drug (21 Nov. 1926, sec. 2, p. 3, col. 1). The *Times* later reported that a Mexican family was said to have gone insane from eating marihuana (6 July 1927, p. 10, col. 6).

86. See *New York Times*, 25 Mar. 1927, p. 4, col. 6; 6 Apr. 1927, p. 13, col. 2.

87. Memorandum from Ralph H. Oyler, FBN agent-in-charge, New York, to Acting Commissioner Anslinger, 6 June 1930.

Chapter III

1. Treasury Decision 35719, 25 Sept. 1915.

2. Ch. 348, 44 Stat. 138 (1927); see Schmeckbier, *The Bureau of Prohibition*, Brookings Institute for Government Research Service Monograph, no. 57 (Washington, D.C.: GPO, 1929), p. 143.

3. Act of 14 June 1930, ch. 488, 46 Stat. 585.

4. Act of 19 Jan. 1929, ch. 82, §5, 45 Stat. 1085.

5. Act of 14 June 1930, Pub. L. no. 71-357, § 4 (a).

6. "1917 Investigation."

7. U.S., Treasury Department, United States Special Narcotic Committee, *Traffic in Narcotic Drugs*, Report of Special Committee of Investigation Appointed March 25, 1918, by the Secretary of the Treasury (Washington, D.C.: GPO, 1919).

8. Kolb and Dumez, "The Prevalence and Trend of Drug Addiction in the United States and Factors Influencing It," *Public Health Reports*, May 1924.

9. See generally A. H. Taylor, *American Diplomacy and the Narcotics Traffic, 1900-1939* (Durham: Duke Univ. Press, 1969), pp. 82-145.

10. Act of 26 May 1922, ch. 202, 42 Stat. 596.

11. O'Connor to W. O. Hart, Bureau of Prohibition, forwarded to Colonel L. C. Nutt, deputy commissioner of Prohibition, 18 Dec. 1928.

12. Act of 19 Jan. 1929, ch. 82, § 5, 45 Stat. 1085.

13. U.S., Congress, House, Committee on the Judiciary, *Hearings on H.R. 12781*, *H.R. 13645*, 70th Cong., 1st sess., 1928, H. Rept. 1652.

14. Wright, "The International Opium Conference," *American Journal of International Law*, 6 (1912), 871. One historian has suggested that the United States delegation favored inclusion of cannabis in the 1912 convention (Musto, "The Marihuana Tax Act of 1937," *Archives of General Psychiatry*, 26 [1972], 102).

15. Addendum and Final Protocol of the International Opium Conference, The Hague, 1912, quoted in W. Willoughby, *Opium as an International Problem* (Baltimore: Johns Hopkins Press, 1925), p. 492.

16. Advisory Committee on Traffic in Opium and Other Dangerous Drugs, "Report to Council on the Work of the Sixth Session," quoted in Willoughby, p. 374.

17. See Willoughby, p. 251.

18. League of Nations Advisory Committee on Traffic in Opium and Other Dangerous Drugs, "Position in Regard to Indian Hemp," Doc. no. O.C. 1542(a), 4 July 1934.

19.   Quoted in Willoughby, p. 539.

20.   Vandenberg to surgeon general, 10 Sept. 1929.

21.   Dr. Walter L. Treadway, Division of Mental Hygiene, Public Health Service, to G. A. Talbert, 27 May 1930.

22.   Draft response from Tennyson to request by Senate Finance Committee for Treasury Department views on S. 2075, 25 Nov. 1929.

23.   Memorandum from Rhees to H. J. Anslinger, secretary of Federal Narcotics Control Board, 15 Jan. 1930.

24.   Anslinger to Reed Smoot, chairman of the Senate Finance Committee, 28 June 1930.

25.   Nutt to Phipps, 25 Jan. 1929.

26.   Nutt to Phipps, 4 Jan. 1930.

27.   Doran to John M. Killet, federal district judge, Northern District of Ohio, 10 Jan. 1930; Anslinger to Smoot, 28 June 1930.

28.   Woodward to Anslinger, 28 Apr. 1930.

29.   Dr. F. O. Taylor, Special Committee of American Drug Manufacturer's Association, to Anslinger, 2 May 1930.

30.   Anslinger to Smoot, 28 June 1930.

31.   Anslinger to Joseph T. Swim, California narcotics chemist, 20 Aug. 1930.

32.   F. R. Gomila and M. C. Gomila Lambow, "Present Status of the Marihuana Vice in the United States," in *Marihuana: America's New Drug Problem*, ed. R. Walton (Philadelphia: Lippincott, 1938), p. 31.

33.   A. E. Fossier, "The Marihuana Menace," *New Orleans Medical and Surgical Journal*, 84 (1931), 247-52.

34.   E. Stanley, "Marihuana as a Developer of Criminals," *American Journal of Police Science*, 2 (1931), 256.

35.   Ibid., p. 257. It should be noted that Mr. Stanley's scientific bibliography was drawn entirely from Fossier's article, and we can presume that Mr. Stanley did not read these references himself. In addition to numerous medical dictionaries and pharmacology texts, the bibliography included a substantial number of foreign studies of cannabis intoxication. Interestingly enough, it also cited the Report of The Indian Hemp Drug Commission of 1893-94, whose conclusions had been diametrically opposed to the views expressed in the article. For some discussion of the state of scientific knowledge at this time, see chapter 7.

36.   Doyle to Hoover, 24 Jan. 1931.

37.   *New Orleans Times-Picayune*, 4 Jan. 1930, article attached to letter from Congressman Oscar De Prest of Illinois to L. C. Nutt, 13 Feb. 1930.

38.   J. B. Greeson, Narcotics agent-in-charge, New Orleans Division, to Anslinger, 29 June 1931.

39.   Will S. Wood to Greeson, 11 July 1931.

40.   Taylor, "Crime and the Foreign Born," *Wickersham Report*, no. 10.

41.   Ibid., pp. 199-329.

42.   Ibid., p. 407; Taylor, "More Bars Against Mexicans?" *The Survey*, 64 (1930), 26.

43.   Newspaper article dated "1931" and headlined "Marihuana, Deadly Drug, As Yet Unregulated by United States State Law," in the files of the Bureau of Narcotics and Dangerous Drugs.

44.   *Rocky Mountain News*, 27 Sept. 1931.

45.   *Denver Post*, 16 Apr. 1929, p. 2; 17 Apr. 1929, p. 2.

46.   *Denver Post*, 21 Apr. 1929; Colorado, *Colorado Laws* (1929), ch. 93.

47.   *Rocky Mountain News*, 27 Sept. 1931.

48.   Hayes and Bowery, "Marihuana," *Journal of Criminal Law and Criminology,*
23 (1932), 1086-94.

49.   See, e.g., *State v. Navaro,* 83 Utah 6, 14-15, 26 P.2d 955, 958 (1933).

50.   Taylor, "Crime and the Foreign Born," *Wickersham Report,* no. 10, pp. 199-
243. Dr. Taylor summarizes his findings on p. 242: "The statistical record of law
violations presented is on the whole, and in varying degrees, somewhat unfavorable to
Mexicans. This seems true, although in places their record is distinctly favorable. But
the use of statistics of arrests or convictions is open to serious criticism because racial
antipathies and political and economic helplessness of Mexicans swell the figures of
their apparent criminality. Mere conflict of codes, too, has the same effect. While the
United States sustains some shock from this conflict with the code brought with him
by the immigrant, it is not to be concluded therefrom that the immigrant is of an
inherently criminal breed." Although Dr. Taylor did not mention marihuana in this
connection, his article did refer several times to the fact that Mexican laborers were
spreading the practice of marihuana-smoking.

51.   Warshuis, "Crime and Criminal Justice Among the Mexicans of Illinois,"
Wickersham Report, no. 10, pp. 265-329.

52.   In a handwritten memorandum, "Subject--Marihuana," 17 Sept. 1931,
Anslinger indicated his personal attention to "Wickersham Commission Report on Crime
and the Foreign Born, pages 205, 281 and 381."

53.   *Wickersham Report,* no. 10, pp. 280-281.

54.   *Christian Science Monitor,* 12 Sept. 1931.

55.   *Christian Science Monitor,* 3 Oct. 1931.

56.   U.S., Treasury Department, Bureau of Narcotics, *Traffic in Opium and Other
Dangerous Drugs for the Year ended, December 31, 1931* (Washington, D.C.:GPO,
1932), p. 51

Chapter IV

1.   Dr. William White to Assistant Surgeon General Treadway, 3 Aug. 1932;
Dr. William Woodward to Dr. S. L. Hilton, 6 Aug. 1932.

2.   See New York, Senate, Joint Legislative Committee to Investigate the Laws
in Relation to the Distribution and Sale of Narcotic Drugs, *Final Report* (Albany, 1918),
Doc. no. 35: "No fixed policy exists for the enforcement of the State statutes except
in the larger cities of the State but their enforcement has been left to the desultory or
spasmodic efforts of local police officials . . .," quoted by Terry and Pellens, *The Opium
Problem* (New York: Prentice-Hall, 1928), p. 834. See also H. S. Becker, *Outsiders:
Studies in the Sociology of Deviance* (London: Free Press of Glencoe, 1963), pp. 137-38.

3.   Sandoz, "Report on Morphinism to the Municipal Court of Boston," *Journal
of Criminal Law and Criminology,* 13 (1922), 54 (emphasis original).

4.   *State Laws* (1931), pp. 31-34.

5.   Ibid., p. 28.

6.   See Special Committee to Investigate the Traffic in Narcotic Drugs, U.S.
Treasury Department Report, 1919.

7.   H. J. Anslinger and W. Tompkins, *The Traffic in Narcotics* (New York: Funk
& Wagnalls, 1953), p. 159.

8.   *1925 Handbook of the National Conference of Commissioners on Uniform
State Laws and Proceedings* (Baltimore: Lord Baltimore Press, 1925), pp. 977-85 (hereafter cited as *19 - - Handbook*).

9. Ibid., p. 978.
10. *1928 Handbook*, pp. 75-78, 323-33.
11. Ibid., pp. 76-77.
12. Nutt to Walter Clephane, chairman, Section on Social Welfare, Conference of Commissioners on Uniform State Laws, 12 July 1928.
13. Nutt to Clephane, 13 June 1929.
14. Nutt to Woodward, 4 Oct. 1929.
15. *1929 Handbook*, pp. 43, 332-40.
16. *1930 Handbook*, pp. 485-97.
17. Ibid., p. 493.
18. Woodward to Anslinger, 28 Apr. 1930.
19. *1930 Handbook*, pp. 126-27.
20. Anslinger to Woodward, Oct. 1932.
21. Anslinger to Woodward, 28 July 1930.
22. Anslinger to Woodward, 7 May 1931.
23. A. L. Tennyson, "Consideration of a Uniform State Narcotic Law by the National Conference of Commissioners of Uniform State Laws at Atlantic City, New Jersey, Sept. 9-12, 1931," memorandum for file dated 16 Sept. 1931.
24. *1931 Handbook*, pp. 127-28, 390-402.
25. *Christian Science Monitor*, 3 Oct. 1931.
26. Anslinger to Judge Deering, 1 Aug. 1932.
27. White to West, 1 July 1932.
28. West to White, 8 July 1932.
29. Woodward to White, 12 July 1932.
30. E. Brookmeyer, general counsel for the National Association of Retail Druggists, to Anslinger, 28 July 1932.
31. West to Treadway, 3 Aug. 1932; Woodward to Dr. S. L. Hilton, 6 Aug. 1932.
32. Woodward to Hilton, 6 Aug. 1932; Woodward to Anslinger, 30 July 1932.
33. Treadway to West, 25 July 1932.
34. Anslinger to Deering, 1 Aug. 1932.
35. Officer of the *Journal of American Pharmaceutical Association* to surgeon general, June 1929; Hugh Cummings to the *Journal of American Pharmaceutical Association*, 10 June 1929.
36. Woodward to Anslinger, 28 Apr. 1930.
37. Brookmeyer to Anslinger and Deering, June 1932.
38. Report of the Preliminary Conference Held in Federal Reserve Board Conference Room, Treasury Department, to discuss the Fifth Tentative Draft of the Uniform State Narcotic Law (Washington, D.C., 15 Sept. 1932), pp. 9-10.
39. Ibid., p. 23.
40. *1932 Handbook*, pp. 95-107, 326; see Tennyson, "Uniform State Narcotic Law," *Federal Bar Association Journal*, 1 (1935), 55; "Illicit Drug Traffic," *Federal Bar Association Journal*, 2 (1935), 208-9, indicating that the simple amendments for marihuana were desired by the bureau so that other drugs could be added in the same way.
41. *1932 Handbook*, p. 107.
42. From our own computations, the total time spent by all the commissioners discussing this act from 1927 to 1932 could not have exceeded one hour. Moreover, the small number of states present at the time of the roll call, as compared with the forty-eight that voted on the Uniform Machine Gun Act the day before, indicated that concern for this act was less than overwhelming.

Chapter V

1.   See, e.g., "New Giggle Drug Puts Discord in City Orchestras," *Chicago Tribune*, 1 July 1928.

2.   See, e.g., *New York Times*, 7 Oct. 1928, sec. 2, p. 4, col. 6.

3.   U.S., Congress, House, Committee on Ways and Means, *Hearings on H.R. 6385*, 75th Cong., 1st sess., 1937, H. Rept. 792, p. 20 (hereafter cited as House, *Hearings on H.R. 6385*).

4.   Dickson, "Bureaucracy and Morality: An Organizational Perspective on a Moral Crusade," *Social Problems*, 16 (1968), 143.

5.   H. S. Becker, *Outsiders: Studies in the Sociology of Deviance* (London: Free Press of Glencoe, 1963), pp. 137-45; see T. Duster, *The Legislation of Morality: Law, Drugs and Moral Judgment* (New York: The Free Press, 1970), pp. 17-19.

6.   King, "The Narcotics Bureau and the Harrison Act," *Yale Law Journal*, 62 (1953), 736-39.

7.   Bureau of Narcotics, U.S., Treasury Department, *Traffic in Opium and Other Dangerous Drugs* (Washington, D.C.: GPO, 1937), p. 59. See also Becker, *Outsiders*. It is interesting to note that Anslinger was reluctant to admit during the early years that the bureau was pressing in any organized way for state action. For example, in 1934 he noted: "I should hardly term it a campaign that is being pursued by this Bureau" (Anslinger to Gertrude Seymour, 14 July 1934).

8.   *New York Times*, 16 Sept. 1934, p. 6, col. 3.

9.   Text of radio broadcast by Isabelle O'Neill over JAR, Providence, R.I., 19 Feb. 1934.

10.   See, e.g., Federal Bureau of Narcotics pamphlet "Why the General Assembly of Virginia should Enact the Proposed Uniform Narcotic Drug Law"; see also Will S. Wood to Elizabeth Bass, 14 Dec. 1936.

11.   See, e.g., Anslinger to Frank Allen of the Cleveland *Plain Dealer*, 22 Oct. 1936.

12.   See, e.g., Anslinger to F. J. Reynolds, director of Readers Research Bureau, P. F. Collier and Son, 23 Dec. 1936.

13.   E.g., Anslinger, "The Reason for Uniform State Narcotic Legislation," *Georgetown Law Journal*, 21 (1932), 52; Tennyson, "Uniform State Narcotic Law," *Federal Bureau Association Journal*, 1 (Oct. 1932), 55. (Mr. Tennyson was legal advisor for the Bureau of Narcotics.)

14.   Anslinger to Stuart J. Fuller, Division of Far Eastern Affairs, Department of State, 29 Sept. 1933.

15.   Draft letter from Anslinger to Woodward, Mar. 1935 (subsequently rewritten).

16.   Will S. Wood, acting commissioner of Federal Bureau of Narcotics, to Woodward, 16 May 1933.

17.   *Washington Post*, 29 Sept. 1934.

18.   "Official Statement on the Need for Uniform Narcotic Drug Act," Federal Bureau of Narcotics White Paper circulated to all legislatures, July 1933.

19.   H. J. Anslinger, "The Need for Narcotic Education," speech over NBC, 24 Feb. 1936.

20.   Anslinger and Cooper, "Marihuana: Assassin of Youth," *American Magazine*, July 1937, p. 18.

21.   Aaron W. Uris to Anslinger, 21 May 1935.

22.   Wood to Uris, 5 June 1935.

23.   Woodward to Anslinger, 25 Oct. 1932.

24.   *Washington Herald, Atlanta Georgian, Detroit Times*, etc., 11 Sept. 1935. Someone should do a study on the activity of the Hearst papers on the drug front during the formative years.

25.   *Washington Herald*, 20 Feb. 1937.

26.   *Birmingham Age-Herald*, 22 Aug. 1935 (editorial).

27.   *Washington Post*, 29 Sept. 1934.

28.   Floyd K. Baskette to Federal Bureau of Narcotics, received 4 Sept. 1936.

29.   Anslinger to Baskette, 21 Sept. 1936.

30.   Anslinger to Frank Allen, 5 Oct. 1936.

31.   *Star-Times* (St. Louis), 17 Jan.-19 Feb. 1935.

32.   See bound yearly volumes of the *Union Signal* in the National Headquarters of the Women's Christian Temperance Union, 1730 Chicago Avenue, Evanston, Ill.

33.   Smith, CBS radio broadcast on "Narcotic Education," 21 Feb. 1935, at 1:00 p.m. (from Chicago studios).

34.   *Union Signal*, 13 Oct. 1934, p. 613.

35.   Ibid., 20 Apr. 1935.

36.   Ibid., 25 Jan. 1936, p. 54.

37.   Ibid., 16 Oct. 1937.

38.   House, *Hearings on H.R. 6385*, p. 24.

39.   *Union Signal*, 13 Oct. 1934, p. 613; 20 Apr. 1935, p. 248; 25 Jan. 1936, p. 53.

40.   *Rocky Mountain News*, 27 Sept. 1931.

41.   *Union Signal*, 20 Apr. 1935 (editorial).

42.   Ibid., 19 Sept. 1936, p. 567.

43.   Smith, "Narcotic Education."

44.   Unsigned memorandum to Surgeon General Hugh Cummings, May 1927.

45.   Dr. William C. White to Dr. Olin West, president of the American Medical Association, 1 July 1932.

46.   *Marihuana or Indian Hemp and Its Preparations*, pamphlet issued by the International Narcotic Education Association and the World Narcotic Defense Association (1936), p. 3.

47.   E.g., *Birmingham Age-Herald*, 22 Aug. 1935 (editorial); *Lansing Journal*, 1 Feb. 1935 (editorial).

48.   *Marihuana or Indian Hemp and Its Preparations*, p. 3.

49.   Wood to Roberta Lawson, president of General Federation of Women's Clubs, 13 Jan. 1936 (copy to Mr. Moorehead).

50.   *Clubwoman*, March 1937.

51.   Ibid.

52.   *Saratogian* (Saratoga, N. Y.), 9 Sept. 1936, p. 5.

53.   Anslinger to Agnes Regan, executive secretary of the National Council of Catholic Women, 28 Mar. 1935.

54.   Anslinger to Rev. John J. Burke, 1 Mar. 1935; see also Anslinger to R. L. Simpson, U.S. marshall, Jackson, Miss., 2 Jan. 1935.

55.   The act passed the house 88-0, *Virginia House Journal* (1934), p. 324, and the senate 34-0, *Virginia Senate Journal* (1934), pp. 300-301. The next month the legislature passed a bill (H.B. 236) prohibiting "use of . . . marihuana and loco weed . . . in the manufacture of cigarettes, cigars," or other tobacco products. Ch. 268 (1934) Virginia Acts of Assembly, p. 411. This law, which amended a 1910 statute prohibiting the use of opium in cigarettes, was the first mention of marihuana in the Virginia code.

56.   Wood to Robert Smith, commonwealth's attorney, 5 June 1935; Anslinger from B. M. Martin, district supervisor, 20 May 1935; J. Clarence Funk, director of Health and Education, to Anslinger, 12 Feb. 1937; Anslinger to Funk, 16 Feb. 1937.

57. *Virginia House Journal* (1936), p. 827; *Virginia Senate Journal* (1936), p. 498.

58. *Richmond Times-Dispatch*, 1 Mar. 1936, p. 12, col. 3.

59. The *Newark Star-Ledger* was surveyed from 20 May to 10 June 1933, a period surrounding the passage on 5 June 1933 of the statute in New Jersey (N.J. Acts [1933], ch. 186 p. 397). On the day of the signing of the bill, there appeared a short article noting that the Uniform Narcotic Drug Act had become law (*Newark Star-Ledger*, 5 June 1933, p. 2).

The statute in Rhode Island (R.I. Acts [1934], ch. 2096 p. 101), was approved 26 Apr. 1934. The *Providence Journal* was examined from 10 Apr. to 28 Apr. 1934. On 12 Apr. there appeared five sentences on the Uniform Act (p. 8). On 21 Apr. the law was described in a short article summarizing the business of the legislative session (p. 7). Neither article mentioned marihuana.

The Salem *Oregon Statesman*, in the period from 8 Feb. to 28 Feb. 1935, contained only one article dealing with drug legislation (21 Feb., p. 2, col. 2).

The Uniform Act was passed in West Virginia on 8 Mar. 1935 (W. Va. Acts [1935], ch. 46 p. 179). The *Charleston Daily Mail*, which carried detailed legislative news, was examined from 1 Mar. to 20 Mar. 1935. On 1 Mar. the legislature reconvened under a special calendar including the Uniform Act. During this period, the act attracted little attention except for an editorial on 7 Mar. (*Charleston Daily Mail*, 7 Mar. 1935, p. 10, col. 1). The bill was mentioned in passing in two other stories on upcoming legislation, and in a report that a federal judge criticized West Virginia's failure to enact the act (*Charleston Daily Mail*, 6 Mar. 1935, p. 6, col. 4).

60. *Charleston Daily Mail*, 7 Mar. 1935, p. 10, col. 1.

61. D. A. Rosboro, member Federation of Women's Clubs, to Anslinger, 9 Mar. 1937.

62. *Washington Herald*, 12 Apr. 1937.

Chapter VI

1. Anslinger to Ms. M. M. Moad, 1 Oct. 1932.

2. Anslinger to Congressman Hamilton Fish, Jr., 28 Aug. 1933.

3. Memorandum from Tennyson to Anslinger, 1 Aug. 1933.

4. Memorandum from B. M. Martin, local supervisor, to agents, 13 Mar. 1934.

5. Memorandum from Will S. Wood to Assistant Secretary Gibbons, 13 Mar. 1935.

6. Morganthau to Senator Fletcher, 13 Apr. 1935.

7. Memorandum on marihuana from Gibbons to Oliphant, 5 Oct. 1936. Musto's research tends to confirm our hypothesis that a "political" decision was made in 1935 to seek federal legislation. See Musto, "The Marihuana Tax Act of 1937," *Archives of General Psychiatry*, 26 (1972), 101, 105.

8. Memorandum from Tennyson to Anslinger, 28 May 1935.

9. Memorandum from Anslinger to Gibbons, 1 Feb. 1936.

10. Ibid.

11. *Missouri* v. *Holland*, 252 U.S. 416 (1920).

12. Memorandum from Oliphant to Gibbons, 13 Oct. 1936.

13. Memorandum from Gibbons to Oliphant, 5 Oct. 1936.

14. Memorandum from Oliphan to Gibbons, 13 Oct. 1936.

15. Taylor, *American Diplomacy and the Narcotics Traffic, 1900-1939* (Durham: Duke Univ. Press, 1969), pp. 200-203.

16.   Memorandum from Anslinger to Thomas J. Morrissey, U.S. attorney for Denver, Colo., 22 Dec. 1936.

17.   It is interesting to note that in testimony before the House Appropriations Committee on the Treasury budget, Anslinger emphasized the marihuana problem but did not indicate that the administration was preparing a bill:

Anslinger: I might say that the marihuana problem seems to be jumping up. . . .

Mr. Ludlow: That is about as hellish a drug as heroin, it it not?

Anslinger: I think it is. It is certainly showing up in the crime situation. We find a number of violent crimes committed while persons were under the influence of marihuana.

(*Union Signal*, 6 Mar. 1937.)

18.   *Union Signal*, 30 Jan. 1937, p. 66. The Hatch Bill was styled S. 325, 75th Cong., 1st sess., Jan. 1937, and the Fish Bill was styled H.R. 229, 75th Cong., 1st sess., Jan. 1937.

19.   *Union Signal*, 6 Mar. 1937, p. 146.

20.   *Union Signal*, 15 May 1937, p. 306.

21.   *Sonzinsky* v. *United States*, 86 F. 2d 486 (7th Cir. 1936).

22.   *Sonzinsky* v. *United States*, 300 U.S. 506 (1937).

Chapter VII

1.   League of Nations, Advisory Committee on Traffic in Opium and Other Dangerous Drugs, Subcommittee on Cannabis, Doc. no. O.C.1707, Report, by Stuart Fuller on 3d Session of Subcommittee on Meetings of June 2, 7, and 9, June 9, 1937.

2.   See Floyd E. Moore, Marihuana Conference (Washington, D.C., 5 Dec. 1938).

3.   Hugh S. Cummings, *Preliminary Report on Indian Hemp and Peyote* (Washington, D.C.: GPO, 1929).

4.   S. Solis-Cohen and T. S. Githens, *Pharmaco-Therapeutics* (New York: Appleton, 1928), p. 1702.

5.   *Marijuana: Report of the Indian Hemp Drugs Commission, 1893-1894* (Silver Spring, Md.: Thomas Jefferson Co., 1969), p. 263.

6.   Memorandum for File written by Guy Johannes 2 Apr. 1925, "Canal Zone Report," 18 Dec. 1925, p. 1.

7.   Letter and memorandum from Edgar A. Bocock to Major Meriwether Smith, judge advocate, 8 Apr. 1923, "Canal Zone Papers," pp. 24-25.

8.   Canal Zone, Committee on Use of Marihuana, testimony of Lt. Col. William C. Rigby, judge advocate, 5 Dec. 1925, "Canal Zone Papers," p. 31; testimony of Capt. Otto Christian, medical corps, before general court-martial, included in letter from Lt. Col. Rigby to Col. W. P. Chamberlain, chief health officer, 16 Dec. 1925, "Canal Zone Papers," p. 112.

9.   Memorandum for File written by Johannes 2 Apr. 1925, "Canal Zone Papers," p. 1.

10.   Memorandum for the governor from Chamberlain, 4 Apr. 1925, "Canal Zone Papers," p. 3.

11.   Preliminary Report on the Physiological Test of Locally Grown Marihuana (*Cannabis sativa L.*), letter from Bates to chief health officer, Balboa Heights, 15 July 1925, "Canal Zone Papers," pp. 18-21; Second Report on the Physiological Test of Locally Grown Marihuana (*Cannabis sativa L.*), letter from Bates to chief health officer, Balboa Heights, 1 Dec. 1925, "Canal Zone Papers," pp. 59-60; Third Report on the

Physiological Test of Locally Grown Marihuana (*Cannabis sativa L.*), letter from Bates to chief health officer, Balboa Heights, 17 Dec. 1925, "Canal Zone Papers," pp. 117-22.

12.   Third Report, letter from Bates to chief health officer, Balboa Heights, 17 Dec. 1925, "Canal Zone Papers," p. 120.

13.   "Canal Zone Report," 18 Dec. 1925, p. 3.

14.   Ibid., p. 2.

15.   Ibid., pp. 133-34.

16.   Article from Alumni Report of the Philadelphia College of Pharmacy, Nov. 1905, quoted in letter from R. F. Chutter, associate export manager, H. H. Mulford Company, Manufacturing and Biological Chemists, to G. E. Hesner, Health Department, Corozal Hospital, 27 Feb. 1925, "Canal Zone Papers," p. 62.

17.   "Marihuana: Mexican Name for Cannabis, Also Called Loco Weed in Certain Parts of Texas," memorandum by Ball, May 1922, "Canal Zone Papers," p. 60.

18.   "The Effects of Haschisch Not Due to Cannabis Indica," memorandum by Ball, "Canal Zone Papers," p. 54.

19.   J. S. Siler et al., "Marihuana Smoking in Panama," *Military Surgeon*, 73 (1933), 269-80.

20.   W. Bromberg, "Marihuana Intoxication: A Clinical Study of Cannabis Sativa Intoxication," *American Journal of Psychiatry*, 91 (1934), 303.

21.   "Use of Cannabis Indica," proof of article to appear in *Journal of the American Medical Association* attached to letter from editor of the *JAMA* to Hesner, 12 Mar. 1925, "Canal Zone Papers," p. 64.

22.   League of Nations, Advisory Committee on Traffic in Opium and Other Dangerous Drugs, Report prepared by Dr. J. Bouquet [O.C. 1542 (0)], 17 Feb. 1937, pp. 33-34.

23.   R. Walton, ed., *Marihuana: America's New Drug Problem* (Philadelphia: Lippincott, 1938), p. 130.

24.   Ibid., p. 139.

25.   T. Ireland, "Insanity from the Abuse of Indian Hemp," *Alienist and Neurologist*, 14 (1893), 622-30, citing Wise study in 1873; see also N. Cheevers, *A Manual of Medical Jurisprudence for India* (Calcutta: Thacker, Spink, 1870).

26.   J. E. Dhunjibhoy, "A Brief Resume of the Types of Insanity Commonly Met Within India With a Full Description of 'Indian Hemp Insanity' Peculiar to the Country," *Journal of Medical Sciences*, 76 (1930), 254-61.

27.   Walton, *Marihuana*, p. 144.

28.   Minutes of Private Meeting of Special Subcommittee on Cannabis of League of Nations Advisory Committee on Traffic in Opium and Other Dangerous Drugs, 2 May 1937 (remarks of Chairman Fuller).

29.   Ibid., 7 June 1937.

30.   Walton, *Marihuana*, pp. 146, 149.

31.   Bragman, "The Weed of Insanity," *Medical Journal and Record*, 122 (1925), 416-18.

32.   J. Mandel, "Hashish, Assassins, and the Love of God," *Issues in Criminology*, 2 (1966), 153.

33.   L. Grinspoon, *Marijuana Reconsidered* (Cambridge: Harvard Univ. Press, 1971), p. 425, n. 2.

34.   Cummings, *Preliminary Report on Indian Hemp and Peyote.*

35.   Stanley, "Marihuana as a Developer of Criminals," *American Journal of Police Science*, 2 (1931), 252.

36.   A. E. Fossier, "The Marihuana Menace," *New Orleans Medical and Surgical Journal*, 84 (1931), 247.

37. *Christian Science Monitor*, 3 Oct. 1931.

38. Circular Letter no. 458 from Anslinger to all agents, 1938.

39 . League of Nations, Advisory Committee on Traffic in Opium and Other Dangerous Drugs, *Position in Regard to Indian Hemp* [O.C. 1542 (a)], 4 July 1934.

40. League of Nations, Advisory Committee on Traffic in Opium and Other Dangerous Drugs, *The Abuse of Cannabis in the United States (Addendum)* [O.C. 1542 (L)], 10 Nov. 1934. (Memorandum forwarded by the representative of the United States of America.)

41. Siler, "Marihuana Smoking in Panama."

42. Bromberg, "Marihuana Intoxication."

43. See Anslinger's confidential note dated 21 Dec. 1934, attached to a letter from the U.S. marshall in Tulsa to the Bureau of Narcotics, 18 Dec. 1934: "The second paragraph in page 2 regarding the killing undoubtedly refers to the murder by the son of Federal Judge Kennamer. U.S. Attorney Eastus at Dallas, Texas also told me confidentially that the killing was attributed to the use of marihuana."

44. E.g., Will S. Wood to Aaron Uris, 5 June 1935.

45. E.g., Wood to Robert S. Smith, commonwealth's attorney, Roanoke, Va., 5 June 1935.

46. Memorandum from Tennyson to Wood, 18 June 1935.

47. Anslinger to Otto and R. Schlabach, 14 Apr. 1936.

48. William Spillard to Anslinger, 30 Mar. 1936.

49. Anslinger to F. J. Reynolds, director of the Readers Research Bureau, *Collier's*, 23 Dec. 1936.

50. Note from H. E. Gaston to Anslinger, 23 Dec. 1936.

51. Anslinger and Cooper, "Marihuana: Assassin of Youth," *American Magazine*, July 1937, pp. 19, 150.

52. See, e.g., *Union Signal*, 30 Jan. 1937, p. 75.

53. H. S. Becker, *Outsiders: Studies in the Sociology of Deviance* (London: Free Press of Glencoe, 1963), pp. 141-42.

54. Walton, *Marihuana*, p. 2.

55. League of Nations, Advisory Committee on Traffic in Opium and Other Dangerous Drugs, Report prepared by Treadway, June 1937.

56. Fossier, "The Marihuana Menace," 247.

57. League of Nations, Advisory Committee on Traffic in Opium and Other Dangerous Drugs, Report prepared by Dr. J. Bouquet [O.C. 1542 (o)], 17 Feb. 1937, pp. 27-28.

58. Walton, *Marihuana*, pp. 10-11.

59. Ibid., p. 13.

Chapter VIII

1. House, *Hearings on H.R. 6385*, p. 30.

2. Ibid., pp. 32-42.

3. U.S., Congress, Senate, Finance Committee Subcommittee, *Hearings on H.R. 6906*, 75th Cong., 1st sess., 1937, pp. 11-14 (hereafter cited as Senate, *Hearings on H.R. 6906*).

4. House, *Hearings on H.R. 6385*, pp. 48-52.

5. Ibid., pp. 32-37.

6. Senate, *Hearings on H.R. 6906*, pp. 14-15.

7. Ibid.
8. See generally H. S. Becker, *Outsiders: Studies in the Sociology of Deviance* (London: Free Press of Glencoe, 1963).
9. Senate, *Hearings on H.R. 6906*, p. 16.
10. House, *Hearings on H.R. 6385*, p. 26.
11. Ibid., pp. 59-65, 67-86.
12. Ibid., pp. 87-88.
13. Ibid., p. 92.
14. Ibid., p. 100.
15. Ibid., p. 118. See also pp. 117, 120.
16. Act of 14 June 1930, ch. 488, 46 Stat. 585.
17. House, *Hearings on H.R. 6385*, p. 93.
18. Ibid., p. 94.
19. Ibid., pp. 94-95.
20. Ibid., p. 95.
21. Ibid., p. 97.
22. Ibid., pp. 100-102.
23. Ibid., pp. 102-5.
24. Ibid., pp. 105-6, 110.
25. Ibid., pp. 115-16.
26. Senate, *Hearings on H.R. 6906*, pp. 33-34.
27. U.S., Congress, House, Committee on Ways and Means, 75th Cong., 1st sess., 11 May 1937, H. Rept. 292, pp. 1-2.
28. *81 Congressional Record* (1937), p. 5575.
29. Ibid., pp. 5689-92.
30. Ibid., pp. 7624-25.
31. Ibid., p. 7625.

Chapter IX

1. Dickson, "Bureaucracy and Morality: An Organizational Perspective on a Moral Crusade," *Social Problems*, 16 (1968), 143.
2. Memorandum from Wollner to Anslinger, 14 Feb. 1938.
3. See, e.g., *State* v. *Diaz*, 76 Utah 463, 200 P. 727 (1930), where a defendant in a first-degree murder prosecution tried to disprove the requisite *mens rea* by showing that he was under the influence of marihuana at the time of the offense. Diaz had claimed that "his mind was an entire blank as to all that happened to him and stated that after smoking the marijuana he became 'very crazy.'" To corroborate his assertion, defendant summoned a physician whose testimony was summarized by the court: "He stated that [marihuana] is a narcotic and acts upon the central nervous system affecting the brain, producing exhilarating effects and causing one to do things which he otherwise would not do and especially induces acts of violence; that violence is one of the symptoms of an excessive use of marijuana. . . ; that the marijuana produces an 'I don't care' effect. A man having used liquor and marijuana might deliberately plan a robbery and killing and carry it out and escape, and then later fail to remember anything that had occurred." In a later case, *State* v. *Navaro*, 83 Utah 6, 26 P.2d 955 (1933), the court rejected a constitutional attack by expounding on the evils of the drug; in this connection, the court relied heavily on the physician's testimony in *Diaz*.

4.   Sidney Benbow to Anslinger, 7 July 1937, quoted in Senate, *Hearings on H.R. 6906*, p. 11.

5.   Richard Hartshorne to Charles Schwarz, 18 Mar. 1937; quoted in Senate, *Hearings on H.R. 6906*, p. 11.

6.   See letters from district supervisors to Anslinger, 12 Nov. 1938, 24 Sept. 1938, 2 June 1938, 14 June 1938, 16 Jan. 1939, 1 Dec. 1938.

7.   Anslinger to Williams, 11 Apr. 1938.

8.   Anslinger to Munch, 14 Apr. 1938.

9.   Anslinger to Williams, 4 June 1938.

10.   Judge J. Foster Symes, quoted in *Traffic in Opium and Other Dangerous Drugs* (Washington, D.C.: GPO, 1937), p. 57.

11.   District supervisor of Philadelphia to Anslinger, 5 Feb. 1938.

12.   D. B. Martin to Anslinger, 19 Nov. 1938. File no. 0380-9-M.

13.   *Traffic in Opium* (1937), p. 80. For a full and effective discussion of the flaws in these drug statistics from 1937 until the mid-1940s due to a confusion over what parts of the marihuana plant were to be weighed in determining how much of the drug had been seized, see Mandel, "Problems with Official Drug Statistics," *Stanford Law Review*, 21 (1969), 998-99.

14.   Confidential memorandum from Anslinger to all district supervisors, 14 Dec. 1937.

15.   The La Guardia Report concluded in 1944 that "the sale and distribution of marihuana is not under the control of any single organized group." Mayor's Committee on Marihuana, *The Marihuana Problem in the City of New York* (New York: Jaques Cattell, 1944), p. 25 (hereafter cited as La Guardia Report).

16.   See Federal Bureau of Narcotics File no. 04 80-36-22, Book 1; File no. 1245, Book 1.

17.   See chap. 11, inf. n. 35.

18.   *Minneapolis Tribune*, 11 Feb. 1938.

19.   Berman to district supervisor, New York, N.Y., 11 Feb. 1938. File: Marijuana and Musicians, 1938-53 (hereafter referred to as M & M).

20.   Joseph Bell to Berman, 15 Feb. 1938; letter from Bell to Anslinger, 23 Feb. 1938. File: M & M.

21.   Detroit Federation of Musicians, *Keynote*, Jan.-Feb. 1941. File: M & M.

22.   Thomas W. Andrew, FBN agent, to Ralph H. Oyler, 19 Mar. 1941.

23.   Memorandum for files from Anslinger.

24.   *Los Angeles Daily News*, 22 Aug. 1941.

25.   Berman to Anslinger, 8 Sept. 1941.

26.   Memorandum for files from Anslinger.

27.   Anslinger to all district supervisors, 7 Sept. 1943.

28.   Joseph A. Manning, district supervisor, to Anslinger, 11 Nov. 1944, 9 Nov. 1944, 7 Oct. 1944, 5 Oct. 1944.

29.   Anslinger to all district supervisors, 19 Dec. 1944.

30.   R. W. Artis, district supervisor, to Anslinger, 9 Feb. 1945.

31.   Memorandum Report, Bureau of Narcotics, New York, N.Y., 4 May 1953.

32.   Draft letter by Anslinger, 22 Nov. 1948.

33.   Testimony of Anslinger before House Ways and Means Committee, 1 Mar. 1949.

34.   *Downbeat*, April 1949, p. 10.

35.   Memorandum, Bureau of Narcotics, District 2, from John T. Cusack, agent, 7 Nov. 1951; Anslinger to M. Sicot, secretary general, International Criminal Police Commission, 26 Feb. 1951; memorandum from Anslinger to agent, returned with "too vague" scrawled across it, 27 Nov. 1951.

Chapter X

1. Memorandum from Wollner to Anslinger, 14 Feb. 1938, p. 1.
2. Ibid., p. 2.
3. Anslinger to Fuller, assistant secretary of state, 9 Nov. 1938.
4. Memorandum from Anslinger to Assistant Secretary Gibbons, 29 Nov. 1938. Participating in the conference were: H. J. Anslinger, commissioner of narcotics; Dr. H. H. Wright, professor of agronomy, University of Wisconsin; Mr. Frank Smith, chief of Drug Control, state of New York; Dr. B. B. Robinson, Bureau of Plant Industry, Department of Agriculture; Dr. John R. Matchett, chief chemist, Bureau of Narcotics; Mr. Henry Fuller, consulting chemist; Dr. James C. Munch, professor of pharmacology, Temple University; Dr. S. Loewe, pharmacologist, Cornell University Medical College; Dr. Walter Bromberg, senior psychiatrist, Department of Hospitals, New York City; H. J. Wollner, consulting chemist, Treasury Department; Dr. A. H. Blatt, Howard University; Mr. Joseph Levine, chemist, Bureau of Narcotics; Mr. Louis Benjamin, chemist, Treasury Department; Dr. H. M. Lancaster, chief dominion analyst, Canadian government; Dr. James Couch, Pathological Division, Bureau of Animal Industry, Department of Agriculture.
5. Report of Marihuana Conference held in the U.S. Bureau of Internal Revenue Building, room 3003, Washington, D.C., 5 Dec. 1938, pp. 133-34, 141-42.
6. Ibid., p. 106.
7. Ibid.
8. For a complete review of these articles see Lester Grinspoon, *Marijuana Reconsidered* (Cambridge: Harvard Univ. Press, 1971).
9. Senate, *Hearings on H.R. 6906*, p. 14.
10. "Marihuana," Federal Bureau of Narcotics In-House Paper (1938), p. 23. Authorship: "IAON/jel."
11. J. D. Fraser, "Withdrawal Symptoms in Cannabis Indica Addicts," *Lancet*, 2 (1949), 747-48, and Marcovitz and Meyers, "The Marihuana Addict in the Army," *War Medicine*, 6 (1944), 382-91, did report withdrawal symptoms in heavy users. And Bouquet, "Marihuana Intoxication," a letter to the *Journal of the American Medical Association*, 124 (1944), 1010-11, reported mild withdrawal in heavy users.
12. Kolb's "An Authoritative Treatise on Marihuana" appeared both in *The Recorder*, 12 Sept. 1938, and in *Federal Probation*, July 1938.
13. George C. Schicks, "Marihuana: Depraver of Youth," *Druggists Circular* (1938), 6. Mr. Schicks was assistant dean, Rutgers University College of Pharmacy.
14. Merrill, "Marihuana: Hashish in Modern Dress," *American Foreign Service Journal*, May 1939, p. 265.
15. Walter Bromberg, "Marihuana: A Psychiatric Study," reprint from the *Journal of the American Medical Association* (1 July 1939), p. 1. This article had been read before the New York Academy of Medicine, 11 Oct. 1938, and also at the Marihuana Conference two months later.
16. S. Allentuck and K. M. Bowman, "The Psychiatric Aspects of Marihuana Intoxication," *American Journal of Psychiatry*, 99 (1942), 249.
17. La Guardia Report, p. 146.
18. E. G. Williams et al, "Studies on Marihuana and Pyrahedge Compound," *Public Health Reports*, 61 (1946), 1059-83.
19. E. A. Murphy, federal narcotics agent, to Garland Williams, assistant narcotics supervisor, 20 May 1938, p. 2.
20. See, e.g., H. J. Anslinger's 1940 compilation "Marihuana Research," reprinted from the 1938 *Convention Book of the Association of Medical Students*.
21. La Guardia Report, p. 141.

22. H. L. Freedman and M. J. Rockmore, "Marihuana: A Factor in Personality Evaluation and Army Maladjustment," *Journal of Clinical Psychopathology*, 7 (1946), 365-82 (Part 1), and 8 (1946), 221-36 (Part 2).

23. Bromberg, "Marihuana: A Psychiatric Study."

24. Allentuck and Bowman, "Psychiatric Aspects."

25. La Guardia Report, p. 51.

26. H. S. Becker, "History, Culture and Subjective Experience: An Elaboration of the Social Bases of Drug-Induced Experiences," *Journal of Health and Social Behaviour*, 8 (1967), 172.

27. T. F. Middlebrooks, district supervisor in Houston to all agents and reply of 16 Apr. 1943. See also Anslinger to Dr. Ball, 18 Oct. 1937, and "Marihuana and Insanity," Federal Bureau of Narcotics file, specifically, Anslinger to Fuller, Kolb, etc., 23 Jan. 1940.

28. M. C. Harney to Anslinger, 12 Mar. 1940.

29. Ibid. See also *Daily Oklahoman* (Oklahoma City), 16 Mar. 1940, reporting the lack of effect of marihuana in the alertness of the dogs in Dr. Lowe's study.

30. Dr. Jorge Sequra Millan, a student of Dr. Salazar-Viniegra, authored a pamphlet in 1939 *La Marihuana, studio Medico y Social* [Marihuana: medical and social study] extolling his teacher's work. A translation of this pamphlet appears in the bureau's files attached to a memorandum to Anslinger from J. Bulkley, 28 Aug. 1943.

31. Ibid., p. 4.

32. Ibid., p. 5.

33. Ibid.

34. "Report of the 5th Session of the Cannabis Subcommittee of the League of Nations." Memorandum from Anslinger to secretary of treasury, 16 June 1939.

35. Ibid.

36. Ibid.

37. B. Martin, district supervisor, to Mr. H. G. McAllister, secretary of the Pharmacy Board of North Carolina, 31 Mar. 1950.

38. See, e.g., F. T. Merrill, *Marihuana: The New Dangerous Drug* (Washington, D.C.: Opium Research Committee, Foreign Policy Association, Inc., March 1938). See generally H. S. Becker, *Outsiders: Studies in the Sociology of Deviance* (London: Free Press of Glencoe, 1963), pp. 141-42.

39. Schicks, "Marihuana: Depraver of Youth."

40. Anslinger to Dr. James C. Munch, 14 Apr. 1938. File. no. 0480-36 Gen.

41. Anslinger to Joseph Manning, 12 Apr. 1938.

42. Circular Letter no. 458.

43. "Hearing Federal Legislation Marihuana will be held before House Ways and Means Committee Ten AM Tuesday Twenty-Seventh stop please Endeavor to attend HJA." Telegram from Anslinger to Munch, 26 Apr. 1937. File no. 0480-36 Gen.

44. T. W. McGeever, district supervisor, to Anslinger, 6 Apr. 1938 (in file on *Sohl* case). This letter followed the agent's interviews with Ethel Sohl and her convicted codefendant, her parents, and the defendants' husbands. In further investigation, Agent McGeever interviewed Mr. McLaughlin, Ethel Sohl's attorney, with reference to a newspaper report that he had introduced marihuana cigarettes into evidence at the trial. The attorney denied he had done so and expressed great anger at McGeever's having interviewed his client in jail without his permission. Moreover, McLaughlin said he thought the publicity the defense had given the marihuana issue would be of great help to all those trying to enforce the marihuana laws.

45. *New York Post*, 7 Apr. 1938.

46. Anslinger to Williams, 9 Apr. 1938. File no. 0480-36 Gen.

47. Ibid.

48. File record of telephone call to Williams, 12 Apr. 1938. File no. 0480-36 Gen.

49. Munch to Anslinger, 19 Apr. 1938. File no. 0480-36 Gen.

50. Kolb stated that "the prevalent opinion that anyone who smokes a marihuana cigarette and becomes intoxicated by it will have criminal impulses is in error." Kolb, "Authoritative Treatise."

51. Memorandum to file by Will S. Wood, acting commissioner, 6 May 1938.

52. Bromberg, "Marihuana: A Psychiatric Study."

53. N. S. Kwager, "Marihuana: Our New Addiction," *American Journal of the Medical Sciences*, 195 (1938), 354.

54. Ibid., pp. 355-56.

55. Allentuck and Bowman, p. 249.

56. Freedman and Rockmore, "Marihuana: A Factor in Personality Evaluation."

57. W. Bromberg and T. C. Rogers, "Marihuana and Aggressive Crime," *American Journal of Psychiatry*, 102 (1946), 825-27.

58. S. Charen and L. Perelman, "Personality Studies of Marihuana Addicts," *American Journal of Psychiatry*, 102 (1946), 674-82; Marcovitz and Meyers, "The Marihuana Addict in the Army."

59. Kolb, transcript of comments on Allentuck and Bowman study, 1942. FBN File no. 0480-36-9.

60. Editorial, "Recent Investigation of Marihuana," *Journal of the American Medical Association*, 120 (1942), 1128-29.

61. Anslinger, "The Psychiatric Aspects of Marihuana Intoxication," letter to the *Journal of the American Medical Association*, 121 (1943), 212-13.

62. Bouquet, "Marihuana Intoxication," letter to the *Journal of the American Medical Association*, 124 (1944), 1010-11.

63. Kolb, transcript of comments, 1942.

64. La Guardia Report, p. 25.

65. Editorial, "Marihuana Problems," *Journal of the American Medical Association*, 127 (1945), 1129.

66. Walton, "Marihuana Problems," letter to the editor of the *Journal of the American Medical Association*, 128 (1945), 283.

67. Bowman, "Marihuana Problems," letter to the editor of the *Journal of the American Medical Association*, 128 (1945), 889-90.

68. Marcovitz, "Marihuana Problems," letter to the editor of the *Journal of the American Medical Association*, 129 (1945), 378.

69. R. N. Chopra and G. S. Chopra, "The Present Position of Hemp-Drug Addiction in India," *Indian Medical Research Memoirs*, 31 (1939), 1-119; "Use of Hemp Drugs in India," *Indian Medical Gazette*, 75 (1940), 356-67; "*Cannabis Sativa* in Relation to Mental Diseases and Crime in India," *Indian Journal of Medical Research*, 30 (1942), 155-71.

70. Anslinger, "More on Marihuana and Mayor La Guardia's Committee Report," letter to editor of the *Journal of the American Medical Association*, 178 (1945), 1187.

71. J. M. Pholen, "The Marihuana Bugaboo," *Military Surgeon*, 93 (1943), 94-95.

72. See, e.g., the quotation attributed to Dr. J. D. Reichard of Lexington Hospital in the 4 Mar. 1947 editorial of the *New York Times* where he allegedly debunked seven myths about marihuana; see also, Report of Agent Murphy transmitted to Anslinger by Supervisor Williams, 20 May 1938.

Chapter XI

1. Act of 2 Nov. 1951, ch. 666, 65 Stat. 767. Between 1937 and 1951 the Uniform Narcotic Drug Act was amended to change the definition of cannabis from the flowering or fruiting tops of just the female plant to include the corresponding parts of the male plant. See *1943 Handbook*, pp. 172-73.
2. 21 U.S.C. § 174 (1964).
3. 26 U.S.C. §§ 4741-76 (1964).
4. Peyton Ford to Congressman Hale Boggs, 14 Apr. 1950. File: 1245 Legislation.
5. U.S., Congress, Senate, Special Committee to Investigate Organized Crime in Interstate Commerce, *Hearings*, 82d Cong., 1st sess., 1951, pt. 14, exhibit 1, pp. 131, 240-41, 266 (hereafter cited as *Kefauver Committee Hearings*).
6. Ibid., pt. 14, p. 235. See also *New York Times*, 19 June 1951, p. 25, col. 1.
7. *Kefauver Committee Hearings*, pt. 14, p. 382.
8. *97 Congressional Record* (1951), pp. 8197-98.
9. Ibid., pp. 8198-8204.
10. Ibid., p. 8211.
11. Ibid., p. 8198 (as quoted by Congressman Boggs). See also *Kefauver Committee Hearings*, pt. 14, pp. 430-31 (testimony of Commissioner Anslinger).
12. *97 Congressional Record* (1951), p. 8198.
13. Ibid., p. 8196.
14. Memorandum from Peyton Ford, assistant to attorney general, to Anslinger, 17 July 1950.
15. Anslinger to Jack Lynch, 21 Aug. 1951. File: 1245 Legislation.
16. "H.R. 8355—Bill Introduced by Representative Boggs to provide minimum penalties for violation of Narcotic Laws," memorandum from Hugh Spaulding to Hansen and Carlock, Treasury Department, 29 Sept. 1950. File: 1245 Legislation.
17. *97 Congressional Record* (1951), p. 8209.
18. Alex Bradford to Anslinger, 26 June 1951. File: 1245 Legislation.
19. *Washington Post*, 12 Aug. 1951, p. 4B, col. 1.
20. *Evening Star* (Washington), 5 Oct. 1951, p. A-10, col. 1.
21. *St. Louis Medical Society Bulletin*, March 1951. File: 1245 Legislation.
22. *Los Angeles Times*, 25 May 1951. File: 1245 Legislation.
23. "Raps Present Law on Dope Traffic Fight," *Los Angeles Daily News*, 18 June 1951.
24. Spaulding to John K. Carlock, assistant general counsel, 24 Sept. 1950; Anslinger to Carlock, 23 Oct. 1951.
25. Congressman Keating questioned the constitutionality of the provision (*97 Congressional Record* [1951], p. 8206). Apparently Keating accepted Congressman Harrison's statement that the language had been in the statutory predecessors for years and had been passed on by the Supreme Court (ibid., p. 8211).
26. *97 Congressional Record* (1951), p. 8207.
27. Ibid., p. 8206.
28. Ibid., p. 8197.
29. P. A. Williams, district supervisor, to Anslinger, 2 June 1953. File: 1245 Legislation.
30. Thomas E. McGuire, federal narcotic agent, to Williams, 28 May 1953 (sic). File: 1245 Legislation.
31. Ibid.
32. *New Orleans Statesman*, 28 May 1954; *New Orleans Times-Picayune*, 28 May 1954.

33. *New Orleans Times-Picayune*, 12 June 1954.

34. Robert J. Caldwell to Pearson, 27 Aug. 1951. File: 1245 Legislation.

35. The FBN reports tend to reflect an increase in seizures and arrests after World War II. For statistics on marihuana enforcement by state and municipal authorities from 1936 to 1941, see Bureau of Narcotics, U.S., Treasury Department, *Traffic in Opium and Other Dangerous Drugs* (Washington, D.C.: GPO, 1935), p. 63 (hereafter cited as *Traffic in Opium*); ibid. (1936), p. 57; ibid. (1937), p. 81; ibid. (1938), p. 80; ibid. (1940), p. 73; ibid. (1941), p. 38. For statistics on the amount of marihuana seized by federal agents from 1939-45, see *Traffic in Opium* (1939), p. 78; ibid. (1940), p. 72; ibid. (1941), p. 37; ibid. (1942), p. 49; ibid. (1943), p. 42; ibid. (1944), p. 34; ibid. (1945), p. 23. For figures on the amounts seized and the number of federal marihuana arrests during the period 1946-51, see *Traffic in Opium* (1946), pp. 23, 27; ibid. (1947), pp. 28, 29; ibid. (1948), pp. 23, 28; ibid. (1949), pp. 22, 26; ibid. (1950), pp. 29, 33; ibid. (1951), pp. 25, 29.

For a full and persuasive discussion of the flaws in these drug statistics from 1937 until the mid-1940s due to a confusion over what parts of the marihuana plant were to be weighed in determining how much of the drug had been seized, see Mandel, "Problems with Official Drug Statistics," *Stanford Law Review*, 21 (1969), 998-99.

36. Statement of Judge Alex N. MacLeod, Passaic County, N.J. File: 1245 Legislation.

37. U.S., Congress, House, Committee on Ways and Means, Subcommittee on Narcotics, *Hearings on H.R. 3490*, 82d Cong., 1st sess., 1951, p. 147 (hereafter cited as *Boggs Act Hearings*).

38. Ibid., pp. 147-48. Dr. Isbell's paper stated: "Any definition [of addiction] which makes (physical) dependence an essential feature will also not include intoxications with such substances as cocaine, marijuana, and amphetamine, because (physical) dependence on these substances is no more marked than is dependence on tobacco and coffee, and yet, in some ways, intoxication with cocaine or marijuana is more harmful than is addiction to morphine. Furthermore, definitions which exclude cocaine and marijuana from the list of addicting drugs would cause endless confusion because, in common parlance and legally, both drugs are regarded as addicting."

39. *Kefauver Committee Hearings*, pt. 14, p. 119.

40. *Boggs Act Hearings*, p. 206.

41. *Kefauver Committee Hearings*, pt. 14, pp. 133, 449; *Boggs Act Hearings*, pp. 62, 105.

42. 97 *Congressional Record* (1951), pp. 8197-98.

The linkage between marihuana and heroin was also supported by some of the testimony by addicts themselves. Of twenty-seven addicts interviewed in part 14 of the *Kefauver Committee Hearings*, fifteen testified that they had started their drug use with marihuana. The association is even stronger because most of the twelve who had not used marihuana were medically based addicts because of illness or were older addicts who had begun using drugs before marihuana was readily available. See *Kefauver Committee Hearings*, pt. 14, pp. 11, 29, 54, 62, 71, 84, 93, 99, 104, 108, 153, 157, 160, 162, 167, 171, 182, 189, 194, 203, 211, 216, 220, 367, 380, 432, 436. Five of the addict witnesses indicated that marihuana did in fact lead to the use of the harder drugs, but only one gave definite reasons why he thought this transition inevitably took place. One male addict, after stating that the average age of marihuana smokers was fourteen or fifteen, stated: "You would very seldom find a person smoking marihuana who does just that, he keeps on, and he gets to the point where he does not have the same drive or feeling that he first had, and it is like a stepping stone, he graduates to heroin." *Kefauver Committee Hearings*, pt. 14, pp. 199-200.

Of course the testimony is consistent with other theses as well. In particular, the addict histories clearly indicate that curiosity and peer-group pressure were the primary factors in the initiation of opiate use (ibid., pp. 12, 32, 94, 108, 254). Moreover, Congressman Boggs introduced some mystery into his statements during the House debates by stating: "A study in February of 1950 of 602 case reports indicates that 53 percent . . . started their addiction to drugs by reason of association with other addicts, and 7 percent of them started on marihuana" (97 *Congressional Record* [1951], p. 8197). This study is cited on the same page with Congressman Boggs' statement that our young people usually start on the road to drug addiction by smoking marihuana.

 43. *Kefauver Committee Hearings*, pt. 14, p. 440.

 44. J. Mandel, "Who Says Marihuana Use Leads to Heroin Addiction?" *Journal of Secondary Education*, 43 (1968), 211-17.

 45. *Traffic in Opium* (1950), p. 6. Anslinger to Senator William Knowland, 4 June 1951. File: Penalties no. 1.

 46. In 1951 seven states (Alabama, Indiana, Maryland, New Jersey, Oklahoma, Tennessee, and West Virginia) and Alaska, passed penalty provisions similar to those in the Boggs Act (*Traffic in Opium* [1951], p. 8). In addition, nine other states (Connecticut, Illinois, Louisiana, Michigan, New York, Pennsylvania, Utah, Washington, and Wisconsin) amended their drug laws to provide more severe penalties, but not the same as in the Boggs Act (ibid. [1951], pp. 8-9). In 1952 four more states (Colorado, Georgia, Kentucky, and Virginia) enacted the Boggs penalties (ibid.[1952], p. 6). Six more states (Delaware, Iowa, Minnesota, Nebraska, Pennsylvania, and Wyoming) followed suit in 1953 (ibid. [1953], p. 9).

 The Ohio law, approved 16 June 1955, provided for imprisonment of anyone found guilty of illegally selling narcotic drugs for a period of not less than twenty nor more than forty years (ibid. [1955], p. 7). The Louisiana measure, adopted the following year, provided severe prison sentences without parole, probation, or suspension for the illegal sale, possession or administration of a narcotic drug. Sentences ranged from a five-year minimum to a ninety-nine-year maximum (ibid. [1956], p. 28).

 47. See generally R. King, *The Drug Hang-Up: America's Fifty-Year Folly* (New York: Norton, 1972).

 48. U.S., Congress, Joint Resolution, 84th Cong., 1st sess., 18 Mar. 1955.

 49. U.S., Congress, Senate, Committee on the Judiciary, Subcommittee on Improvements in the Federal Criminal Code, *Hearings on Illicit Narcotics Traffic*, 84th Cong., 1st sess., 1955, p. 57 (hereafter cited as *Daniel Committee Hearings*); see H. J. Anslinger and W. C. Oursler, *The Murderers* (New York: Farrar, 1961).

 50. Orrin S. Good to Anslinger, 31 July 1954. File: Penalties no. 1.

 51. G. W. Cunningham to M. Akeson, 7 Apr. 1953. Anslinger to George E. Dilley, 13 Sept. 1954. File: Penalties no. 1.

 52. Congressman Boggs, father of the Boggs Act and Chairman of the Subcommittee on Narcotics of the House Ways and Means Committee, stated that "[e]ffective steps to eliminate the unlawful drug traffic requires . . . the imposition of severe punishment by the courts" (102 *Congressional Record* [1956], p. 10689). The subcommittee, which had set out to determine the effect of the Boggs Act on narcotics traffic, began its recommendations with calls for further increases in the penalties for narcotics law violations. Both the House Ways and Means Committee report and the subcommittee report are filled with statements to the effect that harsher penalties are the most effective weapons in the war against illicit narcotics. The Ways and Means Committee conclusion was succinct: "Experience with the Boggs law . . . has clearly demonstrated the efficacy of severe punishment in reducing the illicit commerce in drugs" (*U.S. Code Congressional and Administrative News* [1956], pp. 3291, 3309, 3305, 3281-303, 3286). Finally,

Senator Daniel, speaking for the Senate subcommittee investigating the drug situation in the United States, found "it absolutely necessary for the Congress of the United States to strengthen the hands of our law enforcement officers and provide higher penalties if we are to stop the narcotics traffic in this country" (102 *Congressional Record* [1956], p. 9014). His subcommittee also recommended the kind of across-the-board increases in penalties that the act eventually contained.

    53.   *U.S. Code Cong. and Ad. News* (1956), p. 3305.

    54.   Ch. 629, 70 Stat. 570 (codified at 26 U.S.C. § 7607 [1964]); ch. 629, 70 Stat. 573 (codified at 18 U.S.C. § 1404 [1964]); ch. 629, 70 Stat. 574 (codified at 18 U.S.C. § 1406 [1964]); ch. 629, 70 Stat. 574 (codified at 18 U.S.C. § 1407 [1964]); ch. 629, 70 Stat. 575 (codified at 18 U.S.C. § § 1182 [a] [5], [23] [1964]).

    55.   The House Subcommittee on Narcotics, which produced what became the essentials of the Narcotic Control Act of 1956, revealed its knowledge of the distinction between marihuana and narcotics solely by a footnote to the major heading "Narcotics" which stated in fine print that the term narcotics included marihuana (see *U.S. Code Cong. and Ad. News* [1956], p. 3294).

    56.   *Daniel Committee Hearings*, pp. 58-59.

    57.   102 *Congressional Record* (1956), p. 9015.

    58.   In holding unconstitutional the presumption of knowledge that marihuana was smuggled, the Supreme Court in *Leary* v. *United States*, 395 U.S. 6 (1969), relied on the change in use patterns from 1959 to 1967. We think the presumption was unconstitutional when passed in 1956, both as to importation and knowledge.

    59.   *Daniel Committee Hearings*, p. 18.

    60.   The decline in the number of FBN arrests and seizures is directly related to the increase in local and state enforcement personnel. This thesis is supported by data from California where statewide arrests soared while federal arrests remained stable (Bureau of Criminal Statistics, California Department of Justice, *Crime in California* [1956]). See also A. Lindesmith, *The Addict and the Law* (Bloomington: Indiana Univ. Press, 1965), p. 238. One commentator has suggested that except for the years immediately after the passage of the Marihuana Tax Act, when the bureau wanted to concentrate on its newly acquired enforcement field, the FBN arrest data show clearly its emphasis on the opiates and cocaine (Mandel, "Problems with Official Drug Statistics," *Stanford Law Review*, 21 [1969], 1019-20).

    61.   Cf. House, *Hearings on H.R. 6385*, pp. 13-14 (testimony of Clinton Hester, office of the general counsel of the Treasury Department) with *State* v. *Bonoa*, 172 La. 955, 136 So. 15 (1931). It should be asked whether the information at congressional disposal changed so drastically between 1937 and 1956 as to justify the statutory presumption enacted at that time (21 U.S.C. § 176[a] [1964]), providing that possession of marihuana was presumptive evidence of knowing concealment of illegally imported marihuana.

    62.   Written materials inserted into the record of the Senate hearings included the testimony of an experienced federal Customs official that high quality marihuana was being grown near the Texas cities of Laredo and Brownsville (*Daniel Committee Hearings*, pp. 3488-89). In addition, the attorney general of Ohio noted that marihuana "may grow unnoticed along roadsides and vacant lots in many parts of the country" (ibid., p. 4814). Also, a bulletin issued by the Philadelphia Police Academy recited that "[p]lenty of marijuana is found growing in this city" (ibid., p. 599).

    63.   Blum, "Mind Altering Drugs and Dangerous Behavior," in the President's Commission on Law Enforcement and Administration of Justice, *Task Force Report: Narcotics and Drug Abuse* (Washington, D.C.: GPO, 1967), pp. 21, 24; Bouquet, "Cannabis," *U.N. Bulletin on Narcotics*, 3 (Jan. 1951), 22, 32-33.

64.   Cf. Chein, "The Status of Sociological and Social Psychological Knowledge Concerning Narcotics," in *Narcotic Drug Addiction Problems*, ed. R. Livingston (Washington, D.C.: GPO, 1963), p. 155. Mr. Chein reports a shift in drug use from 1930-60 from old to young and a continued increase in the percentage of drug users who are black or Spanish-speaking.

Chapter XII

1.   *Traffic in Opium* (1960), p. 69.

2.   *People* v. *Mistriel*, 110 P. Cal. App. 2d 110, 241 P.2d 1050 (Dist. Ct. App. 1952); *People* v. *Stark*, 157 Colo. 59, 67, 400 P.2d 923, 927-28 (1965); *People* v. *Glaser*, 238 Cal. App. 2d, 819, 48 Cal. Rptr. 427 (Dist. Ct. App. 1965), cert. denied, 385 U.S. 880 (1966); *People* v. *Aguiar*, 257 Cal. App. 2d 597, 602-03, 65 Cal. Rptr. 171, 174-175 (Dist. Ct. App.), cert. denied, 393 U.S. 970 (1968); *Commonwealth* v. *Leis*, nos. 28841-2, 28844-5, 28864-5 (Suffolk Super. Ct. 1968), affirmed, 355 N. Mass. 189, 243 N.E.2d 898 (1969); *People* v. *McKenzie*, 458 P.2d 232 (Colo. 1969); *Raines* v. *State*, 225 So. 2d 330 (Fla. 1969).

3.   *Washington Post*, 24 Feb. 1970, p. D-1, col 3. See also J. Rubin, *Do It!* (New York: Simon & Schuster, 1970).

4.   See, e.g., George M. Belk, New York district supervisor, to Howard L. Leary, New York commissioner of police, 6 Oct. 1967.

5.   Eddy, Halbach, Isbell, and Seevers, "Drug Dependence: Its Significance and Characteristics," *Bulletin of the World Health Organization* (1965), 728-29.

6.   "Marihuana and Society," *Journal of the American Medical Association*, 204 (1968), 91-92.

7.   Henry L. Giordano, commissioner of Narcotics, to Dr. James C. Munch, 20 Feb. 1968; Giordano to Karl Heyman, 20 Feb. 1968; Giordano to Ronald J. Turner, 5 Mar. 1968; Giordano to Congressman James C. Corman, 17 Nov. 1967. See Munch, J.C. "Marihuana and Crime," *U.N. Bulletin on Narcotics*, 15 (1963), 15-23.

8.   Seevers, "Marihuana in Perspective," *Michigan Quarterly Review*, (1966), 247-51.

9.   U.S., Congress, House, Select Committee on Crime, *Marihuana*, 91st Cong., 2d sess., 1970, H. Rept. 91-978, pp. 108-09.

10.   Quoted in C. Kirk, "The Marihuana Road to Paradise—and Hell," *New York Sunday News*, 17 Dec. 1967, p. 97.

11.   Giordano Testimony Before a Subcommittee of the House Committee on Appropriations, quoted in *Marihuana*, ed. Erich Goode (New York: Atherton Press, 1969), p. 154.

12.   Donald Miller, *Legislative and Judicial Trends in Marihuana Control*, FBN Pamphlet (1968).

13.   R. Mechoulam et al., "A Total Synthesis of a One-Δ^9 Tetrahydrocannabinol, the Active Constituent of Hashish," *Journal of American Chemical Society* (1965); H. Isbell et al., "Effects of Delta-Δ^9 Tetrahydrocannabinol in Man," *Psychopharmacologia* (1967), 184-88.

14.   Miller, *Legislative and Judicial Trends in Marihuana Control*.

15.   Mikuriya, "Contemporary Aspects of Drug Abuse," paper presented at Conference on Drug Abuse, Mendocino Series, 6-8 Feb. 1970, p. 1.

16. *Boston Globe*, 20 Dec. 1967, p. 1; George Gaffney, acting commissioner of Narcotics, to Garrett Byrne, Suffolk County district attorney, 9 Oct. 1967.

17. *People* v. *Stark*, 157 Colo. 59, 400 P.2d 923 (1965); see also *People* v. *McKenzie*, 458 P.2d 232 (Colo. 1969).

18. *Commonwealth* v. *Leis*, nos. 28841-2, 28844-5, 28864-5 (Suffolk Super. Ct. 1968), affirmed, 355 N. Mass. 189, 243 N.E. 2d 898 (1969).

19. *Suffolk Law Review*, 23 (1968), 31.

20. *Raines* v. *State*, 225 So. 330 (Fla. 1969); *People* v. *McKenzie*, 458 P.2d 232 (Colo. 1969).

21. Giordano to Karen Conner, 29 Dec. 1967.

22. Giordano to Congressman Bob W. Wilson, 11 Apr. 1968.

23. Memorandum for Files written by George Gaffney, 13 Oct. 1967.

24. *Baltimore Sun*, 22 Oct. 1967.

25. *Wall Street Journal*, 20 Nov. 1967, p. 8.

26. *New Republic*, 28 Oct. 1967, pp. 7, 8.

27. Pub. L. no. 89-74, 79 Stat. 226 (1965).

28. *Wall Street Journal*, 20 Nov. 1967, p. 8.

29. Pub. L. no. 90-639, 82 Stat. 1361 (1968).

30. John Kaplan, *Marijuana: The New Prohibition* (New York: World Pub. Co., 1970), pp. ix-xii.

31. *Time*, 26 Sept. 1969, p. 69; *Yale Daily News*, 14 Jan. 1970.

32. *Marihuana: A Signal of Misunderstanding*, The First Report of the National Commission on Marihuana and Drug Abuse, Appendix (Washington, D.C.: GPO, 1972), I, 251.

33. Mallabre, "Drugs on the Job," *Wall Street Journal*, 4 May 1970, p. 1, col. 6. This article deals not only with drug use by professionals but also details the increasing trend of drug use on the job.

34. U.S., Congress, Senate, Committee on the Judiciary, Subcommittee to Investigate Juvenile Delinquency, *Hearings on S. 1895, S. 2590, S. 2637*, 91st Cong., 1st sess., 1969 (hereafter cited as Senate, *Narcotics Legislation Hearings*).

35. Ibid., p. 268.

36. "CBS Evening News," 6 Aug. 1970. See also J. Rosevear, *Pot: A Handbook of Marihuana* (New Hyde Park, N.Y.: University Books, 1967), pp. 117-31; *Traffic in Opium* (1966), pp. 2, 40.

37. *Marihuana: A Signal of Misunderstanding*, Appendix II, 612.

38. *Newsweek*, 7 Sept. 1970, pp. 20-32.

39. *Marihuana: A Signal of Misunderstanding*, Appendix II, 889-99.

40. "Court Voids 30-yr. Term in Pot Case," *Washington Post*, 22 Jan. 1972.

41. "Dr. Mead Calls Marijuana Ban More Perilous Than Marihuana," *New York Times*, 28 Oct. 1971.

42. "Marihuana and Society," *JAMA*.

43. For retrospective confirmation see *Marihuana: A Signal of Misunderstanding*, Appendix II, 652.

44. Ibid., pp. 613-94.

45. *U.S.* v. *Kleinzahler*, 306 F. Supp. 311 (E.D.N.Y. 1969).

46. *Marihuana: A Signal of Misunderstanding*, Appendix II, 843.

47. *State* v. *Ward*, no. A-9 (N.J., 26 Oct. 1970). The court affirmed the conviction but modified the sentence. Two justices dissented from the affirmance on the ground that the defendant did not receive a fair trial. They concurred in the sentencing modification on the ground that the sentence was "grossly excessive."

48.   The following account is taken from *Life*, 31 Oct. 1969, pp. 30-31; *New York Times*, 3 Jan. 1970, p. 14, cols. 1-2; *Richmond Times-Dispatch*, 31 July 1969, p. 1, col. 6; ibid., 19 Dec. 1969, p. B-1, cols. 1-2; ibid., 3 Jan. 1970, p. 1, cols. 4-6; ibid., 5 Jan. 1970, p. 12, cols. 1-2 (editorial).

49.   *Life*, 31 Oct. 1969, p. 30.

50.   Ibid., p. 31.

51.   Mention was made of it in the *Richmond Times-Dispatch*, 19 Dec. 1969, p. B-1, col 1; ibid., 3 Jan. 1970, p. 1, col. 1.

52.   In December 1969 the Virginia Commission for Children and Youth recommended that penalties for the possession, use, and sale of marihuana be sharply reduced and that the substance not be classified with "hard" drugs such as heroin. *Richmond Times-Dispatch*, 15 Jan. 1970, p. C-1, col. 7.

53.   *New York Times*, 3 Jan. 1970, p. 14, cols. 1-2.

54.   *Richmond Times-Dispatch*, 5 Jan. 1970, p. 12, col. 1 (editorial entitled "The Pardon").

55.   Ibid.

56.   Ibid., 26 Feb. 1970, p. B-4, col. 1.

57.   Ibid., col. 3.

58.   Ibid., 3 Mar. 1970, p. B-1, col. 5.

59.   Virginia, Virginia Code Annotated, sec. 54-524 (Supp. 1970); Virginia, Virginia Acts, ch. 86, (1934), p. 81, *formerly* Virginia Code Annotated, secs. 54-487 to 54-519.

60.   Virginia, Virginia Code Annotated, secs. 54-524.101(c) (Supp. 1970).

61.   *Richmond Times-Dispatch*, 3 Mar. 1970, p. B-4, col. 6. See also ibid., 15 Mar. 1970, p. F-6, col. 1, (editorial).

62.   See, e.g., J. Giordano, associate director of the Bureau of Narcotics and Dangerous Drugs, to Congressman Clarence Miller, 28 May 1968.

63.   *Leary* v. *United States*, 395 U.S. 6 (1969); *Turner* v. *United States*, 396 U.S. 398 (1970).

64.   Pub. L. no. 89-801, 80 Stat. 1515, sec. 3 (1966).

65.   National Commission on Reform of Federal Criminal Laws, "Drug Crimes," (14 Jan. 1969), study draft in the possession of the authors in Charlottesville, Va.

66.   Pub. L. no. 91-513, 84 Stat. 1236 (1970).

67.   Senate, *Narcotics Legislation Hearings*, p. 909.

68.   Ibid., p. 255.

69.   Ibid., p. 663.

70.   116 *Congressional Record* (1970), p. 797.

71.   Ibid., p. 770.

72.   Senate, *Narcotics Legislation Hearings*, p. 250.

73.   U.S., Congress, House, Committee on Interstate and Foreign Commerce, 91st Cong., 2d sess. H. Rept. 91-1444, p. 13.

74.   Senate, *Narcotics Legislation Hearings*, p. 251.

Chapter XIII

1.   U.S., Congress, House, Committee on the Judiciary, Subcommittee No. 3, *Hearings on H.R. 10019, H.R. 11166, H.R. 14011, H.R. 14012, H.R. 14137, and H.R. 14354*, 91st Cong., 1st sess., 1970 (hereafter cited as House, *Hearings on Commission on Marihuana*).

2. Senate, *Narcotics Legislation Hearings*, p. 252.

3. *Newsweek*, 7 Sept. 1970, p. 22.

4. Ibid.

5. House, *Hearings on Commission on Marihuana*, p. 50.

6. Ibid.

7. U.S., Congress, House, Select Committee on Crime, *Marihuana*, 91st Cong., 2d sess., 1970, H. Rept. 91-978, pp. 108-09.

8. Senate, *Narcotics Legislation Hearings*, pp. 275-77.

9. Auerbach, "Views Shift on Marijuana," *Washington Post*, 25 Mar. 1972.

10. Senate, *Narcotics Legislation Hearings*, p. 278.

11. Ibid., p. 269.

12. House, *Hearings on Commission on Marihuana*, p. 21.

13. Ibid., p. 46.

14. Ibid., pp. 51-62.

15. Ibid., pp. 100-05.

16. Title V of Pub. L. no. 91-296.

17. Title VI of the Comprehensive Drug Abuse and Prevention and Control Act of 1970, Pub. L. no. 91-513.

18. Columnist William Hines, *Chicago Sun-Times*, 22 May 1971, p. 24.

19. "The Leaflet," newsletter of the National Organization for the Reform of Marihuana Laws, vol. 1, no. 2 (Jan.-Feb. 1972), p. 1; *Philadelphia Inquirer*, 20 July 1971, p. 9.

20. 117 *Congressional Record* (1971), p. 60.

21. *New York Times*, 2 May 1971, p. 14.

22. Transcript of president's remarks. Also quoted in Kraft, "Avoiding a Dogmatic Drug View," *Washington Post*, 6 June 1971.

23. *Washington Post*, 20 May 1971, p. A-3, cols. 5-8; *New York Times*, 20 May 1971, p. 50, col. 1.

24. Kraft, "Avoiding A Dogmatic Drug View."

25. *Journal of the American Medical Association*, 16 (1971), 486-92.

26. See, e.g., *Wall Street Journal*, 19 Apr. 1971; *Time*, 31 May 1971.

27. *Miami Herald*, 23 Apr. 1971.

28. "Psychiatrists Testify Marihuana Harms Adolescents," *New York Times*, 18 May 1971.

29. *Journal of the American Medical Association*, 16 (1971), 487.

30. Ibid., p. 492.

31. Ibid.

32. Transcript of Hearings before the National Commission on Marihuana and Drug Abuse, 17 May 1971, pp. 46-47, on file in the National Archives.

33. Dr. Snyder later published *Uses of Marijuana* (New York: Oxford Univ. Press, 1971); see also Snyder, "What We Have Forgotten About Pot: A Pharmacologist's History," *The New York Times Magazine*, 13 Dec. 1970, pp. 26-28, 121-34.

34. Dr. Solomon Snyder to Mr. Keith Stroup, executive director, NORML, 13 May 1971.

35. See, e.g., J. Fort, "Pot: A Rational Approach," *Playboy*, Oct. 1969.

36. J. Fort, "Analysis of April 1971 American Medical Association article on Marijuana," distributed at press conference on 17 May 1971 by the National Organization for Reform of Marijuana Laws, p. 1.

37. E.g., Zinberg, Weil, and Nelson, "Clinical and Psychological Effects of Marijuana in Man," *Science*, 13 Dec. 1968; Zinberg and Weil, "Acute Effects of Marijuana on Speech," *Nature*, 3 May 1969; Zinberg and Weil, "A Comparison of Marijuana Users and

Non-Users," *Nature*, April 1970. Dr. Zinberg has since published, in collaboration with J. Robertson, *Drugs and the Public* (New York: Simon & Schuster, 1972).

38.   Zinberg, statement on Kolansky and Moore article distributed at press conference on 17 May 1971, by the National Organization for Reform of Marijuana Laws, p. 4.

39.   L. Grinspoon, *Marijuana Reconsidered* (Cambridge: Harvard Univ. Press, 1971).

40.   L. Grinspoon, "The American Medical Association and Marijuana," statement distributed at press conference on 17 May 1971, by the National Organization for Reform of Marijuana Laws, p. 4.

41.   Erich Goode, "Ideological Factors in the Marijuana Controversy," paper presented at The New York Academy of Sciences Conference on Marijuana, New York, N.Y., 20-21 May 1971.

42.   Benson, V. "Marihuana 'Study' Critique," *Journal of the American Medical Association*, 217 (1971), 1391; see also Halikas, Goodwin, and Guze, "Marihuana Use and Psychiatric Illness," *Archives of General Psychiatry*, 27 (1972), 162.

43.   U.S., Congress, Senate, Committee on Labor and Public Welfare, Subcommittee on Alcoholism and Narcotics, *Marihuana and Health*, A Report to the Congress from the Secretary, Department of Health, Education and Welfare, 92d Cong., 1st sess., 1971 (hereafter cited as *Marihuana and Health* [1971]); U.S., Congress, Senate, Committee on Labor and Public Welfare, Subcommittee on Alcoholism and Narcotics, *Marihuana and Health*, A Report to the Congress from the Secretary, Department of Health, Education and Welfare, 92d Cong., 2d sess., 1972 (hereafter cited as *Marihuana and Health* [1972]).

44.   *Marihuana: A Signal of Misunderstanding*, First Report of the National Commission on Marihuana and Drug Abuse, 2 vols. (Washington, D.C.: GPO, 1972).

45.   *Marihuana and Health* (1972), p. 31.

46.   *Marihuana: A Signal of Misunderstanding*, pp. 36, 41.

47.   Ibid., pp. 56-57, 64.

48.   *Marihuana and Health* (1972), pp. 13, 121.

49.   *Marihuana: A Signal of Misunderstanding*, p. 59.

50.   *Marihuana and Health* (1972), p. 131.

51.   *Marihuana: A Signal of Misunderstanding*, p. 61.

52.   *Marihuana and Health* (1972), p. 124.

53.   Ibid.

54.   Ibid., p. 131.

55.   *Marihuana: A Signal of Misunderstanding*, p. 64.

56.   *Marihuana and Health* (1972), p. 129.

57.   Ibid., pp. 31-32.

58.   *Marihuana: A Signal of Misunderstanding*, p. 84; *Marihuana and Health* (1972), pp. 125-26.

59.   *Marihuana: A Signal of Misunderstanding*, p. 87.

60.   *Marihuana and Health* (1971), pp. 70-71.

61.   *Marihuana: A Signal of Misunderstanding*, p. 87.

62.   *Marihuana and Health* (1972), p. 9.

63.   *Marihuana: A Signal of Misunderstanding*, pp. 49, 87-89.

64.   *Marihuana and Health* (1972), p. 31.

65.   *Marihuana: A Signal of Misunderstanding*, pp. 73, 76.

66.   Ibid., p. 90.

67.   Ibid., p. 65.

68.   Ibid., pp. 65-66.

69.   Ibid., p. 102.

70.   *Evening Star* (Washington), 12 Feb. 1972, pp. 1, 15.

71.   In February 1971 when NIMH's first *Marihuana and Health* report was issued, Dr. Brown stated that the "general deleterious effects are minimal" for most casual users although "firm scientific knowledge about the effects of long-term chronic use" was still to be achieved. Although presenting a comprehensive summary of the medical literature, the NIMH report carefully avoided the social policy issues, an omission chastized by the press ("U.S. Cites Marijuana's Ill Effects But Foresees Some Medical Use," *Washington Post*, 2 Feb. 1971, p. A-1; "HEW on Marijuana," *Washington Post* [editorial] 3 Feb. 1971).

In testimony before the Marihuana Commission several months later, U.S. Surgeon General Jesse Steinfeld reviewed the history of marihuana control legislation (relying on the authors' previous work), concluding that he knew "of no clearer instance in which the punishment for an infraction of the law is more harmful than the crime." Although insisting that the penalties for marihuana use "should be consistent with the danger and risk to the individual and society," Dr. Steinfeld declined to be any more specific. "Until facts are in, use of marihuana 'is gambling'" (*American Medical News*, 6 Sept. 1971, p. 3).

In contrast, Dr. Brown, testifying before the same panel, was not so reticent. In May 1971 he first stated his own view that the penalties for possession should be "minimal or non-existent . . . a fine, like for a parking ticket." At the same time, he insisted that the still unanswered questions about the long-term effects and the possible behavioral consequences of widespread use justified "keeping marihuana illegal" ("NIMH Director, Narcotics Chief Clash Over Marijuana Penalties," *Washington Post*, 18 May 1971, p. A-1).

Dr. Brown's departure from the official administration line (that uniform misdemeanor penalties would make the law fair) brought him in line with recent statements by Lionel Solursch, the chairman of the Canadian Medical Association's committee on nonmedical drug use, and several of the most respected medical researchers in this field. See, e.g., L. Hollister, "Marihuana in Man: Three Years Later," *Science* 172 (1971), 21-28.

72.   *Marihuana: A Signal of Misunderstanding*, pp. 140, 142.

73.   Ibid., pp. 151-56.

74.   See., e.g., Auerbach, "Views Shift on Marijuana," *Washington Post*, 25 Mar. 1972; Lahart, "Behind Pot Report, Some Pressures," *Newsday*, 27 Mar. 1972.

75.   *Marihuana: A Signal of Misunderstanding*, pp. 149-50.

76.   *Washington Post*, 25 Mar. 1972, p. 1.

77.   See, e.g., remarks of Raymond P. Shafer, chairman of National Commission on Marihuana and Drug Abuse, transcript of "Meet the Press," vol. 16, no. 15, 9 Apr. 1972 (Washington, D.C.: Merkle Press, 1972), pp. 1-2.

78.   Jack Anderson, *Washington Post*, 24 June 1972, p. 31.

79.   *Santa Barbara News-Press*, 26 Mar. 1972.

80.   Ibid.; *Philadelphia Bulletin*, 23 Mar. 1972, p. 3.

81.   *Birmingham News*, 23 Mar. 1972.

82.   Senator Charles Percy to J. D. Whittenburg, executive director, National Council on Youth and Drugs, 24 Apr. 1972.

83.   Senator Edmund S. Muskie to J. D. Whittenburg, 3 Apr. 1972.

84.   *Chicago Sun Times*, 3 Mar. 1972; *Newsweek*, 28 Feb. 1972.

85.   *Long Island Press*, 20 Feb. 1972.

86.   *National Observer*, 26 Feb. 1972.

87.   *Today* (Chicago), 22 Mar. 1972.

88.   "The Leaflet," vol. 1, no. 4 (May-June 1972), pp. 5-8.

89.   Press release by AMORHIA, The Cannabis Cooperative, Mill Valley, Calif., 22 Mar. 1972.

90.   "The Leaflet," vol. 1, no. 4, p. 1.

91.   Jack Anderson, *Washington Post*, 26 Apr. 1971, reprinted in 117 *Congressional Record* (1971), no. 60.

92.   "The Leaflet," vol. 1, no. 4, p. 5.

93.   *Philadelphia Bulletin*, 26 Feb. 1972.

94.   *Marihuana: A Signal of Misunderstanding*, Appendix I, pp. 548-68.

95.   *New York Times*, 21 Nov. 1971, p. 60; *New York Times*, 19 May 1971, pp. 1, 52.

96.   Ann Arbor, Mich. *City Code*, tit. IX, ch. 108, § 9:62 (29) (1972). See generally Note, "The Concurrent State and Local Regulation of Marijuana: The Validity of the Ann Arbor Marijuana Ordinance," *Michigan Law Review*, 71 (1972), 400.

97.   "Judge Sets Aside $5 Marijuana Fine in Ann Arbor, Michigan," *Washington Post*, 22 Oct. 1972, p. G-6.

98.   See *People v. McCabe*, 275 N.E. 2d 407 (Ill. 1971); *People v. Sinclair*, 194 N.W. 2d 878, and *People v. Lorentzen*, 194 N.W. 2d 827 (Mich. 1972); *English v. Miller*, *Criminal Law Reporter*, 11 (1972), 2140 (U.S.D.C., E.D. Va.); *State v. Kantner*, 493 P. 2d 306, cert. denied, 409 U.S. 948 (Hawaii 1972).

99.   *Griswold v. Connecticut*, 381 U.S. 479 (1965); *Stanley v. Georgia*, 394 U.S. 557 (1969); *Roe v. Wade*, 410 U.S. 113 (1973). See generally R. Bonnie and C. H. Whitebread, "The Forbidden Fruit and the Tree of Knowledge: An Inquiry Into the Legal History of American Marijuana Prohibition," *Virginia Law Review*, 56 (1970), 1145-55.

100.   *Federal Register*, vol. 37, no. 174, pp. 18097-98, 7 Sept. 1972.

101.   *National Organization for the Reform of Marijuana Laws v. Ingersoll*, Civil no. 72-1854 (D.C. Cir.). In a decision addressing similar issues, *United States v. Kiffer et al*, Doc. no. 72-2263 (2d Cir. 18 Apr. 1973), the Second Circuit affirmed the conviction of three persons for possession with intent to distribute two tons of marihuana, rejecting their argument that classification of marihuana in Schedule I was irrational.

102.   *U.S. News and World Report*, 4 Sept. 1972, p. 50; *Los Angeles Times*, 10 July 1972, p. 1; *Los Angeles Herald-Examiner*, 23 Mar. 1972.

103.   *Los Angeles Times*, 9 Nov. 1972.

104.   *National Observer*, 26 Feb. 1972.

105.   Internal memorandum of the National Coordinating Council on Drug Education, in possession of the authors in Charlottesville, Va.

106.   Brecher, *Licit and Illicit Drugs* (Boston: Little, Brown, 1972).

107.   *New York Times*, 20 Feb. 1972; *Newsday*, 9 Mar. 1972, 24 Mar. 1972; *Cincinnati Enquirer*, 12 Mar. 1972; *Miami News*, 23 Mar. 1972; *Knoxville News-Sentinel*, 23 Mar. 1972; *Portland Oregonian*, 23 Mar. 1972; *Birmingham Post-Herald*, 24 Mar. 1972; *Philadelphia Inquirer*, 24 Mar. 1972; *Evening Star* (Washington), 24 Mar. 1972; *Louisville Times*, 24 Mar. 1972; *Minneapolis Star*, 25 Mar. 1972; *San Francisco Examiner*, 26 Mar. 1972; *San Francisco Chronicle*, 26 Mar. 1972; *Chicago News*, 27 Mar. 1972; *Wall Street Journal*, 30 Mar. 1972.

108.   *St. Louis Post-Dispatch*, 19 Feb. 1972; *New Orleans Times-Picayune*, 24 Mar. 1972.

109.   "The Time Has Come: Abolish the Pot Laws," *National Review*, 8 Dec. 1972, pp. 1344-48, 1366.

110.   *Savannah Morning News*, 23 Mar. 1972; *Dallas Times Herald*, 24 Mar. 1972; *Chatanooga News-Free Press*, 24 Mar. 1972; *Knoxville Journal*, 24 Mar. 1972; *Tri-City Herald* (Pasco, Wash.), 26 Mar. 1972; *Asheville* (N.C.) *Citizen-Times*, 26 Mar. 1972; *Times Record* (Spencer, W. Va.), 11 May 1972.

111.   *Philadelphia Bulletin*, 26 Feb. 1972; *Sunday Advertiser* (Boston), 27 Feb. 1972; *Allentown* (Pa.) *Call*, 2 Mar. 1972; *Daily Banner* (Cambridge, Mass.), 3 Mar. 1972, p. 10; *Providence Bulletin*, 24 Mar. 1972; *Worcester* (Mass.) *Telegram*, 25 Mar. 1972.

112. *Los Angeles Times,* 26 Mar. 1972.

113. *Los Angeles Times,* 13 Sept. 1972.

114. Thurman Arnold, *Symbols of Government* (1936), p. 160.

115. Statement in possession of authors in Charlottesville, Va.

116. *Los Angeles Times,* 21 June 1972, p. 2; *Washington Post,* 21 June 1972, p. A-2.

117. Raymond P. Shafer to Edward L. Wright, president; American Bar Association, 21 Apr. 1971.

118. Wright to Shafer, 7 May 1971.

119. Gerald Stein, chairman of Committee on Alcoholism and Drug Reform of American Bar Association Section on Individual Rights and Responsibilities, to Shafer, 9 July 1971.

120. Peter Barton Hutt, chairman of Committee on Drug Abuse of American Bar Association Section on Criminal Law, to Shafer, 29 July 1971.

121. *Marihuana: A Signal of Misunderstanding,* pp. 115-16.

122. *Evening Star* (Washington), 7 Feb. 1972, p. A-3; Report of American Bar Association Section on Individual Rights and Responsibilities, in possession of the authors in Charlottesville, Va.

123. *Criminal Law Reporter,* 11 (1972), 2471-74.

124. "Mayor's Committee Recommends Legalization of Marihuana Here," *Washington Post,* 6 Mar. 1973, p. A-1. See also "Marihuana: What Should Society Do?" commentary by Chief of Police Jerry V. Wilson and Dr. Thomas E. Piemme, two members of the committee, *Washington Post,* 26 Mar. 1973, p. A-22.

125. H.B. no. 447, §§ 4.05, 4.06, enacted by Texas Legislature 28 May 1973, signed by Gov. Briscoe, 17 June 1973.

126. *Marihuana in Texas,* Senate Interim Drug Study Committee, S.R. 1442, 62d Texas Legislature, 1972.

127. For example, the Leadership Conference conducted a "National Showdown on Urgent Issues" on 22 May 1973. In preparation for the "Showdown," the foundation disseminated to its members and affiliated organizations a supposedly neutral fact-sheet on marihuana which denigrated the commission's report and recommendations and cited all studies in any way attributing harmful properties to the drug. Memorandum and fact-sheet on file with authors in Charlottesville, Va.

128. J. Thomas Ungerleider, M.D., to Dana L. Farnsworth, M.D., 31 Mar. 1972, quoting from television news-discussion program on KTLA-T.V., Los Angeles, moderated by Mr. George Putnam and visited by Hardin Jones, Ph.D.

129. "Marijuana Seen as Threat," *Montclair* (N.J.) *Times,* 18 Jan. 1973 (pertaining to Dr. Theodore R. Robie). Memorandum from Dr. Robie to each staff member of the National Commission on Marihuana and Drug Abuse, on file with authors in Charlottesville, Va.

130. Campbell et al, "Cerebral Atrophy in Young Cannabis Smokers," *Lancet,* 4 Dec. 1971, pp. 1219-25.

131. "Cannabis Encephalopathy?" *Lancet,* 4 Dec. 1971, p. 1240.

132. See, e.g., A. Friendly, "About Pot and Brain Damage," *Washington Post,* 12 Dec. 1971.

133. G. Nahas, *Marihuana: Deceptive Weed* (New York: Raven Press, 1973), p. 110.

134. Ibid., pp. 319-20.

135. Ibid., p. 308.

136. Address of the President on Crime and Drug Abuse Broadcast Live on Radio From Camp David, 15 Oct. 1972 (White House Press Release).

137.   *Washington Post*, 11 Mar. 1973, p. A-4 ("Text of Nixon's Address on Fighting Crime and Drugs"); see also "Nixon Sets Broad New Crime War," *Washington Post*, 11 Mar. 1973, p. A-1.

138.   In a press conference a few days later, the president indicated that holding the line against marihuana was an integral part of the administration's anticrime package: "equitable punishment" for marihuana use; "mandatory criminal penalties with regard to hard drugs"; and capital punishment for certain classes of offenders (Text of President Nixon's Press Conference on March 15, 1973, in *Washington Post*, 16 Mar. 1973, p. A-18).

139.   *Marihuana: A Signal of Misunderstanding*, p. 91.

Selected Bibliography

This selected bibliography lists many of the published books and articles to which we referred in researching and writing this book. Of equal importance, however, were the letters, papers, and unpublished memorandums in the files of the Bureau of Narcotics and Dangerous Drugs in Washington, D.C., and the microfilm newspaper files in many of the nation's libraries. In many instances, the identifying information for specific memorandums and letters, as well as newspaper clippings, was incomplete. In such cases, we simply recorded the available data, which are included in the preceding compilation of reference material. We have not listed these sources here.

Recent Books of Interest

Bloomquist, E. *Marijuana: The Second Trip*. Beverly Hills: Glencoe Press, 1971.

Brecher, E. *Licit and Illicit Drugs*. Boston: Little, Brown, 1972.

Duster, T. *The Legislation of Morality: Law, Drugs and Moral Judgment*. New York: The Free Press, 1970.

Goode, E., ed. *Marihuana*. New York: Atherton Press, 1969.

Grinspoon, L. *Marijuana Reconsidered*. Cambridge: Harvard Univ. Press, 1971.

Kaplan, J. *Marijuana: The New Prohibition*. New York: World Pub. Co., 1970.

King, R. *The Drug Hang-Up: America's Fifty-Year Folly*. New York: Norton, 1972.

Musto, D. *The American Disease: Origins of Narcotic Control*. New Haven: Yale Univ. Press, 1973.

Nahas, G. *Marihuana: Deceptive Weed*. New York: Raven Press, 1973.

Schofield, M. *The Strange Case of Pot.* Baltimore: Penguin Books, 1971.

Snyder, S. *Uses of Marijuana.* New York: Oxford Univ. Press, 1971.

Zinberg, N., and Robertson, J. *Drugs and the Public.* New York: Simon & Schuster, 1972.

Selected Books and Articles on Marihuana

Allentuck, S., and Bowman, K. M. "The Psychiatric Aspects of Marihuana Intoxication." *American Journal of Psychiatry,* 99 (1942), 249.

Anslinger, H. J. "Marihuana Research." Convention Book of the Association of Medical Students.

——. "The Reason for Uniform State Narcotic Legislation." *Georgetown Law Journal,* 21 (1932), 52.

——, and Cooper. "Marihuana: Assassin of Youth." *American Magazine,* July 1937, p. 18.

Benson, V. "Marihuana 'Study' Critique." *Journal of the American Medical Association,* 217 (1971), 1931.

Bouquet. "Cannabis." *U.N. Bulletin on Narcotics,* 3 (Jan. 1951), 22, 32-33.

——. "Marihuana Intoxication." *Journal of the American Medical Association,* 124 (1944), 1010-11.

Bragman. "The Weed of Insanity." *Medical Journal and Record,* 122 (1925), 416-18.

Bromberg, W. "Marihuana: A Psychiatric Study." Reprint from the *Journal of the American Medical Association* (July 1, 1939), 1.

——, and Rogers, T. C. "Marihuana and Aggressive Crime." *American Journal of Psychiatry,* 102 (1946), 825-27.

——. "Marihuana Intoxication: A Clinical Study of Cannabis Sativa Intoxication." *American Journal of Psychiatry,* 91 (1934), 303.

Campbell, et al. "Cerebral Atrophy in Young Cannabis Smokers." *Lancet,* 4 Dec. 1971.

Charen, S., and Perelman, L. "Personality Studies of Marihuana Addicts." *American Journal of Psychiatry,* 102 (1946), 674-82.

Chopra, R., and Chopra, G. "*Cannabis Sativa* in Relation to Mental Diseases and Crime in India." *Indian Journal of Medical Research,* 30 (1942), 155-71.

——. "The Present Position of Hemp-Drug Addiction in India." *Indian Medical Research Memoirs,* 31 (1939), 1-119.

——. "Use of Hemp Drugs in India." *Indian Medical Gazette*, 75 (1940), 356-67.

Dewey, L. "Hemp." *U.S. Department of Agriculture Yearbook, 1913*. Washington, D.C.: Government Printing Office, 1913.

Dhunjibhoy, J. "A Brief Resume of the Types of Insanity Commonly Met Within India with a Full Description of 'Indian Hemp Insanity' Peculiar to the Country." *Journal of Medical Sciences*, 76 (1930), 254-61.

Fossier, A. "The Marihuana Menace." *New Orleans Medical and Surgical Journal*, 84 (1931), 247-52.

Fraser, J. "Withdrawal Symptoms in Cannabis Indica Addicts." *Lancet*, 2 (1949), 747-48.

Freedman, H., and Rockmore, M. "Marihuana: A Factor in Personality Evaluation and Army Maladjustment." *Journal of Clinical Psychopathology*, 7 (1946), 365-82 (Part 1), and 8 (1946), 221-36 (Part 2).

Gomila, F., and Lambow, M. "Present Status of the Marihuana Vice in the United States." In *Marihuana: America's New Drug Problem*, ed. R. Walton. Philadelphia: Lippincott, 1938.

Halikas; Goodwin; and Guze. "Marihuana Use and Psychiatric Illness." *Archives of General Psychiatry*, 27 (1972), 162.

Hayes and Bowery. "Marihuana." *Journal of Criminal Law and Criminology*, 23 (1932), 1086-94.

Ireland, T. "Insanity from the Abuse of Indian Hemp." *Alienist and Neurologist*, 14 (1893), 622-30.

Isbell, H., et al. "Effects of Tetrahydrocannabinol in Man." *Psychopharmacologia*, 1967.

Kolb. "An Authoritative Treatise on Marihuana." *The Recorder*, 12 Sept. 1938, and *Federal Probation*, July 1938.

Kwager, N. "Marihuana: Our New Addiction." *American Journal of the Medical Sciences*, 195 (1938), 354.

Mandel, J. "Hashish, Assassins, and the Love of God." *Issues in Criminology*, 2 (1966), 153.

——. "Who Says Marihuana Use Leads to Heroin Addiction?" *Journal of Secondary Education*, 43 (1968), 211-17.

Marcovitz and Meyers. "The Marihuana Addict in the Army." *War Medicine*, 6 (1944), 382-91.

"Marihuana Problems." *Journal of the American Medical Association*, 127 (1945), 1129.

"Marihuana and Society." *Journal of the American Medical Association*, 204 (1968), 91-92.

Mechoulam, R., et al. "A Total Synthesis of a 1-D Tetrahydrocannabinol, the Active Constituent of Hashish." *Journal of American Chemical Society*, 1965.

Merrill, F. T. *Marihuana: The New Dangerous Drug.* Washington, D.C.: Opium Research Committee, Foreign Policy Association, Inc., March 1938.

Musto, D. "The Marihuana Tax Act of 1937." *Archivés of General Psychiatry*, 26 (1972), 101-8.

National Women's Christian Temperance Union. *Marihuana.* Evanston, Ill.: National Women's Christian Temperance Union Pub. House, 1928.

Pholen, J. M. "The Marihuana Bugaboo." *Military Surgeon*, 93 (1943), 94-95.

Robinson, V. "An Essay on Hasheesh: Historical and Experimental." *Medical Review of Reviews*, 18 (1912), 159-60, 300-312.

Rosevear, J. *Pot: A Handbook of Marihuana.* New Hyde Park, N.Y.: University Books, 1967.

Schicks, G. C. "Marihuana: Depraver of Youth." *Druggists Circular*, 1938, p. 6.

Seevers. "Marihuana in Perspective." *Michigan Quarterly Review*, 5 (1966), 247-51.

Siler, J. S., et al. "Marihuana Smoking in Panama." *Military Surgeon*, 73 (1933), 269-80.

Simon. "From Opium to Hash Eesh." *Scientific American*, Nov. 1921, pp. 14-15.

Stanley. "Marihuana as a Developer of Criminals," *American Journal of Police Science*, 2 (1931), 252-56.

Tennyson. "Uniform State Narcotic Law." *Federal Bar Association Journal*, 1 (1932), 55.

——. "Uniform State Narcotic Law." *Federal Bar Association Journal*, 1 (1935), 55.

Walton, R. *Marihuana: America's New Drug Problem.* Philadelphia: Lippincott, 1938.

Williams, E. G., et al. "Studies on Marihuana and Pyrahedge Compound." *Public Health Reports*, 61 (1946), 1059-83.

Zinberg and Weil. "Acute Effects of Marijuana on Speech." *Nature*, 3 May 1969.

——. "A Comparison of Marijuana Users and Non-Users," *Nature*, April 1970.

Zinberg; Weil; and Nelson. "Clinical and Psychological Effects of Marijuana in Man." *Science*, 13 Dec. 1968.

Government Reports on Marihuana

Marijuana: Report of the Indian Hemp Drugs Commission, 1893-1894. Silver Spring, Md.: Thomas Jefferson Co., 1969.

Mayor's Committee on Marihuana. *The Marihuana Problem in the City of New York* (La Guardia Report). New York: Jaques Cattell, 1944.

National Commission on Marihuana and Drug Abuse. *Marihuana: A Signal of Misunderstanding,* The First Report of the National Commission on Marihuana and Drug Abuse, and Technical Papers to the First Report. 2 vols. Washington, D.C.: Government Printing Office, 1972.

U.S., Congress, Senate, Committee on Labor and Public Welfare, Subcommittee on Alcoholism and Narcotics. *Marihuana and Health,* A Report to the Congress from the Secretary, Department of Health, Education and Welfare. Washington, D.C.: Government Printing Office, 1971, 92d Cong., 1st sess., 1971.

——. *Marihuana and Health,* A Report to the Congress from the Secretary, Department of Health, Education and Welfare. Washington, D.C.: Government Printing Office, 1972, 92d Cong., 2d sess., 1972.

Articles and Books on Related Subjects

Adams, B. *The Theory of Social Revolutions.* New York: Macmillan, 1913.

Adams, S. H. *The Great American Fraud.* Chicago: Press of American Medical Association, 1907.

Anslinger, H. J., and Oursler, W. C. *The Murderers.* New York: Farrar, 1961.

Anslinger, H. J., and Tompkins, W. *The Traffic in Narcotics.* New York: Funk & Wagnalls, 1953.

Becker, H. S. *Outsiders: Studies in the Sociology of Deviance.* London: Free Press of Glencoe, 1963.

——. "History, Culture and Subjective Experience: An Elaboration of the Social Bases of Drug-Induced Experiences." *Journal of Health and Social Behaviour,* 8 (1967), 172.

Blum, R. "Mind Altering Drugs and Dangerous Behavior: Dangerous Drugs." In the President's Commission on Law Enforcement and Administration of Justice, *Task Force Report: Narcotics and Drug Abuse.* Washington, D.C.: Government Printing Office, 1967.

———. *Society and Drugs*. San Francisco: Jossey-Bass, 1969.

Brill. "Recurrent Patterns in the History of Drug Dependence and Some Interpretations." In *Drugs and Youth*, ed. J. R. Wittenborn. Springfield, Ill.: Thomas, 1969.

Bronaugh. "Limiting or Prohibiting the Possession of Intoxicating Liquors for Personal Use." *Law Notes*, 23 (1919), 67.

Brooks, J. E. *The Mighty Leaf: Tobacco Through the Centuries*. Boston: Little, Brown, 1952.

Brown. "Enforcement of the Tennessee Anti-Narcotic Laws." *American Journal of Public Health*, 5 (1915), 323-33.

Cheevers, N. *A Manual of Medical Jurisprudence for India*. Calcutta: Thacker, Sprinks, 1870.

Chein. "The Status of Sociological and Social Psychological Knowledge Concerning Narcotics." *Narcotic Drug Addiction Problems*, ed. R. Livingston (1963).

Cherrington, E. *The Evolution of Prohibition in the United States of America*. Waterville, Ohio: The American Issue Press, 1920.

Corcoran, A. "Possession Under the State Prohibition Laws." In *Marihuana: A Signal of Misunderstanding*, Appendix, vol. 2. Washington, D.C.: Government Printing Office, 1972.

Curti, M. *The Growth of American Thought*. 2d ed. New York: Harper & Row, 1951.

Dickson. "Bureaucracy and Morality: An Organizational Perspective on a Moral Crusade." *Social Problems*, 16 (1968), 143.

Eberle. "Report of Committee on Acquirement of Drug Habits," *American Journal of Pharmacy*, Oct. 1903.

Eddy; Halbach; Isbell; and Seevers. "Drug Dependence: Its Significance and Characteristics." *Bulletin of the World Health Organization*, 1965.

Eldridge, W. B. *Narcotics and the Law*. 2d rev. ed. Chicago: Univ. of Chicago Press, 1967.

Freund, E. *The Police Power, Public Policy and Constitutional Rights*. Chicago: Callaghan, 1904.

Grinnell. "A Review of Drug Consumption and Alcohol as Found in Proprietary Medicine." *Medico-Legal Journal*, 23 (1905), 426.

Gusfield, J. P. *Symbolic Crusade*. Urbana: Univ. of Illinois Press, 1963.

Hartz, L. *The Liberal Tradition in America*. New York: Harcourt, 1955.

Higham, J. *Strangers in the Land: Patterns of American Nativism, 1860-1925*. New Brunswick: Rutgers Univ. Press, 1955.

Hofstadter, R. *The Age of Reform*. New York: Knopf, 1955.

King, R. "Narcotic Drug Laws and Enforcement Policies." *Law and Contemporary Problems*, 22 (1957), 113, 124-26.

——. "The Narcotics Bureau and the Harrison Act." *Yale Law Journal*, 62 (1953), 736-39.

Kolb. "Factors That Have Influenced the Management and Treatment of Drug Addicts." In *Narcotic Drug Addiction Problems*, ed. R. Livingston. Washington, D.C.: Government Printing Office, 1963.

—— and Dumez. "The Prevalence and Trend of Drug Addiction in the United States and Factors Influencing It." *Public Health Reports*, May 1924.

Lee, H. W. *How Dry We Were: Prohibition Revisited*. Englewood Cliffs, N.J.: Prentice-Hall, 1963.

Lindesmith, A. *The Addict and the Law*. Bloomington: Indiana Univ. Press, 1965.

Link, A. *Woodrow Wilson and the Progressive Era*. New York: Harper & Row, 1954.

Mandel, J. "Problems with Official Drug Statistics." *Stanford Law Review*, 21 (1969), 991, 998-99.

Maurer, D. W., and Vogel, V. H. *Narcotics and Narcotic Addiction*. Springfield, Ill.: Thomas, 1954.

May, H. *The End of American Innocence*. New York: Knopf, 1959.

McGrew, J. L. "History of Tobacco Regulation." In *Marihuana: A Signal of Misunderstanding*, Appendix, vol. 1. Washington D.C.: Government Printing Office, 1972.

Mowry, G. *The Era of Theodore Roosevelt*. New York: Harper & Row, 1958.

National Commission on Law Observance and Enforcement (Wickersham Commission). *Report on Crime and the Foreign Born*, Report no. 10, 1931. Reprint. Montclair, N.J.: Patterson Smith, 1968.

Note. "Narcotics Regulation." *Yale Law Journal*, 62 (1953), 751, 784-87.

Nyswander, M. *The Drug Addict as a Patient*. New York: Grune & Stratton, 1956.

O'Donnell. "Patterns of Drug Abuse and Their Social Consequences." In *Drugs and Youth*, ed. J. R. Wittenborn. Springfield, Ill.: Thomas, 1969.

Rogers. "Life, Liberty & Liquor: A Note on the Police Power." *Virginia Law Review*, 6 (1919), 156.

Rubin, J. *Do It!* New York: Simon & Schuster, 1968.

Safely. "Growth of State Power Under Federal Constitution to Regulate Traffic in Intoxicating Liquors." *Iowa Law Bulletin*, 3 (1917), 221.

Sandoz. "Report on Morphinism to the Municipal Court of Boston." *Journal of Criminal Law and Criminology*, 13 (1922), 54.

Solis-Cohen, S., and Githens, T. S. *Pharmaco-Therapeutics*. New York: Appleton, 1928.

Stanley, E. "Morphinism." *Journal of Criminal Law and Criminology*, 6 (1915), 588.

——. "Narcotic Drugs and Crime." *Journal of Criminal Law and Criminology*, 12 (1921), 110.

Taylor, A. H. *American Diplomacy and the Narcotics Traffic, 1900-1939*. Durham: Duke Univ. Press, 1969.

Taylor. "More Bars Against Mexicans?" *The Survey*, 64 (1930), 26.

Tennyson. "Illicit Drug Traffic." *Federal Bar Association Journal* 2 (1935), 208-9.

Terry, C., and Pellens, M. *The Opium Problem*. New York: Prentice-Hall, 1928.

Timberlake, J. H. *Prohibition and the Progressive Movement*. Cambridge: Harvard Univ. Press, 1963.

U.S., Treasury Department. *State Laws Relating to the Control of Narcotic Drugs and the Treatment of Drug Addiction*. Washington, D.C.: Government Printing Office, 1931.

——, Bureau of Narcotics. *Traffic in Opium and Other Dangerous Drugs*. Washington, D.C.: Government Printing Office, 1932-37.

Vance. "The Road to Confiscation." *Yale Law Journal*, 25 (1916), 285.

Weber. "Drugs and Crime." *Journal of Crime and Criminology*, 10 (1919), 370.

Wilbert and Motter. *Digest of Laws and Regulations in Force in the United States Relating to the Possession, Use, Sale and Manufacture of Poisons and Habit Forming Drugs*, U.S., Treasury Department, Public Health Bulletin no. 56. Washington, D.C.: Government Printing Office, 1912.

Willoughby, W. *Opium as an International Problem*. Baltimore: The Johns Hopkins Press, 1925.

Wright. "The International Opium Conference." *American Journal of International Law*, U1 (1912), 871.

Citations to Current Marihuana Laws

Alabama	414 Sec. 101 et seq. Alabama Uniform Controlled Substances Act (1971)
Alaska	§ 17.12.010 et seq. Alaska Stat. Ann. (1962)
Arizona	§ 36-1001 et seq. Arizona Rev. Stat. Ann. (1962) as amended (Supp. XI, 1971)
Arkansas	§ 1 et seq. Arkansas House Bill no. 409 (1971) and § 1 et seq. Amendments contained in House Bill no. 64 (1972) and § 1 et seq. House Bill no. 71 (1972)
California	§ 11500 et seq. and § 11721 Health & Safety Code, Deering California Code Ann. (Supp., 1972)
Colorado	§ 48-5-1 et seq. Colorado Rev. Stat. (1963) as amended (Supp. II, 1971)
Connecticut	Connecticut Substitute Senate Bill no. 20, Public Act no. 278 (1972)
Delaware	Delaware Code Ann. tit. 16, §§ 4701-4722 (1953) as amended (Supp., 1968)
Florida	§ 398.01 et seq. Florida Stat. Ann. (1966) and (Supp. 14A, 1972)
Georgia	§ 79A-801 et seq. Georgia Code Ann. (Supp. Book 22, 1971)
Hawaii	T19 § 329-19 et seq. Ha. Rev. Code (1969) § 1240-56 Act no. 9 Sess. Laws (IV, 1972)
Idaho	§ 37-2701 et seq. Idaho Code (Supp. VII, 1971)
Illinois	56 1/2 § 1100 et seq. Ill. Stat. Ann. (Supp., 1972)
Indiana	35 § 3301 et seq. Burns Indiana Stat. Ann. (Supp. VII, 1972)
Iowa	§ 204.101 et seq. Iowa Code Ann. (Supp. XA, 1972)
Kansas	§ 1 et seq. Kansas Substitute for Senate Bill no. 347 (1972)

Kentucky	Senate Bill 274 Kentucky Rev. Stat. (1972 temporary Issue)
Louisiana	§ 40.961 et seq. West's Louisiana Stat. Ann. (Supp. XXIII, 1972)
Maine	Tit. 22 § 2361 et seq. Maine Rev. Stat. Ann. (1964) and (Supp. XII, 1972)
Maryland	Art. 27 § 276 et seq. Maryland Code Ann. (1971) and (Supp. III, 1971)
Massachusetts	Ch. 94C § 1 et seq. Massachusetts Laws Ann. (Supp. 3-A, 1971)
Michigan	§ 18.1070(1) et seq. Michigan Stat. Ann. (current material, 1972)
Minnesota	152.-1 et seq. Minnesota Stat. Ann. (Supp. XI, 1972)
Mississippi	§ 6831-70 et seq. Mississippi Stat. Ann. (Supp. 5A, 1972)
Missouri	§ 195.010 et seq. Missouri Stat. Ann. (1972)
Montana	§ 54-129 et seq. Montana Rev. Code (Supp. III, 1971)
Nebraska	§ 28-4115 et seq. Nebraska Stat. Rev. (Supp., 1971)
Nevada	§ 1 et seq. Nevada Assembly Bill no. 107 (1972)
New Hampshire	318-B et seq. New Hampshire Stat. Ann. (Supp. III, 1969)
New Jersey	§ 24-21-1 et seq. New Jersey Stat. Ann. (Supp. XXIV, 1972)
New Mexico	§ 1 et seq. New Mexico Senate Bill no. 35 (1972)
New York	§ 220.02 et seq. McKinney's Stat. Ann. New York Penal Law (Supp. Book 39, 1972)
North Carolina	§ 90-96 et seq. North Carolina Ann. (Supp. II-C, 1971)
North Dakota	§ 19-03.1 et seq. North Dakota Century Code (Supp. III, 1971)
Ohio	§ 3719.01 et seq. Ohio Rev. Code Ann. (1971) and (Supp., 1971)
Oklahoma	Uniform Controlled Substances Act § 2-101 et seq. Ch. 119 Oklahoma Session Laws (1971)
Oregon	§ 474.010 et seq. Uniform Narcotic Drug Act (1971) and § 475.010 et seq. Narcotic and

	Dangerous Drugs (1971) and 167.202 et seq. (1971)
Pennsylvania	§ 1 et seq. Pennsylvania House Bill no. 851 (1972)
Rhode Island	§ 21-28-1 et seq. Rhode Island General Laws (1968) and (Supp. IV, 1971)
South Carolina	§ 32-1516.5 et seq. South Carolina Code Laws (Supp. VII, 1971)
South Dakota	§ 39-17-44 et seq. South Dakota Compiled Laws Ann. (Supp. XII, 1972)
Tennessee	§ 52-1408 et seq. Tennessee Code Ann. (Supp. IX-A, 1971)
Texas	H.B. no. 447, § 4.05-.06, enacted 28 May 1973
Utah	§ 58-37-1 et seq. Utah Code Ann. (Supp. VI, 1971)
Vermont	Tit. 18 ch. 84 §4201 et seq. Vermont Stat. Ann. (1968) and (Supp. VI, 1970)
Virginia	§ 54-524-1 et seq. Virginia Code (1972) and (Supp. VII, 1972)
Washington	§ 69.50.101 et seq. Washington Rev. Code Ann. (Supp. 66 to 69, 1971)
West Virginia	§ 60A-1-101 et seq. West Virginia Code (Supp. XVII, 1972)
Wisconsin	Ch. 219 § 161.001 et seq. Wisconsin Laws of 1971
Wyoming	§ 35-348 to 371 Wyoming Stat. (Supp., 1969)

Citations to Marihuana Prohibitions Enacted 1915-1933 before Uniform Narcotic Drug Act

Alabama	No. 26	[1931]	Alabama Acts 42
Arizona	Ch. 36	[1931]	Arizona Laws 61
Arkansas	Act 213	[1923]	Arkansas Acts 177
California	Ch. 604	[1915]	California Acts 1066
Colorado	Ch. 39	[1917]	Colorado Laws 120
Delaware	Ch. 191	[1933]	Delaware Acts 658
Idaho	Ch. 105	[1927]	Idaho Laws 136
Illinois	Ch. 38	[1931]	Illinois Laws 1027
Indiana	Ch. 189	[1929]	Indiana Acts 616
Iowa	Ch. 282	[1921]	Iowa Laws 306
Kansas	Ch. 192	[1927]	Kansas Laws 247
Louisiana	Act. No. 41	[1914]	Louisiana Laws 71
Maine	Ch. 694	[1914]	Maine Laws 300
Massachusetts	Ch. 694	[1914]	Massachusetts Laws 704
Michigan	No. 310	[1929]	Michigan Laws 841
Mississippi	Ch. 13	[1930]	Mississippi Laws 13
Montana	Ch. 91	[1927]	Montana Laws 324
Nebraska	Ch. 145	[1927]	Nebraska Laws 393
Nevada	Ch. 33	[1923]	Nevada Stat. 39
New Mexico	Ch. 42	[1923]	New Mexico Laws 58
New York	Ch. 692	[1927]	New York Laws 1675
North Dakota	Ch. 106	[1933]	North Dakota Laws 158
Ohio	No. 422	[1927]	Ohio Laws 187
Oklahoma	Ch. 24	[1933]	Oklahoma Sess. Laws 53
Oregon	Ch. 27	[1923]	Oregon Laws 35
Pennsylvania	No. 163	[1933]	Pennsylvania Laws 904
Rhode Island	Ch. 1674	[1918]	Rhode Island 145
South Dakota	Ch. 127	[1931]	South Dakota Laws 100
Texas	Ch. 61	[1919]	Texas Laws 156
Utah	Ch. 66	[1915]	Utah Laws 77
Vermont	No. 197	[1915]	Vermont Acts 336
Wyoming	Ch. 57	[1929]	Wyoming Sess. Laws 67

Index

MARIJUANA MYTHS, MARIJUANA FACTS:
A REVIEW OF THE SCIENTIFIC EVIDENCE
by Lynn Zimmer and John P. Morgan

In this ground-breaking book, Zimmer and Morgan shatter 70 years of myths about marijuana. Chapters address marijuana's physical and psychological effects, marijuana's addictive potential, marijuana's impact on driving, marijuana's use as a medicine, marijuana's long-alleged "gateway" effect and much more. Concisely written and jargon-free, Marijuana Myths, Marijuana Facts is essential reading for parents, teachers, policy-makers, and everyone who believes our response to marijuana should be based on facts, not fear.

"An important contribution to the marijuana and drug policy literature." –Journal of the American Medical Association

"A remarkable book...A miracle of intelligent concision...Legislators who write marijuana laws and judges who sentence marijuana users should...consult this little book."–William F. Buckley, JR.

"A welcome document...the first in-depth examination of all the government's claims about pot...Useful in a policy debate that has often been colored by hysteria."–Rolling Stone

"A clearly written rebuttal of some of the exaggerated claims offered in support of current U.S. marijuana policy." –Science

"An invaluable resource...The most accurate book on the effects of marijuana." –Andrew Weil, M.D., author of Spontaneous Healing

"Accurate, timely, and impressive...clearly written and accessible." –Louis Lasagna M.D., author of the National Academy of Sciences report on marijuana

"An impressive attack on much of the mythology around marijuana." –The British Medical Journal

LYNN ZIMMER IS ASSOCIATE PROFESSOR OF SOCIOLOGY AT QUEENS COLLEGE.

JOHN P. MORGAN IS A PHYSICIAN AND PROFESSOR OF PHARMACOLOGY AT CITY UNIVERSITY OF NEW YORK MEDICAL SCHOOL.